Cosmopolitanism and the National State

Translated by Robert B. Kimber

INTRODUCTION BY FELIX GILBERT

PRINCETON UNIVERSITY PRESS

PRINCETON, NEW JERSEY, 1970

Cosmopolitanism and the National State

BY FRIEDRICH MEINECKE

Contents

FRIEDRICH MEINECKE was the leading German historian in the first half of the twentieth century and an important figure in the development of modern historiography. This should be reason enough to publish a translation of one of his most famous books. However, sixty years have passed since the first appearance in 1907 of *Weltbürgertum und Nationalstaat* (*Cosmopolitanism and the National State*) and republication of a historical work or a first translation after such a long span of time is rare. Such an undertaking usually needs some special justification. In addition to its significance as an authoritative investigation of a historical topic, a work of history can be valuable as a mirror which reflects the political situation existing when it was written, or it can be an important demonstration of a new historical method. Meinecke's *Cosmopolitanism and the National State* deserves attention for all these reasons. It is crucial for the development of Meinecke as a historian because it is the first work in which he shows himself as the master of his craft; the ideas of the book are closely connected with issues which dominated the German political scene in the first decade of the twentieth century; and it is the first impressive display of Meinecke's methods of intellectual history.

Meinecke composed *Cosmopolitanism and the National State* in the middle of his life. Born in 1862, he was 45 years old when the first edition of the book was published, and he died in 1953 at the age of 91. Until the publication of *Cosmopolitanism and the National State* his career had been the usual one of a German academic. Like many other German professors in the nineteenth century, he came from a family of Prussian civil servants and Protestant ministers. Meinecke was perhaps closer to the spirit of the first half of the nineteenth century than many of his contemporaries because he grew up in a small, isolated town of the Mark Brandenburg. In his advanced age he still remembered the sounding of the post horn when the daily mail coach passed the house of his parents. The atmosphere of his father's house was closer to an earlier time in its way of thinking and living as well. It was permeated by a pietistic and conservative spirit. At the beginning Meinecke's scholarly career proceeded along entirely traditional lines. His first publications were concerned with themes of Prussian history and his first large work was a biography of Boyen, one of the reform-minded military heroes in Prussia's fight against Napoleon. After a long period of waiting for academic advancement, in which Meinecke earned his living as an archivist, the publication of the Boyen biography led to his appointment as professor of modern history in Strasbourg in 1901. Five years later, unwillingly but feeling unappreciated by the officials in charge of Strasbourg University, he accepted a chair in the University in Freiburg. Two years later *Cosmopolitanism and the National State* was published.

With the appearance of this book the external circumstances of Meinecke's life and, to a certain extent, the nature of his historical concerns changed. After he had declined various offers of professorships, he accepted in 1914 the most prestigious chair of history in Germany, that at the University of Berlin, and he remained there until his retirement in 1932; he returned again to teaching in Berlin after the defeat of the Nazis. During the years of the Weimar Republic Meinecke became the most influential figure in German historical scholarship. His scholarly interests transcended the Prusso-German framework of his earlier years; both in *Die Idee der Staatsräson (Idea of Reason of State in Modern History)** and *Die Entstehung des Historismus (Origin of Historism)* he tackled political and intellectual problems of a general European character. Moreover, Meinecke became a figure in political life. In the last years of the Empire he became an advocate of reform, particularly of an electoral reform in Prussia which would have broken the hold of the Junkers over German policy. Since, in his opinion, the First World War demonstrated the bankruptcy of the German ruling group, he acknowledged the necessity of a thorough change, and became a somewhat unenthusiastic but loyal defender of the Weimar Republic. All these developments originated from the publication of *Cosmopolitanism and the National State* insofar as with the publication of this work Meinecke had emerged as a person of a well-defined intellectual profile.

At first, today's reader may not get the impression that the political assumptions and concepts of this book are different from those notions which we consider as typical of the political ideas of the first decade of the twentieth century. The main theme of the book is intended to show that when the ideas of nationality and nationalism began to take hold in Germany they were imbedded in a universalistic framework; and it is almost shocking to discover that Meinecke regarded the development from universalism and cosmopolitanism to nationalism as clear,

---

* Translated into English under the title *Machiavellism* (London, 1957).

unquestioned progress. The process which he describes and on which he comments with approval is that of the gradual renunciation of all commitments to cosmopolitan values until at the end the sovereign national state is recognized as the supreme value and final goal of history. According to Meinecke this is a process which possesses "necessity, greatness, and ethical dignity." This glorification of nationalism and of the national state—dangerous and even repulsive as it might appear to us—was in accordance with the political climate of the years before the First World War. These were the convictions and values of the time, and Meinecke shared them to the fullest. He went far in accepting the consequences of this worship of the national state. Because he regarded the state as an entirely independent individuality, he believed that a state had to fight against others to maintain itself. "Struggle, care, and conflict are the destiny of the genuine national state, not peace and calm." Even the Wilhelminian feeling of German superiority is noticeable in this book. But, of course, there are few products of this time that are not infected by the Jingoistic climate of the period.

It is more remarkable that conventional political attitudes can also be observed in Meinecke's remarks on German domestic and constitutional issues. Meinecke's admiration for Bismarck seems unbounded: Bismarck's methods were the only ones suited to achieve German unification. Bismarck might not have solved all the problems of German politics, but what he had done was perfect. Meinecke accepts the need for a strong and independent executive. When he writes approvingly of the parliamentary character of the Bismarckian constitution, he means to acknowledge his belief in the necessity of a parliament, but he does not intend for the government to be dependent on this parliament.

These were views which might be found among most of the high-ranking members of the German civil service, and they do not differ from those which other German political historians expressed. Nevertheless—although it might not be evident at first sight—Meinecke's book goes beyond the conventional assumptions of these groups. It is a work on German unification, on German political history; as such it should center around the actions of the policymakers and explain them on the basis of documentary sources preserved in the archives. Meinecke's book, however, analyzes the thought of philosophers like Hegel and Fichte, of literary figures like Novalis and Friedrich Schlegel, of scholars like Ranke, Droysen, and Niebuhr, and of political thinkers like Adam Müller, Haller, and Stahl. When Meinecke discusses statesmen like Stein or Humboldt or even Bismarck, he is more concerned with their thought than with their actions. Accordingly, the sources for this work are primarily printed books or pamphlets, personal letters, lectures, and only to a very small extent documents from archives. This is a book on the influence of ideas on the course of politics and also on the influence of politics on the development of ideas.

With this approach Meinecke challenged the traditional notions of political history because this concept implied that a political history that was limited to an investigation of the day-to-day business of statesmen remains superficial. The springs of political action must be traced back to the world of ideas which formed the intellectual atmosphere of a time, and out of which the individual shaped his own particular view of the world. There was nothing novel in assigning to ideas a role in history. The two thinkers who exercised the greatest influence on historical thought in Germany in the nineteenth century—Hegel, the philosopher, and Ranke, the historian—had both stressed the importance of ideas in history. But for both of them ideas floated above the events of history; they served to designate the particular character of a period and to distinguish it from others. Meinecke, however, as he said in a letter written during the composition of *Cosmopolitanism and the National State*, employed a "psychological empathizing method." He did not concern himself with ideas as abstracts indicating the common qualities of a variety of phenomena. For him man was the medium through which ideas worked in history; they established a common basis for thought and action among men but they also gave each individual the opportunity for developing a distinctive personality. The interplay between common ideas and the different shapes which they assume in individual minds, the evolution which ideas undergo in consequence of this interplay, the manner in which they pattern the course of action and the manner in which they are transformed as a result of their application to reality—these seemed to Meinecke questions which the historian must study if he wants to achieve a full understanding of the events of the political world.

These views not only represent an enlargement of the concept of political history; they also imply a new approach to the history of ideas. Meinecke's effort to place political history in a broader context had to be complemented by demolishing the compartmentalization which kept the history of ideas isolated from the rest of history. As long as it was regarded as a separate pursuit the history of ideas was fragmented into different histories, each describing the development in different areas of man's intellectual activities—history of philosophy, history of historical scholarship, or the history of economic thought. Or else it meant dealing with the history of single concepts such as immortality, progress, or sovereignty. In this approach the history of an idea has its inner logic. It is the gradual unfolding of all its immanent qualities. In Meinecke's view, however, ideas and actions were interdependent. The emergence and the evolution of ideas had to be presented within the framework of all that which surrounded them. Meinecke developed, therefore, a new method of intellectual history.

He abandoned the traditional procedure of presenting a man's ideas in the form of a closed system into which everything, whatever he had said or written, was fitted, in which earlier statements were used to explain statements in later works, and from which those ideas which did not fit were eliminated as immature or not seriously meant. In analyzing a man's thought Meinecke would adopt a genetic method, i.e., he would follow an individual's intellectual development from step to step, from one written work to the next.

A particularly brilliant example of Meinecke's method in *Cosmopolitanism and the National State* is the long chapter on "Fichte and the Idea of the German National State." In carefully outlining Fichte's intellectual development, he revealed the philosophical assumptions behind Fichte's famous addresses to the German nation. Meinecke demonstrated that the glorification of the German nation, which earlier interpreters had taken as an expression of pure nationalism and as an appeal for a fight against Napoleon, had an educational aim and was the outline of an ideal nation which did not exist in reality. In this interpretation the addresses fitted to the idealistic, ethical concerns of Fichte's philosophy. This approach also involved new emphasis in analyzing literary sources or documents. In elucidating the intellectual development of an individual the key concepts and fundamental assumptions of writings were more important than content. Changes in subject matter might be forced by external circumstances; shifts in key concepts reflect the inner development of an individual. They also allow the perception and definition of the intellectual relationship which exists among various individuals. In this manner Meinecke showed the wide ramifications and the importance of Christian-Germanic romanticism for political thought in the first half of the nineteenth century—one of the discoveries of *Cosmopolitanism and the National State*.

It would be wrong to claim that the genetic method in intellectual history was Meinecke's invention. To find the connecting thread in

European intellectual history had been the lifework of the Berlin philosopher, Wilhelm Dilthey. As a student Meinecke had found little stimulus in Dilthey's lectures, but he began to read him again when he took up the studies which led to the composition of *Cosmopolitanism and the National State* and he was then deeply impressed. Dilthey's *Jugendgeschichte Hegels* (*History of Hegel's Youth*) and his *Leben Schleiermachers* (*Life of Schleiermacher*) were and remain penetrating studies of the intellectual development of important thinkers and opened new perspectives. But Dilthey used the genetic method for purely biographical purposes. Meinecke applied this method to a group of thinkers; in his hands it served to establish a connection between the political and the intellectual world and to show the features which on the one hand tied together, and on the other divided one generation from the next. In *Cosmopolitanism and the National State* Meinecke used the genetic method of intellectual history in such a way that it could be made applicable to broad historical themes.

The application of a new historical method was not the only reason, however, why this work impressed its readers as something novel. We must return once again to the issue which we have discussed before: the political attitude which this work reflects. We have seen that it was permeated with a German nationalistic spirit, characteristic of the period before the First World War and particularly characteristic of the work of political historians of this time. But by demonstrating that the guiding principles of the political world originated in the world of thought—in literature, in philosophy, in scholarship—Meinecke reduced the supremacy of politics and by this implied a sharp criticism of Wilhelminian Germany. He suggested that the exclusiveness of the ruling group in Prussia-Germany represented a weakness because it cut political life off from its creative source, namely, the world of ideas, and the men who generated them. German politics was in danger of becoming sterile and rigid. It could be—it ought to be—revived by granting influence to those classes, forces, and ideas which were growing up outside the narrow Prussian ruling group. These views were not in contradiction to Meinecke's admiration for Bismarck and his work because, although he considered Bismarck's solution of German unification as the only solution attainable in the political circumstance of the nineteenth century, he emphasized that Bismarck's work was unfinished and needed to be completed. Nor were these demands incompatible with Meinecke's belief in the greatness of the Prussian tradition. Like his contemporary and friend, Otto Hintze, the prominent scholar of Prussian institutional history, Meinecke believed that the Prussian reforms in the Napoleonic era consisted of two parts: the one was the modernization of the bureaucracy so that Prussia would have the necessary strength and elasticity to maintain its position among the European powers; the other was a "program for the future" which would realize the principle of the participation of the citizens in political life. While the first part of the reform had been successfully carried out, the program for the future had never been taken in hand.

It might be questioned whether Meinecke would have recognized the importance of this issue if his own move, first to Strasbourg, then to Freiburg, had not given him an opportunity to look upon the Prussian state from the outside; in the relaxed liberal atmosphere of southwest Germany the virtues of Prussia's disciplined and hierarchically organized society may have lost some of their glamor. But whatever the motives of Meinecke's adoption of a progressive outlook were, *Cosmopolitanism and the National State* was viewed as a historical justification of the demands for political reforms—and that was part of its impact. With the appearance of this book Meinecke had taken a position in the liberal camp and had entered upon the political course which he would follow in future years.

Meinecke advocated changes because he wanted to preserve what he considered the true values of the past, not because he believed that the new was better than the old. For this reason some have characterized Meinecke's notion of the history of ideas as an escape from reality, a sign of an unwillingness to enter upon a discussion of the critical social issues which were at the roots of the tensions in political life or to allow social change. In the case of *Cosmopolitanism and the National State* this criticism has no validity. In this book Meinecke proffers a political message; and although it does not aim at revolution, it certainly aims at reform.

The question of the political relevance of Meinecke's most important later works—*Idea of the Reason of State* (1924) and *Origins of Historism* (1936)—presents a much more complex problem. These books are not entirely remote from the political issues of their time. *Idea of the Reason of State* shows the impact of the experiences of the First World War and of the German defeat; Meinecke felt compelled to re-examine the question whether the notion of the sovereign national state as the embodiment of the highest ethical values had validity and whether political necessity could justify the breaking of moral laws. In *Origins of Historism* the political content is more obscure. Here Meinecke's concern is with the development of his own field of scholarship. It is a book of restricted rather than general interest. But his emphasis on the importance of private and individual concerns implied some opposition to the Nazis who reduced man's value to an instrument of politics. Nevertheless, these two works differ from *Cosmopolitanism and the National State*. They are less unified—both are collections of interrelated studies rather than single, closely integrated works. They are less concerned with the description of a general intellectual climate than with analyses of the ideas of a few great individuals—"a walking along mountain crests while the lower valleys remain hidden in clouds," to use Meinecke's own words. Most of all they do not raise political demands nor have they a direct political purpose—they are somewhat like soliloquies in which the author studies the values of others in order to clarify his own thinking.

Meinecke was not without questions and doubts about the value of his approach, and in the later years of his life he wrote and published a large number of essays on problems of historical theory. It is unfortunate that on the basis of these articles some students have constructed a system of historical philosophy. Meinecke—as he himself frequently said—was no systematic thinker, and these studies were meant to define his position in relation to the accepted norms of historical work. He did not intend to set forth a new philosophy of history.

Perhaps it is true that Meinecke did not go to the end of the road which he had entered; he did not pursue the study of intellectual trends to an analysis of the social forces which they represented. Nor did he systematize the insights in the historical process which he had gained. Yet these weaknesses were also a strength. For Meinecke, results or conclusions were only a part—and not the most important part—of the work of the historian. Meinecke's interest was the particular form which ideas assumed in the mind of an individual. It was the richness and variety of the individual that he was primarily concerned with. Meinecke was, as we have said, Germany's most influential historian. But he was not the head of a school in the sense that he prescribed his students to follow his path. He urged his students to find their own way, the way most appropriate to their personality. He could be disquieting; a rather lively and sharp discussion could be suddenly terminated by a long silence in which Meinecke seemed to be far away. The sharp features of his face—a high forehead, an aquiline nose, a firm mouth—were dominated by eyes which, behind glasses, seemed to look into a far distance rather than at what was before them. Meinecke's scholarship was distinguished by the combination of two divergent qualities: he possessed an ability for powerful critical analysis and a gift for intuitive understanding. Though in his work he was more interested in thought than action, he remained a historian to whom life meant more than the abstract truth. And whatever *Cosmopolitanism and the National State* means for our knowledge of innovations in historical method and for an understanding of the political climate in Wilhelminian Germany, it has an immediate attraction as an evocation of the richness of political and intellectual life of a past era.

My two main goals in this translation were accuracy and readability. I cannot claim that either one has been fully achieved, but I hope that my compromise between the two, like Bismarck's solution to the Prusso-German problem, is at least viable, if not a thing of beauty and symmetry.

The 1962 Oldenbourg edition of *Weltbürgertum und Nationalstaat*, on which this translation is based, is essentially a reprint of the seventh edition, published in 1928. In the course of six new editions Meinecke made numerous alterations and added many footnotes, often changing his style of documentation and citing works by different titles. Thus, the footnotes in the original are sometimes ambiguous, sometimes erroneous. I have silently corrected any errors I have found either in the text and in the notes. Also, an effort has been made to clarify the footnotes on the basis of internal evidence in the original, and their form has been changed to conform with current practice in documentation. These changes made the possibility of clerical error more likely, but I think the gains in lucidity far outweigh the risks of error involved.

In a short note preceding the glossary I have tried to explain my strategy for dealing with terminological problems. I hope both the note and the glossary will be of help to the reader in keeping the assorted empires, confederations, and parliaments of nineteenth-century Germany in order.

I would like to express my thanks to Felix Gilbert, who has been reading this translation in pieces and as a whole for nearly as long as I have been working on it. The blunders from which he has saved me are legion. At Princeton University Press I am indebted to the late Dorothy Hollmann for her help with the form of both text and notes, and I am particularly grateful to Linda Peterson, who edited a difficult manuscript with great care and patience. My major debt of gratitude is to Edith Mettke, who helped type the manuscript, read every word of it, and made many suggestions for improvements. Without the criticism and comments of all who have helped me, this book would contain more flaws than it does. For those that remain, the responsibility is all mine.

Cosmopolitanism and the National State

PREFACE TO THE SECOND EDITION

THE FIRST EDITION of this book appeared at the end of
1907. It attempted to search out the origins of the German national
state by seizing on certain major problems and following their development during the past century. The approach had to draw on intellectual history as well as on historico-political materials. I note with
gratitude that my efforts were given a predominantly favorable and
friendly reception and that they have already provided a stimulus
for further research. I have profited from the remarks of my reviewers,
particularly those of G. Küntzel, R. M. Meyer, and H. Oncken, as
well as from several individual studies of the last few years; and I
have consequently been able to provide a number of improvements
and amplifications in the second edition. The publication of Gentz's
correspondence prompted me to characterize briefly his role in the
developments treated in Book I. I hope I have satisfactorily defended
my view of Stein's German and European policies against the doubts
that H. Ulmann has raised. G. Droysen's biography of J. G. Droysen
gave me a welcome opportunity to clarify in Book II the preliminary phases of his plans for the spring of 1848. King Friedrich Wilhelm IV's position on the problems treated in Book II could be
further clarified with the help of material written by him that was
recently discovered in the Hausarchiv. Additional sources that I have
found in the meantime bear on the position of the Erbkaiserpartei.
I have not neglected the arguments raised against my presentation
of the tactics of the Catholic group in 1848; and, finally, H. Oncken's
biography of Bennigsen has provided me with important supplementary material for the concluding chapters.

My book is based on the assumption that German historical research, without renouncing the valuable traditions of its methodology,
must work toward a freer exchange and contact with the major forces
of political and cultural life. Without damage to its basic nature and
aspirations, it can plunge more boldly into both philosophy and politics. Indeed, only in this way will it be able to fulfill its true task of
being both universal and national.

Freiburg i. B., May 21, 1911

PREFACE TO THE THIRD EDITION

THIS NEW EDITION has benefited greatly from the literature of the last few years and offers a number of additions and new notes, particularly in the first and sixth chapters of Book I and throughout all the chapters of Book II. Pastor's book on Max von Gagern provided new sources that filled some gaps in Book II and, to my pleasure, offered confirmation for some of my earlier conjectures.

The printing of this new edition had already begun when the World War broke out. The war will lend form to the twofold ideal of cosmopolitanism and of the national state, an ideal that has provided a beacon for the German nation during its rise to new historical life. Past, present, and future come together now in our souls. While our fighting sons protect us from such dangers as Germany has not had to overcome since the Thirty Years' War and the Napoleonic occupation, we will lift up our inner eyes unto the hills from whence cometh our help and unto those noble spirits of the past who invisibly accompany us in our struggle and bless it. I hope this book, originally a product of quiet contemplation, will prove to be of some value in these troubled times.

In an epilogue to Book II, I have attempted to treat the Prusso-German problem in the light of the present moment.

Berlin-Dahlem, March 19, 1915

PREFACE TO THE FOURTH EDITION

THE WAR HAS KEPT alive interest in the problems treated in this book. This new edition again offers a number of additions, particularly in the first and sixth chapters of Book I and in those chapters of Book II that are affected by Erich Brandenburg's most recent publications from the literary remains of Ludolf Camphausen.

Berlin-Dahlem, January 25, 1917

PREFACE TO THE FIFTH EDITION

RECENT RESEARCH has obliged me to make only slight changes in the text and notes of this edition. However, the crushing fate that has overwhelmed Germany in these weeks touches on the roots of the two problems that are treated in this book. The alert reader will easily recognize the lines of development that lead from my research and considerations to today's grave situation and the tasks it sets for us. The problems that I treated from the possible and feasible perspectives of the period before the war—problems of national egoism, of international confederation, of the relationship of Prussia to Germany, and of the further development of the German constitution under the pressures of international politics—will now require practical solutions that could not be conceived of then. My book must, of course, retain the character it received when it was written. I think, however, that its basic ideas will continue to play a role in the present. But the present will also cast a new light on the past. Just as we are politically obliged to draw the consequences of the World War for our existence, obliged to draw them with determination, unbroken spirit, and loyalty to our national past, so too we are intellectually obliged to reexamine our old historical views in the light of recent experience.

Berlin-Dahlem, November 8, 1918

PREFACE TO THE SIXTH EDITION

THE CHANGES for this edition are limited almost exclusively to additional material in the notes that takes the research of the last few years into account. Book II had to remain unchanged in its structure, but I have added to it an essay of 1921 that treats the further development of the Prusso-German problem.

Berlin-Dahlem, April 24, 1922

PREFACE TO THE SEVENTH EDITION

WHEN I FIRST PUBLISHED this book twenty years ago, a reviewer noted that it dealt for the most part with areas that had remained relatively untouched by other literature. This is no longer the case today. Also, the historical events of these last twenty years have caused me to change my own position, particularly on the problems treated in Book I. Whoever compares my *Idee der Staatsräson* (1924) with this book will easily perceive the change. However, this change is not so profound that I feel obliged to renounce this earlier work. The high and fundamental values that guided my judgment then— state, nation, and humanity—I still hold unshaken. Then, however, I saw them in a clear light. Now I see them indistinctly, as in the mists.

It would blur the historical character of my book if I tried to inject my present views into it. The parts of it based on my original research will, I hope, be able to hold their own among the more recent works that often enrich and refine the details of the picture I sketched in Book I but essentially confirm its basic outlines. I take little pleasure in the recent mass of publications on Romanticism, which, to the extent that they touch on the problems I treated, only inflate what I tried to say briefly and concisely. It is time that young scholars who feel drawn to intellectual history apply themselves to other, more taxing areas of it.

Few changes were made in Book I, and the footnotes call attention to disputes with some of my opponents. Book II, however, profited greatly from Hübner's recent publication of Droysen's papers concerning the year 1848, which contain the minutes taken in the Frankfurt constituent committee of 1848-49. Major gaps in the history of the idea of allowing Prussia to merge with Germany could be filled in with the aid of this material. Since the problems connected with this idea have become vital and pressing again for us today, I hope my book will be of some value to all those politicians who are sensitive to the historical origins of the questions of German political reform being debated at the present time.

Berlin-Dahlem, November 12, 1927

Book I

*Nation, State, and Cosmopolitanism
in the Development of the German
Idea of the National State*

1

···

GENERAL REMARKS
ON THE NATION, THE NATIONAL STATE,
AND COSMOPOLITANISM

IF WE INTEND to investigate how the idea of the national state developed in Germany, we must first try to clarify what constitutes a nation and a national state, and we must also try to define the relationship between the two.

What distinguishes individual nations from each other within the totality of human history? There are no generally valid criteria to help us here. We can see at a glance that nations are large, powerful communities that have arisen in the course of a long historical development and that are involved in continual movement and change. For that reason the character of the nation has something indeterminate about it. A common place of residence, a common ancestry or, more exactly, since there are no racially pure nations in an anthropological sense, a common or similar mixture of blood, a common language, a common intellectual life, a common state or a federation of several similar states—all these things can be important and essential elements or characteristics of a nation, but that does not mean that every nation must possess them all to be a nation. However, a natural core based on blood relationship must be present in a nation. Only on this basis can a rich and unique intellectual community and a more or less clear consciousness of that community develop, and it is this factor that elevates a union of tribes into a nation and makes it capable of assimilating foreign tribes and elements. But experience offers no general laws that explain how this higher community arises and what its components are. Only an investigation of concrete individual cases can provide such explanations. If general laws are at work here, they have remained hidden from our experience. Now and then we may think we have isolated general tendencies, if not general laws, and we may think we have perceived

9

similar basic characteristics and stages of development in all or at least
in many nations. But under closer scrutiny every nation proves to have
its unique individual aspects. If the social sciences try to penetrate as
deeply as possible into the typical and general characteristics of
nations, the true historian will concentrate more on observing the particular features of an individual nation as faithfully and precisely as
possible. This is the goal we have set for our study, but in order to
achieve it, we shall need at least a brief orientation on the general
types and tendencies we can distinguish in the nature and development of nations.

We shall be primarily concerned with nations in their later stages
of development and not in their initial phases, which, as we have suggested, usually result from a merger of small tribes and groups. The
first prerequisite for the development of a nation is the acquisition of
a firm territorial base, a "fatherland." There are, of course, wandering and geographically divided nations as well, but experience shows
that only the ones that have possessed a permanent residential seat,
a fatherland, over a long period of time have been able to acquire and
maintain a rich substance and firm coherence. If we ask now from
what sources this substance derives, two major categories will occur
to us immediately. Despite all the obvious reservations that can be
made, we can still divide nations into cultural nations and political
nations,[1] nations that are primarily based on some jointly experienced
cultural heritage and nations that are primarily based on the unifying force of a common political history and constitution. A standard
language, a common literature, and a common religion are the most
important and powerful cultural assets that create a cultural nation
and hold it together. One of the best authorities on the standard languages of ancient Hellas says of them: "They gained their predominance through literature alone and not through political channels."[2] A similar example is the Irish standard language, which,
completely independent of all political developments, has also been
created and handed down by poets and storytellers.[3] But the cases
are more frequent in which political communities and political in-

---

[1] Cf. A. Kirchhoff, *Zur Verständigung über die Begriffe Nation und Nationalität*
(1905), pp. 52ff. Also, earlier than Kirchhoff but essentially the same, Fr. J. Neumann, *Volk und Nation* (1888), pp. 132 and 149.—On the natural foundations
of the nation (blood relationship and soil), cf. Bauch, *Vom Begriff der Nation*
(1916).

[2] Wackernagel, *Die griech. und latein. Literatur und Sprache*, p. 300, in the
series Kultur der Gegenwart.

[3] Thurneysen, *Die Kelten in ihrer Sprache und Literatur* (1914), p. 15.

fluences have encouraged, if not indeed caused, the growth of a
standard language and a common literature.[4] There is often a close
connection, too, between religion, state, and nationality. The cohesive
force a national religion and church can provide is especially evident in former political nations that have lost their statehood, perhaps
centuries ago, and that are struggling to attain it again.[5] Such cases
also suggest that a cultural nation can be a political nation as well,
and we often do not know whether political ties or the ties of religion
and church are the stronger in holding it together.[6] As a result, it is
difficult to distinguish cultural and political nations from each other
on the basis of either internal or external structure. Members of different cultural nations can live within a genuine political nation, as the
example of Switzerland shows; and a cultural nation, as the example
of the entire German nation has shown, can experience within itself
the growth of several political nations, that is, populations of states
that shape their feeling of political unity into a distinctive individual
form, that become a nation through this process and often consciously
want to become one, but that also remain members of the larger, more
comprehensive cultural nation whether they desire this and are aware
of it or not.

Thus, we may find either a desire or a lack of desire to belong to
a nation and a distinct or an indistinct awareness of nationality. Here
we touch on what may be the most important criterion for defining,

[4] On this point, cf. Mitscherlich, "Der Nationalismus und seine Wurzeln,"
Schmollers Jahrbuch, XXXVI (1925), and Hertz, "Wesen und Werden der
Nation," in *Nation u. Nationalität* (*Jahrb. f. Soziologie*, Ergänzungsband I [1927]),
p. 29.

[5] M. Lenz, "Nationalität und Religion," *Preuss. Jahrbücher*, CXXVII; *Kleine
historische Schriften*, p. 234.

[6] In any case, instances are rare in which a cultural nation arises purely and
exclusively from a common culture without the assistance of any political factor
at all. Although overstated, Dahlmann's remark contains a core of truth: "A people
can be more a nation than a state, but a people cannot be a nation without a
state." (*Politik*, 3rd edn., p. 3) The heritage of the Roman Empire, for example,
contributed to the growth of the Italian cultural nation, as did the political aspect
of the papacy and of the Roman church. But no political nation has probably ever
arisen the other way around, that is, without the assistance of any cultural factors.
But it is rash to declare the entire conceptual distinction between the cultural
nation and the political nation worthless because of these limitations and reservations. Such declarations have occurred repeatedly since the appearance of the first
edition of this book. All historical categories of this sort really designate only
dominant tendencies that seldom appear completely pure and isolated in historical
reality. As the following chapters will prove, the concepts of the cultural nation
or political nation can have at the very least a very definite and characteristic
existence in the consciousness of the single individual.

in broad terms at least, the different elements in the genesis of nations. It has been said that whoever wants to be a nation is a nation. "L'existence d'une nation est un plébiscite de tous les jours."[7] But did the Alsatian who wanted to belong to the French political and cultural nation before 1870 automatically lose the distinctive marks of the German cultural nation from which he took his origins? He retained them longer than he probably cared to, and, in historical terms, he was still a member of the German cultural nation when he no longer wanted to belong to it. But Renan's remark, which is aimed directly at Germany's claim to Alsace, is still valid if we limit it properly and consider the historical premises behind it. It derives from the spirit of 1789, from the idea of the self-determination and sovereignty of the nation, that is, of the political nation that wants to form its own political constitution and to direct its own political destiny. The French were the first to experience the desire for nationhood. Then, in the nineteenth century, this same desire seized the German and Italian peoples as well and led to a new organization of major political nations on the continent. But this later era in which the will to be a political nation emerged so strongly was preceded by a period in which the national will did not take on such a clear and conscious form. In this earlier period we can hardly speak of national self-determination in any full sense of the term. But despite this the French and the English were political as well as cultural nations, and the Germans and Italians were at least cultural nations. Here we encounter a major turning point in the development of the great modern nations, the political as well as the cultural ones. We can distinguish an early period in which nations have a more plantlike, impersonal existence and growth and a later period in which the conscious will of the nation awakens. In this later period, if only through the agency of its leaders, the nation becomes aware of itself as a great personality, as a great historical unit, and it now lays claim to self-determination, the mark and privilege of the mature personality.[8] But it is always a question here of a gradual trans-

---

[7] E. Renan, *Qu'est-ce qu'une nation?* (1882), p. 27.

[8] Eduard Meyer's views on the difference between ethnological group [*Volkstum*] and nationality [*Nationalität*] differ from ours in terminology but agree in content: "Only gradually . . . and *at first half-unconsciously*, does a feeling of closer homogeneity develop, an idea of the unity of the *ethnological group*. The highest gradation of this, the idea of *nationality*, is the most refined and complicated structure that historical development is capable of creating. This idea transforms the actually existing unity *into a conscious, active, and creative will*" etc. ("Die Anfänge des Staats," *Sitzungsber. der Berliner Akademie, phil-hist. Klasse* [1907], June 6). See, too, Meyer, *Theorie und Methodik der Geschichte*, pp. 31ff.,

formation, not a radical one. Even in the more vegetative and dormant periods of national life, there are isolated moments when nations open their eyes, when they speak and think through their intellectual leaders, and when they express themselves in great united actions and manifestations of will. Similarly, the quiet, unconscious life of the earlier phase does not stop in periods of awakened national personality. All the innovations that are carried forward by the conscious will of nations, by their nationally oriented governments, parties, and leaders, only take up and cultivate what has already germinated, what has gradually sprung up from below.

Still, the gradual shift is so great that we can divide political as well as cultural nations into those of an old and those of a recent type.

For as far as political nations are concerned, they arise not only through a demand for self-determination but also through the quiet workings of the state and through a shared political life within the same political system. They arise, we might say, in the course of slow historial growth. We cannot specify the moment when they are born. We can only say that wherever a lively and durable feeling of political community exists, effective both within and beyond the borders of the state, there the population of a state has become a political nation and the state a national state. As the examples of England and of France in the *ancien régime* show, the state can be based on a great cultural nation and simultaneously circumscribe that cultural nation in its main body. But as the example of Prussia in the same period shows, initially at least, the state can also form a par-

---

where he goes a bit too far in his reaction against those who see the basic units of history in nations.—The distinction between "people" [*Volk*] and "nation" [*Nation*] that Kattenbusch undertakes corresponds approximately to the one we make between cultural nation and political nation; cf. "Vaterlandsliebe und Weltbürgertum" (Hallenser Rektoratsrede, 1913). "A people," he says, "is a unit in nature and in some cases in *culture*. A nation is always an intentionally formed organism. . . . Nations always appear as *states* [*Reiche*]. . . . Nations are always *autonomous states* [*Eigenstaaten*]." This narrowing of the term nation cannot be reconciled with common usage. Therefore, I consider our terminology more practical.—The *Verhandlungen des zweiten deutschen Soziologentages*, 1912 (Tübingen, 1913), which concerned themselves primarily with the problem of the nation, produced only one item of great value, the paper by Robert Michels (enlarged under the title "Zur histor. Analyse des Patriotismus," *Archiv f. Sozialwiss.*, XXXVI). His work is important in particular for the development of the modern national idea in France and Italy.—Bubnoff has recently treated in an interesting way the "Begriff der Nation und die Idee der Völkergemeinschaft," *Archiv f. Sozialwiss.*, LI (1923), although his treatment is somewhat too one-sided when seen from the standpoint of axiology.

ticular political nation from parts of a larger cultural nation. The decisive point is that political nations and national states of this older type are formed from above—and to a great extent unconsciously —whether the formative influences are absolutistic or aristocratic-parliamentary. In ultimate terms, of course, the national state of this earlier period is quite imperfect. The entire disjointed and amazingly ornate world of the *ancien régime*, the entire system of the regional, local, and social institutions worked against nationalization from above. The patrimonial powers and the corporations divided and absorbed the public spirit to a great extent. The idea of the whole was visible only in innumerable refractions. Thus, the great power states can only have become strong autonomous personalities by their own momentum, and where a political nation already stood behind them, it was not as ready to initiate such a development as it was to follow in its wake.

But as far as the cultural nation of this earlier period is concerned, its vegetative character becomes evident in the fact that it does not have the inner impulse to become a political nation and to create a national state that would circumscribe it. In this period, it could be more easily content with its existence as a mere cultural nation than in the periods when nations sought the most appropriate means for expressing their personalities. Personality means not only the utmost autonomy but also the utmost autarky, a harmonious unity and a cultivation of all inner capacities and potentials. However, we shall put the purely ideal and abstract concept of the national personality aside at first and consider only the real forces that constitute it, the profusion of individual personalities that form it, and the common factor in these individual wills. If the full consciousness of a great national community is once awakened and raised to an intense longing for national realization, then this longing is like a flood that pours itself into everything it can fill and is not satisfied until everything is nationalized that is at all capable of nationalization. This process is basically a great extension of the individual personality and its sphere of life. The human being needs the community to sustain him and to receive his contributions in turn. The more autonomous, the more individualized he himself becomes, the larger the spheres of his receptivity and influence can be. These spheres of life consequently acquire a richer substance and a clearer outline, and of all the great spheres of life that a man can enter, there is probably none that speaks so directly to the whole man as the nation, none that carries him so strongly, none that renders so faithfully his entire natural and intellectual being, none that can so readily be or become both macroanthropos and fully realized individual.

Thus, it is no coincidence that an era of individualistic strivings for freedom immediately preceded the era of modern national thought. The nation drank the blood of free personalities, as it were, to attain personality itself. It is of no consequence here that this modern individualism was divided in itself. Its one branch, deriving from natural law and democratically oriented, sought to achieve equal rights for all, while its other branch, aristocratically oriented in an intellectual sense, sought to achieve the liberation and elevation of the best minds.[9] Democratic individualism could use the idea of the nation to fight all violations of social equality, and the same idea enabled aristocratic individualism to empathize with the masses, perceiving the forces lying dormant in them and embracing an ideal image of the people, if not the people themselves. Whether or not individualism actually achieved all its goals was not as important as the fact that everything the free and creative personality did served the nation by making its total life richer and more individual.

Both of these individualistic movements, then, were nationally formative. The greater activity of individuals brought with it a greater activity of the nation, and the modern idea of the national state became the liveliest outgrowth of modern national thought. The older national states, France and England, were rejuvenated; France acted rapidly and passionately, England slowly and thoughtfully, to push aside the obstructing forces that had previously interfered with the closer unification of nation and state. Completely new national states emerged from nations that had flourished for centuries as cultural nations. The lofty insight that the state is an ideal supra-individual personality—this insight that sustains and justifies all our thought and concern about the state—could only come to life when the political feelings and energies of individual citizens permeated the state and transformed it into a national state.[10]

Because the existence of the modern national state depends on the highest possible activity of the nation that forms that state, its existence cannot be ensured through external organization and maintenance alone. Those factors create only the outer walls of power.

[9] Cf. Troeltsch, "Das Wesen des modernen Geistes," *Preuss. Jahrbücher* (April 1907), pp. 10ff. He distinguishes between rationalistic and irrationalistic individualism.

[10] Cf. Meisner, *Lehre vom monarchischen Prinzip im Zeitalter der Restauration und des deutschen Bundes* (1913), p. 290.

From these walls, the nation as a political nation can look out on the world, self-confident and armed, and within them, it can strive to enhance and harmonize both its intellectual and social life. At this point, a new impetus appears in the nation as a cultural nation, an increase of activity, a more conscious effort toward self-improvement. This new impetus stimulates nations that are still held back at the stage of the cultural nation, and it rouses in particular those parts of nations that are separated from the politically unified core of the nation and that have only cultural connections with it. This ideal that takes hold of an entire nation is a desire for an integral national community in all the vital areas of existence.[11] The task is infinite because as the means for accomplishing it develop, its difficulties also grow. As the nation becomes stronger, all the spheres of life within the nation also become stronger. Thus, intellectual, political, and social antipathies entrench themselves more deeply within the nation, and new ones emerge, for all the factions benefit from the vital individual forces stirring at the heart of the nation. Indeed, within the nation itself different concepts of the nation come into conflict with each other, and each of them alone claims to represent the nation truly and properly. The fact that part of the nation unselfconsciously and sincerely regards itself as the core and essence of the entire nation is rooted in the very character of national life itself, for national life is mainly determined by the more active and powerful elements, never to the same extent by the sluggish mass,[12] and the ideal image of the nation is always the mirror of what stirs in individual souls. In a certain sense the nation is always *pars pro toto* by nature, but it cannot, of course, do without the totality, any more than the head can do without the body. As a rule, there was no doubt in the earlier national state about who represented the head and who the limbs that obeyed it. In the more recent national state, however, where the most widely differing individualities and social groups seize on the idea of the nation and project themselves into it, there is no end of doubt and struggle

[11] Very good on this is G. Rümelin, "Über den Begriff des Volks," *Aufsätze*, I, 103: "One motive can direct me to this sphere, another to that sphere; my faith can assign me to a group from which the union of community, state, language, and ancestry separates me. But our nature will feel and deplore as a disruption every such division and fragmentation of its spiritual orientation, and the mind will always be haunted by a quiet longing for a unified community. A central group that embodies all our goals in life will be present to the mind as an ideal goal."

[12] On this "stratified character" of the national community, see, too, the recent work by O. Spann, "Über den Begriff der Nation," *Die Geisteswissenschaften*, I, 561, and Binder, *Logos*, X, 294.

over that point. Whoever observes this struggle might well think
that we are moving not closer to the goal of a complete community
but farther away from it and that nations lived in a more unified and
undisturbed way during their earlier vegetative period. But it is not
just unity in itself that appears to the modern sensibility as the highest
value. It is rather a unity replete with life and energy, not just a harmonic chord as such but the richest possible harmonic chord. It
may seem to us that the national life of earlier times, although slighter
in substance, actually had greater strength than the national life of
modern times, which has been splintered by thought and civilization. But let us not be led too far afield by this question, which leads
to purely subjective speculation and which one and the same observer
might often answer differently in different moods. We can never
simply compare the individual features of early and of modern national life. Instead, we must constantly keep the entire and enor-
mous reshaping of all the conditions of life in mind. The early national state was, as we saw, immature and incomplete in its inner
existence. That is the case with the more recent one, too, but for
significantly different reasons. The early national state was lacking
in spontaneous activity stemming from a broad cross section of the
nation. By contrast, the modern national state has rather too much
of this activity and has difficulty in holding together the factions that
differ among themselves and exert their individual pressures on
the state. But because this excess of action springs from fruitful differences within society and between its members, it cannot be the
task of the modern national state to nullify these contradictions and
reduce the national culture to one level. Its task is to achieve a
unified position in certain basic matters and a tolerance and appreciation for whatever diversity and variety it can permit—a peace of God,
as it were, for certain days of the national year. If this task is even
partially achieved, the modern national state can boast of having
accomplished a more difficult and doubtless higher task than the early
national state could manage.

But the same line of thought that ascribed a greater natural energy
and freshness to earlier national life can raise an important objection
to our concept of early and modern national states. One could well
submit that every state that displays a specific national character in
its structure is a national state. If that is so, then it would not be
important for the national state to unite in itself, totally or in its main
body, the nation whose character it reflects. Nor would it be at all
important that it form its subjects into a political nation. The impor-

tant point is simply that its institutions be as free as possible of influences from outside the nation. From this point of view, Russia before Peter the Great would be a purer national state than Russia modernized by institutions from western Europe, and what we have called the modern national state would come under suspicion of not being a national state at all because its constitution has so often been formed after a foreign model. In this view, the genuine national state emerges like a unique flower from the particular soil of a nation, and this soil is capable of producing, besides this one unique state, many other political structures of an equally strong and vivid character. This state is not and does not become national through the will of the people or of those who govern it but through the same means that language, customs, and faith are national and become national—through the quiet workings of the national spirit. The development of the ancient and Italian city-states and of the early German territorial states was probably of this kind. It is the cultural nation, and particularly the cultural nation in its more vegetative period, that produces the national state in this sense, and from this point of view the state is regarded as simply one product of the national culture along with others. This principle of classification therefore follows a different logic than the one first used above. The former principle began with the state; this one begins with the nation, i.e., the cultural nation. The former principle led to the view that there are different types of states and that national states are those containing a political nation, that is, a population with a lively feeling of political community. The latter principle, however, leads to the view that the nation engenders various children of its spirit among which are national states, that is, states that show the special character of a particular national culture. We shall see later on in our study that we are not dealing with idle distinctions here but with crucial ones of great significance for the development of ideals of the national state in Germany.

We have distinguished between cultural nations and political nations, between national states in the political sense and national states in the national-cultural sense. Among national states in the political sense and also among political and cultural nations, we have distinguished between those of ancient and modern type. We have always kept in mind that these different types shade into each other in historical reality. Up to this point we have primarily considered nations and national states as such and in regard to their particular immanent qualities and purposes. But this one point of view alone is not sufficient. For, as we have already suggested above, nations and national states are not merely examples of certain species that either remain pure or cross with each other. Like all historically formed structures, they also display a highly singular character. Singular is not meant here in the sense that everything particular to a nation can be derived exclusively from its own immanent national spirit, as one view of history, influenced by Romanticism, has long maintained. It is meant rather in the sense that a nation's character is also formed, just like that of an individual personality, through conflict and exchange with neighbors. Contacts between nations and national states can thus determine their individual development in the most profound way. A single historical moment, a single great event in the international arena can so affect a single nation or national state that it follows a course that could not have been predicted before on the basis of its past behavior. Outside influences may also encounter certain defensive obstacles in the very character of the nation upon which they operate, and perhaps only those influences that strike an already extant but dormant seed in a nation can truly fructify and transform that nation. We must then ask, too, whether these dormant seeds and possibilities are peculiar to all nations or only to those in which they came into bloom, whether they are qualities of the species "nation" or whether they are unique qualities of certain nations. It is beyond question, however, that certain impulses from without can be a crucial influence on the development of an individual nation and of an individual national state.

What are such external influences but actions in the communal life of nations and states, a life that has a causal coherence in itself? These large communities that unite several nations and states have such fluid and indeterminate borders and are in themselves so fluid and indeterminate that historical research has developed a standard practice of contrasting the world of the nation and of the individual state with the world of the universal. This has led to the idea that the entire history of the world is a unique process, a massive interweaving and crossing of national and universal developments.[13]

We might say that historical research moves on the highest level of its jurisdiction and enjoys the purest air, the clearest view, when it confronts this interrelationship and attempts to elucidate it. If historical research prefers, as we said, to deal with the particular, it will find here the highest form of the particular and the most im-

[13] O. Hintze, "Über individualistische und kollektivistische Geschichtsauffassung," Histor. Zeitschrift, LXXVIII, 67 (Histor. u. polit. Aufsätze, IV, 12).

partial point of view for evaluating everything particular. But one
could well object that the study of the relationships between nations and national groups, between states and systems of states cannot possibly be the principal field of historical research. And one
could object further, with good reason, that however significant, extensive, and widely operative these contacts, thrusts, and counter-
thrusts between nations and national groups are, they are only the
visible manifestations of profound and hidden forces. According to
this view, then, anyone who wants to understand these forces at
their source must study the individual in his historical permutations,
for the entire subject matter of historical research—society, culture,
state, nation, and all of mankind—exists only in and through the
ideas, feelings, and actions of individuals. They are the basic cells of
historical life. Our answer to this objection is, of course, that our
study of this area of contact between national and universal development will not be restricted to the encounters and external actions
of nations and states alone. It will also extend to the inner life of
men, for, after a certain stage of culture has been reached, the remarkable process of interaction between national and universal impulses arises here. There is a universal impulse in the intellectual
friction between individual and environment and in the striving of the
individual to rise from the sphere of the nation into his own particular sphere, because individual values appear as universal human
values to the man who pursues them. But they never are universal,
for they always bring with them a clump of native soil from the national sphere, a sphere that no individual can completely leave
behind. If we turn to history itself, we will immediately find a number of relevant historical examples. Think of ancient culture and
its conflict between national and—we can restore the debased word to
its dignity without hesitation—cosmopolitan thought. One commentator says of the ideal of ancient *humanitas*, of pure humanity: "It was
only from the conflict of two nationalities that the concept and the
word could grow," and this idea was "a first and not entirely conscious
attempt to limit the state's claims on the individual, to distinguish
between nationality and humanity."[14] Think of the development of
Christianity with its massive and fertile encounter between universal
and national religion. Think further of what must be of particular concern to us: think of the first traces of a real German national consciousness in the Middle Ages and of its connection with the universal poli-

[14] Reitzenstein, *Werden und Wesen der Humanität im Altertum* (1907), pp.
4 and 6.

tics of the emperors. "It is not mere chance that the first appearance of the name 'Germans' as a designation for our people coincides almost exactly with the establishment of the Roman Empire of the German Nation."[15] At that time, too, an undertaking beyond national interests helped ignite the national idea in the hearts of men. And finally, did not the France of the Revolution—the first great national state in Europe that was consciously based on the autonomy of the nation—did it not burst forth from the womb of the eighteenth century, from a soil completely imbued with universal and cosmopolitan ideas?

It is only natural to ask whether the rise of the idea of the national state in Germany was the result of a similar tension between universal and national ideas. The current view is that an epoch of cosmopolitan thinking preceded the awakening of the national idea and of the idea of the national state in our country also. If we should demonstrate no more than that in this study, we shall have said nothing new. However, this same view also sees cosmopolitanism and national feeling as two modes of thought that mutually exclude each other, that do battle with each other, and that supplant each other.[16] Such a view cannot satisfy the historical mind that has a deeper awareness of circumstances and that insists on a thoroughly detailed demonstration of every stage in the evolution of ideas. A more subtle view, which the custodians of German culture have always esteemed, is that the true, the best German national feeling also includes the cosmopolitan ideal of a humanity beyond nationality and that it "is un-German to be merely German."[17] This view probably comes closer to the truth, but it postulates a harmony between the cosmopolitan and the national idea that was not always there, and fails to clarify the complex process of confrontation and union. It will be our main objective to illuminate the true relationship of universal and national ideals in the growth of the modern German idea of the national state.

[15] Dietr. Schäfer, *Deutsches Nationalbewusstsein im Licht der Geschichte* (1884), p. 10. Cf. his *Deutsche Geschichte* (2nd edn.), I, 167, and Dove, *Ausgewählte Schriftchen*, p. 302; von Below, *Der deutsche Staat des Mittelalters*, I, 359, thinks he has found a "German consciousness" even before the era of Ottonian politics. He admits, however, that the Italian policy of the emperors certainly contributed to the rise of national consciousness.

[16] Even Wohlwill's study, *Weltbürgertum und Vaterlandsliebe der Schwaben* (1875), which points toward our subject in its title, does not go far enough in its examination of this relationship, although it had already noted accurately the mixture of cosmopolitan and patriotic impulses.

[17] J. E. Erdmann, "Das Nationalitätsprinzip" (1862), in *Ernste Spiele* (4th edn.), p. 221. Similarly, Zeller, "Nationalität und Humanität" (1873), in *Vorträge und Abhandlungen*, II, 433ff.

The nature of the problem requires a thorough, monographic treatment. The examination of political ideas can never be separated from great personalities, from creative thinkers. We must attempt to grasp these ideas at their high source and not on the broad plain of so-called public opinion, in the insignificant political dailies. Also, we shall discuss only a small group of outstanding thinkers, and those whom we select will be considered not in terms of their entire political development but only where they have made a special and crucial contribution to the formation of the German idea of the national state. It is of particular importance that we trace thoughts and concepts back to what is more important than thoughts and concepts, that is, to life and personality. Our emphasis will fall on the period of the Revolution and the Wars of Liberation, on Humboldt, Fichte, and the Romantics. Using examples from the German policies of Stein, Gneisenau, and Humboldt, we shall also examine the political practice of statesmen in relation to our central question. The idea for this study arose from observations I have made both in these areas and on the German policies of Friedrich Wilhelm IV.[18] If we wanted to meet the full challenge of our problem, we would have to expand it to include all the main ramifications of the national idea in Germany, the liberal-democratic one as well as the Romantic-conservative one, and we could even extend it with success to the modern mass parties of the Social Democrats and the Center. But we intend to make only a beginning. We have therefore singled out the Romantic-conservative strand, which is important because it leads from Stein to Bismarck by way of Friedrich Wilhelm IV, Hegel, and Ranke. Also, this branch is generally less known and appreciated than the liberal branch, which is sometimes regarded as the only carrier of ideals of the national state until the time of Bismarck. However, we shall not be able to disregard the liberal branch altogether, and I hope to be able to say something new about it in the second part of my study, which is devoted to the problem of the Prussian and German constitutions.

Yet another point: In attempting to elucidate the history of certain ideas through a monographic treatment of individual thinkers, we shall inevitably have to repeat some observations; and, although the objects of study change, a few simple ideas will have to be expressed over and over again. I do not think this can be avoided, and I appeal to Leibniz' remark that nature is indeed simple in its principles but infinitely rich in the application of these principles.

[18] I have already suggested some of this in my monograph on *Das Zeitalter der deutschen Erhebung* (1906, 3rd edn. 1924).

2

THE NATION AND THE NATIONAL STATE
AFTER THE SEVEN YEARS' WAR

LET US REVIEW quickly the main currents of thought on the nation and the national state in the last decades of the eighteenth century. In doing so, we can begin with the word nation itself, for the uses of this word help us perceive these currents, and they will also serve to demonstrate the mysterious power of language in the development of such ideas.

The word nation had already been in use in Germany for several centuries. It was probably taken over directly from the Latin, from the legal language of the state and church in the fifteenth century,[1] and it is worth noting that this double usage automatically engendered the feeling that a nation could emerge from two sources, from the cultural community or from the political community. Sometimes it was a term for a tribal and linguistic unit, sometimes one that referred to all the members of the Empire.[2] The word nation took on a still richer tone from the use of the phrase *teutscher Nation* in the language of the edicts of the Imperial Diet in the sixteenth century and in Luther's language, a tone that can still be heard in the capitulation of Karl VII. For a long time, then, this word had had a more elevated sense than the word *Volk*, which was more often used for the lowly, the common, and the members of the mass, for the humble population, for soldiers, and so on. The situation was similar in the neighboring countries France, England, and Italy, where the terms *nation*, nation, and *nazione* evoked loftier associations than the words *peuple*, people, and *popolo*.[3] We might say that in the word nation a concept of striving upward toward clarity, eminence, and personality is implicit, while *Volk* is rather the designation for a passive and vegetat-

[1] Fr. J. Neumann, *Volk und Nation*, p. 139. Werminghoff, "Der Begriff: Deutsche Nation in Urkunden des 15. Jahrhunderts," *Histor. Vierteljahrsschrift*, XI (1908), 184ff.

[2] Neumann, *op.cit.*, p. 142.

[3] *Ibid.*, pp. 125ff. Hertz, in *Nation u. Nationalität* (1927), pp. 10ff., also points out exceptions to what is said above.

ing existence condemned to plodding obedience.[4] We can see how the
word nation became more resplendent and richer in content after the
middle of the eighteenth century, first in France, then in Germany as
well. In his *Esprit des lois* of 1748, Montesquieu devotes the nineteenth
book to the question of how laws are related to the principles "qui
forment l'esprit général, les moeurs et les manières d'une nation," and
in these same years appeared Voltaire's work that since 1769 has borne
the title *Essai sur les moeurs et l'esprit des nations*. Both men understand by "nation" an ethnological community [*Volksgemeinschaft*] distinguished by certain intellectual or moral character traits, but both of
them are also aware of the nationally formative power of the state.[5]
A little later, a more vigorous elevation of the concept "nation" began which was exactly parallel to the rise of the *tiers état*. In 1758 a
spokesman of the third estate declared it improper that business-
men, scholars, and artists be considered members of the *peuple*; they
belonged rather to the higher strata of the "nation," which, according
to this view, also included the *peuple* but which could serve automatically as the designation for the actual nucleus of the nation,
too. As we have already noted, the intellectually or politically dominant class of a nation always has a tendency to identify itself with
the nation.[6] Thus, the social, political, and intellectual ideas and
demands of the third estate entered into the concept of the nation
and received through it in turn an idealistic impulse.[7] How strongly
the spell and the significance of the word were felt is evident in
the famous debates by members of the third estate in June 1789,
when they deliberated for a long time whether they should call them-

[4] Voltaire says in *Siècle de Louis XIV*, Chap. 37: "Il y a toujours dans la nation
un peuple qui a nul commerce avec les honnêtes gens, qui n'est pas du siècle, qui
est inaccessible au progrès de la raison."

[5] M. Ritter, "Studien über die Entwicklung der Geschichtswissenschaft," 4.
Artikel, *Histor. Zeitschrift*, CXII, 51 and 61f.; reprinted in his *Entwicklung der
Geschichtswissenschaft* (1919), pp. 229, 239f.

[6] Neumann, *op.cit.*, p. 124, cites an interesting point from J. de Maistre:
"Qu'est-ce qu'une nation? C'est le souverain et l'aristocratie." In Hans von Gagern,
Über Deutschlands Zustand und Bundesverfassung (1818), a higher meaning is
attributed to the term *Volk*; Gagern adds, however (p. 24): "But if I speak of
the views, wishes, judgment, and high interest of the nation, I do not include at
all the child of the beggar. . . . I mean primarily the better, thinking part . . . the
heart of the nation, without further consideration of age, sex, or status."—Jahn
does just the opposite of this in his introduction to *Deutsches Volkstum* (1810)
and tries to restore the words *Volk, Volkstum*, as opposed to *Nation, Nationalität*,
to their dignity.

[7] "La nation, c'est la France lettrée ou riche." Aulard renders thus the conception of those whose thinking was most radical on the eve of the Revolution. *Hist.
politique de la Révolution française*, p. 25.

selves *assemblée nationale* or *représentants du peuple français*. Mirabeau recommended the latter designation because it was less pretentious and more general, but the majority of the assembly favored the more elevated designation. Mirabeau's proposal was designed to keep the way open for a peaceful settlement; the decision of the assembly opened the way for the Revolution.[8]

Carried along by the social movement of the third estate, the idea of the nation in France passed directly into the idea of national sovereignty and of the modern national state. The extensive and profound difference between the German and the French nations is evident in the infinitely greater ramification and slowness of the same development in Germany. This diffusion often seems to suggest a lack of strength, and this impression will arise particularly where the influence of the French example is felt and particularly when it appears in only a pale imitation. But the truth of the matter probably is that the German national idea developed so slowly and matured so late because it had to assimilate so much heterogeneous material and because the historical ground in which it grew was still not as well cleared as the soil of the French nation.

From this uncleared soil, the term "German national spirit" comes to us in Friedrich Karl von Moser's little book of that title, *Vom deutschen Nationalgeist*, published in 1765. In this book, and in some of his other writings from these years, we can sense the vitality that Frederick the Great and the Seven Years' War had awakened in the Germans. In these same works, we also become aware of the tremendous effect of Montesquieu's and Voltaire's new ideas

---

[8] The opposition of *peuple* and *nation* is not always felt as sharply as it is here. The word *peuple* was also chosen as a slogan to express a purely democratic-egalitarian point of view. In his *Contrat social*, for example, Rousseau uses *peuple* predominantly but sometimes interchanges it with *nation* (cf., for instance, Book II, Chap. 8, "Du peuple": "Il est pour les nations comme pour les hommes un temps de jeunesse . . . mais la maturité d'un peuple n'est pas toujours facile à connaître" etc.). The Abbé Coyer in his *Dissertations pour être lues* (Haag, 1755) wants to restore the lowly *peuple* to their dignity as the most essential part of the *nation* as opposed to the grand and the rich.—The differences between the Jacobins and Girondists in 1793 are highly interesting for the further development of the term and idea of the nation in France. The Jacobins acted according to the principle that the heart of the nation—that is, they themselves and the people of Paris—was the nation itself. In opposition to this, Condorcet's draft of a constitution attempted to put forward the totality of the nation and to prevent the possibility of the active and enterprising part of the nation seizing control. He did this, of course, primarily for tactical reasons; for the Girondists, like the Jacobins, tended to regard themselves as the *melior et sanior pars* of the nation and as a *pars pro toto*.

on the life of nations and of the state.[9] Both these men prompted Moser to consider the situation of the German nation, but the core of his ideas was old rather than new. He did, of course, create the term "national spirit," probably taking his clue from Montesquieu's *Esprit de la nation* and Voltaire's *Esprit des nations*.[10] But the new term, with its promise for the future, was applied in an old context that had no future. Its modern tone was out of place in the dusty environment in which Moser used it. As he says himself, he found the "signs of a national spirit" in those parts of Germany where twenty principalities could be seen during a day's journey.[11] It was the patriotism which the smaller and weaker estates felt toward the Empire that he praised. For the most part, that patriotism was only an expression of a feeling of weakness. Beyond that, it was a mélange of pride in the traditional role of the estates, of conservative legalism, of respect for the Emperor, and, finally, of a sincere but often only vague sense of German community. Justus Möser, who reviewed this book at the time,[12] doubtless had good reasons to reject this image of the German national spirit as a delusion. There once was a time, he remarks with bitter resignation, when it was perfectly obvious what a nation was, the time when every Frank or Saxon cultivated his free inherited land, defended it himself, and went to the common local assembly from his own home. At the present time, it was impossible to know what a nation was. But he did not do justice to Moser's deeper intention, for Moser's national spirit was a political national spirit, too. As Moser conceived of it, it was the capacity for independent political conviction and freer political activity.[13] There was al-

[9] Montesquieu is for him a "writer of such rank that one follows and imitates him even in his errors and mistakes." *Beherzigungen* (1761), p. 224. We are immediately reminded of Montesquieu's mode of thinking when Moser says in his *Reliquien* (2nd edn., 1766), under the heading "Spirit of a Nation": "Every nation has its great motivating force. In Germany, it is obedience; in England, freedom; in Holland, action; in France, the honor of the king" etc.—Voltaire is cited in the *Beherzigungen*, p. 362, as the author of the *Esprits des nations*. What is meant here, of course, is the *Essai sur les moeurs et l'esprit des nations*, which, indeed, received its definitive title only in 1796 but which had already contained the phrase "esprit des nations" in the title of an earlier 1756 edition (cf. *Oeuvres compl. de Voltaire* [1878], II, xi, and Kantorowicz, *Histor. Zeitschrift*, CVIII, 297f.)—On Moser, see Bruno Renner, *Die nationalen Einigungsbestrebungen F. K. v. Mosers* (Königsberg dissertation, 1919).

[10] "The French distinguish," it says in the *Beherzigungen*, p. 362, "between *l'esprit et le génie des nations*. We have only one word for both." In this same book, the term "national spirit" is also used occasionally (p. 492).

[11] *Ibid.*, p. 51.

[12] In the *Allg. deutsche Bibliothek*, VI; Möser, *Werke*, IX, 240ff.

[13] "The whole concept of national interest," it says in his *Beherzigungen*, p. 341,

ready something of Stein's spirit in it. From the declining world of the Empire and its knighthood, Stein too carried over into modern times a living element both of common national-political feeling and of the estates' sense of independence.

This old Imperial patriotism contained a fruitful seed that could spring up again in new soil and in a new atmosphere, but it had no future in the soil of the old Empire. The alignments at the time of the League of Princes may well have occasioned a passing interest once again in the national-political situation of Germany, and they may also have given rise to fantasies of a unified Germany under one ruler in the future. But that was nothing more than an interesting thesis, one of many intellectual games one played for amusement.[14] Moser's appeal to the political national spirit of the Germans was made too late or too early, depending on how we look at it. But the idea of a German national spirit as such did not disappear, and it replenished itself in a completely new way. In France it was the middle class and the men of letters together that created the new national idea; in Germany it was almost exclusively the men of letters. In France, the idea was created consciously and intentionally. In Germany, the national spirit emerged as a by-product of the intellectual efforts of the great poets and thinkers of the time. While France moved forward toward a modern national idea characterized, as we said, by conscious activity, the development of the nation in Germany was characterized by unconscious and vegetative growth of the highest order. Men were animated by youthful, overpowering im-

---

"takes for granted a people that have a voice in the important questions that concern their ordered existence and well-being. The people have such a voice in all republics and limited monarchies. In an absolute monarchy where the will and command of the sovereign alone rule . . . this concept is a mere fiction that is dangled before the mob."—See Kantorowicz, *op.cit.*, pp. 298f., on an interesting reply to Moser's book on the German national spirit, i.e., Bülau (?), *Noch etwas zum deutschen Nationalgeiste* (1766). Probably also following the lead of Montesquieu and Voltaire, this author tries to expand the concept of the national spirit further than Moser did and also to extend it to the characteristic features of private, legal, and economic life, etc. It is characteristic of his rationalism, as Kantorowicz remarks, that he is still unaware of the expression of the national spirit in art, literature, and language. Only "learning" is mentioned as coming under its influence. The subject of the national spirit is, moreover, only ironically treated; the book is primarily a bitter satire against the despotic regime of the German princes. Justus Möser offers a characteristic judgment of this book, too (*op.cit.*). On the discussions that Moser's book evoked, see M. Sommerfeld, "Aufklärung und Nationalgedanke," *Literar. Echo*, August 15, 1915, and Renner, *op.cit.*, pp. 44ff.

[14] See Joh. von Müller, *Teutschlands Erwartungen vom Fürstenbunde*, in *Sämtl. Werke*, IX, 332; Wenck, *Deutschland vor 100 Jahren*, I, 117ff.; II, 248.

pulses that left the entire debilitated existence of the prevailing society behind. Who could know just then where the path would lead? But before any predictions could be made, new heights had been reached, and it was clear that these heights were those of the nation as well. But even if it was just the cultural nation—and not even the entire cultural nation, but only its literary activity and a purely intellectual communal feeling in educated circles—that created this new German national spirit, and even if there was doubt while this spirit was being created whether one could speak of a German nation in an intellectual sense,[15] there was soon no doubt at all about the fact of a rich, flourishing, and characteristic national literature. From his own vivid and immediate experience, Herder could write at the beginning of the nineties: "The highest culture of a people does not develop quickly; . . . it flourishes best, and I would add, it flourishes only, in the particular soil of the nation."[16]

It would be an attractive project, but one we cannot undertake here, to trace the development of this intellectual national consciousness from Klopstock and Lessing to Herder and Schiller and to show how its threads drew closer together from one decade to another.[17] It also lies beyond the scope of our study to show how the deeper historical foundations of national coherence had already been revealed in Justus Möser's thought. We want to establish here only the main course of the movement that led from the newly awakened cultural nation to the state and the political nation. To do that, we must begin in the nineties, when, because of the powerful influence of the French Revolution, the state and the relationship of the nation to the state could become objects of interested speculation, if

[15] Lessing, at the end of the *Hamburger Dramaturgie*: "What a noble idea to provide the Germans with a national theater when we are still not a nation! I am not speaking of a political system but simply of moral character." Schiller, "Schaubühne als moralische Anstalt": "If we should see the day when we have a national stage, then we should also be a nation." Herder, *Briefe zur Beförderung der Humanität*, 4. Sammlung, Nr. 53: "We cannot hold it against the magisters if they are still disputing *pro gradu* what governmental system Germany has or whether the Germans are a nation."

[16] *Briefe zur Beförderung der Humanität*, 1. Sammlung, Nr. 10.

[17] On Lessing, see, for example, Baumgarten, "War Lessing ein eifriger Patriot?" *Hist. u. polit. Aufsätze und Reden*, pp. 217ff. See, further, the very thin work by Behrens, *Deutsches Ehr- und Nationalgefühl in seiner Entwicklung durch Philosophen und Dichter (1600-1815)* (Leipzig dissertation, 1891); further, Jastrow, *Gesch. d. deutschen Einheitstraumes* (3rd edn.); Joachimsen, *Vom deutschen Volk zum deutschen Staat* (1916); M. Lenz, "Deutsches Nationalempfinden im Zeitalter unserer Klassiker," *Jahrbuch der Goethegesellschaft* (1915) and *Kleine Historische Schriften*, II.

not of active participation, for German thinkers too. Even Herder made occasional forays into politics. Although he was infinitely more interested in furthering the work of the cultural nation, cleansing the "great uncultivated garden of the nation" and thereby weeding out the folly of national arrogance,[18] he also reflected sometimes, with his great awareness of the totality of life, on the more robust and virile tasks of the nation. It would not be enough, he thought, for the individual German to be courageous and honest. The nation also needed "Illumination, enlightenment, sense of community; the pride not to let oneself be regulated by others and to regulate oneself as other nations have always done, to be German on one's own *well-protected* land and soil."[19] In this way, he called for the political autonomy of the nation but in a spirit that was still not that of the modern autonomous national state. For he shared the illusion of many friends of the Revolution that the nationalization of state life would put an end to strife between cabinets: "Cabinets may deceive each other; political machines may exert pressure on each other until one is shattered. *Fatherlands* do not march against each other this way; they lie quietly side by side and help each other like families. . . . The idea of *fatherland against fatherland* in blood feud is the most horrible barbarity that can be expressed in human language."[20] The national state and cosmopolitanism are seen here from the point of view of the first French Revolution. They are forces that should mutually limit and aid each other in the closest possible union.

In the last analysis, Herder's awareness of the historical world, and of the character of the nation as well, followed from his ideal of humanity, and it was this ideal that in turn imposed limitations on that awareness.[21] In the Sturm und Drang period, in the days of the *Blätter von deutscher Art und Kunst*, of *Goetz* and of *Die Räuber*, thought had taken a direction that might have led to a consideration of the great political problems of the nation. But the universal ideal of humanity that arose purified from the ferment of the Sturm und Drang led thought away from those problems and lessened interest in the political world for a long time to come. Thus Herder's otherwise admirable capacity for imaginatively reliving historical

[18] *Briefe zur Beförderung der Humanität*, 4. Sammlung, Nr. 42.
[19] *Ibid.*, 5. Sammlung, Nr. 57. He had already written in the *Ideen zur Philosophie der Geschichte der Menschheit*, Book IX, Chap. 4: "Thus, the state in its most natural form consists of *one* people with *one* national character."
[20] *Briefe zur Beförderung der Humanität*, 5. Sammlung, Nr. 57, at the end.
[21] See Kühnemann, *Herders Persönlichkeit in seiner Weltanschauung*, pp. 128ff.

phenomena failed him in regard to the state and its desire for power. His historical awareness was therefore not capable of recognizing that the new national state, of which France was the model, represented only a further development of an old national and power state. Preoccupied with the philosophical and human background for the rights and claims of what seemed to be a newly created state, contemporary vision was blind to this state's foundations and previous history. German observers did not see what happened in France after 1789 as the work of concrete, historically conditioned forces but as the work of the free creative spirit of man, regardless of whether its creations were for good or for ill. Praise or condemnation overruled a historical understanding. But these impressions were still constructive for the development of the national idea, for they lent this idea a universalistic and rational tendency, which was precisely what made the idea acceptable to those who demanded such rational motivation. Wieland remarked very characteristically in 1791, "If twenty-four million or even twenty million people out of twenty-five million should unanimously and firmly insist on a revision of their old state constitution, then these twenty million would constitute the nation, and not they but the smaller group that opposed the will of the much larger would be the rebels." But it then follows from these "basic truths" that no European state has the right to force on the French nation any constitution other than the one it wants.[22] That was the new fruitful doctrine of the absolute right of national self-determination, proclaimed, however, as a rational-political truth, not as a historico-political one. Recognition of self-determination brought recognition of the personality of the nation, too, although this was still not what our historical perspective understands by the historically matured personality of the nation. The nation was not much more here than a subdivision of humanity, a frame built out of abstract principles and without individual substance; and the will of the majority, the will that was supposed to create this substance, actually threatened the genuine historical substance of the nation. The profound weaknesses and errors of this formalistically conceived doctrine of national sovereignty are perfectly obvious. But the historico-political error was also a great historico-political force, and this influx of rationalistic, universalistic ideas was indispensable in Germany too for the genesis of the modern national state. Let us keep it in mind for our understanding of later developments, for at first it did not represent much more than a provocative theory

[22] Wenck, op.cit., II, 209.

which only a very few thought of converting into reality and for which reality itself was still not prepared. As long as there was no desire for power from below in the population, there was also no motivation for bringing the state and the nation into a closer relationship to each other.

However, the desire for power was at work from above to create the beginnings of an actual political nation within the broader German nation. Friedrich Karl von Moser was indignant that his German national spirit came up against competition in the North, against the "monstrosity of a militaristic-patriotic government" which had arisen in—and here he expressed himself in the correct legalistic terminology of the Empire—the upper and lower Saxon territories. Conscious goals and careful calculation were the dominating principles everywhere in the Prussian state, and Frederick the Great had wanted to imbue his titled officers, regardless of which province they came from, with a common Prussian spirit, an *esprit de corps et de nation*.[23] He had immediate need of their national spirit. As the most active agents of the state, they also became the first custodians of Frederick's incipient national idea. We can rarely observe as concretely as here how a political nation emerges, how nationalization begins where the pulse of political life beats most strongly. This nationalization had also spread into the lower strata of the Prussian population, from which the king had not yet demanded *esprit de corps et de nation*. The growth of this popular Prussian patriotism was similar to that of the intellectual national consciousness that blossomed in German literature. Unsought and unexpected, it was suddenly there. All the Prussian state had required of its subjects was a sense of duty and steady application to completely unpretentious and prosaic tasks. But because the state thereby made demands on the whole man, the whole man's feelings could also come into play when the poetry of the heroic life and of a battle for the state's existence was added to the prose of routine and peaceful work for the state. This new Prussian national spirit that developed both by design and by chance was essentially only personal enthusiasm for the king and an awareness of the momentous events that he and everyone else with him had experienced, endured, and suffered. But without such experiences of an entirely personal nature, a warmer feeling toward the government could not have been created in a state whose internal and external life was still primarily dependent on the personality of the ruler. People could work for the Prussian

[23] "Polit. Testament von 1752," *Acta Borussica, Behördenorganisation*, IX, 362.

state now and be enthusiastic about the Prussian king, and still another necessary ingredient of a lively political national spirit was also present in a modest incipient form: free political criticism. There is a quantum of political displeasure and disapproval that generates a certain sense of well-being, and this could be found in Berlin at the time. It was not allowed to show itself in the press; but to compensate for that, it was all the bolder in conversation, and the Berliner was proud whenever visitors expressed astonishment and compared his bold speech with that of the English. "The Berliner speaks," one writer testifies, "with equal freedom about religion and the defects of the state, and he judges the king as quickly as he does his neighbor; yet patriotism and love for the king are the basic traits of the nation."[24]

Toward the end of Frederick's reign and under the influence of German literature, a generation of civil servants matured that attempted to fuse German cultural ideas with the Prussian concept of the state. The school of young Prussian officials and officers who later took their places in public life thus present the first significant model of how a political national spirit of modern character could be developed in Germany on the basis of both political and intellectual sources. However, the individual elements of this national spirit still did not fit together very well. The ideas from German cultural life that these young philosophical Prussians wanted to lend to their state were still too large a garment for the state's meager body. It was mainly an illusion if they saw Frederick's military and administrative state as the custodian of the new humanistic idea. And it was partially just a matter of coincidence that the mature period of Frederick's epoch occurred together with the first florescence of the German literary epoch and that the two were entwined together. For although there was an inner relationship between the rigorous spirit of the Prussian political system and the rigorous spirit of the Kantian philosophy, the central ideas of Kant's philosophy and those of the new German humanistic movement were still nowhere near capable yet of permeating the central substance of the Prussian state itself. In his own life Frederick had exercised a high degree of freedom in the sense of personal autonomy, and he had set an example in it, but he did not educate, and could not have educated, his state and his subjects in this same freedom.

For this reason, the Prussian national spirit at the end of the *ancien régime* led a somewhat unsteady and precarious existence. It owed

---

[24] Wenck, *op.cit.*, I, 158; see also Hay, *Staat, Volk und Weltbürgertum in der Berlinischen Monatsschrift* (1913), pp. 46ff.

what existence it had to a king whose manner of governing endangered it and repelled freer thinkers. His successor governed similarly but without offering the compensations Frederick had offered. The first years of the reign of young King Friedrich Wilhelm III aroused some sort of Prussian national feeling and short-lived enthusiasm, but this mixture of noble and trivial illusions with more serious and vigorous ideas first had to undergo the test of fire before the genuine could be separated from the artificial and the idea of a Prussian political nation raised to a position of high and incontestable value.

We can draw one basic conclusion from what has already been said here. The peculiar situation in Germany was that the only usable foundations for a modern national state were not available in the German nation but in the Prussian state. However, this state alone could not supply the intellectual forces that it needed for its nationalization but had to take them from the wide spectrum of the German cultural nation. This fact is well known and almost trivial, but we rarely clarify in detail the tensions and discord that arose from it. Since the German national culture had taken on a clearly universalistic character, the Prussian state also admitted these supra-national, universalistic elements when it used the impulses of this culture to renew itself. Thus, what occurred was a nationalization through partially supra-national, universalistic means, an advance in the formation of the state through the reception of ideas that were, to some extent, highly unpolitical. The result was often like the mixing of fire and water, and Prussian politics had to suffer from this contradiction until Bismarck's time. I hope that these seemingly abstract statements will gradually take on life and color as we turn our attention now to the individual thinkers.

3

··

WILHELM VON HUMBOLDT IN THE LAST DECADE OF THE EIGHTEENTH CENTURY

As EARLY AS his first political writings, the "Ideen über Staatsverfassung, durch die neue französische Revolution veranlasst" (1791) and the "Ideen zu einem Versuch, die Grenzen der Wirksamkeit des Staates zu bestimmen" (1791 and 1792), Wilhelm von Humboldt touches on the subject of the nation and its relationship to the state. In the first of these two works, the reader is immediately struck by Humboldt's far-ranging and independent outlook and by his disinterested and philosophically motivated evaluation of what the French people had undertaken at that time. They had attempted the impossible, he thought, if they wanted to create a constitution according to principles of reason alone, for reason seeks to achieve a harmony of all human energies. Humanity's goal is not harmony, however, but the development of particular powers. "As with individual men, so with entire nations. They can follow only one single path at a time. Thus the differences between them and thus the differences within themselves in different periods."[1] This led to the fruitful insight that nations are great historical individualities, one-sided in their powers and incapable of a purely rational development. But Humboldt did not go to the opposite extreme of wanting to ignore reason entirely as a regulating factor in the life of nations. Besides "time and nature," which must prepare the way, he also makes room for the "wise legislator." Working from a thorough knowledge of his particular era, encouraging or checking impulses in it, the legislator burdens himself—and contents himself—with bringing his age as close as possible to the goal of perfection. We might say Humboldt does justice here to the unconscious as well as the conscious, the elemental as well as the intellectual factors in

[1] W. von Humboldt, *Werke*, ed. Leitzmann, I, 81.

34

the development of a nation. And we might also add that in this view of the relationship of the legislator to national life, he was not too far from the concept of the modern national state, a concept that also clearly demands the government's precise comprehension of the nation's best interests. But then the unhappy memory of his own experience with the pressures of enlightened absolutism intruded itself between nation and state in his thinking. "The principle arose that the government must provide for the physical and moral well-being of the nation. Precisely that is the worst and most oppressive despotism."[2] This experience made him profoundly distrustful of the very institution of the state, because the state was capable of paralyzing the finest human potentials with its deceptively appealing arts of oppression. Humboldt recognized one-sidedness as the lot of individuals and nations and as the source of their strength. And within the entire context of his thinking, this insight represents a confession of a painful, but not total, resignation. His particular ideal was not the strength of single-mindedness, which would have led him to a deeper understanding of the state and a more just evaluation of it, but was instead one of "education" directed toward versatile activity and a harmonious use of all the personality's capacities. But power and education, he had to admit, "always stand in inverse proportion to each other." He adds, of course, that the wise man pursues neither one wholly; both are too dear to him to allow him to sacrifice one to the other. Humboldt was undoubtedly sincere in stating this as a principle for himself and for the individual in general; but even though he had a cool understanding of the power produced by the unifying of national life in the state, he certainly had no warm feelings for it; and as he considered this problem more closely in his second early essay, state and nation drifted even farther apart for him than they had before. As he began to feel stronger and prouder as an individual, his picture of the nation, which he had drawn with such definitive historical character in his first essay, became more colorless and sketchy.

His essay on the limits of the state's efficacy defines his position regarding the nation as follows: "The constitution of the state and the community of the nation should never be mistaken for each other, no matter how closely woven together they may be. If the constitution assigns a certain role to the citizen either by dominance and force or by custom and law, there is still another role he can freely

[2] *Werke*, I, 83.

choose which is infinitely diverse and frequently variable. And it is
this role, the free activity of the nation in itself, which preserves all
those values that men hope to achieve when they come together in
society."[3]

He often uses the word nation, but nowhere does he define the
term explicitly. He speaks, indeed, of the mind and character of the
nation;[4] he hopes that the war may spread its beneficent influence
"on mind and character throughout the entire nation" and that in
the nation may live "the spirit of true soldiers or rather noble citizens"
who "are always ready to fight for their fatherland," but he does not
want the state to aim at training the nation for war.[5] He does not
fail to recognize, further, that some means are needed to bind state
and nation together or, as he rather accommodatingly puts it, to
join "the ruling and the ruled parts of the nation." He regards as
one of these means the "diffusion among the people of an attitude
favorable to the constitution," a method that has brought forth good
results, particularly in antiquity; but he thinks it unadvisable for
the present because it can easily become detrimental to the education of the citizen as an individual.[6] If we look more closely, of
course, we see that he does not entirely reject the nation's love
for its constitution but only rejects premeditated means to awaken
that love. But then, too, the constitution should make itself felt
as little as possible, and the strengthened and expanded private interests of the citizens should replace the activity of the state as
much as possible. The state should be as weak, not as strong, as it
can afford to be. From his knowledge of the human soul, Humboldt knew clearly even then that man is more inclined to domination than to freedom, and as a Prussian subject he knew further that
not only the ruler but also the governed found satisfaction in knowing themselves members of a whole that endures beyond the life
span of one generation.[7] But that was not Humboldt's ideal. He did
not envision a higher level of culture in the activities of domination
but in those of freedom.

    [3] *Werke*, I, 236; see also I, 131: "An undeniably important difference always
remains between a national institution and a state institution. The former has only
a mediate, the latter an immediate power. Thus, in the former, there is more
freedom in the creating, dissolving, and modifying of the union. At their beginnings, all state organizations were most probably nothing other than national
communities of this kind"—a thought that leads to an unusual modification and
loosening of the theory of social contract.
    [4] *Ibid.*, I, 162.   [5] *Ibid.*, I, 140.
    [6] *Ibid.*, I, 234.   [7] *Ibid.*, I, 240.

We see from this that not only the old absolutistic power state was alien to his wishes but also the modern national state, which comes into existence through the will and participation of the people and is based on a strong constitutional life that binds the ruling and the ruled together. Wherever he looks he sees potential chains for the spontaneous individual whose productivity stems purely from inner resources, and his sensitive eye sees every small cloud that could darken the freedom of the inner life. Thus, we can only visualize what he understands by the terms "nation" and "the mind and character of the nation" in as light and bodiless a form as possible—not as a vital *force* that leads and gratifies the individual but rather as a vital *spirit* that arises naturally from the confluent breath of many individual souls. And even if this spirit descends again on the individuals from whom it came and exerts an influence on them, as Humboldt thinks it should, it is still primarily something produced, not something productive.

Perhaps we can make Humboldt's concept of the nation clearer if we first compare it with the one produced by the doctrine of popular sovereignty and the ideas of the French Revolution and then with the one later held by the Romantic period and the historical school of jurisprudence. Humboldt's concept is reminiscent of the former in its neglect of the historical forces at work in the development of a nation[8] and in its conception, influenced by natural law, of the "national community" as a union of a large number of individuals living together at a given moment; but then he has nothing to say about a *volonté générale*, a collective national will that is carried out by the majority or its representatives. Indeed, he rejects the idea of such a collective will. "Even if the state coalition were a national coalition in the strictest sense," he says,[9] "the will of single individuals could still express itself only through representation, and a representative of many cannot possibly be a sufficiently faithful reflector of opinion for each of the represented individuals." As we know, Rousseau did not care for the principle of representation either, but Humboldt even goes beyond Rousseau when he rejects decision by majority vote and declares the assent of every individual as necessary. To be sure, he has in mind here only the question of whether the state may take measures that go beyond the purposes of external and internal security; but it is clear that he also re-

---

[8] For this reason, the concept of the nation in his essay on the limits of the state's efficacy represents a retrogression compared to the "Ideen" of 1791.

[9] *Werke*, I, 131.

fuses to accept the possibility of a homogeneous national will that crushes individual wills that may resist it. "Most of the work," he says at another point,[10] "is always left to the voluntary and united efforts of the citizens."

Just as Rousseau and the French Revolution allowed the will of the nation a degree of power over the individual life that Humboldt did not want to recognize, so historicizing Romanticism later saw the individual directed by an unconsciously functioning national spirit of the people. In both cases the individual is subjugated, but the subjugating national spirit is different in each instance. Humboldt, however, does not tolerate any subjugating national spirit, not one constructed on principles of natural law and democracy or one conceived in historical and conservative terms, neither the consciously and purposefully ruling spirit nor the unconsciously creative one. And if he did in fact use the word nation with warmer feelings than the word state, he did so because for him "nation" implied more freedom for the individual.[11] Among the different factors that form the character of the modern nation, the spontaneity of the individuals that make it up has never been so strongly, indeed so exclusively, stressed.

But it was still an impressive thing that this pure and glowing individualist recognized anything of the nation at all, that he was not satisfied with the mere selfish enjoyment of the personality, and that the free activity of individuals among themselves became for him straightaway the "free activity of the nation in itself." Because of this, however, his concept of the nation became so general that it could merge with his equally indefinite and broadly conceived idea of "society,"[12] and "nation" and "society" threatened to evaporate altogether into mere terms for natural communal life. But as a balance to this vagueness, he had an extremely comprehensive view of this natural communal life and free interaction of men; these factors were present in his mind in as manifold, rich, and powerful a form as possible. His view of them and his feelings for them were so vital and profound that it took only some further experience of life for him to hear the whisper of genuine national spirit in this harmonic movement of human energies. If we were to reproach him for being deaf

[10] *Ibid.*, I, 157f.

[11] "Just as the nation interested him more than the state, so man interested him more than the nation." Haym, *Humboldt*, p. 51.

[12] For particulars on this, see *Werke*, I, 113; Haym, *Humboldt*, p. 55, says, very much to the point: "The image of a noble society presented itself to him as an entire nation living in one state."

to this spirit at that time, we could also counter our reproach with his own words: "He scatters more seeds that are productive in themselves than he erects buildings that show the direct traces of his hand." And those who still think Humboldt's uncorporeal concept of the nation more interesting than some of the many well-intentioned, patriotically German effusions of these decades can comfort themselves with a sentence that directly follows the one just quoted: "We need a higher level of culture to find satisfaction in preparing the way for future achievement than we need to take pleasure in the production of immediate results."[13]

Left to themselves, the energies of the Humboldtian spirit found their way to the concept of the nation. Whoever attempted to penetrate the mystery of individuality as sharply and eagerly, as delicately, yet at the same time as energetically as Humboldt did had to find eventually that the national spirit lived and worked within the individual, too—the genuine national spirit that does not simply blossom from the free social activity of the individual but extends before him and around him as a living historical force. From his study of the Greeks, who were his models of great individualism, it became clear to Humboldt what national character had meant for them and what a valuable and necessary prerequisite it is for the development of individual personalities. Looking at the Greeks, he had to admit: "The education of man in the mass goes before the education of individuals."[14] Another consideration that lay in the original direction of his thoughts could also bring him to a clearer understanding and a higher appreciation of the nation. His individualism did not aim at uniformity but at variety and uniqueness in human life. The ideal of humanity, he thought,[15] does not manifest itself in *one* form but in as many as are possibly compatible with each other, and it never appears in any other form than in the total sum of individuals. But how, then, did this abundance of individuality in the world grow if it was peculiar to the great unions of individuals, the nations, as well as to the individual himself? Humanity requires, he said,[16] the union of many "in order to show, through the great variety of their capacities, the true richness and entire range of human nature." He asked in this connection: Would it not be a loss of valuable char-

[13] At this point, he apparently did not draw a distinction between culture and education, as he did later in his linguistic writings.

[14] *Über das Studium des Altertums und des griechischen insbesondere* (1793), in *Ges. Schriften*, I, 276.

[15] *Plan einer vergleichenden Anthropologie* (1795), in *Ges. Schriften*, I, 379.

[16] *Loc.cit.*

acteristics if even the little Swiss nation were struck from the list of European nations?

We can indeed say that in the years after 1793 the question of the nation headed the list of problems that he wanted to solve. That was apparent even in his letters, particularly those to Goethe and Jacobi. But the real depth of his interest at this time reveals itself in his notes on history and the philosophy of history. For the most part, these notes first became available in the academy edition of Humboldt's works, and they have enlarged our knowledge of his thought tremendously.[17] "The study of a nation," he says there,[18] "cannot help offering all those benefits that the study of history generally provides." Taking the point of view of a rather utilitarian rationalism, he seems to see the benefits of history in its favorable effects on character, capacity of judgment, and knowledge of human beings. He conceives of knowledge of human beings here as deeply and comprehensively as possible. It is "knowledge of man as a whole" and of all the forces and laws that are at work in human life from within and from without. The study of a nation should attempt to examine the state of the nation and its entire situation; and in doing so, the study should provide a biography of that nation, as it were, that elaborates its character from all sides and shows that character in its totality. Such a study should not investigate just the reciprocal relationships of individual characteristics but should also consider their relations to external circumstances individually, as causes or effects. With this demand for a profound causal analysis of the total life of a nation, Humboldt anticipated one of the major tasks that the historians of the nineteenth century set for themselves. A few more quotations will help us estimate the strength of his interest in the character of the nation: "The study of man," he said in the same work of 1793,[19] "would make the greatest progress by studying and comparing all nations in all lands and times." Thus he developed in the following years the idea of founding the entirely new science of comparative anthropology. Its task would be "to search out the character of entire classes of men, par-

[17] Kittel's commendable but too schematic work on W. von Humboldt's historical philosophy (1901) was not able to use these sources. However, Eduard Spranger's excellent book, *W. von Humboldt und die Humanitätsidee* (1909), is based on these sources and, further, on Humboldt's recently published letters to his fiancée and wife. To my pleasure, Spranger's book agrees with my conception of Humboldt's national consciousness.

[18] *Über das Studium des Altertums* (1793), in *Ges. Schriften*, I, 256f.

[19] *Ibid.*, I, 264.

ticularly the character of nations and epochs."[20] The fundamental
idea on which this vast plan was based was this: "Taken alone, man is
weak and able to achieve very little with his own short-lived strength.
He needs heights on which he can stand, a social group that is valid
for him, a heritage to which he can attach himself. He will obtain
these advantages unfailingly the more he cultivates in himself the
spirit of his nation, his people, and his age."[21] Then, in 1796, this
plan for a comparative anthropology receded into the background
before the still vaster plan for a historically oriented work on the nature of humanity in general. Its separate parts were to be written by
different collaborators according to a central plan.[22] He set himself
the task of delineating the mind and character of the eighteenth
century. His first draft of this work, written in 1796 and 1797,[23]
did not get beyond a presentation of his methodological principles, a
careful sharpening of the knife he wanted to use; and because of
that, it indicates perhaps the limits of his capacities. Too often his
conceptions remain mere castles in the air and do not take on any
solid form. However, they do speak to us as though they were alive,
and they give sharp responses to our inquiries. It becomes clear that
despite the rationally and universally oriented tendencies of his age,
Humboldt tried to grasp the spirit of the eighteenth century from the
point of view of national history. In contrast to the French thinkers of
Louis XIV's time, who apparently knew only one form and rule for
everything, Humboldt declares:[24] "We are training ourselves now
to study the unique features of every age and nation, to inquire into
them as much as possible, and to make this knowledge the main
basis of our judgment." We can see from his example how a strict individualism that is honest with itself could come to recognize, by
virtue of its own strength and reflection, the supra-individual forces
of life that surround and limit the individual but also sustain and
fructify him. However important the aesthetic pleasure of discover-
ing these new ideas may have been, it was not, as we know, the
most important thing for Humboldt. The aesthetic was inseparably
fused in his mind with his innermost guiding principle: an intellectual
perspective that always attempted to comprehend itself and the
world at the same time. The strong individual in him that thirsted
for freedom became aware of its weakness and of its dependence

[20] *Plan einer vergleichenden Anthropologie* (1795), in *Ges. Schriften*, I, 384.
[21] *Ibid.*, I, 385.
[22] Cf. Leitzmann's notes in the *Ges. Schriften*, II, 401.
[23] *Ibid.*, II, 1-112.   [24] *Ibid.*, II, 72.

on the nation that bore it. And with gratitude, he looks back toward that nation. He confessed movingly to Goethe from Paris on March 18, 1799:[25] "Knowing the limits of my nature, you must be able to feel how everything that surrounds me outside Germany must remain heterogeneous for me. . . . Whoever occupies himself with philosophy and art belongs to his fatherland more intimately than others. . . . Philosophy and art are more in need of one's own language, which emotion and reflection have formed and which forms them again in turn." To this he adds the highly significant and accurate observation that a finer cultivation of language, philosophy, and art would make the individuality and the differences of nations more marked, the intimate understanding of them more difficult, but also the need for such understanding more general. In the highest human activities, then, he found the live roots of the nation. He did not envisage the development of an increasingly higher culture in a cosmopolitan fusion but rather in a national differentiation that can lead in turn to new efforts at mutual understanding. His Paris journals show how he immediately set about this task himself.[26] In the hectic atmosphere of French life, he felt with quiet pride the uniqueness as well as the superiority of German culture compared to the French.

In these years Humboldt seems to have almost reached the nineteenth-century mode of historical and national thought. But now we must sharply define his limitations as a son of the individualistic and cosmopolitan eighteenth century, limitations he intentionally did not want to transgress. His thinking is the first great example of how the new national idea, even in its most intelligent representatives, was still permeated by the universal, humane ideals of the hitherto existing culture. We should note how Humboldt soon limits the demand he had made in 1793 for a comparative study of nations. Aside from the prohibitive size of such a study, he also came to think it less useful because the degree of intensity with which one nation is studied became more important to him than the degree of extensiveness with which a great number can be studied. The national character most worthy of investigation was the one that best reflected

[25] Bratranek, *Goethes Briefwechsel mit den Gebrüdern von Humboldt*, p. 58. He wrote to Jacobi on October 26, 1798: "I have become an even more inveterate German in France than I was before." Leitzmann, *Briefe Humboldts an F. H. Jacobi*, p. 60; see, also, in the same book, p. 120. Humboldt wrote similarly to F. A. Wolf, October 22, 1798 (*Ges. Werke*, V, 208).

[26] Vol. XIV of the *Ges. Schriften* (1916).

the essential nature of humanity.[27] For him, that was the character of the Greeks. Their aim was "to educate men in the highest possible versatility and unity," and in the Greek character "the fundamental character of humanity in general" is evident.[28] Thus, for Humboldt, the study of a nation is a means to an end: he seeks in history a confirmation of his human ideal. In the final analysis, modern research into national life tries to extract the highest human values from history, too, but it finds the path from nation to mankind and from recorded experience to abstract ideal longer and more difficult than Humboldt thought it to be. It seeks to unite the breadth that Humboldt was willing to forego in his study of nations with the depth that he demanded. At the same time, the ideal of humanity that Humboldt wanted to reach quickly is allowed to recede from the immediate field of study so that the luster of the ideal does not weaken the eye's perception of reality. This does not mean that modern research gives up the ideal, but it does relegate it to other, higher spheres. It attempts only to determine as precisely, comprehensively, and impartially as possible how manifold man is as an individual historical being. How does this compare with Humboldt's definition of the task of comparative anthropology? He thought this science should examine the fixed character of nations with the accuracy of the natural sciences, but: "Although *it is the special concern and indeed the central purpose of comparative anthropology to learn how different man in the abstract can be,* the field must nonetheless take on all appearances of wanting to discover how different men as individuals are." Seen logically, Humboldt's approach probably does not seem too different from that of modern research. Seen psychologically, however, the difference between the two is quite striking.

Modern man is convinced that the limits between the different activities and needs of the human mind must be respected more strictly than Humboldt thought necessary. Modern man is further convinced that if we are to work as empirically as possible, we must first take empiricism as a goal in itself and pursue it relentlessly, not simply play the part of empiricists. This conviction brings both gains and losses with it. The modern thinker loses much of the inspiration and inner satisfaction that enabled Humboldt to rise at any time from the plane of actual man to that of ideal man. He gains, however, all that we can gain from a rational division of labor. The primary purpose of this book is to show how such an act of division

[27] *Ibid.*, I, 264.   [28] I, 270 and 275.

came about in the development of the concept of the nation in the nineteenth century. This concept was gradually separated from the universalistic and universally ethical ideals that were originally attached to it. By means of this separation, it first became usable for the purposes of the state. But we must consider still another division of labor that occurred in the province of the national idea. The concept of the state was divided, we might say, into theoretical and practical spheres. National consciousness became on the one hand a highly useful instrument for research and, on the other, a motivating moral force for state and society. These two impulses are bound together intrinsically, and they can never be separated without endangering them both at their sources. But in practice they act separately, and within a single individual a vigorous, nationally oriented political egoism can exist decisively alongside an affectionate understanding of foreign national character. In this regard, however, Humboldt is still an undivided whole, a close weaving together of theory and moral intention, because, as we saw, he wanted the study of nations to be both contemplative and ethical. His search for the ideal human being represents at once the highest ethics and the highest intellectual vision. In the course of investigating the national, he aimed beyond the national and sought the highest intellectual and moral level attainable. But, we will ask, what are the ethical results of his study of nations, the results that are of greatest interest to modern man and that seem most obvious to him? How did this study affect Humboldt's German sentiments?

We saw how he became gratefully conscious in Paris of what he had received from his fatherland and how he felt himself more German than ever in the midst of this strange and foreign nation. But the German nation to which he felt himself bound was not the entire nation in the full reaches of its being but only an extremely small elite from it. "In Germany," he writes to Jacobi,[29] "one gladly forgets the masses so that one may linger with some individuals." And still more clearly to Goethe:[30] "What binds me to Germany is nothing else but what I have drawn from life with you and with our circle, a circle from which I have been torn nearly two years now." Goethe and his world—that was Germany for Humboldt. Certainly he felt, too, that Goethe's Germany was not simply a circle of free, creative men but that in it that "inner motivation" was at work, that "lively, always active force" that was indispensable for every human being and for

---

[29] Leitzmann, op.cit., p. 64.   [30] Bratranek, op.cit., p. 58.

every nation.[31] Surely he had a consciousness of the national, but did he have a national consciousness?

He found the beauty and greatness of the German national character in the fact that it knew none of the natural limitations that other nations have and raised itself more purely and freely to the universally human. He writes in his essay on the eighteenth century:[32] "People generally censure the German because he denies his inner originality, imitates other nations too slavishly, and plays an easy victory into their hands by willfully staging the battle on a field unfamiliar to him. At present, this reproach cannot be denied. But in a long-range view, this imitation proves to be a temporary phenomenon and an extreme form of a quality that is otherwise worthy of admiration and emulation. Indeed, this imitation appears primarily to be a high-minded striving for idealistic diversity, since it does not arise from a lack of strength but only from the lack of a circumscribed nature, and it is the absence of such limitation that frees the understanding in the formation of judgments and the will in the development of strength."

Such sentiments were still far from being converted into a national political ethos. They did not even suffice for a recognition of what nation and state can mean for each other, nor did they suffice for a purely impartial scientific interest in this problem. Living in the phenomenon of a revolutionized and nationalized French state and eagerly involved in comprehending the French national character in its most minute features, Humboldt wrote to Goethe: "I do not trouble myself with politics, you know."[33] He counted politics among those "circumstances of the times" and "external events" that we must leave aside if we want to make out the permanent character of a nation. He wrote to Jacobi from Paris on October 26, 1798, "I shall not speak about the political mood at all. I am limiting myself simply to what is really national, the trend of opinion and mind, the formation of character, the customs, etc."[34]

What always held him back from political life was the high and ambitious thought that the Germans had been called at that time to become the representative people of all mankind. They were to create the purest mirror of humanity, just as the Greeks, in Hum-

[31] Leitzmann, op.cit., p. 61.

[32] Op.cit., II, 43; see also, in this respect, Humboldt's letter to A. Wolf, August 20, 1797, Ges. Werke, V, 194.

[33] Bratranek, op.cit., p. 49 (Spring, 1798).

[34] Leitzmann, Briefe Humboldts an F. H. Jacobi, p. 61.

boldt's view, had created it before. We know how this thought, in every form of expression from the most trivial to the most sublime, dominated educated Germany at that time. Probably no one expressed it better than Schiller in a prose outline for a poem that apparently comes from the period after the peace of Lunéville and that an editor could later entitle "German Greatness."[35] The prose synopsis reads: "May the German have any pride at this moment when he emerges ingloriously from a grievous war, when two arrogant nations tread on his neck and the victor determines his fate? . . . Yes, he may! He comes defeated from the battle, but he has not lost what constitutes his worth. The German Empire and the German nation are two different things. The majesty of the German never rested on the head of his prince. The German has founded his own value apart from politics, and even if the Empire perished, German dignity would remain uncontested. This dignity is a moral greatness. It resides in the culture and in the character of the nation that are both independent of her political vicissitudes. . . . While the political Empire has tottered, the spiritual realm has become all the firmer and richer."

If the course of the world is indeed planned, his sketch continues, then he who cultivates and masters the mind will come to mastery in the end. Other peoples will then be the flower that falls while the golden fruit remains. While the British search out wealth and the French, glory, the highest reward is destined for the German: "He keeps company with the spirit of all worlds." "Every people has its day in history, but the German's day is the harvest of all times."

[35] "Deutsche Grösse. Ein unvollendetes Gedicht Schillers 1801." First published by Goedeke, then by B. Suphan, Weimar, 1902 (*Schriften der Goethegesellschaft*), in the Cotta centenary edition of Schiller's works, II, 386, and by Lienhard, *Schillers Gedichtentwurf Deutsche Grösse* (1916). Leitzmann, *Euphorion*, Vols. XII and XVII, assigns the outline to the year 1797. I am not convinced by his arguments. Schiller welcomed the Peace of Leoben with great relief, but he regarded the Peace of Lunéville quite differently and bitterly. Also, the world situation that the sketch reflects (especially the expansion of English power) suits 1801 better than 1797. Two comments of W. von Humboldt's to Schiller from 1797 and 1798 have recently been taken as references to the poem "German Greatness" (Ebrard, *Neue Briefe W. von Humboldts an Schiller*, pp. 161 and 235). But these statements certainly do not reveal anything about the theme of the "song" Schiller was planning at that time.—Kuberka, *Der Idealismus Schillers als Erlebnis und Lehre* (1913), p. 35, tries to show from some well-known passages of Schiller's later dramas that the author had "anchored" the political idea of the state "in the ideal of the modern national state." But he fails to recognize the poetic license and human insight with which Schiller approached and treated all political questions and materials. Toennies, *Schiller als Zeitbürger und Politiker* (1905), sees this factor more clearly.

These words have a certain magic about them that becomes all the stronger perhaps because this look into Schiller's notes has been granted only to his descendants and because he seems now, in intimate conversation, to render account about something that is a concern of the heart as well as an item of knowledge. We feel the inspiration of his soul more strongly than we would if he had clothed these thoughts in his glittering verse, which so easily clouds immediacy. The effect of his words rests, however, on something still deeper, on the intimation that we are concerned here with the chaste secret of our national history, with something in our cultural heritage that might seem like delusion or intellectual pomposity to the fault-finder but that appears to a more sensitive mind as the purest of sentiments and at the same time as a sentiment historically necessary and beneficial. That the German Empire and the German nation are two different things, that the culture and the character of the German nation are independent of its political vicissitudes are statements that will seem rash to some people today. However, this thought that strikes the present generation as erroneous was a living truth for many Germans of Schiller's time, and for the most serious among them it was a truth of religious force.[36] Whoever seeks to found the realm of the spirit in this world must begin by saying: My kingdom is not of this world. He must flee the world in order to rule it later with a stronger inner power. We create the highest intellectual and moral values by first raising ourselves above reality. The idea of the nation in Germany gained a new and deeper substance for the very reason that everything political—and how much of the faded and decayed was in it then—was swept out of it and replaced by all the intellectual values that had been newly attained. Through this act, the concept of the nation was raised to the sphere of eternity and religion. And through this, universally oriented culture was made national in such a way that one could not and did not want to say where the universal ended and the national began. A bridge was thus built from the one to the other, and when in the course of time this spiritualized idea of the nation returned to the state, it brought to it a legacy which enabled the state to fulfill its highest mission and to assume in the family of important human values the place the development of mankind attributes to it. For if the modern national state is to remain capable of rejuvenating

[36] I refer the reader here to my parallel and supplementary remarks in my *Das Zeitalter der deutschen Erhebung* (3rd edn.), pp. 27f.

itself, it needs a source of life in the universal sphere and a constant justification before the bench of the highest human ideals.

The course of this development is clear to us today in its large outlines, a development that led from the idea of humanity to that of the nation and finally to that of the state. First, the universal became national and the national universal. Then the state was made national and the nation political but in such a way that the universal note continued to sound for a long time. But the simplicity of this large development breaks up into a baffling, tangled course and a maze of deadends and side streets if we look at it more closely. The genuine historical mind cannot forget the one for the sake of the other. It must rise to a high vantage point at one moment and then at the next descend to where the individual wanderer painstakingly seeks his way. For only in the refraction of a beam of light can we see the colors of the actual life we want to grasp. And when we try to support our general theories with facts, we will have to admit that many individual events may have come about according to principles unknown to us. And these principles may contribute to a final result that they would seem to prevent. Many might think, for example, that Schiller too would have become an orator for the German nation if he had lived past 1806. And as support for this, one could refer to Schiller's personality, to the spirit of his last drama, and finally to what can be heard in his lines on "German Greatness." For despite all his denial of political interest, we can still feel beyond this denial his painful distress about the actual situation of Germany. It could well be that he would have followed Fichte's example. But only a superficial view would claim that he could have done nothing else and would have gone beyond Goethe's quietism. For there was more than one road that led from the universally oriented world of the eighteenth century to the national and nationally political world of the nineteenth century, and the great figures of this period were too individualized and independent to let themselves be sent out on one path alone. The point of departure for all these men was the idea of a universal humanity, and the richness and creative energy of this idea are evident in the very fact that so many different paths took it as their point of origin, for this universalism was also the most vigorous individualism.

4

NOVALIS AND FRIEDRICH SCHLEGEL IN THE YEARS OF EARLY ROMANTICISM

THE END of the last chapter was meant to evoke a quotation from Novalis. By this route, we come from Humboldt and Schiller to the Romantics to inquire how they conceived of the nation and of its relation to the life of the state during their most productive period, the final years of the eighteenth century. From Humboldt's subtle but coherent thinking, we come now to a world of aphorism and fragment, to a puzzling profusion of suggestive and original ideas. Humboldt's path always led clearly and directly toward the "ideal human being" that he had set up as his goal, and he looked at the nation and state from this perspective. The Romantics followed innumerable paths, and no sooner have we committed ourselves to one of them than we see our guide, whom we thought we were following, nimbly flee in another direction. It would seem pedantic if we continued to the end of the path we had started on and sought systematic rigor where often only a vibrant imagination was at work. However, we must make the attempt to establish as many firm points as possible because, especially in the early Romantics, we begin to sense the first signs of the later political Romanticism[1] to which our study will lead. We will clearly not find reflected in the high-spirited turmoil of early Romanticism the bitter seriousness and doctrinaire strictness that Romantic ideas later took on in the circle of Friedrich Wilhelm IV. But we will perhaps be able to see in what context they first appear and with what accompanying ideas they are connected. And further, we will be able to derive some enlightening points from the historical background of those

---

[1] The term "political Romanticism," which has been much maligned lately, retains a worthwhile meaning, and we cannot do without it. It includes not only the political ideas and actions of specifically Romantic poets and writers, but also an entire world of political thought and direction that indeed began with the Romantics but was then handed down and revised in certain political circles until beyond the middle of the nineteenth century.

years and from the effects that the French Revolution and the Napoleonic period had on German intellectual life. This investigation will be limited to those representatives of early Romanticism whose ideas on the nation and state were most richly developed. They are, in order of importance, Novalis and Friedrich Schlegel.

However iridescent and protean the play of their ideas may seem at first, there is still one central idea that holds the others together and that also explains by its own content why that play appears so colorful and manifold. This is the idea that the universe contains in itself an endless profusion of individualities and that its unity is not loosened or shattered by this but is instead strengthened by it, so that the universe is in itself an individual and a personality.[2] "Individuality in nature is quite endless. How greatly this view animates our hopes about the personality of the universe."[3] Similarly, for Friedrich Schlegel, God is an "abyss of individuality"[4] on the one hand and, on the other, "the essence of the individual to the highest degree."[5]

Merged together in these ideas are old pantheistic impulses, religious elements of a mystic or pietistic nature, and new individual-

---

[2] We are touching on this central idea here only to the extent that is necessary for an understanding of our problem. We will not consider its broader philosophical implications and its relationship to the philosophical systems of the time, especially Schelling's. The recent well-known writings of Ricarda Huch, Marie Joachimi, Kircher, Poetzsch (*Studien zur frühromantischen Politik und Geschichtsauffassung*, 1907) offer suggestive material for an understanding of Romantic philosophy in general. Also useful here are Walzel, *Deutsche Romantik* (5th edn., 1923); Elkuss, *Zur Beurteilung der Romantik und Kritik ihrer Erforschung* (1918); Schmitt-Dorotić, *Politische Romantik* (1919; 2nd edn., 1925); Nadler, *Berliner Romantik 1800-1814* (1921). The more recent books about Romanticism by Mehlis (1922), Stefansky (1923), and Kluckhohn (1924) do not offer anything particularly new in our area of study. More useful here is Borries, *Die Romantik u. d. Geschichte* (1925). A. Weise, *Die Entwicklung des Fühlens und Denkens der Romantik* (1912), offers many interesting political observations collected from magazines of the Romantic period. In his investigation of the Romantic "psyche," Weise lets Lamprecht's influence mislead him into neglecting the actual personalities and circles that stood behind individual magazines. He consequently makes the error of treating Fichte's Machiavelli essay of 1807 (see p. 77, below), which was reprinted in the *Musen* of 1813, as evidence of North German-Prussian Romanticism in 1813.—The political views of Novalis and Fr. Schlegel have also been treated recently by Metzger, *Gesellschaft, Recht und Staat in der Ethik des deutschen Idealismus* (1917), pp. 224ff. However, precisely those parts of Metzger's commendable book that would interest us most do not get beyond the stage of excerpting from these authors. In contrast, Samuel's penetrating book, *Die poetische Staats- und Geschichtsauffassung Fr. v. Hardenbergs (Novalis)* (1925), is highly successful as a whole.

[3] Novalis, *Schriften*, ed. Heilborn, II, 371 and 653.

[4] Friedrich Schlegel, *Prosaische Jugendschriften*, ed. Minor, II, 289.

[5] Marie Joachimi, *Weltanschauung der Romantik*, p. 39.

istic tendencies closely related to those of Goethe and Humboldt. The entire philosophical movement of the period since Kant led in this direction, and Schelling in particular was extremely influential here. Thus, a completely new and appealing attitude toward life arose. A quietistic, emotional abandon to all the interrelationships of the universe was united in it with an intense enjoyment of one's own individuality and that of others. But we do not want to concern ourselves with the background of these ideas in intellectual history or with their effect on personal life. Their application to the life of the nation and state is what interests us here. It becomes clear at the start that the ideas of all the early Romantics became so infinitely fluid and flexible that in looking down into the "abyss of individuality" these Romantic thinkers could become intoxicated with their vision of God and the world. They were serious about interpreting every impulse of life as an individuality. "We can say," Novalis writes, "that every thought, every stirring of our spirit is a highly individual manifestation of a thoroughly unique whole."[6] Since everything, indeed, *everything* could be resolved into its individual character, the eye became sharpened to every particular phenomenon of history and of the life of the state, too; and the early Romantics were readily inclined to acknowledge the special status of this area of life. But whoever is willing to acknowledge everything is in danger of affirming nothing. How often the objects of the Romantics' spirited reflection slipped through their fingers because they did not have the power to grasp and hold fast. But with their strong desire to expand their intellectual range, they penetrated quickly and overwhelmingly into areas that were still of little interest to Classical Idealism. Novalis often speaks movingly and profoundly about the state and the relationship of the individual to it: "The more spirited and lively the members are, the more lively and personal the state is. The spirit of the state glows forth from every genuine citizen just as in a religious society a personal God reveals himself, so to speak, in a thousand forms. The state, God, or any other spiritual being does not appear in one form but in a thousand various forms."[7] We can sense how the elements that come together here to conjure up the image of the state as a living personality can immediately disperse again in endless phantasmagoria. But still, Novalis actually did see the state as a coherent individuality—"the state has always been a macroanthropos"[8]—indeed, as an individual-

---

[6] *Schriften*, II, 243.   [7] *Ibid.*, II, 543.
[8] *Ibid.*, II, 217; cf. II, 291.

ity in the historical sense, not in the rationalistic sense of those who wanted the perfect normative state; for, he says, "states will remain different as long as men are different,"[9] and he chides those poor Philistines who see no other salvation than in the new style of the French Revolution.[10] With a sound feeling for life, he saw the close association of state and family and observed the elements of the family in the character of the state.[11] Prussia therefore captured his attention because at that moment the young ruling couple, Friedrich Wilhelm III and Luise, seemed to be initiating a new and propitious era there. He became absorbed with the animating effects that such a ruling couple generated, and he saw them in a symbolic light that anticipated the mood of Prussia's rise against Napoleon and also that of the Restoration period that followed it.[12] The simple patriarchical royalism of the first period and the mystic patriarchical royalism of the second both begin to show themselves here, but in a form still completely free, fluid, and poetic. For even though Novalis turns away sharply from the idea of popular sovereignty, the sovereignty of the individual still shines through in his thinking.[13] It was

[9] *Ibid.*, II, 291; cf. II, 526.

[10] *Ibid.*, II, 42. His attitude toward the French Revolution, about which he had been extremely enthusiastic in his early youth, does not by any means become one of total aversion even in later years. (See Heilborn, *Novalis*, p. 45; *Friedrich von Hardenberg [Novalis]: Eine Nachlese*, p. 58; Andr. Müller, *Stellung der deutschen Romantik zu den Ideen der franz. Revol.* [Münster dissertation, 1924; typed MS], pp. 30ff. Müller read my book poorly, however, and takes from it just the opposite of what I had said concerning Novalis' attitude toward the idea of the national state and toward Catholicism.) This ambivalent attitude toward the Revolution distinguishes Novalis from Burke as well as from later political Romanticism. He says acutely of Burke (*Schriften*, II, 31) that he "wrote a revolutionary book against the Revolution," and he presumably counts Burke among those "most brilliant opponents of the Revolution" who "urgently recommended castration." "They doubtless noted that this alleged sickness was nothing more than a crisis of incipient puberty" (*loc.cit.*; cf., too, II, 660, and his essay on Christendom, II, 418, where he displays a remarkable empathic understanding of revolutionary pathos). This does not, however, preclude the possibility that he might have learned something from Burke. Samuel, *op.cit.*, pp. 76ff., has recently shown this to be plausible.

[11] Samuel, p. 99; Kluckhohn, *Persönlichkeit und Gemeinschaft*, p. 48.

[12] Haym, *Romant. Schule*, p. 344, rather one-sidedly emphasizes only the last point when he says: "All the main attitudes of the later Restoration and Romantic theory of the state are already present in these aphorisms."

[13] Cf., for example, *Schriften*, II, 40: "It is incorrect to call the king the first official of the state. The king is not a citizen of the state and consequently not an official of it either. This is precisely the distinctive point of a monarchy. It is based on the belief in a man of higher birth than the rest, on the voluntary acceptance of an ideal man. . . . The king is a man raised to the role of fate on earth. This poetic idea inevitably presses itself upon men. It alone satisfies a higher yearning of their nature. All men should become worthy of the throne. The educational

thus possible to dream of an ideal monarchy that would also be a genuine republic at the same time, because for Novalis genuine republicanism meant simply "general participation in the entire state, close contact and harmony of all the members of the state."[14] He could demand that the state enter into the life of the individual in quite a different way than it had up to that point. "The state is too little proclaimed among us. There should be proclaimers of the state, preachers of patriotism. Most members of the state stand in a very poor relationship to it now, almost an antagonistic relationship."[15] In the course of such considerations, the value and productive power of the state grew in his estimation. "All culture," he was bold enough to say, "arises from the relationship of man with the state."[16] He also became more and more convinced that the state contained a long-slighted and neglected source of strength for elevating and invigorating the individual existence: "Man has tried to make the state into a cushion for his indolence, but the state should be precisely the opposite,—it is an armature of all activity. Its purpose is to make man totally powerful, not totally weak, to make him the most active, not the most indolent of beings. The state does not relieve man of any cares but rather increases his cares infinitely, not, however, without infinitely increasing his strength."[17]

Thus, even this visionary poet and philosopher is an articulate witness of a quiet change in German intellectual life at that time, of the germinating, in a previously unpolitical soil, of ethical and political impulses that came to view so strikingly in those years. Unsatisfied with the pure idealism of his great contemporaries, he undertook to raise it into magical realms. We might object that there is little substance to this heralding of the state, that this preacher of patriotism and of sympathy for the state is in truth no preacher at all but only a poet, an extremely sensitive and receptive artistic mind that discovered that the state and life in the state also have their beauties. We shall let the objection stand and then try to discover the strength in what appears to be a weakness. Do we not have before us again one of those hidden paths by which the German spirit came to the German state—a significant application of Schiller's principle of aesthetic education? The gate of beauty should lead not

means to this distant goal is a king. He gradually assimilates the mass of his subjects. Every man springs from an ancient line of kings. But how few still bear the marks of this heritage?" Cf., too, *Schriften*, II, 659f.

[14] *Ibid.*, II, 49; cf. in general, II, 35ff.   [15] *Ibid.*, II, 393.
[16] *Ibid.*, II, 543.   [17] *Ibid.*, II, 528.

only to the land of knowledge but also to the land of moral action. We
can indeed doubt the strength and will of the poet to enter the
land he had glimpsed or to grasp in reality the state he had praised.
But it was at least a gain that he saw it in the strength of its battle
array and in its splendor. The new, living state that he demands,
however aesthetically tinged his demand may be, is still the same
one that more ethical natures like Schleiermacher, Arndt, and
Fichte demanded then and in the following years. Also, a concrete
core to Novalis' ideal of the state is not missing either, because, as
we noted, it was bound to the attitudes of the old inherited patriarchical royalism. Thus we can see here how men could come to the genuine national state from this historical foundation and by following
the aesthetic and Romantic tendencies of the times. For it is Novalis'
view that the state should be based on the active participation
of the citizens in the community and on a conscious, mutual interaction of civil and political life. His sympathies for the national
state are evident in his opposition to the mechanistic state of Frederick the Great's monarchy. "No state," he said,[18] "has been admin-
istrated more like a factory than Prussia since the death of Friedrich
Wilhelm I." That was a reproach that had been made by many
since Mirabeau, both by adherents of the French ideas of freedom
and by adherents of the old feudal system and patriarchical order.
Novalis may have been influenced by both sides when he took up
this reproach. The reproach was not entirely just, but it belongs to
the historical injustices that must be committed if we are to make
progress in history ourselves. His great and fruitful achievement was
that he not only criticized the largest German individual state but
also idealized it and that he recognized in it the calling and the capacity to be a genuine national state.

If Novalis' interests in this area had been more pronounced, he
might have gone further as a political thinker than he did. But precisely because this single-minded interest was lacking in him, his
thoughts on the state never went beyond mere philosophizing and the
establishing of important principles. He looked back on his own revolutionary tendencies in his youth as something he had overcome.
"These years pass for most of us, and we feel ourselves attracted by
a more peaceful world where a central sun directs our steps, and we
prefer to be planets rather than to join in a destructive dance that
is only the beginning of the real struggle."[19] The basic Romantic

---

[18] *Ibid.*, II, 47.   [19] *Ibid.*, II, 660.

tendency to let the forces of the universe rock us in blissful contemplation thus became predominant in him. Politically, he became tolerant and relativistic, and he praised the "mature mind's independence from every individual form that is no more valuable to it than a
necessary tool."[20] Because of this sublime indifference to the individual forms of the state's existence, he did not develop the fruitful
beginnings of his theory of the national state any further. This man
who perceived personality and individuality everywhere else had surprisingly little to say about the personality of the nation as a whole.
He demanded the animation and glorification of the state more
for the benefit of the individual than for the entire nation, and he
did not yet make the element of German nationality useful for the
state in any specific way. As his aphorisms on the Prussian monarchy clearly indicate, he understands the term nation to mean a
political nation in the narrower sense of a people within the borders
of an already established state, in this case, the Prussian people.[21]
The German nation, however, is purely a cultural and not a political
nation for Novalis, just as it was for Humboldt and all the great thinkers of this period.

And as such it dissolved for him immediately into the realms of
universality and humanity as a whole. "There are Germans everywhere. The German character is no more limited to a particular
state than Roman, Greek, or British character. Those are general
human traits that have become particularly dominant in one place
or another. German nature is representative of genuine humanity and
is therefore an ideal."[22] He writes in the same vein to A. W.
Schlegel:[23] "German nature is cosmopolitanism mixed with the strongest individuality." "The instinctive tendency of the Romans toward
political universality exists in the German people too. The best thing
that the French gained from the Revolution is a portion of the German
character."[24] "No nation can compete with us in vigorous universalism."[25] Novalis the Romantic shared with Schiller and Humboldt's
circle this belief in the universal calling of the German nation and the
belief that the German people were the representative nation of all

[20] *Loc.cit.*
[21] Thus he speaks in *Schriften*, II, 49, of the wish of the king of Prussia "to
become the true reformer and restorer of his nation and his time."
[22] *Ibid.*, II, 16.
[23] November 30, 1797. *Friedrich von Hardenberg (Novalis): Eine Nachlese*,
p. 169; Raich, *Novalis' Briefwechsel mit F. u. A. W. Charl. u. Carol. Schlegel*,
p. 41.
[24] *Schriften*, II, 15.   [25] *Ibid.*, II, 70.

mankind, but he gave this view a particularly Romantic coloring. It was specifically Romantic to conceive of the universal and the individual always in and with each other and to practice a type of epicurism in keenly perceiving each of the two elements in the other. "Everything national, temporal, local, and individual can be universalized . . . this individual hue of the universal is its romanticizing element."[26] At another point, Novalis gave still another definition of romanticizing: "The world must be romanticized . . . I romanticize the common by giving it a high significance, the ordinary by giving it a mysterious appearance, the known by giving it the dignity of the unknown, the finite by giving it the appearance of the infinite."[27] Great and glowing as this demand was and powerful as the impulses were that it was able to give to modern thinking, we can easily understand that it let thought wander off into brilliant play and that in the end the "appearance of the infinite" could emerge victorious over the finite. Similarly, the universal overshadowed everything that was individual and concretely defined, and the idea of total humanity won ascendency over the idea of the nation.

We can understand further how a universalistic element emerged in his view of the state, and it was this element that could no longer recognize or approve the unconditional autonomy and individuality of single states. "States must finally realize," he says, "that the achievement of all their goals is only possible through collective measures. Systems of alliance. An approximation to a universal monarchy."[28] What he meant by this he worked out coherently in his remarkable essay of 1799 on "Die Christenheit oder Europa."[29] We can see in it now, more clearly than before, the connecting links between subjective early Romanticism and the later political Romanticism of the Restoration period.

Novalis presents here both a concept of history and an ideal for the future. He outlines a glowing picture of the Christian European culture of the Middle Ages. He sees dark shadows fall on the Reformation and on the intellectual and political development that followed it, but he thinks that the morning of a new and splendid day in the life of Europe is breaking, that the glorious period of the Cath-

---

[26] *Ibid.*, II, 129.   [27] *Ibid.*, II, 304.   [28] *Ibid.*, II, 285.
[29] *Ibid.*, II, 399. The essay was originally planned for the *Athenäum*, but it was withdrawn by the magazine itself and set aside for special publication. It is known that Goethe spoke against its publication in the *Athenäum*. Samuel, *op.cit.*, 230; Dilthey, *Das Erlebnis und die Dichtung*, p. 231 (3rd edn., p. 298); Haym, *Romant. Schule*, pp. 462ff.; Raich, *Novalis' Briefwechsel*, pp. 133 and 145ff.; Spenlé, *Novalis* (Paris, 1903), pp. 274ff.

olic Middle Ages will rise up in a new, rejuvenated form. But it is dangerous to reduce his thoughts to so simple and tangible a formula, for their outlines dissolve in haze and luster if we look at them more closely. Language serves the ineffable here, and ideas do not serve what can be thought but only what can be felt and seen. He speaks in extravagant tones of the Catholic Church of the Middle Ages and its cult, of the "holy, exquisitely beautiful lady of Christendom," even of the eternal value of the Jesuit order; but who would dare to sift these words and take his catholicizing sentiments seriously when he praises Schleiermacher as one of the heralds of the new era and when he speaks of a final form of Christianity that is nothing else than "belief in the ability of everything earthly to be the wine and bread of eternal life." Thus, everything earthly and historical is only a symbol for him or a means of approaching the invisible and infinite, the incomprehensible and miraculous, those depths where humanity and universe flow together. He takes such a high position above actual history that he sees heaven and earth melt into each other, and it is just this sublime spectacle that makes him patient, irenic, and understanding in regard to the isolated historical event. Thus, even his verdict on Protestantism and its bad religious and political effects finally resolves into a kiss of brotherhood for the entire world.

But his verdict, with the consequences that follow from it, remains nonetheless, and it must be taken into account. It is very instructive for us to see how his sympathy for the Middle Ages is essentially a sympathy for their universalistic nature. He compares the "general Christian community" of this epoch with the disruption of the community of states in recent times. He blames this disruption on the Reformation, which has allowed secular and earthly elements to win the upper hand. "Modern politics did not arise until this point in time, and single powerful states have tried since then to take possession of the vacant universal seat, which has taken on the form of a throne."[30] The rise of the great power states of modern times, the urge for expansion and autonomy, in short, the secularization of politics seems to him to be a secession and a usurpation. He will not allow the state to stand firmly on the solid ground of its own particular interests. "All your supports are too weak if your state continues to lean toward the earth. But if, by a higher striving, you bind it to the heights of heaven, if you give it a bearing on the universe, then

[30] *Schriften*, II, 406.

you will have a source of energy in it that will never wear out, and you will see your pains richly rewarded."[31] Taking a high vantage point, he can understand that even the murderous battles of states and nations have a higher historical purpose because these closer and more manifold contacts of peoples with each other are only a preliminary step toward a European community and a "state of states." But the task of bringing this about cannot devolve upon the states themselves but only upon a universal power that stands above them and is at once both worldly and otherworldly, i.e., the hierarchy and the church, for "it is impossible for secular powers to bring themselves into balance. . . . Only religion can waken Europe again and reconcile its nations."[32]

This is, in a cursory but not unclear sketch, the program for a religious-ecclesiastical cosmopolitanism[33] and also a plan for its dominance in the area of politics. The medieval idea of the *corpus Christianum* comes to life in it again, an idea which also dominated early Protestant thinking in the form Luther had given it. Novalis' program became a prelude and a companion piece to the theories of de Maistre, Bonald, and—as Dilthey has recognized—to the Holy Alliance.[34] Novalis is, of course, despite his Catholic sympathies, still essentially a pantheistic Protestant, and it is one thing when he speaks about the church and hierarchy and their call to leadership in the Christian world of states and quite another thing when the Catholics Bonald and de Maistre speak of the same thing. For however antagonistic Novalis was toward Protestantism and the Enlightenment, he was by no means ready to do without the inner intellectual freedom that was their greatest achievement. He dreamed of a harmony of individual freedom and universal unity.[35] But such ideals, drawn to their heights and spiritualized to their extremes, can seldom survive in such pure form. We soon ask for the palpable and physical again. Even Novalis was not satisfied with his invisible church of the future and wanted Christendom to "form a visible church again without regard for national boundaries." He called for a "worthy European council" to realize his dream. The road

---

[31] *Ibid.*, II, 412.   [32] *Ibid.*, II, 417ff.

[33] He speaks directly at one point about "religious cosmopolitan interests" (*Schriften*, II, 405).

[34] "It was an unhistorical view that lent a Christian appearance to the Holy Alliance." *Das Erlebnis und die Dichtung*, p. 230 (3rd edn., p. 298).

[35] "No one will protest against Christian or worldly oppression any more, for the very being of the church will be genuine freedom itself" (*Schriften*, II, 420).

back to Rome from here was not a long one, and it could attract flagging spirits. Friedrich Schlegel is an illustration of that.

Let us turn now to those aspects of Schlegel's development that touch on our problem.[36] The yield from the most interesting and richest years of his thought—again the final years of the eighteenth century—is clearly not as fruitful as it was with Humboldt and Novalis. But his dominant position in early Romanticism and his further development that leads directly to the political Romanticism of the Restoration period demand that we take a look at the political and national thought of his youth. This universal thinker undoubtedly had a passionate interest in political subjects. "I shall be happy when I can finally revel in politics," he wrote to his brother in 1796.[37] But this political interest was not in the state as it was but in the state as it should be according to his ideas. His "Versuch über den Begriff des Republikanismus" (1796)[38] still stands on essentially the same rationalistic and nonhistorical foundations as Kant's essay on eternal peace, which Schlegel discusses here. Schlegel's essay is still more theoretical and unrealistic than Kant's, in whose discussion we can always sense the solemn earnestness of the political reformer. Schlegel's political argument, influenced by Fichte's thinking, is more an attempt to incorporate politics into his world scheme. He could thus make further concessions to the ideas of the French Revolution than could the more cautious and experienced Kant.[39]

One of the ideas in which he joins Kant and then goes beyond him demands our attention here. To achieve a lasting peace, Kant

[36] R. Volpers, *Fr. Schlegel als politischer Denker und deutscher Patriot* (1917), offers a careful collection of material but without sufficient penetration and unification. H. Finke's solid prorector's address in Freiburg in 1918 (cf. particularly pp. 55ff.) offers new perspectives for a higher evaluation of Friedrich Schlegel in general and of his attitudes toward the nation as well. However, I think I must still stand by my own presentation, which intended to seek out only those elements of Schlegel's thinking that fall within our field of inquiry. On the ideas of his brother, August Wilhelm, that belong here, cf. Haym, *Romant. Schule*, pp. 804ff., 824, 850ff., and above all O. Brandt, *A. W. Schlegel, der Romantiker u. die Politik* (1919), and Andreas Müller, *op.cit.*, pp. 123ff.

[37] Walzel, *F. Schlegels Briefe an seinen Bruder August Wilhelm*, p. 278.

[38] Published in the magazine *Deutschland*. Friedrich Schlegel, *Prosaische Jugendschriften*, ed. Minor, II, 57ff. Cf. the characteristically positive judgment of him by the French author Rouge, *Fr. Schlegel et la génèse du romantisme allemand* (1904), pp. 169ff.

[39] However, leanings toward a historico-empirical treatment of politics do occur in Schlegel's essay (*Jugendschriften*, II, 69f.). Cf., too, Baxa, *Einführung in die romant. Staatswissenschaft* (1923), pp. 23f. Cf. Andr. Müller, *op.cit.*, pp. 42ff., on Fichte's influence.

had called for a federalism of free states, an international league for peace. Kant would have been content with that step, and he rejected the idea of a world republic as impracticable. Schlegel, however, thought an international state both conceivable and possible. "The idea of a world republic has practical validity and distinctive importance."[40] Like Kant, he conceived of the individual nations as independent and autonomous within this international state. But this autonomy was not the same as the autonomy we have in mind in this study. It is not the autonomy of a concrete, historical state entity but the autonomy, the sovereignty, of a people as Rousseau and natural law defined it, an autonomy that is based on general human postulates of reason[41] and that sees individual states only as subdivisions of humanity. Thus, the idea of uniting these states into a republic is understandable. Where Novalis recommended a religious-ecclesiastical cosmopolitanism, Schlegel revived the idea of a cosmopolitanism derived from natural law and democracy.

Curiously enough, he belonged to the un-Romantic world as a political thinker although as a poet and aesthetician he had known and heard for a long time the "soul and voice of the nation,"[42] the genuine, historical nation. As a young author he had the wish as early as 1791 "to grasp everything in the rich individuality of our nation," and he claimed then "to have discovered that our people have a great character."[43] Irreconcilable as the two extremes may seem, we are really breathing the air of those years when, in 1793, we see Schlegel become enthusiastic about "German values and spirit" at one moment and about "French freedom" at the next.[44] Like Humboldt and Herder before him, he too had gained further understanding of national character through the inspiration of Hellenic culture. It became clear to him from Greek poetry that it had drawn its strength virtually and exclusively from the soil of the nation,[45] whereas modern poetry, he thought, had become artificial because it had drawn back from this soil and taken on a general European character.[46] Surveying

[40] *Jugendschriften*, II, 59.   [41] See p. 29, above.
[42] "Über das Studium der griechischen Poesie" (1795-96), *Jugendschriften*, I, 175f.
[43] To his brother, in Walzel, *op.cit.*, p. 26.
[44] Walzel, pp. 132 and 145.
[45] "Greek culture in general was thoroughly original and national, a whole complete in itself, which achieved the highest peaks through mere internal development and, after running full circle, sank back into itself. . . . Its poetry was not national just in its beginnings but was also continuously national in the entire course of its existence" (*Jugendschriften*, I, 143).
[46] *Ibid.*, I, 94.

the phenomenon of Greek culture as a whole, he could not stop at the idea of Greece as a cultural nation alone but was forced to appreciate it as a political nation too and to see the connection between its intellectual and political life. Greece did not offer him the spectacle of a collective national state but a spectacle that was perhaps even greater in his view: a group of national states that were intrinsically related and united but that remained free and autonomous in themselves. He explains in his *Geschichte der Poesie der Griechen und Römer*,[47] written in 1798, that not every nation has a style or character in the higher sense of the word. "A nation achieves that only through a certain fortunate correspondence between the moral and intellectual disposition and the external environment and through a balance of original elements at the beginning of its formation when the general character has become capable of independence; through unlimited freedom in its own development and destiny and through vigorous battle with another people of contrasting nature; through sociality and community of all individuals, through the uniting and fraternizing of the free states . . ." and finally: "through the striving for universality and completeness of culture in a cosmopolitan sense that does not scorn the acceptance of something foreign that might transform oneself."

His wishes and ideals for his own nation shine through the ideal picture of the Greek people that he sketches here. He can even readily fuse his early dream of an international state and a world republic with his specifically national consciousness. The autonomy of the individual free state as well as of the nation as a whole is conceived of much more concretely and historically here than it was in his political essay of 1796. Thus he sketched the image of a great, independent, and unique cultural nation that underlay a number of independent, unique, but still related and connected state structures. We shall see later how meaningfully this thought could be worked out. But Schlegel himself did not carry it any further then. He was always drawn beyond the national and political sphere to a purely intellectual one. "Do not squander faith and love in the political world," he wrote in 1799, "but sacrifice, in the divine world of learning and art, your innermost life to the holy and fiery stream of eternal creativity."[48] Concerning his own German character, his feel-

---

[47] *Ibid.*, I, 358; cf., too, I, 361: "But how ineradicably this character endures once such a mixture of wandering and indigenous peoples of similar but not identical origins comes together in a nation or even in a system of republics" etc.
[48] "Ideen" (*Athenäum*), *Jugendschriften*, II, 300.

ings were similar to those of Novalis and Humboldt. To be German was to have the inspiring awareness of serving the highest goals of mankind more purely than other nations serve them. "It is a national characteristic only among the Germans to honor art and learning as divinities just for the sake of art and learning themselves.[49] . . . Art and learning are the national gods of the Germans, not Hermann and Wodan."[50]

With this, we return again to the most influential source of the ideas that have concerned us so far. Both Novalis and Schlegel made initial steps toward a profound appreciation of the national state and also toward a political universalism that limited the autonomy of the individual state in turn. In Novalis this universalism is bound to a medieval, theocratic universalism, in Friedrich Schlegel to the cosmopolitan ideas of the Revolution. Schlegel's universalism, though, is only tenuously connected to these ideas, and it is not decisively influenced by them. But stronger and more profound in its effects than either the Middle Ages or Rousseau was the basic character of German culture at the time: its high intellectualism, its exclusive esteem for the ideal values in life, its energetic devotion to the inner life of the human mind, its inclination to let only those elements of the outer world affect it that would nourish the inner life best and most easily. In this respect, the early Romantics were still the genuine sons of the generation that had created the humanistic ideal, the generation of Herder, Goethe, Schiller, and Kant. And even if they carried in themselves the seeds of a new, richer conception of the life of the state and of a stronger leaning toward reality, their spiritual and intellectual interests were still more important to them than politics. They could be enthused at one moment about a state that made a powerful and active being of man and then, in the next moment, feel themselves repulsed by the spectacle that the interaction of states presented, this wild battling of political egoisms in which no inner human values could be found. While the other European countries were occupied with war, speculation, and factionalism, Novalis thought, the Germans were diligently educating themselves to be members of a higher epoch of culture.[51] As we can easily see now, other European nations were fighting for the realization of this same new cultural era, but the dust of battle prevented them from see-

[49] Ibid., II, 302.
[50] Ibid., II, 304. Cf., too, a similar statement from his later period in Finke, op.cit., p. 57.
[51] Dilthey, Das Erlebnis und die Dichtung, p. 224 (3rd edn., p. 291).

ing the real object of their struggles. And in Germany the political soil of the fatherland was not yet ripe for the high ideals that the early Romantics served. Thus it was understandable that whenever Novalis and Schlegel thought about a desirable political situation for men in Europe, they converted their intellectual universalism into political universalism and dreamed of an international peace, an international confederation, an international state, and a world republic.

5

FRIEDRICH SCHLEGEL IN THE TRANSITION TO POLITICAL ROMANTICISM

NOVALIS' LIFE, writing, and thought were like a wonderful and consummate dream, and his early death strikes us as an aesthetically necessary conclusion to this dream. It was Friedrich Schlegel's lot, however, to outlive his period of fire and genius by nearly three decades. This is not the place to discuss the reasons for the decline of his mind. We are only interested here in the further development of his thoughts about the nation and the national state in the period when, by his conversion to the Catholic Church (1808) and his attachment to Austria, he transformed a free, individualistic Romanticism into a Romanticism bound to politics and the church. Intellectual and personal reasons led him in that direction, but there is no doubt that the political vicissitudes of the times were a contributing factor. We can see this in his altered views on national and international problems. The luxuriance and freedom of early Romanticism could flourish without restraint in the years after the Peace of Basel when North Germany lay outside the stormy regions. The early Romantic dreams of an international peace and confederation were also linked to the optimistic mood of these years, a mood that could only be optimistic because of its detachment from the world. But when the old Empire collapsed at the beginning of the new century, this optimism came to an end. Now, when the political independence of states and nations was threatened, the alarming question arose of how the intellectual freedom and independence that had been so nonchalantly enjoyed up to this point would fare. Thus, the situation of these years from 1801 on was the strongest external stimulant for the further development of the national idea, and Friedrich Schlegel probably accepted its effect on him all the more willingly because he needed a new supply of materials for his gradually failing mind. When he takes up the cause of free nationality against the dominant power of France—mainly in the philosophical and political lectures of the years 1804 to 1806 (*Philosophische Vorlesungen*)[1] and then in the Vienna lectures on modern history in 1810 (*Über die neuere Geschichte*)[2]—we are conscious everywhere of a vitally interested mind and sometimes too of a trace of warm conviction, but the real battling spirit, the immensely powerful intensity of Fichte and Arndt, is missing. He lacks something of that ethos which would be able to convince us of the inner necessity of whatever new ideas he has to offer. The only new items that strike us as convincing and completely genuine are ones that proceed directly from his earlier line of thought. They are a clear awareness of the incomparable intellectual value of a free and distinctive national development and the view that the richness and vitality of European culture depends on such development.[3] But when he goes further and considers the political aspect of national life more closely than he did before, we are soon aware that he is experimenting uncertainly and finally looks for support in a political constitution that will best fit in with the ecclesiastical restraints of the Catholic system.

He first proposes the bold idea that language is the best principle by which to divide states, not only because it is the means of intellectual communication but also because it offers the proof of similar origin. Unity of language proves common ancestry; and "the older, purer, and less interbred the race, the more customs there will be; and the more customs there are and the more true persistence in them and attachment to them, then all the more will the group having them be a nation."[4] This concept of the nation was meant to be highly historical, yet it suffered from the historically false assumptions that a nation is always based primarily on blood relationship and that unity of language can only be explained by common ancestry. What remains then of the freedom and character of national life he praises so highly? Freedom was reduced to the nativistic doctrine of opposing all foreign influence, and character

---

[1] *Philosophische Vorlesungen aus den Jahren 1804 bis 1806*, ed. Windischmann (2 vols.; 1836-37). See esp. II, 385.

[2] *Über die neuere Geschichte. Vorlesungen, gehalten i. J. 1810* (Wien, 1811).

[3] Cf. his *Vorlesungen von 1810*, p. 11: "If the Germanic peoples had not succeeded in casting off the Roman yoke, if, rather, the remaining northern part of Europe had been assimilated to Rome and the freedom and individual character of its nations also destroyed . . . , then that magnificent struggle, that rich development of the human spirit in the modern nations would never have taken place. And it is precisely this richness, this variety that makes Europe what it is, that gives it the advantage of being the foremost seat of human life and culture." In a similar vein, p. 116; see also the *Vorlesungen von 1804-6*, II, 358.

[4] *Vorlesungen von 1804-6*, II, 357 and 259.

was equivalent to the strictest maintenance of tradition, to stagnation and archaism in the characters of nations. We encounter here probably for the first time in Germany the specifically conservative interpretation of the principle of nationality. The more conservative a nation is, we are told, the more it is a nation, and Schlegel was indeed much more concerned with justifying and praising the old social orders and customs than he was with elevating national language communities to national political systems. The real national state for him is accordingly the feudal state as it is found, he thinks, in the noblest nations;[5] and he sees the basic strength of the nation contained in the nobility, which must also be the national estate κατ' ἐξοχήν, the highest "strength and bloom of the nation."[6] For all practical purposes, the rule of the nobility represents the achievement of nationality for him. This is most evident in the fact that Schlegel makes the nobility into a warrior caste whose primary duty is to take over and direct the defense of the nation,[7] and that he approves of general conscription only in an emergency but rejects it decisively as a general principle. Schlegel's national state, then, taken as a national state in the political sense, represents completely the type of the older national state; but it also comprises what we previously called a national state in the national-cultural sense, because it requires that the state emerge from the pure, unadulterated native soil of the nation. As we saw, of course, he called only a state that had preserved a feudal system pure and essentially national. He thereby did violence to the concept of national character and originality by prescribing what these qualities should consist of and by declaring every deviation from that prescription to be a corruption and degeneration. Beyond that, he made canon and dogma out of a single stage of development in political life which had not been peculiar to one particular nation alone but to all the Romance and Germanic nations. A more likely thesis is that the character, the individual genius of these nations did not become evident at this stage of their development but rather in the way they overcame and transformed their original, common feudalistic system, the one earlier, the other later, the one by revolution, the other by reform. Anyone who raised the feudal system to the position

---

[5] "If a nation remains true to its customs and its constitution, the relationships between the estates will not be easily blurred, and if such blurring does occur, it is always a sign of corruption and decay." O. Brandt, A. W. Schlegel, p. 48, shows that it is likely that Friedrich Schlegel was influenced here by his brother August Wilhelm.

[6] Vorlesungen von 1810, pp. 561, 563.   [7] Vorlesungen von 1804-6, II, 360ff.

of a normative system for nations did exactly the same thing in principle as the man who considered democratic constitutionalism to be the norm. Whether Schlegel was aware of doing so or not, he set up a supra-national, universalistic norm for the political life of individual nations. This extremely important phenomenon is fundamental to our study, and we must look into it somewhat further. This setting up of general governmental ideals for individual Romance and Germanic nations was clearly not mere doctrinarism. It could be historically and nationally justified by the fact that these nations were similar and, to a great extent, related to each other. The emergence and proclamation of these universalistic ideas, whether they originated in the aristocratic or democratic camp, were a symptom and effect of this cultural community and relationship between the individual nations, and represented a revival of old traditions. But where was the border between what we might call this common European pasturage and the individual property of a nation, between what conformed to the particular character and the particular stage of development of the individual nation and what it could share with other nations or receive from them? Friedrich Schlegel was not predisposed to such a purely empirical and, in the true sense, historico-political examination of the governmental forms of a nation. His whole generation was not so predisposed nor were the immediately following generations, for the universal and national spheres flowed together for them. Thus, they thought all too often and in good faith that they were serving the national idea when their thinking was actually universalistic.

Friedrich Schlegel was informed with both conscious and unconscious universalism. This was evident in the way he defined the relationship of individual states to each other. We saw that in the early stages of his thinking, when he dreamed of an international state and a world republic, he favored a democratic cosmopolitanism based on natural law. Now he too plunged into that religious-ecclesiastical Romantic universalism that Novalis had advocated. All the new universalistic movements of the Enlightenment, of the new humanistic ideal, and of the French Revolution show, as secularized universalistic movements, so to speak, a historical continuity with the Christian universalism of the Middle Ages.[8] The two Romantics turned away from these worldly offshoots and returned to the holy mother in their

---

[8] Cf. Kaerst, *Das geschichtl. Wesen und Recht der deutschen nationalen Idee* (1916), p. 8. J. Mausbach, in *Hochland*, IX (1912), has fruitfully presented the current Catholic conception of "Nationalismus und christl. Universalismus."

search for solid land during the storms of the times. They doubtless probed too for the foundations of the national state; not of the modern secular state, however, but of the one surrounded and dominated by Christian universalism. It is true, of course, that Schlegel called for the autonomy of the state's personality with a firmness that seems to exclude any doubt. "Every state is an independently existing individual. It is completely its own master, has its own particular character, and governs itself according to its own particular laws, customs, and usages."[9] He also explicitly rejected the rationalistic idea of an international state, an idea he had previously advocated himself, only to recommend now in its place the Romantic idea of a universal empire, "empire seen as specifically different from a kingdom, seen as a kingdom over kings. It is assumed that the nation which exercises a certain dominion over its neighbors by means of the empire will be a strong nation, if not the strongest. It must, then, be suited to do that by its political and moral constitution. The idea of an empire is a much more effective one than that of an international state for bringing about an ethical relationship among nations. A comparison of the Middle Ages with modern times proves that. This system is also better suited to the natural relationship in which nations stand because of the great differences in their levels of education."[10] We can probably assume that the greatest event of the times, the founding of the Napoleonic empire, is reflected in these thoughts. But then, as the lectures of 1810 go on to explain,[11] these same thoughts had intended to contrast true empire with the false empire of Napoleon and to oppose Napoleon's universal system, based on an egoistical lust for power and on lifeless political machinery, with a universal system based on ethical and religious ideas.[12] The intellectual foundations and assumptions of the Holy Alliance and the Restoration period become increasingly clear to us here. They are reflected in the idea that the feudal form of government—a constitution based on estates—would necessarily create a bond among all the nations that possessed it, and Schlegel, the catholicizing Romantic, had no difficulty in seeing the hierarchy as still another universal bond among nations and praising it as such. Thus, he could think of nationalism and universalism as being in

[9] *Vorlesungen von 1804-6*, II, 382.   [10] *Ibid.*, II, 383.
[11] *Vorlesungen von 1810*, p. 350.
[12] Gervinus, *Gesch. des 19. Jahrhunderts*, I, 358, says correctly: "In this way, Schlegel wanted to oppose one type of universal monarchy, mass rule, and dynasty with another."

the purest harmony. "The demands for both division and union between nations will be satisfied by an empire with an all-inclusive feudal system and a hierarchy."[13]

But this solution was only possible at the cost of the genuine political autonomy of states and nations. We saw in the case of Novalis how his Christian universalism blinded him to the great struggles for power in preceding centuries and to the rise of the modern states. Schlegel judged these phenomena just as adversely as Novalis had. The desire of the states for power, he thought, destroyed the bond between the Christian nations and destroyed the national feudal systems within them. He knew very well that the beginnings of such modern politics were to be found in Renaissance Italy.[14] He praised the culture of the Renaissance as a blessing for Europe, but Renaissance politics had been a poor example for the European courts because they had given rise to wars in which each state was pitted against every other state.[15] Thus, in this Romantic-universalistic conception of history, the entire political aspect of modern history was pushed to one side. And even the desire of nations for unity and freedom had to suffer curtailment. The older Italian patriots of Dante's time who only wanted a strong emperor with a love of fame and justice were, Schlegel thought, "on a better path than the false patriots of a later Florence who always talked of nothing but the liberation of Italy."[16]

That is the essence of this Romantic's battle for national freedom against French universal despotism. The concept of the nation and of its autonomy was entwined and entangled with ideas that threatened to suffocate it. Universal, cosmopolitan thought was so integral a part of this generation that it reappeared even where a Romantic predilection for the national seemed to have overcome the cosmopolitan Enlightenment. We call cosmopolitan and universal those ideas which were ethical and religious in substance. The cos-

---

[13] *Vorlesungen von 1804-6*, II, 387. We need not go into the further fantastic elaborations of his idea (uniting of the learned class with the hierarchy, creation of an intermediate group between the hierarchy and the nobility in the form of a religious order of knights from which a pope-emperor could then be chosen to unite the highest secular and ecclesiastical powers, etc.).

[14] He is not, of course, familiar with the term "Renaissance," which became current in France in later decades.

[15] *Vorlesungen von 1810*, p. 235: Karl V and the Austrian rulers, on the other hand, had been "guided by the much higher concept of a Christian republic, a free and peaceful international European state" (pp. 272 and 337).

[16] *Ibid.*, pp. 275ff. It need hardly be said that his judgment here has a distinctly Austrian tinge.

mopolitan Enlightenment had already had an ethical and—*cum grano salis*—religious substance. Romantic universalism, too, was ethical and highly religious. The ethos was fundamentally different in some respects, but Enlightenment and Romantic thinkers had a common enemy in what they thought was the unethical state of the *ancien régime* but what was in reality the power state in general. They both deprecated as blind lust for power what was fundamental to the nature of the state, what was a product of its drive for self-preservation and autonomy. They moralized from without instead of understanding the nature of the state from within. It was not clear to them that ethics have an individually determined aspect along with their universal aspect and that the apparent immorality of a power-hungry political egoism can be justified from this individually determined side. For nothing that springs from the deepest individual nature of a being can be immoral.

These considerations are not as far removed from our subject as it may seem. The idea of the complete, genuine national state could only be achieved if the autonomy of the state in general was again achieved and recognized and if the tangled vines and creepers of universal, ethical ideas that sought to choke it were torn away and the proper energy of the state with its mighty roots revealed.

6

....

FICHTE AND THE IDEA
OF THE GERMAN NATIONAL STATE IN
THE YEARS 1806-1813

THE CASE OF Friedrich Schlegel shows that very limited and particularistic interests—the interests of the feudal state—attached themselves to the universal and national ideas that rose up against the system of Napoleon. But for a better understanding of the developments that led to the political philosophy of Friedrich Wilhelm IV and of his associates, we must return once again to the great main currents of the new national thought in Germany, currents that are free of particularistic interests but that still exhibit a mixture of universal and national ideas. Of the many routes that lead from the cosmopolitan world of the eighteenth century to that of the national state in the nineteenth, we shall devote ourselves mainly to the complicated and tortuous ones rather than to the most direct. We can find the most direct routes in the thinking of a patriot like Ernst Moritz Arndt. He had called for a "unity of people and state," as an ideal at least, as early as 1802 in his book *Germanien und Europa*, but he was also forced to admit to himself with sorrow that only prodigious events could achieve a "unity of the people" in Germany.[1] A natural rustic instinct and a warm, full heart, together with the various educational influences that had affected him in his youth, led him along this path. Although the individualistic and humanistic ideal of the waning eighteenth century had also taken a forceful hold on him, he still resisted the tendency of his contemporaries to detach this ideal from earthly weight and ballast. He sought an outlet for the release of human potential on earth and in the manifold reality of national and individual life, not in the ether of pure thought. In this way he came upon the idea of the national state, if only in a vague inkling of its future form—a

[1] *Germanien und Europa*, pp. 420, 426.

71

national state, moreover, that was to be grounded on an intimate interaction of the state with the cultural nation as well as with the political nation.[2] The cold utilitarianism of Friedrich II's political machinery repelled him, but he did not set up a mere image to oppose it, some empty, abstractly concocted ideal of a free national state. He must be given full credit for recognizing the hard realities of political life even though his awareness of them was vague and general. The state, he said, is formed out of practical necessity; it is made up of practical elements, and it can only be sustained by them. Simple, practical laws hold for the state. But, he submits, what "if these practical laws were eternal laws sufficient for the forming and sustenance of both world and states?" That thought had occurred to him, he added, simply as a notion, a chance bolt of lightning in the night.[3] He was on the verge of taking the course that Ranke later followed, the course of searching for eternal laws in earthly and empirical facts, searching for the dominating forces of history and the state in history and the state themselves, not above them. We cannot help being moved when we see here the first glimmerings of the historico-political realism that the nineteenth century went ahead to develop.

Arndt did not have enough intellectual power and was not enough of a thinker to pursue this fruitful notion further. His permanent contribution to the development of the idea of the national state lies more in the practical than in the theoretical field. Fichte, however, was destined for the greatest accomplishment in both fields. His theoretical contribution is remarkable despite the fact, or rather because of the fact, that he had to travel a much more difficult path to achieve it than Arndt did. The greater and richer intellectual work he had to perform, the obstacles he had to overcome to approach the idea of the national state—these are the factors that make his thoughts about it so interesting.

Arndt could reach the idea of the national state quickly and surely

[2] His view about the relationship between language boundaries and geographical boundaries in his postulated national state shows how the doctrinaire and the practical were mixed together in his thinking. "The factors for determining the natural boundaries of every country are, first, that it have access to the sea and, second, its language" (*ibid.*, p. 385). But he concludes from this, for example, that if Poland were still a state it would have to rule the Germans in Prussia and the Kurland "because it would have to have access to the sea there" (p. 355). On the other hand, though: "The country that is now called Germany must possess the Rhine entirely and the sea on both sides of the Rhine as its natural border." On Arndt's early ideas, see Müsebeck, *Arndt*, I, 50, 54, 61ff., 102ff.

[3] *Germanien und Europa*, pp. 260, 263.

because he had so much of what Fichte did not have or, to put it more precisely, did not even want to have: an earthy patriotism that clung to "a patch of land, the river, the mountain." Fichte looked down on this patriotism of the soil as late as 1804 in his *Grundzüge des gegenwärtigen Zeitalters*, and he delegated to the "enlightened mind" the task of rejecting the state if the state has decayed and of turning toward the quarter "where light and justice are."[4] Then the cosmopolite of 1804 became the orator to the German nation of 1807. This great change of heart has often been regarded with amazement and explained as the result of necessity and experience.[5] But as early as 1800, when Fichte urged the Berlin Masons to adopt the objectives of his philosophy as their own,[6] he did not want to have anything to do with a cold and lethargic cosmopolitanism; he saw cosmopolitanism and love of fatherland "intimately united" in the educated man, and he asserted that love of fatherland is realized in such a man's deeds; cosmopolitanism is realized in his thoughts. The first is the manifestation of the spirit; the second, the spirit itself, "the invisible in the visible." The inner connecting link is evident here although, or rather because, the emphasis is more cosmopolitan than national. The more profound Fichte scholars, even if they were not aware of these often neglected statements, have always seen that the step from the cosmopolitanism of 1804 to the nationalism of 1807 was not a long one and that the two tendencies were very closely related. "The cosmopolitanism of the *Wissenschaftslehre* and the patriotism of the *Addresses* are one and the same concept," Kuno Fischer writes,[7] and Windelband comes to the conclusion that "This patriotism of the *Addresses to the German Nation* [*Reden an die deutsche Nation*] resembles Fichte's cosmopolitanism as one twin brother does the other."[8] The connecting link between

---

[4] *Sämtl. Werke*, VII, 212.

[5] Zeller, *Vorträge und Abhandlungen*, I (2nd edn.), 184; Lasson, *Fichte im Verhältnis zu Kirche und Staat* (1863), p. 200.

[6] *Briefe an Konstant*, printed in the *Eleusinien des 19. Jahrhunderts*, II (1803), 37. Reprint: *J. G. Fichtes Philosophie der Maurerei*, ed. W. Flitner (1923). Cf. Medicus, *Fichte* (2nd edn., 1922), pp. 189ff., and L. Keller, *Fichte und die Grossloge Royal York in Berlin*, in *Schriften d. Ver. f. d. Gesch. Berlins*, Heft 50. —In the concluding passage of *Der geschlossene Handelsstaat* of 1800 there is also, as Metzger, *Gesellschaft, Recht und Staat*, p. 189, has noted, a reference to the nation ("If we were only peoples and nations"). It is not, however, a reference to the historical nation but to the one that is to be newly and artificially created. Haymann, *Weltbürgertum und Vaterlandsliebe in der Staatslehre Rousseaus und Fichtes* (1924), p. 57, overlooks this in his examination of the passage.

[7] *Fichte* (3rd edn., 1900), p. 627.

[8] *Fichtes Idee des deutschen Staates*, p. 11.

the ideal of 1804 and that of 1807-8 can be seen both in the "Erlangen University Plan" ("Ideen für die innere Organisation der Universität Erlangen") of the summer of 1806[9] and in the "Patriotic Dialogues" ("Der Patriotismus und sein Gegenteil. Patriotische Dialogue"), the first of which also falls in the summer of 1806.[10]

In the "Erlangen University Plan" Fichte contrasted a limited and unthinking patriotism, which we could call Spartan patriotism, with a self-critical, or Attic, patriotism. The latter can easily merge with cosmopolitanism and with the German national spirit, and it does indeed merge with them in every strong personality. Fichte expresses his dismay at the fact that "after recent events a German nation can probably exist only in the republic of letters." But the intellectual gulf between the German nation and its neighbor to the West still did not seem as deep to him then as it did later when he made his *Addresses to the German Nation,* for he could still suggest that the relationship of the particular character of the German tribes to the general character of the German nation formed a parallel to the relationship of the total national character of Germany to the new general European character. In both cases the particular always arose from the general. His mood on the eve of the catastrophe of Jena was therefore one of painful resignation and growing national sensibility, but still not one of protest against intellectual community with the nation's most dangerous enemy. He still seemed to consider the general the higher concept as opposed to the particular, which he saw only as a derivative from the general.

His ideas become even clearer to us in the "Dialogues." Here he develops the view "that cosmopolitanism cannot really exist at all and that in reality it must necessarily become patriotism." What this suggests is that both of his tendencies have drawn together, and if we look at the essential elements of what he now calls true patriotism, we can easily understand how this happened. This patriotism is completely universal. Its objectives are those of mankind in general, as Fichte's *Wissenschaftslehre* defined them. By its very nature, he says, a will bent on these objectives must have and can have an immediate effect only on its immediate environment, i.e., its sphere of influence is the nation. To this extent he becomes a patriot, but he remains a cosmopolite "in that the ultimate purpose of all na-

---

[9] *Nachgelassene Werke,* III, 275ff., and W. Erben, *Fichtes Universitätspläne* (1914), pp. 50ff.
[10] *Nachgelassene Werke,* III, 223ff. New edition based on the manuscript: *Der Patriotismus und sein Gegenteil,* ed. Hans Schulz (1918).

tional culture is to extend itself to the entire human race."[11] National culture here is still not individual. It is not a national culture in the historical sense at all. It is nothing more nor less than the highest human culture possible.[12] It was the German nation, of course, that had the potential to create this culture, but in its capacity to do this, as I understand Fichte here, the German nation was only a representative people, and only in this sense was its child—that is, its culture—the son of all men.

Seen from this point of view, the German individual states were essentially nothing more than given spheres of influence within which the individual German was to work for the dissemination of the national culture, i.e., of human culture.[13] In this sense, Fichte claimed to be a German-Prussian patriot, but this does not mean he found richer cultural resources in the Prussian state or in any one German state at all: "The separation of Prussians from other Germans is artificial and based on arbitrary arrangements brought about by chance; the separation of the German from other European nations is based on nature,"[14] that is, on the common language and national character. Using this view as a basis, Fichte could easily have postulated a unified German national state, but he apparently had no need for it. He is satisfied if the new culture achieves dominance in the individual state; and beyond that, as a secondary goal, he approves of the Prussian's working for the integrity, standing, and well-being of the Prussian state.[15] In any case, he points out, the German becomes a Prussian only when he becomes fully aware of being a German. "Only in this way is a true, genuine, proper German a proper Prussian." That is almost the exact opposite of Bismarck's detached remark that "German patriotism usually requires the mediation of dynastic attachment to become active and effective."[16] Fichte probably would have drawn back in horror from this kind of patriotism. "But for that very reason," Windelband says,[17] "what he calls true patriotism is completely divorced from reality, and his Germany is utopian."

[11] *Nachgelassene Werke*, III, 229; Schulz edn., p. 11. Also III, 233; Schulz edn., p. 16.

[12] Wundt's view, *Fichte* (1927), p. 186, should be rejected.

[13] "The German living and working within the Prussian state will desire and work for the emergence of the German national character for the first time and in its most perfected form in this state unit, then for the diffusion of this national character among the related German tribes, and gradually among all mankind" (*Nachgelassene Werke*, III, 233; Schulz edn., p. 15).

[14] *Ibid.*, III, 232; Schulz edn., p. 14.   [15] *Ibid.*, III, 233; Schulz edn., p. 15.

[16] *Gedanken und Erinnerungen*, I, 290   [17] *Op.cit.*, p. 12.

If we wanted to give an ungenerous interpretation of the national idea expressed in these two dialogues, we could say that it was primarily meant to be a vehicle for the dissemination of Fichtean philosophy and that his image of the nation was really nothing but an extension of the philosopher Fichte himself. In more benevolent terms we might say that he lends his own flesh and blood to his image of the nation and could not do otherwise if he wanted to remain true to the deepest thoughts of his philosophy, for this philosophy wanted from the beginning to do nothing other than prepare the way in this world for an empire of moral freedom, freedom understood in the highest and most spiritual sense. All his rather odd-looking positions on the state and nation were but shifting deliberations about the most effective means for reaching his ultimate ideal goal of delivering humanity from the ban of material existence and raising it to a higher world of freedom and to its divine origin. He saw in that world, as he said then,[18] the only true reality, life itself undisguised. For that reason, the only thing in the nature of the German nation that was open to him was what he felt stirring in himself. What he regarded as the very being of the nation, the idea of human enlightenment, did not circumscribe national existence entirely, but it was the genuine, firstborn child of the German nation of that time. In the last analysis his position was not much different from Humboldt's and Schiller's: beneath his cosmopolitan national thought stirred a far more genuine and earthy affection for the fatherland than he wanted to admit.[19] As a significant force which he was not aware of himself, it gave subterranean nourishment to his new ideas; but these ideas were too imperious and inflexible to let him admit that fact. "Theory has seldom remained so far behind an instinctive grasp of reality."[20]

Yet not long after this he penetrated the realities of political and even of national political life in a way possible only to someone who has either extensive practical experience or a disinterested intellectual grasp of the stuff of experience. We can see this in Fichte's

[18] *Nachgelassene Werke*, III, 257. The proof of this has been demonstrated in splendid fashion by Nico Wallner, *Fichte als politischer Denker* (1926).

[19] Erben, *op.cit.*, pp. 18ff., has pointed, with too much emphasis perhaps, to traces of such national feeling in the "Erlangen University Plan" and has at the same time made it seem likely that the beginnings of Fichte's national feeling lie in his Jena period, when he saw young men of all the German tribes "living robustly together" and smoothing away the poor qualities of their tribes through their contact with each other. Cf. also M. Lenz, *Gesch. der Universität Berlin*, I, 112ff., on the "Erlangen University Plan."

[20] Windelband, *op.cit.*, p. 12.

essay on Machiavelli ("Ueber Machiavelli"), which he wrote and published in Königsberg in 1807.[21]

It is a remarkable essay and one that seems, at first glance at least, to have no place in the context of Fichte's development. For we shall see later that the ideas on which we have just focused in his "Patriotic Dialogues" lead directly to the *Addresses to the German Nation* and these in turn to the political ideas of the last year of Fichte's life. In all these stages of Fichte's thought, political and empirical considerations are subordinate to nonpolitical and supraempirical ones. But here we see a man who has thoroughly understood Machiavellian *Realpolitik*, who finds a hard but sound kernel in it, and who wants to replant this seed in his own time. We can fully understand this favorable reaction to Machiavelli if we take Fichte's character into account as well as the moment in history when he concerned himself with Machiavelli. One strong-willed man stood face to face with another; one radical searcher for truth faced another. What impressed Fichte so favorably was the inflexibility and assurance with which Machiavelli pursued the course of his thought and thrust all encumbrance aside without even taking notice of it. "Whatever the consequences are, he states them and looks all around to see what the further consequences might be; then he states them. He is concerned only for the correctness of his conclusions, and he recognizes no other considerations whatsoever." But beyond that, in his constant search for the most effective means toward his ultimate ideal ends, Fichte had never scorned force as a way toward freedom. In the *Addresses* he calls for national education by force, and in the political writings of 1813 for a despot to enforce education in the elements of the German character. The system of rational despotism that Machiavelli outlined was able to impress the despot in Fichte. Furthermore, as early as 1804 in the *Grundzüge des gegenwärtigen Zeitalters*, he had not only causally explained the general struggling and fighting of states with each other but had also justified it morally with the statement that the most cultivated state in the European republic of nations was always without exception the most ambitious one.[22] Also, the period when Fichte was so ready to learn from Machiavelli could well call to mind the thought that Ranke has attributed to Machiavelli,

[21] *Nachgelassene Werke*, III 401ff., based on the abridged reprint in the *Musen* of 1813. New edition by Hans Schulz (1918) based on the original printing in the *Vesta* of 1807.

[22] *Sämtl. Werke*, VII, 210f.

namely, that poison was the only possible remedy for the desperate condition of his fatherland; for Fichte's essay is a sharp indictment of the weakness and laxity that had characterized Prussian politics and that were being severely punished at the time. If, as we noted, his "Erlangen University Plan" mirrored the resigned but not yet radical mood on the eve of Prussian catastrophe, he rose up now under the crushing experience of that catastrophe to a radicalism that sought the most effective weapons and found them in Machiavelli.

But all this still does not reveal the deepest reason for Fichte's leanings toward Machiavelli nor the reason why this affinity was not total and permanent. I think the reason can be found in the immense tension that existed between Fichte's ideals and reality. His goal was a radical spiritualization and civilization of men, but shortly before the time when his national political ideas began to take shape he believed that the current condition of man was one of complete sinfulness, as he explains in his *Grundzüge des gegenwärtigen Zeitalters* (1804). The more brilliant his goal appeared, the more repulsive was the sight of humanity around him. He was such a harsh pessimist about his own times precisely because he was such a glowing optimist about the future. The idealist, Schiller noted,[23] "thinks so grandly of mankind that he runs the danger of despising men." This is perhaps an example of a contrast similar to that between the transcendental ideals of the medieval church and its pessimistic view of actual human conduct. Like the church, Fichte too could draw the conclusion that men must be treated as though they were evil, that they must be dominated and constrained. He explicitly approved Machiavelli's principle that "whoever founds a republic or any kind of state and whoever forms its laws must assume that all men are evil." But to be able to unite this cheerless axiom with his belief in the destiny of mankind he developed his ideas further: The essential point is not whether men actually are so constituted. The important thing is that the state as a restricting institution must necessarily assume them to be so and only this assumption can form the basis for the existence of a state. This same assumption must be taken as a point of departure for the relationship of states to each other. It must be assumed here, too, that every state will make use of every opportunity to harm another if it thinks it can gain an advantage by doing so. For it is always possible that things will take such a course. Once Fichte had entered into this line of thought,

---

[23] "Über naive und sentiment. Dichtung."

drawn to it by the course of recent events, he pursued it with all the energy and fearlessness of his mind. The security of the state, he continued, does not depend on conditions within its own territory alone but "on everything to which you can extend your influence and by which you can consequently enlarge yourself."

Fichte thus saw with great clarity the life of European states in its true form, the image of states and nations vigorously stirring and expanding. At this point, he forgot the pessimistic assumptions with which he had begun and yielded to the stronger urge to find the meaning and rationale for what seemed to be purely egoistical impulses and to bring these impulses into harmony with his highest human ideals: "Furthermore, every nation wants to disseminate as widely as it possibly can the good points that are peculiar to it. And, as far as it can, it wants to assimilate the entire human race to itself in accordance with an urge planted in men by God, an urge on which the community of nations, the friction between them, and their development toward perfection rest."

That is one of the most profound and significant statements of this period. It brings both the reality of the old political struggles for power and the new national impulses into harmony with the cosmopolitan and universalistic ideals of German thought up to this time. The individual character of the nation is much more clearly and emphatically recognized now than it was in his earlier thinking. The nation no longer appears simply as a creation and modification of a higher universal. On the contrary, the primal and individual impulses of nations appear to be the force that creates the general and supra-national.[24] A perspective is opened here that looks directly toward Ranke's concept of history. The decisive step was made here. The power impulse of the state was recognized as a natural and healthy impulse and was placed in the context of a moral world view. Machiavelli's lesson and Antimachiavelli's previous objections to it were both partially overcome here, both partially enhanced and reconciled. This was possible only because the new concept of the nation had been added to those of state and humanity and because this concept cast a new light on the state. If the state was not ruled merely by the will of a prince alone nor merely by interest in its own

[24] This is what distinguishes the justification of state power and expansion politics given here from that given in the *Grundzüge des gegenwärtigen Zeitalters* (cf. p. 86n., below). In the *Grundzüge*, the culture which the conquering state may and should disseminate throughout Christian Europe is still purely universal and not conceived of as individual and national.

self-preservation but was maintained by a living national community, and if this national community became valuable for mankind precisely because of its own particular character, then the voracity of the state, too, was ennobled and elevated. Let us look at Fichte's own words here: "The people are not the property of a prince in the sense that he can regard their welfare, their independence, their dignity, their destiny in the totality of the human race as his private affair. . . . The prince belongs to his nation just as wholly and completely as it belongs to him. Its destiny under divine providence is laid in his hands, and he is responsible for it." In his private life the prince is bound to general moral precepts. In relation to his people, he is bound to law and justice. But in relation to other states "there is neither law nor justice except the law of strength. This relationship places the divine, sovereign rights of fate and of world rule in the prince's hands, and it raises him above the commandments of personal morals into a higher moral order whose essence is contained in the words *Salus et decus populi suprema lex esto.*" That was not all that could have been said about the new, developing national state, but one basic characteristic of its nature had been established: its right and its duty of ruthless self-preservation and of self-determination in defining its interests.

With this "more serious and forceful view of the art of government" Fichte's mind reached the most worldly phase of which it was capable. If we read the *Addresses to the German Nation* after this essay on Machiavelli, we feel that we are being led in the same direction in some respects, only to find ourselves suddenly in an entirely different world at the end.

Let us first look at those ideas in the *Addresses* which follow the direction of Fichte's Machiavelli essay and which consequently represent an advance over the "Dialogues" in his national and political thinking. We note this advance first in the fact that he weaves together more closely the connecting threads between nation and state, i.e., between the German nation and the German individual state. In the "Dialogues" he had distinguished two levels of activity in the German individual state as represented in Prussia: activity on the German-Prussian level, which ultimately becomes activity on the human level in general, and activity on the purely Prussian level, activity directed toward a subordinate goal. In the *Addresses* this scale of values for state activity and objectives has nearly disappeared.[25] The spheres of the individual state and the nation have been drawn together now. The state, Fichte says, has its armed power "only and for no other reason" than to serve the objectives that love of fatherland dictates to it.[26] He seems, then, to hold fast to the idea of the national state adopted in the Machiavelli essay: a national state whose power is exclusively in the service of the nation; and the rational, nonhistorical, Enlightenment ideal of the state seems to be left behind when we read these sentences:[27] "The rational state cannot be artificially constructed out of any and all available materials. The nation must first be educated and brought up to a level that allows such a state." Windelband formulates the basic idea of the *Addresses* in this way:[28] "The state of the future can only be the national state, and in particular, the German national state.—That is, as far as philosophy could formulate it, the program for nineteenth century political history, in which the main interest was the consolidating of national state structures and the actual focal point and dominant event, the establishment of the German Reich." Let us say more precisely that this was the program as far as the Fichtean philosophy could formulate it, and let us note here, too, the traces of previous thought that still remain in his conception of the national state.

A closer examination of the words quoted above shows that Fichte has still not given up the "perfect state," the "rational" state at all. The only fault he found with the Enlightenment thinkers was that they had attempted to build such a state without the national foundations necessary for it. Fichte's introduction of the nation as a new resource here is an immense advance in thought. But because he did not give up the old goal of the rational state, this new element of the nation could not be the real nation either but only a kind of rational nation: "The nation that first learns to educate the perfect man will also be the first nation to achieve the perfect state."[29]

Fichte thus transformed the new way of thinking that he had just adopted back into the old. In the *Addresses*, we can see the same

[25] We are aware of this, for example, in the fact that he separates the "immediate" and "ordinary goals" of the state (preservation of domestic peace, of property, of personal freedom, and of the life and well-being of all) from its higher objectives (*Sämtl. Werke*, VII, 384 and 386).

[26] *Sämtl. Werke*, VII, 386.   [27] *Ibid.*, VII, 353.

[28] *Op.cit.*, p. 8.

[29] *Sämtl. Werke*, VII, 354. Binder, "Fichte u. die Nation," *Logos*, X (1922), obscures this aspect of Fichte's concept of the nation.

thing happening in his development of the principle of autonomy for state and nation that was put forward in the Machiavelli essay. As a true state, he says decisively, the state "must be able to act and make decisions independently and of itself."[30] At another point he says that wherever we find a specific language, we also find a specific nation "that has the right to take care of its affairs independently and to govern itself."[31] In the same connection we are told that the language and literature of a nation would degenerate through the loss of political independence. We can note with some satisfaction that Fichte recognized the relationship of national culture and political independence. But we must also note his peculiar motive for this.[32] "What kind of a literature can that be, the literature of a nation without political independence? What are the intentions of a rational author and what can his intentions be? Nothing other than to have a voice in common and public life and to form and remodel it according to his own ideas." He wants to think for those who govern; "therefore, he can only write in a language that is used for governing, the language of a people who constitute an independent state." That sounds very much in keeping with our idea of the modern national state, for we cannot imagine a genuine modern national state without a great, free, national-political literature. But what Fichte had in mind is not what we understand by national-political literature but rather the kind of writing that eighteenth-century philosophers cultivated when they concerned themselves with the state, that is, the establishment of norms for those who govern and the rule of philosophers over those who govern, in order, as Fichte himself said, "to give form to public life and create a human order in the world."[33] For that kind of literature he requires and demands the political independence of the nation. The nation provides the basis for the sovereignty of learning in the state, of national learning, we might say; but that would hardly render the deeper sense of what Fichte actually meant by learning. It went beyond the sphere of the national, indeed, beyond the sphere of learning in a narrower sense altogether. It meant for him "the transformation of knowledge, reason, and wisdom into life itself and into the highest sources and impulses of life."[34]

Thus, working from a sublime point of view which is also an entirely nonpolitical and supra-national one, Fichte justified his de-

30 *Sämtl. Werke*, VII, 432.   31 *Ibid.*, VII, 453.
32 *Ibid.*, VII, 452.   33 Cf., too, *ibid.*, VII, 492.
34 "Rede an seine Zuhörer," February 19, 1813, in *Sämtl. Werke*, IV, 604.

mand for political independence. But he did not pursue the genuinely political aspects of this demand any further, although he had already shown considerable understanding of them in the Machiavelli essay. He did not pursue them because he did not find the nature of the power state a matter of lasting interest. He could see it only as a means toward a higher end, never as an end in itself. As we said above, an essential aspect of the power state is its energetic expansive thrust, its contact with neighbors in friendship or enmity, its voracity. The state makes use of its autonomy and independence primarily for this purpose. According to Fichte, the state should, on the contrary, use them to isolate itself from the power struggles of other states.[35] He still had the idea of an "isolated mercantile state" in mind. What use would the freedom of the seas be to the Germans? "May a kind providence protect the German from an indirect share in the spoils of other worlds just as it has protected him from a direct share."[36] He cuts off all *Realpolitik* at the roots when he declares at the end: "The confused and variegated mixture of sensuous and intellectual impulses should be deprived of its dominance in the world, and the mind alone, pure and stripped of all sensuous impulses, should take the helm of human affairs."[37] All the other lights burning in the world, so to speak, should be extinguished, so that this one flame of Fichte's ethical ideal might remain, tended by the German nation in its capacity as the primal nation, the chosen people. He wants political independence and power for this people in order to realize this ideal. Just as his philosophy had always demanded a transformation of individuals into men of intellect, he demands now a radical transformation and intellectualization of political and national life in the world.

This was the function that he assigned to the German state. Once we have grasped this basic idea that runs through all of Fichte's thinking, we can no longer regard the national state of the *Addresses* as a practical political construct, and we might consider a further examination of his political ideas unnecessary. But Fichte's ideals and illusions with all their ramifications and consequences are always

[35] We need not go any further into the distinction between natural and unnatural conquest that he makes in the thirteenth *Address* because it is too crass to be of any use for actual politics. We might venture a guess that the change in mood compared to that of the Machiavelli essay (in which a demand for forceful power politics was made) can be traced back to the change in the political situation. Earlier, Fichte was under the influence of the fresh impressions of the war. Now he felt the resignation of the defeated.

[36] *Sämtl. Werke*, VII, 466.   [37] *Ibid.*, VII, 496.

worth examining, and for our purpose of showing how nonpolitical ideas entered into the political life of Germany, there is no more significant figure among the pure thinkers than Fichte. Let us inquire further, then, into his ideas on the form and constitution of the German state. Most important here is his position on the choice of a centralized state, a federal state, or a confederation of states.

In the ninth *Address* he considered the possibility of a German individual state seeking to unite the entire German nation under its rule and to introduce an autocracy in place of the traditional model of a republic of nations. "Every noble spirit throughout the land would be obliged to resist that,"[38] not because of dynastic or particularistic scruples, but because Fichte saw the finest source of German culture and the primary means of insuring its character in what we call the plurality of states and in what he called "republican constitution." He also feared that the autocracy of an absolute ruler might crush individual shoots of native culture in Germany for the term of that ruler's life. Such an autocracy did not strike him as hopeless and totally unbearable because Germans would still govern Germans and the German nation would still remain in existence; however, a monarchical centralized state for Germany did not seem at all desirable to him. It is clear that he favored a centralized state in republican form,[39] but it is equally clear that the actual shape that any centralized state took as such was not of great importance to him. He says of the "German state" quite simply: "Whether it appears to be one or many does not make much difference; in reality, it is only one state." He clearly makes a fundamental distinction here between the external appearance of a state and its inner character. The entire German state can manifest itself in the form of a centralized state, but it can also manifest itself in the form of a plurality of states. The important thing is, according to his words immediately preceding these remarks, "that German national affections themselves either sit at the helm of the German state or be able to reach it with their influence."[40] We see here that Fichte was not overly friendly toward

---

[38] *Ibid.*, VII, 397.

[39] *Ibid.*, VII, 397: ". . . but it would, of course, have been a misfortune if the established unity of the government had had not a republican but a monarchical form instead."

[40] *Sämtl. Werke*, VII, 397; cf., too, VII, 384, 396, 428. Wallner says correctly, *op.cit.*, p. 205: "The nation, a thoroughly cultural and individual value, stands in close contact with the state that serves it. The nation should infuse the state with its 'life,' but it is not the state as such." We could perhaps claim that in the first *Address* (VII, 266) and in the synopsis of the thirteenth *Address* (VII, 464) Fichte deplores Germany's plurality of states and says of their separate existences

the German individual state either. He praises the German plurality
of states as the source of German culture, but he does not approve
of territorial-dynastic patriotism or of attachment to the individual
state. Individual states are permitted, but he denies their citizens
any profound feelings for them.

If we take Fichte's premises as our own, we can conclude that
there would be no need for an external, federative bond between individual states—either as states in a confederation or as members of
a federal state—if one condition were fulfilled, namely, that the national spirit either rule in the life of the German state or be able to
come to power in it. For this reason, Fichte could even find the
condition of Germany before 1806 quite tolerable when state and
nation, "as in the times of ancient Greece alone," were outwardly separated but lived, so he thought, in harmony with each other. He
could therefore proclaim that every informed man ought to have
desired a continuation of that state of affairs.[41] We might object
that he was not thinking of a desirable arrangement but only of a
tolerable one, in contrast to the intolerable circumstances of the period in which he himself lived, and that he was putting forward only
minimal demands for German political life. One might also say that
it was a ticklish business to demand more at that time. But Fichte
was much too bold a thinker to hide his basic principles completely,
and we must therefore assume that he actually settled for what
strikes us as an absolute minimum. He could do so because he was
relatively indifferent to the form of political organization. His sole
interest was to achieve a spiritual unity in German political life. He
envisioned this ideal unity of state and nation at the highest level,
but it "lay in utopia," and only a preestablished harmony could have
made possible its realization and the unifying of all the individual
states as one mind. In his view the German state, like any state, does
not develop according to its own principles but receives its principles
from the national spirit. But according to the *Addresses*, this national
spirit is and should be only the truly human spirit, the highest
and purest cultural ideal. State and nation are certainly bound to-

---

that they "go against nature and reason." But we may assume, following the argument of the ninth *Address*, that he is not looking for unity in the external form
and that he accordingly does not condemn the form but the spirit of the plurality
of states, the spirit "of separate existence." Cf., too, the eleventh *Address* (VII,
437): "It is a good thing for us that there are still different German states separated from each other. What has so often worked to our disadvantage can perhaps
be to our advantage in this important national concern (of education)."

[41] *Sämtl. Werke*, VII, 392, 396f.

gether here in the closest way, but only under the dominance of universal ideas.

As we noted, Enlightenment, Classical Idealism, and Romanticism came together in this universalism. As we have already seen and shall see again later, the Romantics still retained their penchant for the universal as they plunged deeper into the world of the national; and Romanticism awakened Fichte's interest in the nation and influenced his evaluation of it. His universalism, too, is so deeply tinged with Romanticism that direct influence seems more than likely. We remember how enthusiastic Novalis and Friedrich Schlegel were about European political life as it existed before the rise of the great individual powers, how they extolled the unity of Christendom in the Middle Ages and mourned its disintegration in the power struggles of recent centuries. Let us compare Fichte on this point. In the course of opposing the doctrine of a European balance of power, he writes: "If Christian Europe had remained united as it originally was and should have stayed, we would never have had occasion to develop such an idea. A unity rests complete in itself, maintains itself, and does not divide itself into belligerent powers that have to be brought into balance with each other. That idea gained meaning only in a Europe grown unrighteous and divided."[42] Faced with the division of Europe, Fichte plays the universalist, but faced with the thought of a universal monarchy, a frighteningly imminent possibility at the time, he immediately plays the idea of the nation off against it. He found the idea of a universal monarchy despicable and irrational. "Spiritually informed nature was able to express the reality of humanity only in the most highly varied gradations of individuals and of individual groups, i.e., of nations. Only if each of these nations is left to itself . . . and develops and takes form according to its own being, can the image of divinity be

[42] *Ibid.*, VII, 464. He was thinking along these same lines as early as the *Grundzüge des gegenwärtigen Zeitalters* of 1804 (VII, 197 and 200) where, with a completely Romantic polemic against those who are not able to imagine their way into the spirit of other times, he praises the crusades as the "ever memorable vital expression of a Christian totality despite the division into single states which that totality had suffered." Fester, *Rousseau u. d. deutsche Geschichtsphilosophie*, p. 41, rightly emphasizes that Fichte is the first German philosopher to do justice to the Middle Ages and that this is all the more significant because he stood completely apart from the reactionary, catholicizing tendencies of the Romantics. But this does not, of course, preclude the influence of the Romantics on him in the points discussed above. Cf., too, Kluckhohn, *Persönlichkeit und Gemeinschaft*, p. 45.

properly reflected."[43] Once again he wanted to "leave the nations to themselves." We see here, confronting each other face to face, the two principles that guided Fichte's evaluation of the national impulse: a tendency to see the higher value in the general and a quickening understanding for the special value of the particular.[44] The contradiction would be irreconcilable if we did not remind ourselves again that he was only concerned with the spirit of national life, not with its outward political form. As a desirable ideal, then, he envisioned a Europe that would achieve unity and brotherhood throughout the entire continent yet still allow individual nations to develop independently.[45] But given his premises, this independence and autonomy of nations and national states could not be of a truly political nature. Political independence and autonomy were subordinated to broader human objectives.

THE *Addresses to the German Nation* do not represent Fichte's last word on the nation and the national state. As we might expect, the experience of the following years enabled him to penetrate further into this new world that he, like Columbus, had discovered without knowing that it was a new world. We have two documents from the great year of 1813, which was also the last year of Fichte's life: his *Staatslehre* and, more important, a draft for a political essay from the spring of 1813 that we can describe as the last will and testament among his national-political writings. Here, Heinrich von Treitschke said somewhat triumphantly in 1862, we see Fichte "as the first prominent herald of the ideas that motivate Germany's national party today. . . . Here for the first time

---

[43] *Sämtl. Werke*, VII, 467.

[44] Bubnoff, "Der Begriff der Nation und die Idee einer Völkergemeinschaft," *Archiv f. Sozialwiss.*, LI, 123 and 153f., without knowing my book, has also recently noted the parallel existence of these two principles in Fichte's consideration of the German nation. Troeltsch, "Über Massstäbe zur Beurteilung historischer Dinge," *Histor. Zeitschrift*, CXVI, 14, and again in *Historismus u. seine Probleme*, p. 125, has also emphasized that the idea of the profusion of individual national spirits as the mirror of divinity—perhaps the most effective and illuminating idea of the *Addresses*—occurs in the *Addresses*, surprisingly, without previous preparation. Wallner, *op.cit.*, p. 196, derives the new sense of the individual aspect of the nation from Fichte's "religious mysticism," which, from about 1800 on, was joined to his constant and dominant penchant for natural law. It is more correct to say that Fichte draws closer to an objective idealism of a Hegelian nature from about 1800 on, and that because of this the possibility of seeing the individual as a colored refraction of the one eternal beam of the absolute is opened to him.

[45] On the confederation of nations as the main objective in the *Rechtslehre* of 1812, cf. Wallner, *op.cit.*, p. 236.

an eminent man decisively proclaimed the plan of placing the king of Prussia at the head of the entire fatherland as a 'despot to enforce education in the elements of the German character.'" And even if Fichte still envisioned a "republic of Germans without princes or hereditary nobility" as his highest goal, as Treitschke admits, he also realized that this goal would not be achieved in the near future.[46]

For the question we are dealing with here, it is not a matter of primary importance whether Fichte favored a republican or monarchical unity for Germany at that time. What we want to know is how near Fichte came to the idea of the modern national state at all, be it republican or monarchical. However, every step that Fichte made in the direction of the national state was also a step into the real political world and away from purely rational constructions. It would be clear proof of his more highly developed political sense if he had actually postponed the realization of his republican ideals and proclaimed a Prusso-German empire as the immediate goal. Only with caution will we be able to use these fragmentary and often self-contradictory notes as a source for determining Fichte's final position. However, even though Fichte's thoughts are at first pessimistic and doubtful about the future of the Germans, they gain in clarity and weight in the course of these notes; and while he seems at first to expect nothing from Prussia for the German nation,[47] he soon comes to the realization that in Prussia there is already present a "truly German state" that is forced by the spirit of its previous history "to move forward in freedom and in its progress toward empire. Only in this way can it continue to exist. Otherwise it will perish."[48] In that statement, the old Fichtean propensity for postulates of the absolute was again aptly linked with profound insight into the actual. But we should not overlook the fact that his a priori postulate was still stronger than his empirical insight. As Fichte goes on to develop his ideas here, we see again that the concept of a Prusso-German empire, like all his earlier programs for the state, is only an interim means toward an end. The goal of a republic, which he could previously envision only in the distant future,[49] moves all the closer as he develops his ideas and, we should note, as his hopes rise. The result is that he finally rejects the heredity of the German kaiserdom, or, as he expresses it, of a German despotism. "Bring on a despot to enforce education in the German

[46] *Hist. u. polit. Aufsätze*, I, 136.   [47] *Sämtl. Werke*, VII, 549.
[48] *Ibid.*, VII, 554.   [49] *Ibid.*, VII, 553.

character! It does not matter who; may our king earn this merit! A senate after his death,—it can thus be underway." This "it" is the education for freedom that Fichte assigns to the despot as his first duty. The course toward the republic should, then, if we may so interpret Fichte, be taken immediately after the death of the Prusso-German emperor or despot.[50]

But is the German republic he desires a real German national state in our sense of the term? To put the question more precisely, does the actual nation find the political expression of its particular nature in such a republic? The negative answer is inherent in the question, for the special characteristic of the German nation was precisely that minds with strong ties to territorial states and to particular ethnological groups within the nation could accept, and had to accept, the nation as a whole. Nevertheless, we must admit that Fichte's insight into the real factors of nationality in general and into those of German nationality in particular has grown considerably. "Nations are individualities with particular talents and the possibilities of exploiting those talents," he says in a passage similar to one in the *Addresses*.[51] He also writes with understanding about the historical origin of nations and national characters: "A common or a divisive history affects the national development of a people in a crucial way, . . . common history consists of common deeds or suffering . . . also of a common governing house that is a palpable representative of the people's unity: love of fatherland and love of its ruler are often united. . . . A richer and more brilliant history creates a firmer national character (this raises the Prussian above the Saxon). A firmer national character also develops if the

---

[50] The passages on the rule of the Prussian emperor or despot are *Sämtl. Werke*, VII, 554 and VII, 565. Statements follow (VII, 570f.) that contradict them and that do not promise anything for the German people from Prussia ("If, for example, Austria or Prussia conquered Germany, why would that produce only Austrians or Prussians and no Germans?" "No existing ruler of a single country can make Germans; they will all become Austrians, Prussians, etc."). According to this, Fichte either became skeptical about Prussia later; or, what seems more likely, the section beginning on p. 565 (which follows the passage about the despot) comes from an earlier stage of this work. Without examining the manuscript, we will not be able to answer the question of how closely the printed sequence of the sections corresponds to the sequence in which they were written, particularly since divergences of thought occur within the individual sections. Cf., for example, the contradictory statements on the national significance of German literature, pp. 565, 568, and 572. Page 568 represents the earliest stage, while the passage on p. 565 (in parentheses in the printing) seems to have been added after the passage on p. 572 was written.—The new edition of this work by A. Strecker: Fichte, *Polit. Fragmente*, in Philosoph. Bibl., Vols. 163f. (1925), is just a reprint.
[51] *Sämtl. Werke*, VII, 563; cf. VII, 467.

people are given a greater part in the government and are allowed to exercise free judgment in it, if they are utilized not as dumb machines but as conscious and worthy coworkers (that raises Prussia above Austria). National pride, honor, and vanity adhere, as with individuals, to everything and serve to strengthen ties."[52] At the end of this fragment, Fichte took still another essential step toward the recognition of the national factor. Earlier in this study we distinguished between the elements that make up the character of a nation, and we separated those of a political nature from those that are based on a common culture. Fichte, too, made this same distinction. After establishing that the remarkable feature of the national character of the Germans up to that point was "precisely their existence without a state and beyond the state, their purely intellectual development," he then continues: "We must now distinguish more profoundly between the national factor that is formed only by the state (and that swallows up its citizens in the state) and the national factor that lies beyond the state."[53]

Who can say how much deeper Fichte might have penetrated into the character of national existence if it had been granted him to complete his apprenticeship in those great apprentice years of the German nation? He himself seems to feel sometimes that his categories are insufficient to grasp the substance of this new wonder of the nation that overwhelmed his feelings, and it is a grand spectacle to see how he struggles to master it. He tried with all his power to fuse his old problem of the will, "How can we achieve the kingdom of reason?" with his new problem of the emotions, "How can we achieve a single German nation?" But because his will never gave up its dominance over the emotions, we can probably assume that he would never have left the cosmopolitan and rationalistic ground in which his ideas had their roots. In any case, such a foundation is evident everywhere in the political fragments and in the *Staatslehre* of 1813.

He did not draw the conclusion that we would expect from his insight into the historical and territorial-dynastic background of actual German national feelings. To him, the national pride of the Prussians, Saxons, and Austrians is a "fanatical peasant pride," which,

---

[52] *Ibid.*, VII, 567.

[53] *Ibid.*, VII, 572. At the beginning of the fragments (VII, 549), he had tried to define the essence of the nation in the area of politics alone as "mutual understanding between representatives and the represented and a mutual trust founded on that understanding."

he thinks, more than any other factor, has divided the Germans among themselves.[54] He is unable to close his eyes to the insight that such irrational bonds are essential for the self-awareness of a people: "But a people always wants them and cannot let them go; the unity of the concept does not remain alive in the people." But Fichte still does not want to accept this state of affairs. He was not satisfied to bridge these territorial feelings with a common German national consciousness. Instead, he wanted to dispose of these foundations of a historically developed national consciousness altogether. He says toward the end[55] that "the concept of unity for the German people would not put emphasis on any specific regional characteristic but should create the free citizen." He therefore does not want to concede, either, that a mere federation could form a people into a nation.[56] Instead, according to the introduction and also to the *Staatslehre*, the individual states into which Germany is now divided will have to disappear in the future, having served simply as means toward a higher end.[57] But the essential point here is that the German national spirit he advocated was not a product of historical life but a postulate of reason. Let us examine this statement more closely.

He notes that the Germans up to this time still have no national character or pride. Other peoples have national character because of their history. The Germans have had no history as such in recent centuries. "What bonds have we had, what common history?"[58] In some passages we may be able to hear a trace of regret that this is the case; but then a certain satisfaction about this also shines through the regret. This conflict in feelings represented a conflict in the mode of thought of the eighteenth and nineteenth centuries. There is no doubt about which of these was stronger in Fichte, the regret or the satisfaction. This great idealist, who always aspired toward the eternal in the temporal, was delighted with the discovery

---

[54] *Ibid.*, VII, 568.   [55] *Ibid.*, VII, 573.
[56] *Ibid.*, VII, 565, 569. These notes of 1813 show Fichte more intent on the unity of the nation than he was in the *Addresses* (cf. p. 84, above) because the form the unit takes is no longer a matter of indifference to him.
[57] *Sämtl. Werke*, VII, 547, 573; IV, 423. Lask, *Fichtes Idealismus und die Geschichte* (1902), thinks, p. 267, that "we should not see a blind zeal against local patriotism" in Fichte's rejection of the territorial state but that we should instead recognize in it the profound insight "that every state is deeply ailing in which political organization does not coincide with the 'national spirit.'" That is correct, but we must add that his "national spirit" was not the historical, concrete spirit of the German nation.
[58] *Sämtl. Werke*, VII, 565, 568.

of a national spirit that had no history behind it and with the task of creating a national spirit that would be entirely the product of conscious reason and freedom. In his view, precisely this lack of a history seemed to make the task easier. In any case, this lack was a proof for him that there was something "truly primal," something supra-historical in whatever of the German character had survived.[59] As early as the *Addresses* he had claimed this "originality" for the German language and for the German nation, the only "primal people," the "people as such." We can see that his concept of "originality" means something quite different from what we have in mind when we praise a nation as particularly primal. We mean a sound and natural freshness that has been preserved from previous and simpler cultural stages, but we always mean something historically conditioned. Fichte meant, on the contrary, something *not* historically conditioned.[60] The consequence of this must be that historically formed national characters in general are inferior and that they belong to the world of subjugation. Fichte drew this very conclusion. The French, he says, "have no self-created self at all, but only a purely historical one based on their unified experience. The German, on the other hand, has a metaphysical self."[61]

There is, however, another point in these notes where it seems as if Fichte were willing to entrust at least the future development of the German nation to the stream of history. The character of the Germans, he says,[62] "lies in the future: it consists now of the hope of a new and glorious history. The beginning of this history is that the Germans consciously create themselves. That would be the most glorious destiny. The basic character of the Germans is thus: 1. Be-

[59] "The Germans . . . have grown up without a history" (*ibid.*, VII, 565; cf. VII, 571).

[60] The *Addresses* (*ibid.*, VII, 374) make that eminently clear: "The actual basis for a distinction (of the nature of the German) lies in whether we believe in an absolutely primary and original factor in man himself, whether we believe in freedom, in infinite perfectability, or whether we do not believe in all this. . . . Now, finally, a philosophy has come to a stage of clarity at which it can hold before this nation a mirror that lets the nation clearly recognize what it has naturally and unconsciously become up to this point." Cf. Kuno Fischer, *op.cit.*, p. 718: "Fichte based the origin and beginnings of cultural history on a hypothesis that is contradicted by the laws of development, namely, on the hypothesis of a primal and normative people . . . that is, he puts revelation in place of development and thereby makes a riddle of history." On the connection of the idea of a normative people with Rousseau, see Fester, *op.cit.*, pp. 133ff., 146, 153.—Lask, *op.cit.*, p. 257, fails to recognize the fundamental opposition that Fichte himself (*Sämtl. Werke*, VII, 565) established between the "primal" and the "historical."

[61] *Sämtl. Werke*, VII, 566.   [62] *Ibid.*, VII, 571.

ginning of a new history. 2. Self-realization in freedom. . . . 3. The Germans should therefore not be a continuation of their old history: this history achieved nothing for them." But is this "new history" that is in store for the German nation "history" in our sense of the word? The sharp caesura that Fichte puts between the old and new history of the nation contradicts our idea of history. We cannot accept such jumps in development; we cannot believe that a people can have an old and a new history so divided that the one has run its course to no effect whatever and the other bears no relationship to the past at all. Fichte was able to believe in such a leap across the abyss only because his new history is not genuine history: the beginning of this history should be that the Germans "consciously create themselves" and "realize themselves through freedom." In this view of history the factors that are crucial to the nature of genuine history are missing, the factors of necessity and of the irrational. Fichte has therefore two totally different conceptions of history before him. One of these is applicable to the "old" history of the Germans and to the history of other peoples. This concept of history comes close to our own. Fichte scorns it and puts it to one side because of what we might call its impure and ignoble elements. The other concept, based exclusively on the factor of free, conscious creativity, lies beyond the sphere of the truly historical.[63]

The "new history" is, then, a rational and ideal history, just as Fichte's state is a rational state and his nation a rational nation. It is still the voice of human rights and of the first years of the Revolution that speaks in his great prophecy: "And so a true empire of justice will be realized first among them (the Germans) in a form that it has never taken in the world yet. It will incorporate all the commitment to the freedom of the citizen that we see in the ancient world but without sacrificing the majority of the people as slaves, which the old states needed to exist, a commitment to freedom based on the equality of all who bear the name of man."[64] Words like these have an infinitely more substantial effect on us than the similar-sounding phraseology of the Girondists and Jacobins, but only because they have a more profound meaning as Fichte uses them; because all his seemingly abstract ideas on freedom and justice are the live

---

[63] I cannot accept Lask's opinion, p. 269, that sees in the passage from Fichte quoted above an "unmistakable proof" that Fichte "in fact advocated a concept of 'history' that encompassed past and future and that was totally inconceivable for the eighteenth century."

[64] *Staatslehre*, IV, 423; VII, 573.

experience of a great soul, of an unusual human being; because his
demand for freedom is nothing other than the demand for moral
autonomy, the strongest root of all great culture. It is the great measure of personal involvement and of historically motivating energy that
makes Fichte's ideas on the nation and the national state seem more
modern and historical to us than they really are.

I do not think our reservations and limitations will diminish Fichte's
immense contribution to the development of the idea of the nation
and of the national state in Germany. Perhaps they will do just
the opposite. The drama in the development of this new idea becomes all the more impressive when we remember the strength and
vitality of the old one from which it emerged. We usually tend to see
this drama in much too simplistic a fashion. Cosmopolitanism did
not merely sink to the ground, pale and exhausted; and the new national idea did not then spring up in its place, unimpeded and victorious. Cosmopolitanism and nationalism stood side by side in a
close, living relationship for a long time. And even if the idea of
the genuine national state could not come to full bloom within
such a relationship, the meeting of these two intellectual forces was
by no means unfruitful for the national idea. Indeed, the confrontation of nationalism and cosmopolitanism first lent this idea a life
and character of its own. Within this context, the national idea was
not the object of disinterested, academic contemplation. On the contrary, it was roundly affirmed and infused with a great pathos. At
the time Fichte considered the problems we have just discussed here,
it was impossible for a mind like his to derive that pathos from the
torn soil of the nation. Thus, he took it instead from the heights of
a universal ethical ideal.

7

ADAM MÜLLER IN THE YEARS 1808-1813

ONCE FICHTE had gained an insight into the essence of the power state, he put this knowledge aside again, because the ethical impulse in his thinking was too strong to tolerate the permanent autonomy of any other power. The ethical will that led him into the world of the state and the nation also formed the barrier that hid the total character of these forces from him. Thus, it fell to a mind of much lesser strength but of greater receptivity to achieve a deeper understanding of the national state than Fichte had. This was Adam Müller, who, a year after Fichte's *Addresses*, lectured in Dresden in the winter of 1808-9 on *Die Elemente der Staatskunst*.[1] Fichte had spoken to the German nation, and whatever listeners had been present had represented that nation for him. Adam Müller, who held a high post at the court of Weimar at the time, spoke before an assembly of statesmen and diplomats and in the presence of a prince of Weimar. He too told his aristocratic audience things they wanted to hear. His friend Gentz believed, and advised accordingly, that Müller could have established a very comfortable existence for himself with a book defending the principle of nobility by birth.[2] The important point here is not whether Adam Müller was susceptible to such materialistic considerations at the time or not. What is clear is that we, in moving from Fichte to Müller, are passing from the pure air of an inflexible ethical purpose to an environment of a particular social character in which the author himself felt at home and which was not renounced in his theory.

Adam Müller had once studied with Heeren in Göttingen. He dedicated the *Elemente* to his former teacher and received extremely warm thanks from him for the book.[3] Whether Heeren actually led Müller into deeper historical studies cannot be determined with cer-

[1] Appeared in 1809 in 3 volumes. Reprint by Baxa (1922) in 2 volumes with commentary.
[2] Gentz to Müller, 1808, in *Briefwechsel zwischen Gentz und Müller*, p. 140.
[3] Heeren to Müller, Jan. 1, 1810, in Baxa's new edition of the *Elemente*, II, 439.

95

tainty from Müller's writings alone. His historical sense was not the
sort that a writer acquires from active political life. He had been
deeply involved in politics from time to time, and as a journalist
he had had contact with statesmen,[4] but he was never able to adjust himself intellectually to the political currents of the times as
well as Gentz had in his best period. Along with a strong sense of
the actual, he also had a visionary, speculative tendency, and he
brought these two elements into such a tight union that his most
realistic insights always had a component of fanciful vision as well.
We can easily understand his enthusiasm for Heinrich von Kleist,
whose work shows similar characteristics. Kleist, however, was not
only more forceful and original but also worked with greater self-
discipline than Adam Müller. But whatever their differences,
Müller's best period was that of his friendship and contact with Kleist,
and it thus coincided with the critical times after the Peace of
Tilsit.[5] But strong as the stimulation of this period was for Müller's
thinking, it was he who was more interested in practical politics, and
it is possible that Kleist, who had already begun to perceive the
crisis of the fatherland, was drawn into patriotic concerns by Müller.[6]
Müller's ideas may have even inspired the concept of the state in
the *Prinz von Homburg*.[7] Müller's sensitive nature was not capable

[4] As in 1803; see *Briefwechsel Gentz-Müller*, p. 18, and Wittichen, *Briefe von
und an Gentz*, II, 410.

[5] Cf. Steig, *H. v. Kleists Berliner Kämpfe*; Kayka, *Kleist und die Romantik*, pp.
120ff.; Rahmer, *Kleist*, pp. 174f. Rahmer does not do justice to Müller's significance
because he emphasizes almost exclusively the weaknesses of his character. After
the appearance of the first edition of this book, a lively interest in Adam Müller
arose and led sometimes to overestimations of him. Schmitt-Dorotič, *Politische
Romantik* (1919; 2nd edn., 1925), reacted to them with a decided under-
estimation. I have discussed Schmitt-Dorotič's position in the *Histor. Zeitschrift*,
CXXI, 292ff. Of the more recent literature on Adam Müller, I mention here,
besides Baxa's panegyric and not very penetrating *Einführung in die romant.
Staatswissenschaft* (1923), the subtler but somewhat precious work of Reinke-
meyer, *Ad. Müllers eth. u. philos. Anschauungen im Lichte der Romantik* (1926),
also A. v. Martin, "Die polit. Ideenwelt Ad. Müllers," in *Kultur- und Universal-
geschichte*, Festschrift f. W. Goetz (1927), and the highly important Berlin dissertation by Georg Strauss, *Die Methode Ad. Müllers in der Kritik des 19. u. 20.
Jahrh's* (1922). Cf., too, Weinberger, "Das neuere Schrifttum über Ad. Müller,"
Archiv f. Sozialwiss., LI (1924), 808.

[6] Kayka, *op.cit.*, pp. 120ff. and 178. Rahmer is more skeptical on this point,
op.cit., pp. 34 and 218.

[7] B. Luther, *H. v. Kleists Patriotismus und Staatsidee*, in *Neue Jahrb. f. d. klass.
Altertum*, Vol. 37 (1916). The inspiration applies, of course, more to the problems raised than to the solution of the problems. Nadler, *Die Berliner Romantik
1800-1814*, pp. 179ff., has recently uncovered subtler relationships between Adam
Müller and H. v. Kleist.

of the great patriotic passion that Kleist developed, but it was rich and fine enough to absorb the image of national impulses awakening on all sides and to construct a theory of national political life that represents an initial and fruitful step toward a new form of life. But this was only an initial effort and not an exhaustive one.

It was not by chance that Müller combined artistic, aesthetic, and philosophical interests with political ones. In a letter of February 6, 1808 to Gentz[8] he stated that he had never subscribed to a separation of the so-called fine arts from the serious concerns of life. "My view of the world is total and complete." He could not imagine real and ideal views of life excluding each other, and in this respect he was a true friend of Kleist's. "In my view and in me, which is the same thing, everything is, as you call it, idealistic, completely idealistic. . . . But if other people, from other points of view, say that I am completely realistic and complain about my realism, then you will permit me to regard this as a proof that I am in the right, although I require no such proof of this myself." He had his ideas on art in mind here, but in political studies, too, he had the same ambition of founding a theory that could just as well be called "idealistic" as "realistic" and that would show both the philosopher and the statesman the way to the heart of the state. "Totality" is one of his favorite words, and he had a strong urge to achieve an all-inclusive view of civil and political life. He had a feeling for movement in life and for the coherence of its vibrations, for the interaction of all the parts of a whole, and he also had a lively awareness of the fact that invisible forces are at work behind the external phenomena of historical life.[9] He was particularly proud of his distinction between idea and concept, a distinction that other thinkers of this period had already touched on[10] but that he developed further in a more historical fashion. For him the idea was the living element in

[8] *Briefwechsel*, p. 126.

[9] Fr. Schlegel, very neatly but also with some protest against the men who had called early Romanticism into existence, criticizes Müller's way of thinking as "a certain pantheism of feeling that would gladly dissolve everything conceivable into harmony" (in a review of Müller's *Vorlesungen über die deutsche Wissenschaft und Literatur* [1807], in *A. W. und F. Schlegel*, ed. Walzel, in *Deutsche Nationalliteratur*, Vol. 143, p. 415).

[10] Fichte in *Die Grundzüge des gegenw. Zeitalters*, in *Sämtl. Werke*, VII, 69; Schelling (see Friedrichs, *Klassische Philosophie und Wirtschaftswissenschaft*, p. 202; cf. Schmitt-Dorotič, *Histor. Zeitschrift*, CXXIII, 382); Fr. Schlegel (see Kluckhohn, *Persönlichkeit und Gemeinschaft*, p. 69); Görres (see Baxa's new edition of *Die Elemente der Staatskunst*, II, 294); J. J. Wagner (see Kluckhohn, p. 83). Cf., too, Metzger, *Gesellschaft, Recht und Staat*, p. 260.

historical events, which could not be analyzed by means of a dead concept. Here we see one of the greatest effects of Kant's epistemology. Kant had destroyed confidence in the concept and its capacity to express the essence of things, and without meaning to, he had opened the way for attempts to grasp the essence of things by the new method of inspired intuition and speculation. Concepts, Müller said, are merely the rigid forms[11] ordinarily used in the study of the state, of life, and of man. "But there is no concept for the state." If "the mental image that we have developed of such a sublime object expands, if it moves and grows just as the object grows and moves, then we do not call that mental image the concept of the thing but the idea of the thing, of the state, or of life." Thus he demanded of political science, and of all higher studies, that they be a matter of *experience*, not just of learning and understanding.[12]

With such ambitions, he could have become one of the greatest of political thinkers if he had been able to fuse the "ideal" with the "real" in politics as well as Kleist had in art, if he had been able to base his great general conception of the state on an abundance of concrete experience,[13] if he had been able to do justice not only to his "ideas" but also to his "concepts," and if he had not sometimes been lacking in precision and clarity of thought. He still remains highly stimulating today, and certain of his ingenious ideas and the flight of his thought in general can still arouse the highest expectations, but he does not satisfy these expectations to the same degree that he awakens them, and what takes flight in his thinking sometimes vanishes into the incomprehensible.

We shall not do him an injustice if we deny him intellectual originality and see instead, even in the most original and best things he produced, a fortunate application and development of what he had

---

[11] *Elemente*, I, 27f.   [12] *Ibid.*, I, 22.

[13] Rehberg, a political thinker who stood close to Müller in his basic conservative tendencies but was quite different from him in having his roots in experience, missed this in him even then. Rehberg's review of Müller's *Elemente* (*Sämtl. Schriften*, IV, 245) says, "Scholarly works on subjects that concern legal and ethical relationships among men are by no means the worse if they take on a clearly noticeable taste of the earth in which they have grown." These words are not aimed directly at Müller in the context in which they stand, but they are surely meant for him, as another comment, pp. 249f., shows: "Whoever looks everywhere (in the practical world) for ideas alone, instead of developing a clear picture of individual men and their circumstances, is simply chasing will-o'-the-wisps. The writer of these lectures does just that." Rehberg was clearly not capable of grasping the value of Müller's idealistic mode of vision, and he was equally unable to do justice to Herder, with whom he classified Müller.

learned in a great epoch[14] and from men greater than himself.[15] From the influences that most affected him, we shall single out the most relevant ones for our study: Edmund Burke, early Romanticism, and Fichte.[16]

If we mention the name Burke, we must first consider the influence of Friedrich Gentz, the first exponent of Burke in Germany as well as Adam Müller's teacher and closest political friend. According to his own statement,[17] Müller was indebted to Gentz for his interest in the concrete facts of social life, in world affairs, in the state, and consequently for helping him surmount pure speculation. The main questions of our study are also the center of interest in Gentz's political thought. He developed a keen awareness of the relationship between national culture and the national state, and he was able to describe vividly what he had seen of it in England.

[14] Cf. his own words, *Elemente*, I, 9: "Thus, the times in which we live are a great school of political wisdom."

[15] Wilhelm Grimm's comment of 1811 is very symptomatic of the divided impression that Müller made even on his contemporaries: "It is strange that the good things in his writings annoy me, but they do, because I have the feeling he has borrowed them all." Steig, *op.cit.*, p. 526; Humboldt's judgment of Müller is cited in this same work, p. 296 (cf., too, Bratranek, *Goethes Briefwechsel*, p. 236). For contemporary judgments on the *Elemente*, see Baxa's new edition, II, 442ff.

[16] Schelling's influence is of particular importance for Müller's philosophical basis (cf. Wittichen, *Briefe von und an Gentz*, II, 347, note 2; Stahl, *Geschichte der Rechtsphilosophie* [3rd edn.], p. 569; Metzger, *Gesellschaft, Recht und Staat*, pp. 260 and 267f.; Friedrichs, *Klassische Philosophie und Wirtschaftswissenschaft*, pp. 164ff.). Critics have repeatedly reproached me for not having emphasized Schelling's influence. However, they fail to realize that, in the framework of my book, I did not want to write a monograph on Adam Müller but rather wanted to present his position in the development of a particular problem, and was therefore obliged to treat only those influences that have a direct bearing on this problem.—Heller's assumptions, *Hegel und der nationale Machtstaatsgedanke in Deutschland* (1921), pp. 139ff., that Müller had already been influenced by Hegel through Schelling and Gentz and especially that his theory of the national character of the power state goes back to Hegel are in urgent need of close scrutiny. On the other hand, the strong influence that Burke in particular had on Müller has been more thoroughly demonstrated by Frieda Braune, *Edmund Burke in Deutschland* (1917), pp. 182ff., than it could be here. I felt justified in omitting from the study the question of how much Müller was affected by the French writers of the counterrevolution, because the problem of nationality was not an important one for them. In his lectures on Friedrich II (p. 109), Müller praises Bonald's *Traité sur le divorce*. In *Vermischte Schriften*, I, 312ff., he discusses Bonald more thoroughly but freely admits that he had first become acquainted with Bonald's *Législation primitive* in the spring of 1810. Cf., too, Schmitt-Dorotič, *Politische Romantik* (2nd edn.), pp. 88ff., and Kluckhohn, *Persönlichkeit und Gemeinschaft*, p. 50.

[17] Wittichen, *Briefe*, II, 348.—The work of A. Gerhardt, *Romant. Elemente in d. Politik u. Staatsanschauung Fr. Gentz'* (Leipzig dissertation, 1907), is not quite up to its task.

He fought for the individual life and individual rights of nations and states, and seriously considered the problem of how these individual rights were to be limited by the collective rights of the European society of states. In his best years, he saw the means for developing Germany's future national greatness[18] in the universal struggle against France and felt himself to be the bearer of "plans for liberating and changing the world," felt himself to be more a world citizen who fought for a cause than a servant of a particular state.[19] Thus, the ideas Gentz represented definitely belong to the problem we are examining, but the man that stood behind them does not belong there wholly. It has been correctly observed that by becoming an advocate of *Realpolitik* he "stepped out of the line of development that German political life was to take up to the emergence of Bismarck."[20] We might add that he was too much of an epicurean. He enjoyed the profound substance of his life and even his political passion more than he grasped their importance. To adapt a phrase applied to his view of religion, he had more of a feeling for the value of ideas than for ideas themselves. His ideas were therefore lacking in what they needed to make them homogeneous with those of his contemporaries, and his struggle for the freedom of nations was also lacking in true national ferment and in deep inner pathos.[21]

Müller and Gentz complemented each other in a most fortunate way in that one always had what the other did not have but still valued. The one was driven by his nature to an idealistic view of actuality, the other to a realistic view of it. But the ideas that Müller could have taken from Gentz were only the reflection of a stronger light that emanated from Burke and that Müller soon encountered directly for himself.

Burke's observations on the French Revolution were a revelation for Müller. He called Burke the last prophet to appear on this dis-

---

[18] 1804, Wittichen, *Briefe*, II, 251. [19] 1804, *ibid.*, II, 244.

[20] F. C. Wittichen, "Gentz' Stellung zum deutschen Geistesleben vor 1806," *Histor. Vierteljahrsschrift*, XIV, 35.

[21] A remarkable letter to Adam Müller, allegedly written in late 1809, in which language and nationality are declared to be "the true borders and the only borders of individual state territories," has raised some doubt among critics because the original of it is not available. See Wittichen, *Briefe*, II, 418. Dombrowsky, *Aus einer Biographie A. Müllers* (Göttingen dissertation, 1911), pp. 58f., disagrees with him and offers reasons worthy of consideration for the authenticity of the letter. But even if the letter is authentic, we cannot be dealing with a deeply rooted view of Gentz's here.

enchanted earth.[22] Here, he exclaimed joyfully,[23] is real life; here is intellect and theory; here the statesman and the student of the state appear in *one* man. "His works cannot be distilled; concepts cannot be drawn off from them and stored in sealed bottles . . . nor can practical tactics be learned from him. But if we understand the actual historical case that he describes, then we understand his mind at the same time. If we understand the idea that motivates him, then we see that same idea expressed in actual life, correctly and powerfully expressed." Burke affected others as deeply as he did Adam Müller. Not only did he provide the opponents of the Revolution with their most powerful intellectual weapons, but, more important still, he struck the first decisive blow against conceptions of the state that the eighteenth century had formed on the basis of natural law and added elements to all speculation about the state that are permanently relevant. He taught us deeper respect and understanding for the irrational components of the life of the state, for the power of tradition, customs, instinct, and impulsive feelings. We cannot exactly say that he discovered them, for every advocate of *Realpolitik* in modern times from Machiavelli on has recognized them and used them. To the practical man, they had previously seemed to be only the obvious weaknesses of man, which were to be exploited or indulged accordingly. To the rationalizing theoretician, they seemed more a pudendum. If a thinker recognized them at all, he did so resigned to a diminution of the true ideal of reason. That was the case with Montesquieu and, as we saw, with Wilhelm von Humboldt. But a true joy in history and an inner emotional relationship to it were lacking in this purely negative mode of historical thought[24] to which the most incisive—we might say, the most enlightened—men of the eighteenth century held. Only a man who achieved an emotional relationship to history could discover its true values. Möser was probably the first to find this new source of joy in the field of political and social institutions. But in depth of political understanding and in breadth of influence he was surpassed by Burke, whose thinking found verification

---

[22] *Über König Friedrich II.* (1810), p. 52.

[23] *Elemente*, I, 26; other passages on Burke are to be found in the *Lehre vom Gegensatz* (1804), pp. xiif.; in the *Vorlesungen über die deutsche Wissenschaft und Literatur* (2nd edn., 1807), pp. 27 and 149; in the *Elemente*, I, 86; and in the *Vermischte Schriften* (1812), I, 120, 252ff.

[24] Gunnar Rexius, "Zur Staatslehre der historischen Schule," *Histor. Zeitschrift*, CVII, 500, coined the fitting expression "negatively historical tendency."

in the times and in the spectacle of the collapse of pure reason in France. He taught the greater practicality of understanding much that had previously been regarded as weakness or irrationality and of recognizing the kernel of wisdom in the husk of prejudice. He taught respect and even love for this entire interwoven mass of natural and half-wild growth that winds its way through the private existence of the individual just as visibly and invisibly as it does through the society and state as a whole and that provides both a snug cocoon and a hidden support for everyone. Everywhere, in the totality and in the details, one could perceive, if one only had the eye for it, the "entire glory of the precious and diverse ideas that the heart encloses and even the intelligence approves because it needs them to disguise the inadequacies of our naked, fragile nature."[25] Thus, through Burke, a new, warm light fell on a whole world of facts that had previously been neglected or scorned. Social and political life seemed much more complicated but also much richer and, because of this richness, more beautiful than before, when men had been accustomed to considering it in the light of only a few concepts. "Man's nature is intricate; the affairs of social life are infinitely compounded," Burke said.[26] The consequences of this insight for Burke and for his student Adam Müller were a deep respect for the hidden wisdom in everything the living had taken over as a legacy of the past and therefore a deep mistrust of the wisdom of those who wanted to cut the bonds with the past. Natural law and the law of reason retreated before positive law, which then rose to the position of true natural law. "We can confidently reject," says Müller,[27] "all natural law outside of or above or before positive law; we may consider all *positive* law *natural* law since all the infinite specific elements that positive law involves have their origin in nature."

A further effect of this new sense of the complicated and deeply rooted nature of the state was that the relationship between the public and private spheres was seen in a different way. They could no longer be sharply and strictly separated from each other according to their different concepts and aims. The effects of one and the same spirit were felt in both spheres, a spirit that was of permanent duration, that bound the living together both with each other and with their ancestors, and that found expression in the humblest as well as

---

[25] Burke, *Betrachtungen* (trans. Gentz, new edn., 1794), I, 108. Since the influence of Burke in Germany stems primarily from this translation, I shall quote from it, although it blurs the original here and there.

[26] *Ibid.*, I, 84.   [27] *Elemente*, I, 75.

in the highest values of life. Burke consequently did not teach a conception of the state as a practical union—nor indeed as a purely rational institution at all—but as a living community existing far beyond the span of a single generation. "It would be outrageous to regard . . . the state as an ordinary commercial association that one maintains as long as one cares to and gives up when one no longer sees any advantage in it. A state is a union of a very different sort and of a very different importance . . . it is a community of everything that is worth knowing, of everything beautiful, of everything valuable and good and divine in man."[28] We see the extent to which Müller is indebted to Burke when we read his definition of the state:[29] "The state is not merely a factory, a dairy, an insurance company, or a mercantile society; it is the close uniting of the entire physical and intellectual needs, the entire physical and intellectual richness, the entire internal and external life of a nation into a great, energetic, infinitely dynamic and vital totality." "The state is an alliance of preceding generations with the following ones and vice versa."[30] Perhaps more consciously than Burke, he removed the barriers between private and public existence. As long as the state and the citizen serve two masters, he said, then the heart, too, will be inwardly divided.[31] We must reach a point at which "private life is nothing but national life seen from below and public life, in the last analysis, nothing but that same national life seen from above."[32]

It is clear how far we have come from Humboldt's ideas of the nineties. There the individual was valued above the state and nation; or, in Humboldt's later view, the nation is at best only a foundation and means of education for the individual and of importance only in its relationship to him. But now, in Müller, the individual existence is only a part and a link in a great, powerful whole that is composed of past and present. Within this whole, the individual and the present are limited by the supra-individual and the past. Man is accordingly "a being with many aspects, a being woven into nature on all sides and bound to the past and the future by a thousand physical and moral threads."[33] But the nation is "the sublime com-

---

[28] *Betrachtungen*, I, 139f. The strong words "outrageous" and "divine" come from Gentz. Burke says: "The state ought not to be considered as nothing better than a partnership agreement in a trade etc. . . . it is . . . a partnership in every virtue and in all perfection."

[29] *Elemente*, I, 51; a similar definition in his *Vermischte Schriften*, I, 221.

[30] *Elemente*, I, 84.   [31] *Über König Friedrich II.*, p. 37.

[32] *Ibid.*, p. 45.   [33] *Vermischte Schriften*, I, 145.

munity of a long series of past, present, and future generations that
all belong to the same large, close union both in life and in death."[34]
It was this spectacle of the unity of historical life that fascinated
and cheered him, this spectacle of permanence in change, of the
coherence of the generations among themselves, a process in which
the individual man, he thought, must always act with the knowledge
that he does not act alone but that all of nature around him acts too.

Along with Burke's influence, we must also note the ideas Müller
drew from early Romanticism. The main thing Burke taught Müller
was an awareness of tradition and of the bonds uniting the generations. Early Romanticism showed him the infinite dynamism of
the whole, the forces in it working through and with each other,
and the individuality of each of these forces. These two influences
cannot be precisely separated, the less so because early Romanticism
itself had been influenced by Burke.[35] As we saw, Novalis, too, had
wanted to restore the lost continuity with the Middle Ages and
had extolled the state as the "armature of the total activity" of man.
One could also learn from Burke that the essence of individuality
was not limited to the human individual and that it could be found
everywhere in history and nature, an idea that was also important
in early Romanticism. "It was Burke and some Germans" who perceived "the mystery of personality in possessions, in the laws of men,
in states, and in all nature," Müller said.[36] But here Müller shows an important modification as compared to early Romanticism. In Novalis,
along with surrender to the unity of the whole, the sovereignty of
the individual still always shone through, and it was this idea that
joined early Romanticism with Classical Idealism. But in Müller
the glow of this idea is already fading; and, if we may state his position this way, the individuality of the supra-individual powers has
won the victory over individual man, and individual man has lost his
sovereignty to the historical life forces that surround him. But despite all that, Müller still retains deep traces of Romantic subjectivism.

In any event, though, the gap between Müller and Fichte is
wider than that between Fichte and early Romanticism; and for this
reason, the influence that Fichte had on Müller cannot, in my opinion,
be of any central importance. But it is still evident, nonetheless, for
we can observe throughout this entire period a drawing together
of different minds from different points of origin until some of their

---

[34] *Elemente*, I, 204.   [35] See p. 52n., above.

[36] *Vermischte Schriften*, I, 120. See, also, on Novalis: *Lehre vom Gegensatz*, pp.
27 and 77; *Vorlesungen über die deutsche Wissenschaft und Literatur*, p. 73.

paths finally become inextricably entangled with each other. The unification of previously separated spheres of life was a basic need for
these thinkers. In Müller's opinion, learning and scholarship should no
longer be separate from the community of state and national life.
He wanted to show that they "decline and disperse, that all their
necessary vitality, all their warmth, heart, and force dwindle as
soon as they choose to leave a union with the state and seek to rule
and hold sway for themselves." No scholarly discipline can continue
to exist if it does not participate in social life.[37]

This idea of the relationship of knowledge to the state and society was still fairly new in Germany at the time. The political life of
the eighteenth century had had its scholarly assistants in the form
of the learned jurists and cameralists, but they were essentially auxil-
iary troops that had been detached from the centers of scholarship.
The new disciplines that had emerged from the recently awakened
intellectual life had at first turned away from the state rather than
toward it in their development. But that changed with the turn of
the century, partially through the influence of important events of
the period and partially through the inner needs of the disciplines
themselves—or, to put it more precisely, of the men who devoted
themselves to these disciplines. Fichte had thus been able to say
shortly before Adam Müller expressed the same conviction: "Even
thought at its highest levels does not release us from the more general intellectual obligation of understanding our times. All higher
thought must seek to affect the immediate present in its own
way, and whoever is truly involved in such thought is also involved
in the present." When Gentz read this passage in the *Addresses to
the German Nation*,[38] he was struck by its similarity to his friend
Müller's mode of thought: "Everything in the genuine depths of mankind must lead to one final result; otherwise, how could thinkers like
you and Fichte, who begin with such totally different premises, finally
come together again in certain crucial conclusions?"[39]

But if we look closely at this meeting of minds, we shall still see
in it a characteristic difference between the two men. Fichte, too,
wanted to draw learning out of its isolation and bring it into close

---

[37] *Elemente*, I, 63ff.   [38] *Sämtl. Werke*, VII, 447.

[39] June 27, 1808, *Briefwechsel*, p. 148. This similarity cannot, of course, refer
to the quotation above taken from the *Elemente der Staatskunst*, because these
lectures were held only in the winter of 1808-9. It refers to earlier similar statements of Müller's in the *Vorlesungen über die deutsche Wissenschaft und Literatur*
(1807), pp. 116 and 136.—On Müller's relationship to Fichte, cf. also Schmitt-
Dorotič, *Politische Romantik*, p. 124.

community with nation and state. "What is the purpose of all our efforts in even the most remote fields of learning?" Their ultimate purpose was clearly "to give form to public life and create a human order in the world at the appropriate time."[40] Adam Müller could not allow learning such unlimited dominance. In Fichte, learning must give and the state receive. In Müller, there is giving and taking on both sides, and the two functions form an inseparable unity. "Learning and the state are just what they should be when the two are one, just as body and soul are one in a single life."[41] Fichte could have said that, too, but with a different emphasis, an emphasis on the unconditional primacy of learning.[42]

On the other hand, Müller's struggle against the dead "concept" and for the living "idea" of the state is reminiscent of Fichte's early effort to overcome the formalism of concepts and to develop, for the totality of the state, a unifying bond that lies "beyond concepts."[43] Here, once again, the two thinkers immediately part ways in their views of what this unifying bond and this soul of the state should be. For Fichte it is still only the pure ethical will of his *Wissenschaftslehre*, and his goal of all goals is still freedom, i.e., the coming to life of the ethical law to the point where it ceases to be law. We search in vain in Müller for an idea of freedom that derives so completely from the depths of the inner life. He too recognizes an idea of freedom that must function as a great, unabating force in society.[44] But he defines this idea of freedom only as a "desire to assert one's individuality, to introduce and enforce among others one's views, one's mode of action, one's activities, one's entire way of life." The idea of law works as an eternally resistant centripetal force against this centrifugal idea of freedom, but no matter how much Müller emphasizes the vitality and adaptability of this idea of law, there is no doubt that its primary function is to defend historical law and the forms of existence created by previous generations against the individual's desire for freedom. He is fully convinced that a mysterious rationality, an obscure instinct of justice, has held sway from the very beginning in this work of centuries. In his lectures of 1804 on

[40] *Sämtl. Werke*, VII, 453.   [41] *Elemente*, I, 64.

[42] If Köpke and Rahmer's theory (Rahmer, *Kleist*, pp. 189 and 429) is correct and an anonymous essay on scholarly deputations in the *Berliner Abendblätter* is indeed by Müller, then Müller demanded a primacy of the state over learning in this case.

[43] Lask, *Fichtes Idealismus und die Geschichte*, pp. 250 and 256; Fichte, *Reden*, VII, 386.

[44] *Elemente*, I, 209.

the present age, Fichte had divided the development of humanity into an age of unconsciously functioning rational instinct, one of sinfulness, and one of conscious rationality. Müller the Romantic grants validity only to the first of these three eras, that of the unconsciously creating rational instinct, and he takes up his existence in it entirely. Fichte's idea of the national state was directed toward the future, was based on the concept of an entirely new kind of historical development, and had no use for the mere maintenance and preservation of the traditional.[45] Müller's optimism about the past was just as naïve as Fichte's about the future, and in the years of the Restoration it became stronger still and led to a complete, quietistic acceptance of what had taken place and to a subordination of reason to faith.[46]

At this point, he was able to see clearly the deep abyss that separated him from Fichte. But before that, in the years after 1807, his conservatism and historicism had not yet petrified to the point where he could no longer learn from the Fichte of that period and perhaps even take on some aspects of his mind and character. We can see in his correspondence with Gentz what a deep impression the *Addresses* made on him.[47] A passage in Müller's Berlin lectures on Friedrich II reads:[48] "What is the magnetic element in Fichte, the element that his students, with good reason, find irresistible? Certainly not the significance of the material or the objective value of the theory but the inexorable, military disposition of the mind, the self-defense up to and beyond the point that makes a counter-attack unlikely." What impressed Müller and what made this remarkable contact between two otherwise antipathetic intellectual worlds possible, was that everything in Fichte was transposed into life, energy, and movement.[49] Fichte's accomplishment was to make rationalism dynamic and to transfer the dynamics of reason and the free ethical will to the realm of the state. He was not able to actually

[45] "There is no real, genuine life and no decisiveness at all in the preservation of the traditional form of laws and of the welfare of the citizens" (*Sämtl. Werke*, VII, 386).

[46] See the letter of May 2, 1819 to Gentz (*Briefwechsel*, p. 279), where he discusses Fichte's rationalism and intellectualism: "Whoever obeys because of faith and whoever believes in the laws of God and in His absolute ordering of the world *not because these things are reasonable* but because the centuries tell him that these things come from God . . . that man is orthodox; he is a Christian" etc.

[47] *Ibid.*, p. 148. [48] *Über König Friedrich II.*, p. 317.

[49] Müller had written a polemic as early as 1801 (*Berliner Monatsschrift*, December 1801; cf. *Vermischte Schriften*, I, 324) against Fichte's *Der geschlossene Handelsstaat*.

conquer and transform this realm, but he was able to imbue it with an
inner vitality that it had never possessed before. The dynamics of
state and social life that Müller wants to present to us are of a different nature but also of the greatest inner vitality. Life engenders life,
and we can doubtless venture the guess that in the picture of the
vigorously active state and national life that Müller developed, some
of the forceful strokes were derived from Fichte's ideal of the state.

To us this ideal seems thoroughly antihistorical and unempirical;
Müller's state, by contrast, historical and concrete. But the contrast is
not that simple. By advocating the possibility of a continuing development and elevation of the state through reason and ethical
strength, Fichte put himself among those thinkers who, operating on
ethical, rationalistic premises, prepared the way for modern ideas of
evolution. Adam Müller, however, acknowledges neither an ethical
idea nor the modern historical idea of evolution in the field of political life. Only in a few unprejudiced judgments does he show any
trace of modern historical thinking. He essentially sees only a
rigid opposition and dualism of the genuine and the degenerate, of
the organic-natural and the mechanistic-artificial state life. For him,
the mechanistic and artificial was only the appearance of life, and
he believed that beneath the surface, nature continued on its own
course in defiance of all the pressures of political manipulation. But
does not this dualistic opposition between the genuine and the false
life of the state remind us again of Fichte and his severe distinctions
between the primal and the degenerate, between ancient and modern history, between true and specious existence? Thus, Müller, the
Romantic, and Fichte, as a product of the Enlightenment, both stood
on the border between the eighteenth and the nineteenth centuries
and between historical and absolute modes of thought. Both persisted in a dualistic division of the phenomena of state life; both
were unable to use historical insight to analyze historical phenomena
that did not happen to fit into their schemes of thought. Müller, in
opposition to nonhistorical rationalism, asserted the importance of
historical forces in general; but in doing so he failed to recognize
the historical force at work in rationalism itself. As a result, he begins
his historical thinking with a highly antihistorical act.

We have seen how Novalis and Schlegel did the same thing. The
newly revealed historical life was for them a music full of energy and
harmony to which they abandoned themselves but in which they
acknowledged only the harmonies and not the dissonances. But that
in itself was a great and fruitful gain, and the Romantic conception

of the universe as infinitely rich in individuality had to lead eventually to the historico-political realism of the nineteenth century; and, just as inevitably, it had to overcome the idea of a normative or ideal state which still survived in Romantic as well as non-Romantic minds. The principle of individuality, applied to the state, led men to see in each individual state a personality that had to be understood on its own terms and according to its own inner laws. The first step in this direction was to regard the state in general as an individuality, as a rounded, vital, particular unity. We saw how Novalis led the way here. Müller's important views on this subject must be considered now.

He touches on this subject at the very beginning of his book on statesmanship[50] and says in objection to the theory of Adam Smith that it does not give sufficient consideration "to the unified personality of states, to their rounded character." "If we regard the state as a massive individual that includes smaller individuals within itself," he continues,[51] "we see that human society as a whole can take no other form than that of a sublime and complete human being. Consequently, it will never be possible to subject the inner, essential features of the state or the form of its constitution to arbitrary speculation." Another passage[52] declares that the state is "not merely a plaything or instrument in the hands of a person, a Friedrich. It is instead *a person itself*, a free and growing whole that develops independently through the infinite interaction of ideas that oppose each other and then achieve reconciliation." This kind of state personality is entirely different from the state personality that some thinkers, working from a basis in natural law, referred to when they constructed the legal or moral person of the state or nation.[53] It is a living being that overflows with vitality and intelligence in all its parts and functions and that exists in turn only in the total context of a universe fully imbued with personality. For Müller everything in the state—its laws, institutions, material possessions—produces life. That is precisely the meaning of the great "mystery of personality in possessions, in the laws of men, in states, and in all nature."[54]

Müller drew consequences of the greatest importance from this animation and personifying of political life, from this transforma-

---

[50] *Elemente*, I, 18. [51] *Ibid.*, I, 256.
[52] *Vermischte Schriften*, I, 221.
[53] Cf. Gierke, *Althusius* (2nd edn.), pp. 158ff. and 189ff.; E. Kaufmann, *Über den Begriff des Organismus in der Staatslehre des 19. Jahrhunderts* (1908), p. 5.
[54] *Vermischte Schriften*, I, 120.

tion of all political concepts and categories into living, concrete
forces. The first of these was a new and deeper understanding of
the contact and struggles between states. The commonly held conceptions of international law and the balance of power were too formal and external for him, too much dead concepts, to offer any
sense of reality. The term "balance of power" could have validity only
if it were used to suggest "uniform growth, an alternating rise of
states in relation to each other."[55] If they come into conflict with
each other, the resulting "legal dispute is too large for any single
human being to judge, for how could he completely understand
the life of these massive individuals?" Precisely because they are individuals, they collide with each other. "All these states that we
have presented as massive human beings, human in body, tempera-
ment, thought, action, and life, must be independent and free like
the individual man in the individual state. . . . In their particular national form and style, they must grow and live and assert themselves
among their fellows."[56] Indeed, it is this very friction between them
that helps them develop as individuals.

War, too, is seen here in a special light. It belongs to the nature of
the state and is the great educator of the individual character of the
state. It is war "that gives states their outlines, their firmness, their
individuality and personality."[57] State conflicts over political interests were therefore to be judged by other standards than those a moral-
izing public was accustomed to apply to them. "Neither the opinions of cabinets nor the caprice of rulers ever arranged a war,
although a weakened and degenerate rabble may have liked to
think so. There were always deeper reasons that lay in the inevitable structure of relationships between the states. An inner drive for
vital growth, an urge derived from the impetus of earlier generations
and totally unconscious in the generation of the times, was the actual
motivation of the wars that individual nations have undertaken in
recent centuries in order to enlarge themselves."[58] We can see
how this anticipates Ranke in many ways: the state seen as a historically developed individuality, the constancy and continuity of
whose life and being reach beyond the span of the individual existence; a new awareness that the struggles of states for power and

---

[55] *Elemente*, I, 283.   [56] *Ibid.*, I, 283, 285.
[57] *Ibid.*, III, 6; cf. also I, 15 and 107.
[58] *Ibid.*, I, 287f.; similarly, I, 107. Thus, Dombrowsky's view, "Ad. Müller, die
histor. Weltanschauung u. die polit. Romantik," *Zeitschrift f. d. gesamte Staatswissenschaft* (1909), p. 389, is completely incorrect: "His philosophy obliged him
to reject cabinet politics etc."

in their own interest are an expression of their life function and are derived from inner necessity; in short, a deeper understanding and appreciation of politics at the international level. In Ranke, of course, this is all presented more clearly, has a better empirical foundation, and takes truly scholarly form. But the Romantic origin of some of his main ideas becomes perfectly evident here, and it is likely that he received more direct stimulation from Adam Müller than we had realized before.[59]

All these fruitful ideas of Müller's culminate, however, in the idea that "nationality" is the actual life-principle of states. The word was quite new at the time[60] and even less settled in its meaning than in later periods. Thus, anyone who wanted to use it to suggest something specific was perfectly justified in first defining what he meant by it. Müller did just that. Nationality, he said,[61] is "the divine harmony, reciprocity, and interaction between private and public interests." He clearly had the same meaning in mind at another point[62] when he called nationality "the training and solidifying of the civic community existence" or when he equated the "longing for nationality" with the "longing for unity and mutual effort among men."[63] In his lectures on Friedrich II,[64] of course, he equated "true

---

[59] In Ranke's selected correspondence (*Zur eigenen Lebensgeschichte*, p. 173), Müller's name occurs only once (1827) in a purely personal connection.

[60] Cf. F. J. Neumann, *Volk und Nation*, pp. 152ff., and Kirchhoff, *Zur Verständigung über die Begriffe Nation und Nationalität*, pp. 59ff. Kirchhoff is doubtless correct when he writes: "The term 'nationality' . . . does not seem to go back much further than the beginning of the nineteenth century." The earliest I have found it in the course of this study was in Novalis in 1798 (*Athenäum*, I, 1, 87; *Schriften*, ed. Heilborn, II, 15): "Our previous nationality was, it seems to me, genuinely Roman. This is logical enough because we developed in exactly the same way as the Romans etc."; then in Wilhelm von Humboldt in 1800 (*Briefwechsel mit Goethe*, p. 168), who said of Mme. de Staël: "It is an amazing thing to find people sometimes in the midst of a nation who display a foreign mentality within the limits of this nationality." Similar usage appears in Görres (*Polit. Schriften*, pp. 57 and 201) in the same year (1800) and in Hegel as well, at about the same time, Fr. Rosenzweig tells me. Fr. Schlegel uses it repeatedly in his *Philosophische Vorlesungen* of 1804-6 (II, 358, 386); Ad. Müller in 1805 (in Maurer-Constant, *Briefe an Joh. v. Müller*, III, 103); Gentz in 1806 in his preface to the *Fragmente aus der neuesten Geschichte des politischen Gleichgewichts in Europa*, in *Ausgew. Schriften*, ed. Weick, IV, 19; Fichte in the *Reden* (VII, 485) and in his *Staatslehre* of 1813 (IV, 429). By this time, the term had become very common. Cf. Heeren's essay of 1810, "Über die Mittel der Erhaltung der Nationalität besiegter Völker," in *Histor. Werke*, II; Heinichen, *Die Staatsweisheitslehre oder die Politik von Johann v. Müller* (1810), pp. 172ff.: "Wodurch wird die Nationalität einer Nation bewahrt?"; Stein in 1807 (Pertz, I, 437) and in 1811 (see Chap. 8, below); Niebuhr in 1811 in his *Römische Geschichte*, I, 7 and *passim*.

[61] *Elemente*, II, 166.   [62] *Ibid.*, II, 240.

[63] *Ibid.*, III, 253.   [64] *Über König Friedrich II.*, p. 37.

nationality" with "true freedom and independence," but neither one
can exist "as long as the state and the citizen serve two masters . . .
as long as the heart is divided with two desires, the one, to live in
a civic order in the state . . . the other, to abandon the civic order
to separate oneself from this same state with one's home and entire
private life and with one's most sacred feelings, indeed, even with
one's religion."

It is obvious here that his concept of nationality is completely political and represents a close union and interpenetration of state,
nation, and individual, of public and private life. Müller's concept
thus bears some relation to Novalis' brilliant concept of the nation, but it is fundamentally different from Fichte's. Fichte's concept
originated in the cultural nation, the linguistic and cultural community of the entire German people which he elevated to a representative position for all humanity. He had no interest in the German
individual state, and he valued the state in general only in its role as
a "cultural state"—a term that Fichte probably first coined[65]—and
as a means toward the kingdom of reason. Adam Müller, on the other
hand, like Novalis and even Friedrich Schlegel, begins with the
historically given state communities. In Fichte's nation the universal
element is dominant; in Müller's, the element of historico-political
character.[66] He speaks explicitly of a "Prussian" nation and of an
"Austrian" one.[67] What he says about the Prussian nation and nationality is particularly instructive. He sees them as the result of historico-
political events. "Prussian nationality was little more than the product of seven years of exertion,"[68] and because it rested on too
weak a foundation, conscious labor would be required to complete
the work begun. But unlike many others who passed a similar judgment both before and after him, he did not see the deficiencies in a

[65] He uses it in 1804 in *Die Grundzüge des gegenwärtigen Zeitalters*, in *Sämtl.
Werke*, VII, 200, and in 1806 in the "Patriotische Dialoge," in *Nachgelassene
Werke*, III, 230.

[66] On the basis of this, we can explain the origin of some of Müller's views that
have a trace of modern historical thinking about them. I touched on these views
on p. 108, above, and Dombrowsky, *op.cit.*, pp. 390ff., mentions them, too. Dombrowsky's discussion is primarily concerned with the scorn Müller felt for those
who wanted to imitate English institutions, even though he admired England
immensely himself. This scorn does not result, as Dombrowsky thinks, from a
modern historical consciousness, but originates instead, apart from its political
orientation, in the Romantic belief that the individuality of historical phenomena
was unique and could not be transferred to other phenomena. To the extent that
this belief denied the possibility of transferring institutions of one nation to another
it became completely unhistorical.

[67] *Vermischte Schriften*, I, 268.   [68] *Elemente*, III, 193.

purely negative light but also realized that they offered a high challenge. "Although it may not seem to be her calling, the Prussian monarchy is destined by nature above all other European states to create consciously and artfully the nationality that nature seeks to deny her."[69] Thus, this Romantic thinker could finally allow planned, conscious action its place in historical life and could concur with Fichte on this point.

Now that we know Müller's views on the character of the nation in general, it will be of great interest to see how he dealt with the problem of the German nation. Since it did not form any state unity he could hardly see it as a nation in his sense of the word, i.e., as a complete political individuality. Despite this, in his *Elemente der Staatskunst* he still ventures to claim on the basis of his observations of economic life in Germany that Germany's economic existence requires political unity. Here the pan-German mood on the eve of the Austrian war of 1809 is reflected. But the depressing experiences of 1809 robbed him of his ideal again, and he declared in his lectures on Friedrich II: "I too have dreamed a great deal of a unification of that larger nation to which we belong as the limb of the tree belongs to the trunk, and I have waited vainly for revolutions and heroes and changes in the feelings of the people that might lend aid to the dream."[70] Now, though, he concludes, the important thing is to fulfill our immediate tasks and develop enthusiasm for our particular fatherland, our particular ruler, and his hundred-year-old crown.

In this same connection, however, Müller developed views on the relationship between Germany and Europe that immediately strike us as familiar and that remind us of all the thinkers we have discussed before: "The great federation of European nations that will come, sure as we live and breathe, will be of German character; for everything great, fundamental, and eternal in all European institutions is surely German.—That is the only certainty that remains to me from all my hopes. Who can single out and separate the German element from the European character! In the recent storms that have blown over the nations, the seed of German life has been scattered farther than ever across the soil of our part of the world. This seed will continue to increase, and from imperceptible beginnings it will gradually bring about immense results. We must entrust its growth to eternal nature."[71] Müller also shared, then, that same

[69] *Über König Friedrich II.*, p. 16.   [70] *Ibid.*, p. 58.
[71] There is a similar passage in the *Vorlesungen über die deutsche Wissenschaft und Literatur*, p. 54.

idea of the sublime universal mission of the German people which we have already found in various forms in Humboldt, Schiller, Novalis, Schlegel, and, finally, in Fichte. We see, too, how the cosmopolitan ideals of German culture up to this time also reach into Müller's Romantic, historico-political world of thought. If Müller, following Novalis and opposing Fichte, took a step forward in recognizing the German individual state as a national state in the political sense, he certainly took a step backward with Fichte where the problem of the German nation as a whole was concerned. Fichte, too, conceived of the German nation as a representative people for all mankind, but he first wanted to secure its position as a closed entity in itself. For Müller, the calling of the German spirit was to spread itself throughout Europe, to be absorbed into Europe and enrich it so that German and European life could form an indivisible spiritual unity.

This cosmopolitan cultural plan was not the only remaining element of cosmopolitan thought in Müller. His historical realism was, of course, perfectly evident in his analysis of European struggles for power and in his lively conception of the great personalities of the European states. He had made it his particular task to oppose the cosmopolitan leanings of Germans "by vindicating the essence of *national* and *civic* character which can alone give substance to a shallow cosmopolitanism that spreads itself thin all over the world."[72] He knew very well how difficult it would be for his contemporaries to leave the ground of the old general and absolute state ideal for that of the individual national state. "Our age resists this idea of the particular state and nationality as no age before it ever has."[73] He could be justifiably proud of having shown the necessity of separate states for the development of mankind more clearly than anyone else had.[74] But the individual national state did not entirely absorb his political thinking and activity. The new truths that he had helped to discover were not enough for him. He still required something of the old universal nourishment along with the new national fare. "In the heart of the individual man, no matter how happy the circumstances in which he lives as a citizen or how powerfully the fatherland absorbs all his impulses . . . there still remains an unsatisfied area: despite all national satisfaction there is still room for longing."[75] From this longing arose the idea

[72] *Elemente*, III, 171; cf. Rahmer, *Kleist*, p. 35.
[73] *Elemente*, III, 223.   [74] *Ibid.*, III, 212.   [75] *Ibid.*, III, 234.

of a future European federation, an idea we have already come to
know as a standard item of cosmopolitan politics, and Müller was no
less serious about it than he was about his national state. "Make up
your mind to believe in two things resolutely and with the sacrifice
of everything you call your own! *First, in the state*, in the national,
inherited . . . form of a civic community, of a union in life and in death
for a particular, local, and national idea of the realm. . . . Second,
and this follows from the first article of faith: in a *legally founded
community of genuine states*, even if there should temporarily be
only two or three of them."[76] "We feel," another passage reads,[77]
"that pure patriotism in the form in which the ancients cultivated
it no longer exists. A form of cosmopolitanism must accompany it and
properly so, for two things are essential: the fatherland and the
confederation of states. The one without the other is no longer
desirable."

As we mentioned before,[78] it was possible at that time, on the
basis of purely historical and empirical observation, to arrive at the
firm conclusion that state life within the circle of Romance and
Germanic nations was not exclusively devoted to the instinct of self-
preservation of individual state personalities or to the struggle for
existence, and that great similarities existed between these nations,
not only in their historical origins but also in their natural interests
and goals. The world situation was conducive to the recognition of
these similarities and, as the example of Müller's friend Gentz
shows,[79] to a strong emphasis on them, because they were needed
to help protect the threatened autonomy of the individual states. Furthermore, on the basis of modern experience, we can add that the
increasing differentiation of the larger individual states and the more
forceful inner development of their features by no means lessened this store of similarities but rather increased it. However,
Adam Müller was not capable of such a purely realistic appraisal
of international values. His ideal of a European community of
states did not arise merely from a historico-political world view but

[76] *Loc.cit.*   [77] *Ibid.*, III, 296.   [78] See p. 67, above.
[79] Cf. Gentz, *Über den Ursprung und den Charakter des Krieges gegen die
französische Revolution* (1801), in *Ausgew. Schriften*, ed. Weick, II, 195ff., and
his *Fragmente aus der neuesten Geschichte des politischen Gleichgewichts in
Europa* (1805 and 1806), *ibid.*, IV, 18 and 66ff. On Gentz's relationship to
Romanticism, see Varrentrapp, *Histor. Zeitschrift*, IC, 50, note 2; F. W. Wittichen,
"Gentz' Stellung zum deutschen Geistesleben vor 1806," *Histor. Vierteljahrsschrift*, XIV, 44ff., and Groba, "Gentz," in *Schlesische Lebensbilder*, II, 147.

from a religious one as well. In his view,[80] laws and treaties alone could not create this sublime community. The church had created it once before, and only the church could restore it. "There must be a law, a compact of mutual assurance between states, that is higher than the self-preservation of the individual state; and the necessity of this law must permeate every single citizen and every single state to the depths of its being. Where else can this spirit be found but in the religion of brotherhood which once bound peoples of the most manifold languages and customs closely together?"[81]

Adam Müller was converted to Catholicism by 1805, and we must note here that this step had a different meaning for him than it did for some of the other Romantic converts. He doubtless renounced undisciplined subjectivism, but not out of exhaustion or the need to renounce a freedom that had proved troublesome. On the contrary, he accomplished his most fruitful and interesting intellectual work in the years immediately following his conversion, and he remained free enough in his voluntary restriction to admit that it was the Protestantism he had given up that contained the "sacred, inalienable principle of freedom and, consequently, of the omnipresence of religion."[82] But we see here that his Catholicism was still of a highly Romantic and subjective nature. Another genuinely Romantic feature in it was that it immediately reached into the political field and strove toward a union of the religious and political spheres. For him, the great failing of the times was that the political aspects of the Christian religion were forgotten. He opposed the view that religion had nothing to do with so-called worldly affairs. He demanded that the invisible yet still so powerful and adaptable "law of religion" regulate the relationships of the great European states with one another.[83] The clergy—and here we are reminded of Friedrich Schlegel's similar ideas—has the important task of joining the states together and binding the individual member of the state to his society, of "leading all errant might back to the right path through the power of the idea, and, finally, of maintaining the spirit of a certain ethical conformity and mutual Christian esteem in all civic affairs."[84] If such views were to gain any practical political meaning, they could achieve it only through a revival of ultramontane claims of rule. I do not think that Müller himself drew these

---

[80] *Elemente*, III, 224f.   [81] *Ibid.*, III, 226.
[82] *Ibid.*, III, 323. He also praises the profundity of Schleiermacher's *Reden über die Religion* (*ibid.*, III, 255).
[83] *Ibid.*, I, 297.   [84] *Ibid.*, II, 106.

ultramontane consequences from his lofty ideas. These ideas arose from the Romantic's desire for a totality and unity of the entire world. But in this way he came to oppose the consequences of his own realism. He feared that if he gave in to that realism too much, he would arrive at an irresolvable conflict, an intolerable breach between a Christian and pagan view of life. In the last analysis, he simply did not want to admit that self-preservation was the primary duty of the state.[85] He thought that one who recognized only this duty could not achieve a complete inner calm about the destiny of the state and would have to feel a kind of political fear of death whenever he thought about the lessons of history and the changing fortunes of states. But then, he adds, both in jest and in earnest, did Christ not come into the world to deliver states from death, too? Do not the personalities of states also have need of an intercessor?

We shall not dwell on such romanticizing mysticism. Our purpose here was to show that Müller's tentative steps toward historico-political realism in the manner of Ranke were hindered in their progress by universalistic phantasies in which mystical Romantic elements and hierarchical Catholic ones merge.[86]

[85] *Ibid.*, III, 233ff. and 226.
[86] His correspondence with Gentz in the years 1820-21 shows how his thinking on European federalism and on the role of the Roman church in it developed further along lines established by de Maistre.

8

STEIN, GNEISENAU, AND WILHELM VON HUMBOLDT IN THE YEARS 1812-1815

IT WILL HAVE BECOME clear from our discussion so far that the ideas we have treated derive from two main sources. The unusual blending of both national and universal, political and non-political elements in these ideas can be understood in terms of two major factors: first, the developments within intellectual life itself and second, the influences and impulses arising from the world situation. Filled with a new need to find ideas reflected in reality and to shape reality in the image of ideas, the German mind seized on the idea of the nation and fused it with the highly universalistic tendency of contemporary thinking. Hastened by the crushing fate of Germany after the Peace of Lunéville and the fall of the old Empire, this fusion was carried forward with increasing intensity. The world situation created by Napoleon's universal domination also forced nations and states to hold closely together if they were to maintain themselves. National autonomy and universal federation impelled each other like two engaged gears. It is therefore understandable that the massive pressure of events that urged such cooperation also led thought and sentiment still further in the direction they had already begun to take. But now we shall have to inquire into the ideas and decisions of active statesmen. If they did indeed take both national and European interests into account, did they do so under the pressure of intellectual ideals as well as of the political necessities of the moment? We can be sure of the influence of political necessity on their actions, but for that very reason it will be all the more difficult to trace an intellectual influence. One could also object that an investigation of motives in terms of intellectual history is superfluous where we can elucidate our problem more easily and appropriately from the standpoint of political

118

expediency. The difficulty that a systematic investigation encounters here is that the purely political task of the individual state and the individual nation was virtually identical with the universalistic task of unifying and liberating Europe. Sound state egoism and the universalism of political Romanticism both had essentially the same goals. We shall therefore have to proceed with the greatest caution whenever we think we have discovered the influence of these intellectual ideals. More important still, we shall have to distinguish very carefully between personalities. We will not be able to measure men of lesser stature—the political eclectics, or even the statesmen motivated by expediences of politics and power—by the same standards we use to measure those in whom human and intellectual qualities play an important role along with the qualities of the statesman. In the first group the influence of ideas is more limited than in the second, and where ideas seem dominant at first glance, they often serve only to disguise concrete interests. Who would even attempt to find deep motives and impulses based on intellectual ideals in the notes of diplomats or in the *préambules* of political agreements?

But the situation is different in the case of the three men whose ideas on the future formation of Germany in the critical years of 1812-15 we want to examine here. For them, the ideals of their time were not mere oratorical decorations, nor were they simply an educational influence to which even the finest statesman could well afford to submit himself. They were a constant source of vital nourishment which these men could never entirely do without, even in the thick of political activity. Because these ideals were so deeply rooted, it was possible for them to become not only conscious moral convictions but also unconscious presuppositions for thought and action. Anyone who has the least knowledge of these men would probably admit this claim about their national ideals, usually only to add, however, that they used these ideals to oppose the cosmopolitan spirit. This approach is particularly evident in the standard view of Freiherr vom Stein. But now we understand the real nature of this antithesis, and we also know that Romanticism, whose influence on Stein has been convincingly demonstrated by his latest and most important biographer, did not represent nationalism alone but also cosmopolitanism of a new order. We can therefore venture the proposition that even in those years when Freiherr vom Stein worked and planned most energetically for the future of the German nation, he also contributed to the development of that system of Romantic political thought that later took the form of the Holy Alliance. He had the German national state in mind, Lehmann says,[1] but we must add that it was not an autonomic national state but one circumscribed by universalistic principles.[2]

We must note at the outset that Stein did not see the political liberation of Germany as a purely German concern but also as a European one requiring European aid. His emphatic statement of 1809 seems to deny this: "Only Germany can save Germany,"[3] but by 1812 he had relinquished this ideal of national autarky that had overwhelmed him in a buoyant moment. In September 1812 he pointed out to Graf Münster[4] that Germany was in a situation like the one that existed at the time of Gustavus Adolphus. Stein was looking toward England for a foreign liberator. England was sure of the support of both Russia and Sweden and enjoyed the complete confidence of Germany because Germany was convinced that its true interests and those of England were identical. One could object here that this must be understood as the only alternative open to a German patriot at the time. Germany itself bore arms for Napoleon, and Czar Alexander was pursuing plans for the restoration of Poland. Stein considered these plans absurd and dangerous because they would alarm Europe and deter Austria, the largest German power, from taking sides with Napoleon's opponents. He wrote to Pozzo di Borgo[5] on November 12, 1812 that for this very reason, England would now have to be the leading power. In this same letter he made his famous demand that Germany and Italy be reshaped into major units. This was one of the first provisions for peace in Europe in the face of French violence. The idea of urging

[1] *Stein,* III, 191.

[2] I do not find convincing the objections that Ulmann, "Über eine neue Auffassung des Frh. vom Stein," *Histor. Vierteljahrsschrift* (1910), 153ff., has raised against this view, but they have led me to a more precise version and justification of my argument at various points. In the *Histor. Zeitschrift,* CXXXI, 177, I have briefly answered another opponent of my view, Hans Drüner, "Der nationale u. der universale Gedanke bei dem Freiherrn vom Stein," *Histor. Vierteljahrsschrift,* XXII (1924), 1. I have carefully considered his arguments and also G. Ritter's brief remarks directed against me in his address on Stein, *Archiv f. Politik u. Gesch.* (1927), 7, but I have found no reason to change anything in my argument. My footnotes here contain the essential points of my defense against Drüner and Ritter.

[3] To Gneisenau, February 20, 1809, in Lehmann, *Stein,* III, 25; this is reminiscent of Adam Müller's statement (*Elemente,* III, 148): "Nations should rescue themselves through their own efforts."

[4] September 10, in Lehmann, *Stein,* III, 157; Pertz, *Stein,* III, 152f.

[5] Lehmann, III, 193; cf. Pertz, III, 208 and 210.

independent existence on the partitioned nations throughout Europe had great merit, but it was not fundamental for Stein. Lehmann notes regretfully that Stein was able to give up this idea later, at the negotiations in Paris:[6] "He expected of the Italians what he vigorously rejected in the name of his own people." Lehmann considers this an intolerable inconsistency. I believe it is a tolerable one if we do not try to see an advocate of modern national thought in Stein. He helped to create such thinking as much as anyone, but he still did not essentially grasp it himself. Even when he called for the national organization of both Germany and Italy, he did so because of a universalistic predisposition. He saw Europe as a community formed into organic national units, or as a community that should be so formed, to oppose the threat of France; and at the time, England was the leading power of this community. If we were dealing with an unimportant diplomat here, we would regard these phrases as routine flourishes of diplomatic language. But coming from the pen of Stein, who despised such flourishes, they have a completely different tone. Had he used such phrases to win England the way a representative of an independent power would have used them to gain the alliance of another state, then he would not have conceded to England those rights he did concede her in the parts of Germany that were to be liberated, rights that Lehmann considers equivalent to dictatorship. In a letter of September 19, 1812 to Münster, he wrote that in those parts of Germany occupied by English troops England should exercise a dictatorship, just as she did in Portugal. An administrative council was to be formed in which Graf Münster would be the representative of the prince regent of England and Stein the representative of Czar Alexander. Some other leading Germans, a Russian minister, and an English minister might also be members. England should also appoint the commander of the army that was to be formed from the liberated German population.

This display of confidence in England's political disinterestedness is understandable in terms of a policy that relied not only on a temporary alliance of the opponents of France but also on their permanent European solidarity.[7]

[6] Lehmann, III, 377.
[7] "It is hardly possible," Ulmann notes (*op.cit.*, p. 158), "to make this view coincide with the fact that Stein had conceived of a similar role for Russia shortly before this statement was made (Lehmann, III, 146)." However, Stein is not speaking of Russia alone but of "Russia and her allies." The foreign dictatorship,

Stein's memorial of September 18, 1812 on the German constitution is informed by this same spirit. "The peace of Europe requires that Germany be so established that she can resist France, maintain her independence, admit England to her harbors, and prevent the possibility of France invading Russia." The future preservation of national independence is closely associated with the idea that it can be defended only through a close alliance with England and Russia. He does not seem to take into account the possibility that Germany could ever have other allies than these or an opponent other than France.

This memorial was, of course, intended for the czar. "Stein is speaking here," Lehmann says,[8] "with a non-German who is militarily responsible not only for the independence of Germany but for the independence of all the western nations." We must certainly take this into consideration; and, as above, we can again question the conclusive value of a single document. But if we repeatedly come upon the optimistic illusion that Germany's national interest is in good hands with England and Russia, then we must be on our guard. In another memorial on Germany's future, one that Stein gave to Lord Walpole on November 1, 1812 for Walpole's trip to Vienna, we find still another passage that arouses our interest on this point: "German affairs must be regulated by England, Austria, and Russia, and Prussia must be carried along, too."[9] It was left to France's enemies in Europe, then, to tell the Germans what kind of constitution they should have.

But even if we grant that all these statements were not designed merely for their recipients but also grew from Stein's genuine convictions, we could still object that these convictions were created by the pressing needs of the moment and did not represent a firm doctrine like the one the Gerlachs later created by their elevation of

---

of course, was to serve a highly national purpose. It was the only available means of achieving this purpose at the time, but the striking point here is that Stein did not see this as a necessary evil or feel it as such.

[8] III, 160.

[9] Pertz, III, 202. The expression "carried along," Ulmann thinks (p. 160), can refer only to the pressure exerted on Prussia to join the anti-French coalition. The precise meaning of the passage and its position at the end of Stein's sketch of Germany's future contradict this view. Ulmann thinks this constitution would have been so advantageous for Prussia that it would not have been necessary to "force" Prussia to accept it. I agree with him completely here, but "to be carried along" is not the same as "to be forced." In any case, though, we cannot avoid the fact that in Stein's view the constitution and, along with it, the advantages that Prussia was to receive were to come from England, Austria, and Russia.

the idea of the Holy Alliance. But anyone who examines the origins of such a doctrine must be prepared to find them reflected at first only as a momentary insight—an insight, however, that could be absorbed by certain categories of thought already present and that was also affected in turn by the doctrinaire, a priori elements of that thought. Let us pursue these hints further in the hope of coming to firmer ground.

In Stein's same memorial of November 1, 1812 we also find ideas about the political formation of the non-German parts of Europe that clearly point to such a doctrinaire a priori in his thinking. Even if these ideas are meant to serve the national interests of Germany, they are still derived from an entirely nonnational world of thought and show no regard for foreign nationality and historical state personality. As punishment for its loyalty to Napoleon, Denmark was to be totally dissolved. Sweden would take over Norway and the Danish islands; England would receive Jutland. Schleswig and Holstein would be united with Germany. Holland, however, would be united with England, which would then have to reach some mutual agreement with Germany concerning free access to the Rhine and Maas estuaries. Lehmann finds this revision of the map of Europe somewhat antiquated, and concerning the fate of Denmark, he reminds us of the plans of Karl X of Sweden and his friend Cromwell. But a historical explanation of this revision must go further than that. We are not dealing with a mere anachronism here. This is a genuine remnant of absolutistic thought, that well-known view that it is possible and practicable to rearrange parts of European countries for particular purposes and without any regard for their political and historical backgrounds or the desires of their populations. This mechanical-teleological conception of the malleability of the European political system first arose from the naïve practices of the conquering and covetous power states and was also compatible with a mode of thought characterized by natural law and rationalism. Sorel writes:[10] "As a consequence of these ideas and historical facts the division of a state came to be regarded not merely as a resolution of rival claims and as an inevitable result of wars of succession but as a 'ressource normale' of diplomacy, as a means of preventing wars by satisfying in advance the ambitions that threatened to clash with each other." The statesmen of the Vienna Congress have been often and justly reproached for this kind of arbi-

[10] *L'Europe et la révolution française*, I, 39.

trary dealing with nations. It is highly important to note here that even the statesmen and thinkers of the Prussian reform, the champions of national regeneration and spontaneous life in one's own state, could not refrain from toying and tinkering with other states. Gneisenau, Boyen, and even Niebuhr to a certain extent, desired and encouraged the intentional and artificial creation of the new kingdom of the Netherlands.[11] Boyen devised the most remarkable plans for the creation of hybrid states,[12] and the ideas expressed by Gneisenau in the fall of 1812 can help us to understand Stein's thinking along these same lines. In a letter of November 2, 1812 to Münster,[13] Gneisenau rejected Stein's suggestion, mentioned above, for the formation of an administrative council in Germany. He did not reject it because he considered English influence in Germany questionable but because he found the form it was to take impractical and impossible. "Now that things have taken the turn they have, we have to pursue another course. England must conquer on its own, give all the conquered territories its constitution, and unite them with it as an integrated part of the British Empire. The nations united with Britain in this way will be completely satisfied under a free constitution and I hardly need mention to your Excellence that the British government itself would gain in executive power by such an amalgamation."

Again, one could attempt to qualify this remarkable idea that seems just as un-German as it is un-Prussian by noting the situation in which it was expressed and the recipient for whom it was intended. One could show that, considering the state of the Prussian alliance at the time, Gneisenau could well have despaired of Prussia's future, that despite the news of the burning of Moscow, his hopes were still not high, and that he was preparing himself for the collapse of Russian resistance and the czar's strength.[14] But he still clung to an only slightly altered version of this idea even when the proportions of Napoleon's catastrophe in Russia were fully known to him and when he had reason to hope that Prussia too might rise up again. The alteration in his plan was to discard the idea of the direct unification of northwestern Germany with England and to recommend instead the founding of a large North German Guelf empire which the Guelf dynasty would retain if it should

---

[11] *Histor. Zeitschrift*, XCV, 448.
[12] See my biography of Boyen, I, 380; II, 70.
[13] Pertz, *Gneisenau*, II, 423.   [14] *Ibid.*, II, 422.

lose the English crown, a possibility that seemed likely at the time.[15] The English princes supposedly considered this idea as early as 1809. Gneisenau had also favored it then,[16] and it is known that Graf Münster in particular had advocated it.[17] This North German Guelf empire would have the possibility of separating itself from England and, as one could well point out here, the possibility of becoming a purely German state again. But there was no guarantee that this Guelf state would ever be able to emancipate itself completely from England, and Gneisenau himself clearly did not think it could. On January 6, 1813[18] he wrote from London to Chancellor Hardenberg: "I have worked for this plan partially because it provides a powerful influence on England to assure her active participation in our continental affairs and partially because such a state, *defended by England*, would be a bulwark of defense for Prussia and would prevent France from ever attacking us again." Finally, a few days before his departure from England at the end of January 1813, he even readopted his original formulation of the idea in a memorial to Castlereagh. He wanted to give England the choice of either making the as yet unconquered territories between the old bor-

---

[15] The presumed heir to the throne at the time was the prince regent's daughter, who could have brought a new dynasty to England by marriage.

[16] Pertz, *Gneisenau*, I, 469; *Histor. Zeitschrift*, LXII, 505.

[17] Pertz, *Stein*, III, 238, quotes a passage from a letter of December 7, 1812 addressed to the prince regent, in which this plan was developed. He attributes this letter to Graf Münster, but in the life of Gneisenau (II, 439ff.) he gives the complete text, signed this time by *Gneisenau*. He explicitly retracts his earlier assignment of authorship to Münster and notes (*ibid.*, p. 674) that he has taken the complete text now from "papers in his own [Gneisenau's] hand." He probably had the draft in French in Gneisenau's hand before him, and we can feel sure here that Gneisenau was indeed the author. This is all the more likely because the style of the document is similar to his. One sentence in it ("I first presented [these plans] to the British government three years ago.") is more likely to refer to him than to Münster. There is, however, an anonymous copy in the Nassau Archives, but it is in the hand of Münster's secretary and bears a note by Stein in the margin: "From Graf Münster to the regent" (Stern in Schmidt, *Geschichte der deutschen Verfassungsfrage 1812-1815*, p. 43n.; and Lehmann, *Stein*, III, 263n.). Stein also ascribed the document to Graf Münster on March 16, 1813 (*Histor. Zeitschrift*, LIX, 298), but this is not sufficient evidence to reject, as Stern does, the incontrovertible attribution based on archival findings in Pertz's life of Gneisenau. Thus, I think Stein must have made a mistake in attributing this letter to Münster, from whom he apparently received the copy.—Gneisenau's memorial of December 14, 1812 to the Foreign office, in which the project mentioned is developed again and made plausible to the British government, is quoted incompletely and in translation by Pertz, *Gneisenau*, II, 454ff. Stern quotes the complete original text in French in *Forsch. zur brand. u. preuss. Gesch.*, XIII, 180ff.

[18] *Histor. Zeitschrift*, LXII, 514.

der of France and the estuary of the Elbe "into a secundogeniture
for the presently ruling house or of annexing them to its empire and
benefiting from that."[19]

It is understandable that Gneisenau mentioned the second of
these alternatives only to English or English-Hanoverian ears and
not to Prussian ones. But this is a matter of little importance, and it
would be overemphasizing a matter of equally little importance if
one were to hold up to us the fact that Gneisenau wanted to lure
the English armed forces to Germany with this unrealistic scheme
of a northwest German Guelf empire. As Pertz has already noted,[20]
the plan was certainly only a means for Gneisenau, and not an end
as it was for the English princes and for Münster. But that Gneisenau, the champion of the Prussian national state who could dream a
year later of a national unification of Germany with Prussia, could
ever resort to such tactics is an astounding fact that is in urgent
need of a more exacting historical interpretation than it has received
up to now. We can see that Gneisenau's Prussian and German national feelings were of a different sort than ours are today. They
were more variable and malleable than ours, which are more closely
attached to a particular historically and politically formed community. Here we see an individual in a much freer relationship to
his native state and nation. State and nation appear to be things that
a man can create or search out to suit his ideas and needs. We are
reminded here in the most forceful way of Fichte's famous statement of 1804: "The earthbound may remain citizens of the state
in its decline. The enlightened mind will be irresistibly drawn to,
and will turn toward, that quarter where light and justice are."

We do not fail to recognize here, of course, what lies between
the Fichte of 1804 and the Gneisenau of 1812. What Gneisenau had
experienced and done for Prussia and Germany bound him to them
with bonds that were fundamentally indestructible but that were still
more elastic and ductile, more intellectual and personal, and less
natural than those that bound the great patriots of the second half
of the nineteenth century to their fatherland. Gneisenau certainly did
not think he was being disloyal to his nation by working for the establishment of an Anglo-German political system. It was precisely
in this way that he meant to serve it. But we can say that for him
the nation was primarily the incarnation of freedom, independent
moral impulses, and culture. It was an intellectual substance that

[19] Pertz, *Gneisenau*, II, 493.   [20] *Gneisenau*, II, 674.

was not necessarily confined within the borders of a single community. It was a flame that could be transferred to another hearth if the original hearth grew cold. Anyone who is at all aware of the influence that great intellectual currents have on individuals will easily recognize the background of these ideas in the individualistic and cosmopolitan thought of the eighteenth century. Whenever Gneisenau depicts the good fortune of the peoples conquered by Britain and united with it, we are reminded of a characteristic statement that Ewald von Kleist made during the Seven Years' War: "How fortunate those countries would be if the king should conquer them." As Wenck has already pointed out,[21] it was a tendency of cosmopolitan thinking "to find justification for the conqueror in the blessings he brought to the conquered." Liberation was now a new factor that was to accompany conquest and the blessings of conquest. But did not the idea of liberation in these decades often have a highly cosmopolitan aspect? Gneisenau's idea of a free and satisfied Anglo-German constitutional state rests on essentially the same basis as the Mainz clubbists' dream of a Franco-German free state. No matter how opinions differed, as they still do, on the composition of the state, there was general agreement that it should be based on universalistic premises and that the current struggle was one between world freedom and world slavery. Gneisenau stated this unequivocally in the fall of 1812: "The world is divided into those who are forced to fight and those who choose to fight; and whether by choice or by force, they fight for or against Bonaparte's ambition. *The crucial point here is not so much to which country a man belongs but to which principles he adheres.*"[22]

The objection could still be raised that Gneisenau considered the founding of a Guelf state between the Scheldt and the Elbe perfectly compatible with the permanent as well as the temporary interests of the Prussian state and even counted on the silent approval of Hardenberg and the king. If that were really the case, it would only show that Gneisenau thought differently about these interests of the state than a politician would who was standing on the actual soil of this state or who was thinking of Prussia's role in Germany's future as we would think of it today. The boundary line on the Elbe

---

[21] Wenck, *Deutschland vor hundert Jahren*, I, 148.

[22] Pertz, *Gneisenau*, II, 369. Gneisenau makes this remark in connection with the fate of Tiedemann, who was killed fighting on the Russian side against his own Prussian countrymen and who, Gneisenau thought, went to his death intentionally.

was a border that prevented Prussia's expansion into Germany and forced it back toward the East into the Slavic world. But the faith in a permanent harmony of English, English-Guelf, and Prussian politics displays still another cosmopolitan feature. It fails to recognize the constant change of world conditions and state interests that could unite England and Prussia today and separate them again tomorrow. It makes a permanent system out of the present conflict in the world, a dualistic system in which the enemies and friends of the world's freedom confront each other face to face and in which the latter can live together in brotherhood and work toward their common goals.

In another thinker of this circle, Ernst Moritz Arndt, Lehmann has noted this same dominating dualism that minimizes the importance of the interests of individual states. In the first edition of the *Soldatenkatechismus*, which appeared in October 1812, Arndt had preached the radical theory that no soldier was bound by his oath to allegiance to any prince who followed Napoleon. "The collapse into the realm of evil as the author of the *Soldatenkatechismus* had witnessed it in Napoleon's state seemed to him" to dissolve any legal bonds between the prince and his vassal. "We are reminded of Augustine's *civitas terrena* when we read Arndt's description of this state."[23]

That was the common political ground on which the three great patriots, Stein, Gneisenau, and Arndt, stood in 1812 and at the beginning of 1813, the year of liberation. They had the following points in common: they divided Europe into a free area and an unfree area; they judged the particular aspects of German and Prussian political life by this principle; and they saw Prussian and German nationality, universal freedom, and the essential freedom of the individual flow together into a single golden image. This is understandable enough as the result of the unusual and singular events of this year, events that had drawn them away from the soil of a particular state. But we can only comprehend it completely if we note the foundation of cosmopolitan and individualistic thought which was present in their education and to which the events of this year forced them to revert.

Similarities in the basic view did not exclude variety in methods. On the contrary, this basic view encouraged such variety because, detached from the solid ground of the state, political fantasy be-

[23] Lehmann, III, 182.

came independent and could indulge itself in innumerable possibilities. With the exception of the one sharp dividing line separating Europe into two military camps, the borders of states became as variable as they had been for the politicians and philosophers of the eighteenth century. We have seen this happen in Stein's plans for northern Europe, and we find it happening again in his plans for Germany in 1812. On September 18 he recommended the division of Germany between Austria and Prussia, and on November 2 he said that he had no objections to the dissolution of Prussia if it were practicable.[24] Even Gneisenau found this inconsistency excessive, but under close examination the criticism he turned against Stein shows the same premises, to a certain extent at least, as those that formed the basis of Stein's experimenting. He wrote to him at the end of December 1812:[25] "In an earlier letter . . . you want to give all of northern Germany to Prussia. In your most recent one, you want to organize all of Germany into a unit under Austria. With the first of your two suggestions, we would come upon most violent resistance in the local (English) ministry and even among the various German peoples involved. Furthermore, we would make ourselves guilty of ingratitude. The model of better times in the past is what we should use to win public opinion for us, and only with the aid of public support can Prussia recover. This state is a sick body with an afflicted soul. It can only regain its strength through the care and gentle treatment of its neighbors, and you want to suggest now that this sick state begin its cure by driving its neighbors off their own land. That is as unpracticable as it is unjust. For the second of your suggestions, I, at least, must deny my support. A division of Prussia is doubtless practicable, but whoever recommends and supports such a revolutionary step must also calculate whether the disappearance of states of Prussia's importance might not destroy the balance of power in some other way."

[24] In reply to Ulmann, *op.cit.*, p. 157, I do not consider this manipulating of the borders of the German states to be universalism as such, but I do think it is closely related to it. The points of identity are in neglecting the particular historical life of states and in applying general rational norms. The cabinet politics of the eighteenth century, to which Ulmann traces this manipulation of borders, were, to recall Sorel's statement (see pp. 123f., above), by no means untouched by the intellectual currents of the eighteenth century, nor were the Jacobins, whom Ulmann mentions in this respect. His view that they were the champions of a "modern" French national idea completely fails to realize that their nationalism was also deeply tinged with cosmopolitanism.

[25] Around December 22, Pertz, *Gneisenau*, II, 467; Lehmann, *Stein*, III, 279, note 1.

The protest against revolutionary changes in Prussia and northern Germany and the appeal to the "model of better times in the past" show the spirit of the Restoration period and an understanding of the need to preserve the historical individuality of states and nations. This understanding was wakened in him by the times and by his environment, by the milieu of English-Hanoverian interests in which he was living. Gneisenau had the capacity to understand his surroundings, and it was an important element of his greatness that he could derive something vital from every situation in which he was placed and assimilate it into his own being. Thus, transplanted back into Prussian soil, he was soon able to sink his roots into it again much deeper than the less flexible Stein ever could. But at that time he saw the Prussian state from without, and he saw it not only from the standpoint of a *Realpolitiker* but almost from that of a philanthropic educator. He was a skillful statesman, following given precepts, who wanted to revive the weak Prussian organism with the help of universalistic ideas and with the universalistic participation of the neighboring states. Prussia should not be destroyed, but it should not become too large, either, because the balance of power in Germany and Europe demanded that it claim neither more nor less than its due. Here again we see the genuine spirit of artificial manipulation but not just that alone. Personal experience, disappointments, the difficulties of his Prussian years, yet an unabated inner involvement, too—all these things are evident in the pessimistic yet sympathetic view that Gneisenau had of Prussia at the time. Remnants of an old life and impulses of the new come together here.

Stein and Gneisenau did not know then that Prussia had an abundance of its own new life, too, even though they had helped to provide that life themselves. However, they both recognized this vitality when it began to appear in 1813. As we mentioned earlier, Gneisenau took up the Prussian national state again. But what was Stein's position? Let us examine his plans for a German constitution in the period from 1813 to 1815 in terms of our main problem.

If the idea of the struggle for liberation had been forced to take refuge in foreign countries only a year before, it now returned to the native soil of the nation. It still relied heavily on allied foreign powers, but now it was carried and enhanced by the spontaneous energy of the nation. We would expect the ambitions of a statesman striving for more complete national autonomy to be set higher than they were in the straits of the previous years, and we actually do find high and ringing tones in Stein's memorial of August 1813.[26] He presents here as an ideal, although one unattainable at the moment, "a single independent Germany," the raising of the nation "to a powerful state that includes in itself the elements of power, of knowledge, and of restrained and legally regulated freedom." This does not, however, represent any increased demands in his idea of the national state. As early as October 1811, he had wanted a constitution for Germany "based on unity, strength, and nationality,"[27] and in September 1812 he had desired a state "that would contain all the ethical and physical elements of strength, freedom, and enlightenment."[28] But now as before, he did not think he could do without the cooperation of foreign powers. He appealed to Europe and to the "honor and duty of the statesmen who control the momentous affairs of nations" to consider the framing of a German constitution with all seriousness and caution. At the end of 1812 he had thought of England, Russia, and Austria as the organizers of Germany who would have to win Prussia's cooperation for their plans. Now, in September 1813, he had lost some of his confidence in Austria, regained his confidence in Prussia, and retained his confidence in Russia and England. He wrote in a letter of September 16, 1813 to Münster that since nothing was to be gained with Metternich, "England together with Russia and Prussia [must] give its serious attention to the founding and maintaining of a sound settlement of German affairs." Once again, toward the end of 1813, he advocated a German constitution "that provides strength for resisting foreign powers,"[29] and in almost the same breath he called for the czar's support for this project. He thought the czar should begin the preliminary work for a German constitution by forming a commission made up of Stein, Rasumowsky from Russia, and Stadion from Austria. This was, Lehmann very rightly says,[30] "a demand that could do nothing but evoke the strongest criticism when seen from a national point of view." It is understandable, he thinks, only in the light of the czar's meritorious efforts on behalf of Europe and Germany and because of the political insignificance of the other two heads of state in the continental coalition. We must certainly grant some importance to these factors but not to them alone. I doubt that they would have had any effect if Stein's national

[26] Schmidt, *op.cit.*, pp. 59ff. [27] Pertz, *Stein*, III, 46.
[28] *Ibid.*, III, 418.
[29] December 25, 1813, *Histor. Zeitschrift*, LXXX, 260.
[30] *Stein*, III, 350.

feelings had not been essentially different from modern national feelings, if they had not remained rooted in European universalism.

This assumption is also supported by the tasks Stein wanted to set for the Congress of Vienna. His memorial of September 17, 1814,[31] written for the Russian cabinet, reads: "It is the great powers that have risked their moral and physical existence, that have made vast sacrifices, that have shed the blood of their people in torrents. . . . Therefore, because of their devotion to the cause and to victory, the great allied powers should now receive the office of arbitrator and the right to settle the questions that still remain to be decided." Only France should be prevented from having any part in German affairs. According to Stein, the three German powers, Hanover, Prussia, and Austria, should settle these affairs alone. However, "the final results will be presented to the allied powers so that they can judge the results from the standpoint of the European balance of power."[32]

The fact that Stein repeatedly, both before and during the Congress of Vienna, invoked and used the support and intervention of the czar in the cause of the German constitution is well known, and need not be discussed in further detail here. One could well say that he had to use them because he had no other power behind him. In the difficult situation in which Stein found himself, even a statesman of the most rigorous national-political convictions would probably not have scorned the aid of foreign powers. But the question we must now ask is whether the appeal to foreign powers was a temporary tactical device or whether it was also colored by the universalistic illusion of a permanent harmony of interests between Germany and the foreign powers invoked. I think we have demonstrated clear signs of such an illusion, but I also admit that they are only indications, however strong, and do not yet constitute conclusive proof. Thus, to reach any conclusions here, we shall have to inquire not only into the contemporary situation of those years when Stein's national policy could not do without foreign assistance, but also into the goals and final form that Stein envisioned for Germany. Did he want to prevent foreign influence in the most important affairs of the German nation forever? We concede at the outset that this proud man would probably have indignantly rejected any doubt that this

[31] Pertz, IV, 110ff.

[32] This concluding sentence alone refutes Ulmann's view, op.cit., p. 163, that the major powers' role as arbiter was to regulate only general affairs and not German ones.

was his intention. At the end of October 1814, Gentz had shown the crown prince of Württemberg a memorial which recommended that Austria be allied with southern Germany and France to maintain the balance of power against Russia, which would always draw Prussia and northern Germany into its sphere of influence. Stein wrote of this in his diary:[33] "I made him aware of the ruinous effects of a system that would destroy . . . unity in Germany, put southern Germany under the influence of France, northern Germany under the influence of Russia, and maintain a harmful schism between Prussia and Austria." He wanted national autonomy; but the question is now, to come to the heart of the problem, whether the national autonomy he wanted is identical with the one that a national consciousness arising from the developments of the nineteenth century demands. We must answer this question with an emphatic no. Two items of incontrovertible evidence show that Stein considered national autonomy compatible with foreign obligations that we would consider intolerable today.

Humboldt had suggested in a memorial of December 1813 that the great powers of Europe, Russia and England, take over the guarantee for the security of the German Confederation. Stein commented on this:[34] "A foreign guarantee must be regarded with great caution. In any event, only England or Russia should be allowed to have part in it." In Humboldt's view, this guarantee should only apply to the defense of Germany against foreign attacks and should not lead to any interference in internal German affairs. But it is clear that a guarantee limited in that way was still not limited enough and was incompatible with genuine national independence. We can see that Stein had his doubts, but we can also see that he stopped halfway in a situation where modern national feelings would have remained thoroughly consistent and condemned any constitutional loophole whatsoever that might allow foreign interference in the free exercise of a nation's power politics.[35]

The second piece of evidence is Stein's memorial of March 1814,

---

[33] *Histor. Zeitschrift*, LX, 396. [34] *Histor. Zeitschrift*, LXXX, 264.

[35] Drüner, *op.cit.*, pp. 44ff., cites expressions of Stein's distrust of Russian and English policies. But that Stein could still consider the Russian and English guarantee for the German constitution tolerable despite such distrust only confirms our view. Drüner commits the methodological error of ascribing a unified and consistent mode of thought and action to a thinker who lived in an epoch of transition and struggle between old and new ideas. He also makes the error of seeing only those characteristics in Stein that reflect *Realpolitik* and modern national thought, characteristics that I do not deny either.

in which he suggests that a four-part directorate made up of Austria, Prussia, Bavaria, and Hanover be created to serve as the highest German federal authority.[36] Hanover, however, was England. "England and Bavaria, then," Delbrück correctly concludes,[37] "were to have the same rights over Germany that Prussia had." Stein apparently did not find this prospect disturbing.[38]

Let me repeat again that Stein did not consider his thinking inconsistent with national interests. He considered the joining together of English, Russian, and German politics more beneficial than harmful if it were kept within the limits he defined. But it is this belief that we have discarded since Stein's time and that we regard as alien, as universalistic thinking.[39] It was a product of the ideal and the

[36] Pertz, Stein, III, 719; Schmidt, op.cit., p. 131.

[37] "Die Ideen Steins über deutsche Verfassung," Erinnerungen, Aufsätze und Reden, p. 95.

[38] Ulmann, op.cit., p. 162, cites the fact that Stein rejected the domination of non-Germans in our midst as an insult to national honor. Clearly, he did not want any un-German influence, but the fact that he could tolerate the English influence that was streaming in through Hanover proves that he distinguished between German and un-German differently than we do. When Ulmann adds, further, that Stein's national feelings were more autonomous than the law still valid today (sc. before 1918) that holds German thrones open to collateral lines, then we must reply: (1) that this law was only a positive, traditional law, not an expression of contemporary feeling about law, and (2) that it could be tolerated because, on the basis of historical experience, one hoped sooner or later for the nationalization of these foreign collateral lines.—In reply to Ulmann, p. 165, I should note further that I do not see just the "cosmopolite" in Stein and nothing else. I claim only to see a strong admixture of ideas of cosmopolitan origin, an admixture that was not always operative in him but that was operative at certain important moments.—I cannot accept the examples of Bismarck's concessions to foreign influences that Ulmann cites, p. 166, as analogous to Stein's concessions. There is no evidence at all that Bismarck, in 1850, wanted to grant the claim on Germany of the guarantors of 1815. Earlier, in his controversy with Fester on the address of Olmütz, Histor. Vierteljahrsschrift (1902), p. 55, Ulmann saw the Bismarck of 1850 as more conservative than he really was. Ulmann has meanwhile been decisively refuted by a remark of Bismarck's made on November 21, 1850, and handed on by Ludwig von Gerlach, II, 116: "Friedrich II of 1740 was his example." [Translator's note: reference is apparently to Ernst Ludwig von Gerlach, Aufzeichnungen aus seinem Leben und Wirken, ed. Jakob von Gerlach (2 vols.; Schwerin im Meckl., 1903), cited hereafter as: Ludw. v. Gerlach.] Here again, Ulmann was not able to recognize the interweaving of different lines of thought within the same historical personality. Bismarck's abandonment of Luxembourg in 1867 concerned a country that was internally only half German, and Bismarck's action was a realistic political step of autonomous national policy that had a completely different character than the policy of Stein and Friedrich Wilhelm IV.

[39] Oddly enough, G. Ritter, op.cit., p. 20, thinks he refutes me with his statement: "Stein did not take the nature of general European interests too much into account but too little." As the text shows, my actual view is that because of universalistic and ethical leanings, Stein saw the policies of England and Russia in

real. The bond of shared interests between Germany, England, and Russia that had been solidified by necessity and struggle was real. But the creation of permanent plans on the basis of a temporary state of affairs was the work of an ideology that failed to recognize the egoism of politics and overestimated the similarities of European nations.

Stein's well-known views on the relationship of Prussia and Austria to Germany and the German Confederation must also be seen in this light. If Germany and anti-French Europe had a dominating common interest, Austria, Prussia, and Germany had a still greater one. The forms in which Stein wanted to hold these three powers together varied in his projected plans, but the optimistic assumption that they would stay together did not vary. He felt that he could be completely certain of Prussia's commitment to Germany.[40] He was less certain of Austria, and he was fully aware of the barrier between Austria and Germany. In a memorial dated February 17, 1815 he characterized it with the matter-of-factness of complete political realism: "The interest that Austria takes in Germany will always be subordinated *à ses convenances momentanées*." But in the hope of overcoming that barrier the *Realpolitiker* immediately surrendered the field to the idealist when he suggested binding Austria to Germany by offering her the imperial throne. The throne was to lead Austria back to her German calling and train her for the German cause. Stein no doubt believed that this educative process would succeed,[41] and it is the Enlightenment that stands behind this belief—the Enlightenment's politically applied rationalism that thinks it can regulate the life of states and correct their immanent natural drives by means of properly chosen institutions. He was aware of the egoistical impulses of the Austrian state, but he ignored them nonetheless be-

---

too optimistic a light and did not properly recognize their real interests in the cases cited. He was looking at an ideal, not a real, Europe. Thus, I could even subscribe to Ritter's statement. Ritter also traces Stein's efforts of 1814-15 back to a first unsteady attempt at *Realpolitik*—efforts to base his plans on the major European powers' interest in the liberation of Central Europe—and he presents this in a way that suggests I did not recognize this attempt. This is a misunderstanding, too, as the passage on pp. 132f. above shows.

[40] Memorial of August 1813, §§ 28 and 30, Schmidt, *op.cit.*, pp. 65f.; memorial of February 17, 1815, Pertz, IV, 744; cf. Lehmann, *Stein*, III, 439.

[41] See the entry in his diary on February 11 that deals with his conversation with Hardenberg (*Histor. Zeitschrift*, LX, 430). "Hardenberg expressed his aversion (to offering the imperial throne to Austria) and justified it by the dullness of the Austrian dynasty and government. I remarked to him: These imperfections were temporary; the main thing here was the governmental institutions" etc.

cause he believed that the similarities Germany and Austria shared would draw them together. Once the proper state organization was created for them both, Austria would change her inner nature and become a German state again.

But still other elements of intellectual history came together with rationalism in the idea of an Austro-German empire. Historical Romanticism and recollections of the Empire must also have been influencing Stein's thinking when he suggested giving the crown back to the Hapsburgs "because they had possessed it a long time and the nations were accustomed to this."[42] Historical Romanticism condemned manipulation in political affairs and praised historical growth instead. More precisely, it did not extoll such growth itself as the basis of state life, but extolled instead whatever had reached maturity through historical growth. Here we see Stein as the rationalist and Romantic, as the advocate of both manipulation and growth. Lehmann has correctly identified the third and doubtless most influential element in Stein's thinking.[43] "We are dealing," Lehmann says, "with the greatest flaw in his argument, but it is also the most human and most forgivable of flaws. He assumed that practically every German was filled with the same love for the fatherland that animated him and his fellow workers." We see the national idea here in its highest manifestations as an ethical force and as a faith in its power over the entire life of the nation. But it is also entangled with other ideas that prevent it from becoming truly political, prevent it from merging with reality and from being converted by that merger into the reality of an autonomous national state.

We could carry this analysis still further. We could show particularly that Stein's fanciful ideas in the summer of 1814 were based on a conception of the state that had still not fully grasped the nature of state personality. Stein's plan at this point was to split up the Prussian and Austrian states by drawing into the German Confederation the Prussian provinces east of the Elbe and the Austrian ones that were attracted to southern Germany. In the examples of Stein's thinking we discussed earlier we saw how Stein ignored the autonomy of the state personality. In this case, he ignored its inner unity and coherence. He did not want to accept the fact that the state is primarily a power and a power that acts in accordance with its own impulses. He did, of course, demand power for the state and particularly for the German national state he envisioned,

[42] Memorial of August 1813, § 27, Schmidt, *op.cit.*, p. 65.
[43] *Stein*, III, 441.

but for him the essential function of this power was to repel France, the traditional enemy, and to preserve freedom within the state.

As far as I know, he does not use the term "traditional enemy" for France, but he does call it the "eternal, indefatigable, destroying enemy" of the Germans.[44] The term "traditional enemy" expresses a more basic national feeling. Stein had more than a little of that feeling in him, and he nourished it on the history of past centuries.[45] But his concept of the "eternal enemy" as he used it also reaches into the area of the ethical and raises the national conflict to a universalistic one, to that dualism of the good and evil principle that we have encountered before. According to Stein, France brought evil into Germany: "If we examine the history of state administration in Bavaria, Württemberg, and Westphalia, we can see clearly how a mania for innovation, insane arrogance, unlimited extravagance, and bestial voluptuousness have succeeded in destroying all happiness for the pitiable inhabitants of these once flourishing lands."[46] The German constitution, he urged, should rebuild the walls that once protected Germany. In his eyes, Germany's foreign and domestic problems were closely related. For him the German constitution was an outer bulwark for the defense not only of German independence but also of the independence of other nations, and it was also an inner bulwark against the despotism that had been awakened in the princes by France. Germany, then, was to be both a buffer territory in Europe and a province in the empire of ethical freedom.

Stein's biographer, Max Lehmann, has shown this predominance of ethical thinking over *Realpolitik* with great force and sympathy, sometimes with rather crass pathos, but also with the necessary critical approach. He says of Stein's conception of the Congress of Vienna: "The entire Congress did not seem to him to be a struggle for power but rather a struggle between good and evil."[47] The cosmopolitan factor in Stein did not escape Lehmann either. He calls Stein "the child of an era that lived with the idea of mankind," the "warrior of an epoch that had taught nations to stand together."[48] Lehmann very correctly traces Stein's objection to the czar's plans for

---

[44] Memorial of August 1813, Schmidt, *op.cit.*, p. 59.

[45] Drüner, *op.cit.*, pp. 29ff. and 67, overlooks this point and fights an unnecessary battle against me with his demonstration of Stein's earthy patriotism. The whole point here is to single out a feature of Stein's thought that has been disregarded and to see it in a larger context. I have attempted a supplementary total estimation of Stein in my *Das Zeitalter der deutschen Erhebung* and in *Preussen und Deutschland im 19. und 20. Jahrhundert*, pp. 125ff.

[46] Schmidt, *loc.cit.*   [47] *Stein*, III, 477.   [48] *Ibid.*, III, 484.

Poland back to "considerations of a universalistic nature" rather than
to specifically Prusso-German feelings. "The powers of the Western
world were to unite in resisting any universalistic monarchy whatever, and he urged Prussia as well to adhere to the principles of
the balance of power."[49] The old idea of the European balance of
power that had been so often reduced to a mere phrase was revital-
ized in Stein. In him, the ethical and cosmopolitan seed inherent in
this idea could finally develop in pure form. My view that ethical
and cosmopolitan elements merged with national ones in Stein is cor-
roborated by Lehmann when he characterizes Stein's ideas as
"ethico-religious ideas of a half-national, half-universalistic nature."[50]
Thus, we have simply taken a path here that Lehmann first discovered but did not follow far enough. In his view of Stein there is still
an unbridged gap, if not a complete contradiction, between Stein
the champion of the national state and Stein the champion of a
universalistic balance of power.[51] He was both, but these two aspects of his character did not lead separate existences. Instead, they
were related in such a way that his cosmopolitan ideas unobtru-
sively and half-unconsciously guided and limited his idea of the nation
and of the national state.

IF WE COMPARE Wilhelm von Humboldt with Stein and
Gneisenau, we would expect to find the cosmopolitan element more
pronounced in him than it was in the two statesmen. Stein and
Gneisenau matured in Prussian governmental and military service,
Humboldt in the world of classical literature and philosophy and in
an atmosphere of protest against state expansion. As we saw before,
he apprehended the national spirit from a purely human point of
view. We would expect Humboldt as a statesman to be particularly
intent on subjecting nationally regenerated Prussia and Germany
to universalistic codes. We would also expect that he would want to
restrict the autonomy of the state power and of the politically united
nation. But if we examine his ideas on the German constitution during the years 1813-16 with this in mind, we come to the astonishing
conclusion that he came much closer to the idea of the autonomous
national state than Stein did. We saw how Stein instinctively limited Germany's foreign policy to repelling the "eternal enemy"

---

[49] *Ibid.*, III, 423f.   [50] *Ibid.*, III, 374; cf. II, 81.
[51] Drüner, *op.cit.*, p. 39, has misunderstood me here, too. I do not claim there
is a "contradiction" here. I only say that one could infer such a contradiction on
the basis of Lehmann's presentation.

France and how he regarded this as an international task for Germany because he saw Europe divided into free and unfree zones. Because his thinking was instinctively universalistic and, in its fashion, farsighted, it was shortsighted as far as German power politics were concerned. Humboldt recognized this shortsightedness. He actually engages in a polemic against Stein, without admitting to it, when he writes to him in a memorial of December 1813:[52] "In discussing the future of Germany, we must avoid limiting ourselves to merely securing Germany against France. Even if the independence of Germany is indeed threatened only from that quarter, this one factor alone cannot serve as a basis for planning a permanently beneficial situation for a great nation. Germany must be free and strong not just to defend herself against this or that neighbor or against any other enemy but because only a nation that is outwardly strong can preserve within itself the spirit from which all its inner blessings derive. Even if she should never be put to a test, Germany must be free and strong so that she can develop the self-confidence necessary for her to pursue her national development quietly and undisturbed and to be able to assume permanently that beneficent position that she now holds in the midst of the European nations."

That is one of Humboldt's most imposing political statements and one of the most imposing statements of this entire period as well, a declaration that stands on the divide between two epochs, making clear the route that has led to that divide and also affording a wide view of what is to come. Germany's universalistic task as a European nation has not been forgotten, but it does not interfere with her free political action, as it did in Stein's thinking. Nor do freedom of movement and autonomy serve the increase of power alone, as they did in the autonomous politics of absolutism. Power is put into the higher service of the spirit, and the spirit Humboldt means here is no longer the purely individualistic spirit but one united with the entire life of the nation. The individual, power and spirit, nation and humanity, politics and culture—these factors that led such a lively existence in the thinking of this period and that were consequently so unstable finally achieved equilibrium here. We cannot say, of course, that Humboldt saw the state and the national state as clearly as Ranke and Bismarck did later. He did not see them in their naked form, in their pure autarky and autonomy, in the unlimited exer-

[52] *Gesammelte Schriften*, XI, 96; Schmidt, *op.cit.*, p. 104.

cise of their immanent desires for power. In Humboldt, there is
still a light but substantial veil of ethical and intellectual postulates
lying over the state, a veil that should in no way put restrictions on
the state and its power, a veil that ennobles them but does not obscure them.

Thus, Humboldt understood the national power state better than
Stein did, although the state as such was less important to him than
it was for Stein. But perhaps this is the very reason why he could
understand it. The observer, looking at a given object, will often
see more than the man of action will. But Humboldt, too, looked at
the political fate of the German nation with deep personal involvement now, and this affectionate if not passionate interest helped increase his understanding of it. The individual had been his primary concern. Then, in the nineties, the nation began to take precedence over the individual. Later still, he came to understand
more and more profoundly the basic and natural connection between
the two. He says in the same memorial: "In the way nature unites
individuals into nations and divides mankind into nations, there is
an extremely profound and mysterious agent at work that guides
the individual, who is nothing by himself, and the species, which
exists only in individuals, in such a way that their powers develop
gradually and in direct proportion to each other." It is very likely
that he recognized and encouraged the spontaneity and autonomy
of the politically united nation now because he had once recognized and encouraged them in the individual. Where did our historical and political mode of thought originate, our awareness that
supra-individual human unions have an individuality of their own?
It originated in an individualism that kept probing the nature of the
individual over a long period of time until it had discovered its
deepest roots and the connecting elements that bind the life of the
individual to the life of human groups and organizations. Everywhere we look we see individuality, spontaneity, and the urge for
autonomy and expanding power. We find the same things in the state
and nation, too. "Nations," Humboldt says now, "like individuals,
have tendencies that politics cannot alter." This was a protest against
the rationalism of Stein and even of Gneisenau, rationalism that
posed a threat to this form of life. We need not take up here the
transcendent question of how the autonomous life of the ascending
categories ranging from the individual to the state can be compatible with their intellectual dependence on each other. Our purpose
was only to understand how it was that Humboldt, unswayed by

the universalistic idealism of his contemporaries, could grant the national state its rightful claims and develop a more realistic position on this question than Stein could.

But in the last analysis, he did not hold to his purpose either, nor was he spared relapses and inconsistencies. We saw how Stein's optimistic confidence in Prussian and Austrian harmony within Germany derived from the same ethical ideal that nourished his political universalism. Humboldt's plans for a German constitution also counted on the permanent cooperation of the two great German powers. "The firm, uninterrupted friendship of Austria and Prussia is the keystone of the entire structure," he writes in a memorial of December 1813; and he says in his important memorial of September 30, 1816[53] on the German Confederation: "The most important thing is for Prussia and Austria to lead the Confederation together." He called the Confederation "one of the surest means to insure their harmony." But he does not seem to have always been completely satisfied with this arrangement. If we read his statements from December 1813 that the formation of the Confederation depends entirely on this one factor of Austro-Prussian agreement, that this factor is a political one, and that it is based on a purely political principle, then we again see very clearly that Humboldt, unlike Stein, forced himself to take a practical, hardheaded view and tried to put all nonpolitical considerations aside. But did he really believe that politics alone would insure friendship between Austria and Prussia? The reasons he uses to convince himself of this sound forced.[54] If he had really thought it possible that Austria could maintain a permanent harmony of interests with Germany and Prussia on a purely political basis, he would not have objected in 1815 to granting the imperial throne to Austria. He argued then that this would still not guarantee Austria's support of Germany. "Si l'on croit que l'Autriche ne se décidera pas à des transactions nuisibles à l'Allemagne précisément à cause de la dignité Impériale, on oublie qu'une puissance doit

---

[53] *Gesammelte Schriften*, XII, 82; *Zeitschrift für preuss. Gesch.*, IX, 109.

[54] "But by providing no further commitments in the relationship of Austria and Prussia than any other alliance would contain and by making this (assumed harmony between Austria and Prussia) the basis of the welfare of all Germany, welfare which includes the welfare of Austria and Prussia too, one would strengthen this harmony through a feeling prompted by both freedom and necessity. This feeling would be reinforced by the fact that a delegation or division of power would not be allowed between the two countries and there would be no possibility of acting for selfish interests." Schmidt, *op.cit.*, p. 108.

toujours agir ainsi que son intérêt réel l'exige impérieusement."[55] It
also became clear to him in 1816, on the basis of his most recent experience, that Prussia could not count on Austria at all "if there
should be plans that required energetically putting something
through against the majority of the others."[56]

Thus, he was more skeptical than Stein about Austrian politics
in Germany and the possibility of Austro-Prussian cooperation,
but he could not bring himself to act on his skepticism and completely deny the viability of a confederation that rested on such
a fragile basis.[57]

As the situation stood then, the only course available was to experiment with the Confederation and with Austro-Prussian cooperation within it, and we can readily understand how a realistic
statesman like Humboldt tried to make the best of what necessity
dictated and looked as kindly as he could on a none too promising
arrangement. But this still does not vindicate Humboldt from the
suspicion of nonpolitical idealism, for we can find clear signs of it
elsewhere in his writings. We noted earlier that in his constitutional
plan of December 1813 Humboldt had made the unfortunate suggestion of transferring the guarantee for the German Confederation to
the great powers of Europe, namely, to England and Russia. In the
next breath, he tried to limit this guarantee and make it harmless
by precluding the interference of foreign powers in Germany's domestic affairs.[58] But in international political matters bearing on her

[55] Memorial of February 23, 1815, *Gesammelte Schriften*, XI, 300; Schmidt,
op.cit., p. 420.
[56] *Gesammelte Schriften*, XII, 65.
[57] Treitschke, *Deutsche Geschichte*, II, 144, goes too far and sees too much of
an advocate of his own view in Humboldt when he calls Humboldt's view of the
German Confederation "hopeless" as it is presented in the memorial of September
30, 1816. Besides the pessimistic statements that Treitschke refers to, there are
also noteworthy optimistic views on p. 65: The unfortunate situation will "never
prevent Prussia from achieving *through the Confederation* what she can justifiably
demand," and p. 67: "All provisions for common defense will (with a correct
Prussian approach) be able to be achieved successfully."
[58] Accordingly, they should not have a direct part in the creation of the constitution either "qui ne peut être qu'on ouvrage national." Memorial of April 1814,
Gesammelte Schriften, XI, 207; Schmidt, *op.cit.*, p. 146. Immediately following
this, he himself became unhappy about even a limited guarantee exercised by
foreign powers, for, while he had still spoken of "puissances garantes de la constitution" in April 1814, he tried to show in a memorial of September 30, 1816
that the inclusion of the Act of Confederation in the Act of the Congress did not
represent an actual guarantee. "Thus, in the true sense of the word, there is no
guarantor of the German Confederation and its constitution except the Confederation itself" (*Gesammelte Schriften*, XII, 97). As Treitschke, II, 140, points out,

power and very existence, Germany should, on the basis of the constitution, be able to fall back on the brotherly aid of both the great foreign powers. This is, I think, Humboldt's position on the matter.

Along with this erroneous idea, Humboldt shared still another with Stein. This second idea, already mentioned above, was that the English government should be granted a constitutionally defined role in the direction of the German Confederation by way of Hanover. Indeed, Stein's idea in March 1814 of establishing a four-part directorate composed of Austria, Prussia, Hanover, and Bavaria only develops further what Humboldt had already suggested in January 1814.[59] He told Gentz that if there were some hesitation about entrusting the right to declare war to Austria and Prussia alone and denying it to Bavaria and Hanover, "then the difficulty could easily be removed by allowing them to participate in this right, although I would not entirely approve of this." But his disapproval did not apply to the participation of England-Hanover. On the contrary: "This would cause little difficulty because England, which is one with Hanover, would always have a voice in the matter, and even if Bavaria seemed to have a voice, it would still have to yield to the larger powers."[60] Since he had said shortly before that Germany would have to be armed against every enemy and not just against one neighbor or another, he apparently did not think that England could ever become Germany's enemy.

Thus, he did not adhere consistently to the great idea of national autonomy for Germany either, although he was one of the first to sharpen its definition, nor did he give up the belief that all states share common features that can be counted on politically and that provide a foundation for the existence of one's own nation.

But to understand Humboldt completely, we must both supplement and limit what we have already said about him. We said that the ethical and intellectual postulates he advanced for the national and political existence of Germany did not necessarily represent limits on the character of the state and on its power. But he did not remain consistent here either. His ideas on the organization of Germany and on the degree of political unity he wanted to give

---

this was "unfortunately a by-no-means incontestable legal opinion." See also Chap. 9, pp. 148f., below.

[59] Correctly noted by Gebhardt, *Humboldt als Staatsmann*, II, 114.

[60] *Gesammelte Schriften*, XI, 113 (Humboldt to Gentz, January 4, 1814).

it show this. In the same memorial of December 1813 in which he advanced the ideal of the autonomous nation, he also extolled the division of Germany as the source of variety in its intellectual life, and he therefore did not want to put an end to this division entirely. Also, his often surprising capacity for grasping the hard facts of a situation offered support for this wish, for he adds: "The German is only conscious of being a German when he feels himself to be an inhabitant of a particular territory within the common fatherland." These words anticipate Bismarck's famous chapter on the dynasties and tribes, and, considering the nation's stage of development at the time and judging by the most rigorous critical standards of *Realpolitik*, we cannot deny the justice of his opinion that Germany was not ready to be a unified centralized state. It is striking, in this connection, that he limits Germany's natural tendency toward unification to the modest goal "of being a confederation of states," in contrast to France and Spain, which have been "melted together into one mass." He recognizes no intermediate stage between a confederation of states and a centralized state. He does not envision, or at least does not attempt to achieve, a federal state which combines inner variety with outer unity and strength. But we must admit again that he had a good reason for disclaiming the federal state, a reason that shows insight of a highly realistic nature. Several years later, in a memorial of September 30, 1816, he said: "The truth is that a genuine federal state is no longer possible when two of its members (not to mention the others) have become so powerful."[61] But when we read this same memorial we will not be able to avoid the impression that still other reasons besides those of *Realpolitik* determined and limited his goals for Germany. "We must never forget the true and genuine purpose of the Confederation in the context of European politics," he wrote.[62] "This purpose is to insure peace. The entire existence of the Confederation is calculated to maintain the balance of power. This balance would be disturbed if, in addition to the great German states taken individually, still another new, collective state should emerge in Europe, a state whose actions would not be motivated by a disturbed balance of power but would be arbitrary. At one moment, it would act in its own interests; at the next, it would offer either aid or a pretext for action to one or another of the great powers. No one could then prevent Germany as Germany from becoming a con-

[61] *Ibid.*, XII, 83.   [62] *Ibid.*, XII, 77.

quering state, and no true German can desire that, for we know what intellectual and cultural heights the German nation has reached as long as it has been without political ambition, but we cannot know what effects such ambition would have on our cultural life."

We see how much more limited the general objectives for Germany are here than they were in the imposing words of 1813. The sole purpose of the Confederation internationally is "to insure peace." How modest that sounds after the inspiring prospect of a strong, free Germany ennobled by self-confidence! The occurrences between December 1813 and September 1816 make this reduction of hopes understandable for the most part. After the constitution of the German Confederation had turned out to be so much poorer and weaker than Humboldt had desired, the basis of Germany's entire foreign policy was changed. In a confederation as Humboldt had conceived of it in December 1813, decisions of war and peace in Germany were to be in the hands of the two leading powers. Such a confederation could have represented Germany better internationally than a confederation whose radical failing Humboldt described as "a complete lack of all executive power." Deception and intrigue could be expected of a confederation with such inadequate executive powers, but not a great national policy. We can understand why Humboldt warned against "seeing more unity" represented in the Bundestag than it actually had and thereby awakening hopes that the Confederation could not fulfill in its given form. He made his judgment like a realistic physician who properly appraises the weaknesses of his patient, and he also made his judgment as behooved any Prussian statesman who wanted to prevent a weak confederation and the politics of many small states from infringing on Prussian independence. His abandonment of strong and independent German representation in foreign affairs was, then, another understandable concession to reality. But if we compare what he said in 1813 and in 1816, we shall not be able to deny that his cultural ideal prevented him from desiring Germany's development into an autonomous power state in the full sense of the term, and that his national political ideal was limited both by ideas that derived from the cosmopolitan culture of the eighteenth century and by the concept of Germany's calling as the nation of culture and humanity. One could object here that he simply wanted to prevent Germany from becoming a conquering state, i.e., a state that overextended its desire for power. But whoever tries to prevent the misuse of power by hiding it mistrusts it altogether. Humboldt was unhappy about

any "political ambition" whatever in the German nation. This is criticism of a more basic nature than his disapproval of the foreign
policies of the Bundestag, disapproval he might well register as a
Prussian statesman and as a realistic critic of the constitution of the
Confederation.

Thus, this memorial of September 30, 1816 displays keen political
insight in close conjunction with demands of a completely nonpolitical nature. The document as a whole is particularly interesting because it seems increasingly subtle with each new examination.
Still another feature of it is important for our main problem and
demands our attention here.

We claimed that from the standpoint of *Realpolitik*, Humboldt was
justified in wanting to limit the activity of the Bundestag in the
form it had taken so that it "would remain a more defensive, negatively effective agency for preventing injustice rather than an initiating agency for achieving positive results."[63] If we take this into
consideration, we shall probably come to a more charitable view of
the historical effectiveness of the Bundestag. We shall exchange complaint and ridicule for understanding, and we shall regard the un-
productivity of the Bundestag as the natural and normal result of
the situation created in Germany in 1815. Were the consequences
of this situation fully clear to Humboldt? I think not. His position
was self-contradictory. He wanted to clip the wings of the Confederation and the Bundestag, but he still expected them to fly to certain
heights nonetheless. It was an irresolvable antinomy to expect
the Bundestag to prevent injustice on the one hand yet refrain from
initiating any positive action on the other, to expect the Confederation to insure Germany's independence and organize its defense yet
not develop an independent foreign policy. Anyone who is to
prevent effectively must also be able to initiate effectively, and anyone who is to defend effectively must also have at least the capability to attack effectively. A political system, even if it was only a confederation, needed a greater freedom of movement than Humboldt
was willing to allow if it was to achieve what he expected of it. He
did not realize that one cannot deprive a tree of nourishment and
still expect it to bear fruit, even of the most modest sort. With this
point, we are again touching on the central problem of our study:
the Confederation was expected to exercise national political functions without enjoying national political autonomy.

[63] *Loc.cit.*

Humboldt arrived at this error by other and more involved routes than Stein did. Political and nonpolitical elements intermingle much more subtly in him. But the basic source of his error also lies in remnants of a nonpolitical view of the state that he could not completely overcome despite his incisive political insight.

9

TRANSITION TO THE RESTORATION PERIOD:
A GLANCE AT PUBLIC OPINION

TWO MAIN IDEAS carried over from earlier universalistic culture into the newly awakening national ideas and merged with them. One is the view that the German nation, as the purest intellectual and cultural nation, is the representative nation of all mankind. The second is the postulate of a pan-European union of states. The advocates of the classical *Humanitätsideal* cultivated the first idea. During the years of early Romanticism, Novalis, Friedrich Schlegel, and Fichte entertained both ideas, but Fichte placed a much greater emphasis on the first. Adam Müller and the later Friedrich Schlegel did just the opposite, shifting the emphasis to the second idea. Both these ideas stimulated but also inhibited national and political life. The force that Fichte lent to the idea of the representative nation of all mankind helped awaken political enthusiasm during the Wars of Liberation, but we have just seen in Humboldt's case how this idea also helped dampen the nation's desire for political power. In the instance of Stein we saw how the second idea affected political life even more directly and how the intellectual movement and the world situation had an ever greater bearing on each other than was the case with the first idea. Because we are dealing with extensive intellectual currents here, we must remember that the examples we have treated are representative of something more inclusive and widespread and that certain phenomena that would seem inexplicable in isolation become clear within this context. It seems strange, for example, that the Heidelberg jurist Thibaut, in making his famous demand for a unified legal code for all of Germany in 1814, could extoll the "truly Germanic nature" of this demand and at the same time suggest realizing it through an "international treaty with the solemn guarantee of the great foreign allied powers."[1] We know that this idea of a foreign guarantee for a na-

[1] "Über die Notwendigkeit eines allg. bürgerl. Rechts für Deutschland," in

148

tional arrangement could not have been so intolerable to the national feeling of that time as it is to our own because Germany's position in Europe was seen differently from the way we see it now. With this in mind, we will be better able to understand why the first eleven articles of the German Act of Confederation were incorporated into the Final Act of the Congress of Vienna (Treaty of Vienna) and why considerable claims of the European signatory powers to a guarantee of the German constitution and to a right of intervention were created even though no binding guarantee was achieved. In urging the incorporation, Metternich himself had wanted to achieve a binding guarantee. One passage in a declaration of the German conference of June 5, 1815 reads: "The Austrian plenipotentiaries should demand that before the close of the Congress, the Act of Confederation, like the other resolutions of the Congress, be placed under the guarantee of the European powers."[2] He had, of course, nothing in mind here but Austria's interests as he saw them; but the fact that he could make this demand at all, and that the inclusion of the Act of Confederation in the resolutions of the European Congress could then follow without difficulty, suggests a concept of the German Confederation that saw in it an institution of European as well as of national character and of a constituted and chartered European character at that. We saw how even Humboldt defined the "true and genuine purpose" of the Confederation according to this principle, and we shall not be surprised to find similar ideas again in an essay by the Göttingen historian Heeren entitled "Der deutsche Bund in seinem Verhältnis zu dem europäischen Staatensystem."[3]

Zivilistische Abhandlungen (1814), p. 443. I am indebted to my Freiburg colleague Alfred Schultze for this reference. Thibaut could also say about the political unity of Germany "that a politician will hardly be able to prove that complete unity is more useful to the Germans than their division. Large states are always in a condition of unnatural tension and exhaustion" etc. (p. 408).

[2] Klüber, *Akten des Wiener Kongresses*, II, 523. The term "protection" is used in the conference protocol instead of "guarantee" (p. 511). This question and the repeated attempts of foreign powers in the following decades to interfere in the domestic affairs of Germany on the basis of this claimed right of guarantee should receive closer study.—Of the statements of these years in which the idea of placing Germany under the guarantee of the great powers is recommended, I cite, further, the not uninteresting essay "Über Deutschlands und Europens Staats- und Nationalinteresse bey und nach dem Congress zu Wien," in *Germanien* (1814). The idea of a European confederation of states, a confederation to which all the independent nations of Europe would belong, was also advocated, for example, by Mallinckrodt, *Was thun bey Teutschlands, bey Europens Wiedergeburt?* (1813).

[3] 1817. *Histor. Werke*, II, 423ff.

The German Confederation, we read here, is deeply involved in the general and particular interests of Europe. Therefore, how the "central state of Europe" is formed cannot be a matter of indifference to the foreign powers. If this state were a great monarchy with close political unity and equipped with all the material power for political ends that Germany possesses, would any kind of peace be possible for them? Would such a state be able to resist very long the temptation to seek domination of Europe for itself? Practical politicians have been aware of this for a long time, Heeren continues; and for this reason, the "preservation of German freedom" has been an important problem for Europe as well as for Germany since the Peace of Westphalia. The allied powers have wisely recognized now that a political body must be created that is weak in its offensive capability but strong in its defensive one, a "European state devoted to peace."

Heeren conceives of this state devoted to peace in the heart of Europe as the complete logical opposite of a universal monarchy. It would have universal functions, too, but on a completely different basis. "It must be the defender of the principle of legitimate ownership because without this principle it would soon not have any security itself." Thus, responsibility for the preservation of legitimate ownership and of legitimate European dynasties would not lie outside this state's sphere of interest. Just as Europe would protect and sustain it, it would help protect and sustain Europe.

These are the constructions and fantasies of a man who, as a sober, historical thinker, was able to grasp the nature of autonomous power politics and who had faithfully defended German national character in the years when it had been most seriously threatened.[4] We see here again how thoroughly the political atmosphere of these years was saturated with universalistic elements. These were the same years that had given back to the European nations both their independence and a sense of their own independence. But this independence was not really complete, nor was the sense that the Germans in particular had of it a sense of complete independence. The Germans felt that they had a contribution of universal significance to make and that they were therefore entitled to speak and act for the entire world. But while other nations would base a claim to

[4] Cf. his essay "Über die Mittel zur Erhaltung der Nationalität besiegter Völker," written in 1810 and published in the same year in Perthes' *Vaterländ. Museum,* also in *Histor. Werke,* II, 1ff.; and Marcks, *Bismarck,* I, 100f. On Heeren's relationship with Adam Müller, see p. 95, above.

world dominance on this feeling, the Germans of this period derived from it an obligation to serve the world and bore this yoke joyfully.

This obligation to serve, this neutralization of German national strength through the German Confederation and the great European powers that surrounded it in a friendly and patronizing manner, became one of the major determining factors of European history in the following decades. In Heeren's essay we see the ideas of legitimistic politics of intervention and of the Congresses of Troppau, Laibach, and Verona emerging. The tangled vine of legitimistic universalism was not limited to German soil alone. It also thrived remarkably well in the French school of political Romanticism, the school of de Maistre, Bonald, etc. But it could only spread so widely and become so significant because the spirit of the autonomous national state had still not awakened in the center of Europe.

There were individual signs and isolated statements of those political and national truths that have been realized in the modern national state, but for the most part they lay dormant. Friedrich Gottlieb Welcker had sensed at a remarkably early stage, however, that the life of individual nations might be threatened by the solidarity of the European ruling houses and the politics of the European congresses:[5] "The entire picture of international relationships is altered if a new one-sided power, a sovereign power above all individual sovereign powers, is formed by a treaty and if laws can be 'sanctioned by all of Europe' without the knowledge and assent of Europe or of most of the larger individual peoples of Europe." That the Germans had not been granted their constitution as a nation, Welcker continues, and that they had not even been granted the territories they could rightfully demand could only be explained by the fact that they, who should again have begun to exert some influence on their governments, really "were insignificant as far as the foreign powers were concerned, whereas the ruling houses were all-important." He anticipated the idea that was to motivate governments and peoples in the following decades and bring them into conflict with each other: If the princes establish a union on principles that run contrary to the nature and constitution of the individual states, "then the peoples will tend to reach understandings and

---

[5] "Über die Zukunft Deutschlands," written in December 1815. Some supplementary material was added later, and the essay appeared in *Kieler Blätter*, II (1816), 345ff.—Other opinions expressing fear of foreign influence on Germany can be found in Hagen, "Öffentl. Meinung in Deutschland etc.," *Historisches Tagebuch*, N. F. VII, 639f. and 696.

hold together on disputed issues." In the last analysis, then, the nations would not have any ties to their princes nor the princes to their nations.[6] Europe would be divided again—and we know to what extent this prophecy has been fulfilled—into two universal camps with the solidarity of the legitimate governments on the one side and the nations struggling for freedom and autonomy on the other.

As long as this situation continued, an individual national state uniting government and people was impossible, and the idea of national autonomy to which the oppressed people appealed was not a true national idea but a universalistic and rational axiom dominated by the spirit of the eighteenth century. It was at this time that the national idea took on the formal and stereotyped character that it possesses in the theories of Napoleon III and that we find often enough in the expression of national sentiments in Germany before the revolution of March 1848. People were capable of honest enthusiasm about the freedom, independence, and power of all the neighboring nations as well as of their own nation without realizing that this close union of free nations of which they dreamed was not a national but a cosmopolitan idea. But it is clear again that both ideal and real factors gave rise to these political errors. The real historical element was the inner tension between the governing and the governed that the struggle for freedom and the rise of the middle classes had evoked. The conflicting social and political forces that occasioned this tension were active at first only within one state and nation, but analogous forces and tensions existed almost everywhere else as well. These conflicts thus took on an international aspect which the continuing ideal influence of the cosmopolitan spirit reinforced.

But as we saw in Welcker's comments, there was no lack of awareness, at the very beginning of this era, of how unhealthy this universal tension between the governing and the governed was. What Welcker expressed negatively, Luden expressed positively when he wrote in 1814:[7] "State and nation always try to come together with what we might call a tender longing to sustain or win the other. . . . If state and nation are one, the highest wish and the most sacred aspiration of man is to preserve this unity. If they are separated, the effort, if not the wish, is always there to achieve this

---

[6] Welcker, op.cit., p. 364.

[7] "Das Vaterland oder Staat und Volk," Nemesis, I (1814), 16f. It is evident from p. 211 that Luden himself is the author.—As Heller, Hegel und der nationale Machtstaatsgedanke in Deutschland (1921), pp. 142ff., has shown, Luden, perhaps under Hegel's influence, had emphasized the idea of the power state more strongly in his Handbuch der Staatsweisheit oder der Politik (1811).

unity. The members of a nation seek to unite themselves in one state. The citizens of a state seek to become one nation. Sometimes the former dominate, sometimes the latter, and the most momentous changes and the most interesting phenomena in the life of our kind arise from these efforts. But undisturbed growth, continuing peace, lively culture, and general happiness will only be found where the unity of nation and state has been achieved."

Luden also knew that struggle, care, and conflict are the destiny of the genuine national state, not peace and calm.[8] Ottokar Thon, the adjutant of Karl August of Weimar and a young, energetic thinker whom Treitschke valued highly, wrote:[9] "It is fundamentally impossible for states to attract each other. Nature intends them to repel each other." For this reason, he recognized the impossibility of what Stein and Humboldt constantly struggled to think possible, namely, that two states as independent as Austria and Prussia could ever travel one and the same path together. "They will travel it as long as their common interests are served by it. They will abandon it as soon as their views and interests are divided." What makes this judgment doubly valuable is that it comes from a man who knew and understood not only the nature of the power state but also the strength of nations, "what a nation can accomplish when it desires something with decision and energy." Few predicted as concisely and clearly as he the course of German destiny in the nineteenth century: the displacement and banishment of Austria to the east, the subjugation of the smaller German states, and the establishment of the German national state by means of the victorious Prussian sword.

We move to a still higher level in our rapid survey of the voices of public opinion when we examine Niebuhr's famous pamphlet *Preussens Recht gegen den sächsischen Hof* (1814) in terms of our problem. As in Thon, we find political understanding and national feeling united, but here the argument is more profound and thoughtful. Once united, these two factors would inevitably lead to the idea

[8] In earlier editions of this book, I did Luden an injustice when I claimed that he had not achieved this insight. Elisabeth Reissig, "H. Luden als Publizist u. Politiker," *Ztschr. f. thür. Gesch. u. Altertumskunde,* XXXI and XXXII, and Heller, *Hegel und der nationale Machtstaatsgedanke in Deutschland,* pp. 142ff., have shown instead that he belonged to the first advocates of the idea of the power state.

[9] *Was wird uns die Zukunft bringen?* (Vienna, March 1815). Published under the title *Aus den Papieren eines Verstorbenen,* printed as a manuscript (1867). Cf. Treitschke, I (5th edn.), 682, and my study *Die deutschen Gesellschaften und der Hoffmansche Bund,* p. 51.

of the autonomous national state. "Only a political entity that is independent and capable of wilfully asserting itself and claiming its rights can be called a state, not an entity that cannot entertain such a thought at all, that must align itself with a foreign will, submit to it, and follow it whenever such action seems most favorable to survival."[10] For him, the unwritten law of great forces at work in history was higher than the formal, written law; but in recognizing this unwritten law, he did not give up ethical ideals and simply proclaim the brute law of strength: "Whoever gains strength and assimilates it forms with it new life which is good or bad, beneficent or destructive, in accordance with the spirit that makes use of this strength."[11] He did not recognize the law of brute strength but the law of life, a law that could not be nullified by the victory of any stronger party. Thus, imbued with the most vital elements of the recent eventful years, he did not hesitate to subordinate even the individual state to the rights and needs of the nation. "The community of nationality is higher than the political circumstances that unite or separate the different peoples of a nation. Through national type, language, customs, tradition, and literature, a fraternal union exists among them which distinguishes them from other nations and which makes any division wicked that supports a foreign country against one's own nation."[12]

But does this statement not limit the autonomy of the individual state for the sake of a nonpolitical principle? It does indeed, because the national idea that Niebuhr places above the individual state is, we find on examining his statements in their context, closer to the idea of the cultural nation than to that of the political nation.[13] There is an "invisible bond of unity"[14] woven together out of great natural and intellectual similarities, and he conceives of it in such broad terms that it includes the Dutch, the German Swiss, and even the English to a certain extent.[15] With pride and emotion he recognizes

[10] *Preussens Recht gegen den sächsischen Hof*, pp. 29f.
[11] *Ibid.*, p. 70.   [12] *Ibid.*, p. 19.
[13] In *ibid.*, pp. 77f., he distinguishes carefully between "nationality" and "political individuality" when he says: "There is no Saxon nationality any more than there is a Pomeranian or Brandenburg one. We have to do here only with the sacrifice of political individuality." When he still occasionally speaks of the "Saxon nation," he uses the term only for the sake of convenience.
[14] *Ibid.*, p. 28.
[15] "Separated from a very large nation like the German nation, an emigrated group like the English, settled in a distant and completely separate country, can develop into a separate nation. But the original relationship still does not disappear, and although circumstances become more complex, a natural union continues to

the existence of a "genuine Prussian nation," a political nation, in the strict sense, within the larger cultural nation. But this still does not negate the primacy of the cultural nation as opposed to the individual state; and what is most important here, and highly characteristic of Niebuhr, is that this Prussian political nation is not a unified political nation. Accordingly, Prussia cannot be a completely unified autonomous national state either. "Prussia is not an isolated country. It is the common fatherland of every single German who distinguishes himself in learning, in arms, and in administration."[16] Thus, for him, Prussia actually becomes the quintessence of Germany and the champion of German nationality, whose rights, he says explicitly at one point, will still not be surrendered "even if only the smaller part of the nation and not the larger is aware of this and possesses the heart and spirit to act on it."[17]

If we consider the consequences of what Niebuhr says about the nature of the state as such and about the nature and rights of the nation, i.e., the German cultural nation, we can easily see that there is a dualism here, a tension between two different principles. He was not completely aware of this tension himself because he was completely absorbed with the idea that the two principles went together naturally and harmoniously. This idea also forced him to see the history of the Prussian state as quite different from what it had actually been. It had been the history of an ambitious power state striving for autonomy. But he thought that, until 1740 at least, no royal house had shown greater "loyalty to the common German cause" than Brandenburg-Prussia.[18] He is therefore the first significant representative of what has been called the Borussian conception of history, and a forerunner of Droysen and Treitschke. The national

---

exist with the other state in its parts and in its entirety, and the violation of this alliance is always punished." On the Dutch and the German Swiss, we read: "They cannot negate the rights of the nation from which they want to separate themselves. The allies' right of intervention in Switzerland is based on this" (*ibid.*, pp. 20f.). Niebuhr does not stand alone in possessing these Greater German and pan-Germanic ideas. See, for example, W. von Humboldt, *Gesammelte Schriften*, II, 136; Janson, *Fichtes Reden an die deutsche Nation* (1911), p. 34. It would be a rewarding task to study the spread of these ideas and, most important of all, their motivation. On A. W. Schlegel, see O. Brandt, *A. W. Schlegel, der Romantiker u. die Politik*, p. 179. Further, on this general subject, Rapp, *Der deutsche Gedanke* (1920), pp. 82ff., 115, 127. The journalistic material for the period 1848-49 has been collected by Haufe, *Der deutsche Nationalstaat in den Flugschriften 1848 bis 49* (1915), pp. 63ff.

[16] *Preussens Recht gegen den sächsischen Hof*, p. 79.
[17] *Ibid.*, p. 22.   [18] *Ibid.*, p. 68.

postulate dimmed his political insight. This insight was obscured particularly when the justification of Prussia's claims against Saxony was in question, claims that were not based on the German idea and on the German mission of the Prussian state alone but primarily on Prussia's own material and egoistical interests. Niebuhr failed to take those interests into account, but this error of his accurately reflects the thinking of the times and the tendencies that were beginning to appear. A striving away from the nonpolitical cultural nation and toward an existence as a national state was present. But the goal that lay at the end of the road, the goal of the autonomous German national state, was hidden; and it was able to conceal itself from those who were most familiar with political affairs and who realized from experience that the simplest solution to the problem was also the most difficult.[19] But because they could not give up the desire to solve it, their effort to unite state and nation could never become more than an effort to unite two things that were still incapable of unification. This is why the great historical and political thinker Niebuhr also stumbled here. By placing the nation over the state and by forcing the Prussian individual state to serve the German idea, he pointed the way to the future, but in his view of the past and present he did violence to the true personality of the autonomous Prussian state. He saw two parallel lines before him, as it were, that would only come together in the distant future, but he wanted to see them come together immediately, and only by bending one of them could he make this happen.

Here we touch on the problem that will occupy us in Book II of this study. We have had to mention it here because we wanted to make clear how closely the genesis of the idea of the national state in Germany is linked to the invasion of nonpolitical ideas into the state. But among the examples of this invasion, Niebuhr's attempt to establish the relationship of state and nation is significant for its intelligence and profundity and for its congeniality, we might say, with the political as well as with the nonpolitical sphere. He was more deeply committed to the political sphere but more equally committed to both spheres than Humboldt was. But even in Niebuhr's thinking about the nation and the state, the element of universal ideals and postulates was not missing, ideals and postulates that put limitations on the natural life of states as well as on the natural life of nations, which he considered superior to states.

[19] Cf. Delbrück, "Die Ideen Steins über deutsche Verfassung," *Erinnerungen, Aufsätze und Reden,* pp. 93ff.

For he, too, puts forward the idea that the Christian states of Europe should form a unity and that the violation of this unity would be just as nefarious as any treachery that an individual state could commit against its own people. "An alliance with Mohammedans for the purpose of attacking Christians has always been considered an unforgivable crime in the view of Protestants as well as Catholics." He even went so far as to approve in principle the legitimistic crusade against the French Revolution. "If the coalition against the French Revolution had not been led in the weak and thoughtless way that doomed it to obvious failure from the start, then there would really be no reason to object to the doctrine by which the first alliance was formed. This doctrine was that the European states had an existence as a group even though they were not bound together in an actual federation, and every state was obliged to take part in the affairs of Europe."[20] Like Stein and the Romantics, he too saw the universal affairs of Europe and the affairs of the nations as indissolubly bound together.[21] Thus, the ideas of two epochs, the Revolution and the Restoration, met in him: his bold assertion that nationality stands above the state would have been unthinkable before 1789; and after 1815, the statesmen of the Restoration felt it to be highly revolutionary. Yet Niebuhr himself wanted to be a conservative statesman, not a revolutionary one; and even though he had opened himself to the national energies that the Revolution had released, he still thought he would be able to oppose the Revolution with the idea of nationality as he understood it.

This Niebuhrian idea of nationality, which was based on common ancestry and on a common cultural heritage, was the joint product of Romanticism[22] and of the epoch of the Wars of Liberation, and because it was so closely connected with the historical past of nations it could be further developed in a very conservative direction.[23] But if it were to be suitable for this conservative role, the sharp blade it turned against the legitimate dynasties had to be dulled again. It could not be used to place definite demands on the policies of the

[20] *Preussens Recht*, pp. 20f.

[21] It is highly characteristic that he regards the fall of the Republic of Genoa as punishment for supporting the "common enemy," and he also regards this support as "a crime against the nationality of Italy" (*ibid.*, p. 21).

[22] It is characteristic of the particular influence of Romanticism on Niebuhr, for example, that he held up to the Saxon government as proof of its un-German and limited thinking the prohibition it had issued against the reprinting of *Volksbücher* like the *Haymons-Kinder*, etc. (*ibid.*, p. 81). Praise for the "profound Burke" is not missing either (p. 96).

[23] Cf. pp. 66f., above.

individual states. It could not be used as a dominant principle of state life but only as a supporting one, supporting in the sense that the political life of a nation, no less than its cultural life, was regarded as a unique blossom and fruit of the national spirit. Consequently, it was a simple matter to justify and sanction all historically established institutions and forms by appealing to the instinctively creative national spirit from which they arose, and it was equally simple to reject any arbitrary interference in the quiescent life of states as a violation of what had come about naturally and of what was genuinely and originally national. The historical school of jurisprudence under Savigny's leadership effected this step, which had already been anticipated by Romanticism and Schelling's theory of the unconscious development of the absolute spirit.

"All law," he wrote in his book against Thibaut, "arises through custom and national belief. It always arises, that is, through hidden, quietly operative forces and not through the arbitrary action of legislators."[24] Or, as he formulated it in founding his journal for historical jurisprudence: "The historical school assumes that the components of law are provided by the entire past of the nation and not by any arbitrary action that could have shaped them just as well one way as another. The components of law emerge from the inmost character of the nation and its history."[25]

Savigny himself limited his theory to his own field of law, but the state was also law in a broader sense of the term,[26] and the conse-

[24] *Vom Beruf unserer Zeit für Gesetzgebung und Rechtswissenschaft* (1814), p. 14 of the 2nd unrev. edn. (1828).
[25] I, 6 (1815).
[26] Savigny himself expressed this broader conception of law later, around 1840. See Brie, "Der Volksgeist bei Hegel und in d. hist. Rechtsschule," *Archiv f. Rechts- u. Wirtschaftsphilosophie*, II, 199. This work of Brie's, Moeller's essays in the *Mitt. d. Instituts f. österr. Geschichtsforschung*, XXX, and Edg. Loening's in the *Internation. Wochenschrift* (1910), as well as Landsberg's *Gesch. der deutschen Rechtswissenschaft*, 3. Abt., 2. Halbband, have clarified the development of the doctrine and term of the "national spirit" [*Volksgeist*] considerably since the first edition of this book, although many differences of opinion still remain. Savigny's doctrine, for which the master later took over the term "national spirit" from his student Puchta, essentially has its beginnings less in Hegel than in Schelling and Romanticism. As Borries, *Die Romantik u. die Geschichte* (1925), pp. 128ff., clearly shows, the beginnings of the doctrine of the national spirit stood from the very beginning in opposition to the universal-European concept of history that culminated in Ranke. Jak. Grimm and Achim von Arnim are of particular importance for the development of the actual doctrine of the national spirit. See Kantorowicz, *Histor. Zeitschrift*, CVIII, 311f.; Rothacker, "Savigny, Grimm, Ranke," *Histor. Zeitschrift*, CXXVIII, 415ff.; and Herma Becker, *A. von*

quences of his theory were soon drawn for the state, too. The national idea was driven back, then, as it were, out of the sphere of free political action and away from the clarity of the political world, where it could be harmful, into the dark earthy realm of the nation. But there it could gather new strength to break forth into the world again, richer and stronger than before.

Arnim in den wissenschaftl. und polit. Strömungen seiner Zeit, pp. 30ff. and 36ff. Arnim uses the term "living national spirit" as early as 1805, but then, as Herma Becker shows, he puts forward the Romantic theory of the national spirit in a more modern and less doctrinaire version. See further Fr. Schlegel, *Über die neuere Geschichte* (1811), p. 213. In 1806, in the first part of *Geist der Zeit* (6th edn., p. 192), Ernst Moritz Arndt conceives of the "mysterious spirit of the nation, eternal like its nature and its climate," more as an invariable primal force that appears only in extraordinary men and circumstances when society has reached a certain level of culture. In contrast to that, Niebuhr's interesting passage in the *Röm. Geschichte*, II (1812), 42, to which J. Partsch called my attention, shows a Romantic outlook along with a clear understanding of the mutability of historical forces: "Although the national spirit, in its unconscious functioning, is the most powerful and purest guarantee for the permanence of primal characteristics, it changes unnoticeably and often to the point of the most complete revolution of attitudes." But at the same time, the "national spirit" in the quietistic version of later political Romanticism was played against Hardenberg's regime by the old feudal opposition and in particular by the circle of the brothers Gerlach, which sympathized with Savigny's views. Wilhelm von Gerlach writes to his brother Leopold in December 1810: "We are living, to use Savigny's phrase, in the era of artificial law-making. . . . In our new laws you will find the *Zeitgeist*, i.e., the French spirit, mentioned frequently. *The national spirit is never mentioned.*" On this same subject, see Leopold von Gerlach's essay "Ein Wort über die jetzige Gesetzmacherei," December 1810, in Leonie von Keyserling, *Studien zu den Entwicklungsjahren der Brüder Gerlach* (1913), pp. 36f. and 132ff. There is new literature on the question of the national spirit in Kluckhohn, *Persönlichkeit und Gemeinschaft*, p. 89.—Loening has corrected my guess on p. 245 of the first edition of this book that Hegel first used this term in the way the historical school used it. There is a clear difference between Hegel's national spirit and the national spirit of Savigny and the Romantics (see Chap. 11, below). But they still have an evolutionistic element in common, while the liberal-political use of the term "national spirit," which is fairly frequent in these years, is completely free of it. However, the liberal and Romantic elements seem to flow together in the *Aufruf* of Kalisz: "primal spirit of the nation" [Ureigener Geist des Volkes].—The term "national spirit" already appears in a non-Romantic sense toward the end of the eighteenth century. F. K. von Moser used it in 1787 in *Über die Regierung der geistlichen Staaten in Deutschland*, p. 167 (pointed out to me by Dr. B. Wachsmuth). Fr. Kluge also drew my attention to the following passage written by Campe in 1794, in *Reinigung und Bereicherung*, II, I, Vorrede, p. 20: "ennobling of the national spirit and the national consciousness." Kantorowicz, *Histor. Zeitschrift*, CVIII, 300, indicates further that Hegel knew the term as early as 1793. See, too, Rosenzweig, *Hegel und der Staat*, I, 21ff.; Heller, *Hegel und der nationale Machtstaatsgedanke in Deutschland*, p. 31; and Metzger, *Gesellschaft, Recht und Staat*, pp. 317f. Arndt uses it after the turn of the century. Müsebeck, *Arndt*, I, 61, 121.

10

HALLER AND THE CIRCLE OF
FRIEDRICH WILHELM IV

OF THE TWO MAIN CURRENTS of thought regarding the nation and the national state, the liberal and the Romantic-conservative ones, we shall follow only the latter[1] from here on, and we shall try to determine the path that led from the ideas of Novalis, Schlegel, Adam Müller, and Savigny and from Stein's German policy to the policy of Friedrich Wilhelm IV and his circle. But now we encounter a system of thought that seems built directly across our path, the system of Karl Ludwig von Haller. In the years of peace after 1815 he exercised a powerful influence on men with both Romantic and political leanings and particularly on the members of the younger generation who were preparing themselves for government. Despite the fact that he had practically nothing to say about the nation, his influence was still highly significant, and because of it we cannot pass Haller by altogether. We must at least consider those aspects of his character and his political theory that touch on the nation and the national state, however indirect that contact may often be.

In 1808, the same year that Adam Müller began his lectures on the *Elemente der Staatskunst*, Haller published his *Handbuch der allgemeinen Staatenkunde*, which already contained all the essential elements of his theory. But he did not make a great impression on the public until the quieter years of peace, when, from 1816 on, the six volumes of his *Restauration der Staatswissenschaft* began to appear.

---

[1] Dock's book, *Revolution und Restauration über die Souveränität* (1900), which treats the theories of the counterrevolutionary school in detail, is completely unfruitful for our problem. It contains practically nothing but excerpts, and in its seemingly original concluding remarks (p. 269), it is dependent on Stahl's ideas (*Geschichte der Rechtsphilosophie*, VI, 1; 3rd edn., pp. 548f.). H. O. Meisner's work, *Die Lehre vom monarch. Prinzip im Zeitalter der Restauration und des deutschen Bundes* (1913), is more penetrating and independent, but it is not particularly relevant to our inquiry.

He found no echo in the intellectual mood that had led to and then sustained the struggle for national liberation. We do not sense in him any of that high conviction that the German nation has unique, irreplaceable intellectual values to defend, nor do we sense any of that desire for an inner nationalization of the individual state that the Prussian reformers and also the Romantics from Novalis to Adam Müller had felt. Although the Romantics were enthusiastic about the old feudal order, their enthusiasm still arose from a new spirit that made something else of the old order, or at least imagined it to be something other than it really had been, and surrounded it with ideals and illusions of a poetic and philosophical nature. Haller idealized the medieval state for his purposes, too, when he created the term and the concept of the patrimonial state,[2] but these purposes were anything but idealistic. In a blunt and direct fashion he eulogizes the happiness of the old rulers who possessed power and their own wealth and were free to enjoy them. A materialistic and egoistical element permeates his theory, and whenever it calls on God and divine agencies for aid there is no mysticism or even any inner religiousness but rather a self-satisfied attitude that sees God's dispensation and blessing clearly revealed in one's own possessions and in the world order that sustains them. Power and domination are the results of both natural law and divine law. That is the core of Haller's theory.

He says at one point[3] that it is really not a man who rules over you but the power that is given to this man, and if you see the situation exactly and philosophically, God is and remains the only Lord both as the creator and as the legislator and regulator of all the power that is divided among men. With this, of course, he opened the door for a cult of power, for the worship of success itself; and the step from this theory to a doctrine of the struggle for existence and of natural selection is not a very big one. He comforts the weak and oppressed[4] by asking whether the highest level of happiness ever remains eternally unattainable to anyone. Do we not see in the entire world and in all history a constant change in all things? Do not the rich become poor and the poor rich, the mighty weak and the weak mighty? Do not obscure peoples rise to glory and others who have been famous sink into obscurity? His premises took him much further than he intended, for he wanted only to oppose the power of revolu-

---

[2] Von Below shows this in *Der deutsche Staat des Mittelalters*, I, 6.
[3] *Restauration der Staatswissenschaft*, I (2nd edn.), 386.
[4] *Ibid.*, I, 387.

tionary forces and to justify and rehabilitate the power of the old patrimonial state. He therefore used the good Lord not only to sanction power as such but also to control its uses in such a way that it could not assume any forms other than those it had taken in the Middle Ages. We need not dwell any longer on these highly naïve and emotional arguments and attempts to distinguish between legitimate and illegitimate power and between its proper and improper use, for by now it must be clear that it is not thought but will that dominates this entire system—a will, moreover, that is completely formed by traditional ideals. What Haller advocated was not genuinely medieval: it was the vestiges of medieval forms of life. The old epoch found expression once again here through one of its most devoted sons. He did not have to reawaken it in himself by means of fantasy and reflection, as the Romantics did. It was naturally alive from the very beginning in this proud and hardheaded Bernese patrician.[5] The traces of the Enlightenment and of rationalism present in his early education[6] and even in his later theory[7] were

[5] See his typical statements in *Restauration*, VI, 571f.: "Some seem to think the system I have developed so far is simply drawn from the history of the Middle Ages. . . . I openly confess to never having read a single book about the so-called Middle Ages. . . . We have derived these eternal laws from everyday social relationships themselves as they exist before our eyes, not from ancient and unknown times" etc.

[6] Cf. Looser, *Entwicklung und System der polit. Anschauungen K. L. von Hallers* (Bern dissertation, 1896), pp. 2ff. On Haller's life and political legacy, see Ewald Reinhard, *K. L. von Haller*, Vereinsschrift der Görresgesellschaft (1915).

[7] He is in complete agreement with natural law in that his theory, like that of the advocates of natural law, takes the condition of nature as the point of departure and does not go any further. Neither his theory nor that of natural law moves ahead to social contract. His points of contact with the antistate and purely individualistic tendency of the Enlightenment, with Rousseau, whose *lucida intervalla* he praised, and with Siéyès and the *Illuminati* are all to be seen in this context. Savigny immediately (1817) grasped this rationalistic element in Haller ("extreme rationalist in history and politics"); see Varrentrapp, "Rankes *Historisch-polit. Zeitschrift* und das *Berliner Polit. Wochenblatt*," *Histor. Zeitschrift*, IC, 40; see also Singer, "Zur Erinnerung an Gustav Hugo," *Zeitschr. f. Privat- u. öffentl. Recht*, XVI, 285 and 311. Stahl characterizes him quite well in *Geschichte der Rechtsphilosophie* (3rd edn.), p. 560: "He is the rationalist among the counterrevolutionary writers. He does not, like the others, pursue varied, individual aspects, but, like natural law, traces a dominant principle through everything with logical consistency. But, as we showed above, this dominant principle still rests on concrete experience."—It has also been noted by others that Haller himself does not get away from Rousseau's contract theory, which he had so passionately opposed. As Ancillon pointed out against him, he merely converted the ingot into small coins by replacing the general *contrat social* with a vast number of small private contracts. (Cf. F. von Raumer, *Über die geschichtl. Entwicklung der Begriffe von Recht, Staat und Politik* [2nd edn., 1832], p. 190.) A similar point is made by R. von Mohl, *Geschichte und Literatur der Staatswissenschaften*,

not incongruous in the last bewigged generations of this period, for
these traces were evident only in their dress, as it were, and not in
their basic nature. The Bernese ruling class of the eighteenth century
had been an energetic, well-to-do, and hearty aristocracy that lived
from the production of a rich country and did not need to annoy its
subjects with fiscality, did not want to annoy them with red tape,
and was particularly kind and patriarchical toward the peasants.[8]
This way of life found justification for itself in the pleasant thought
that it had been attained through the great activity and energy of
one's ancestors, and it found additional justification in the consciousness that one was worthy of this existence, that one indeed had the
right to enjoy it undisturbed. And did one not feel oneself morally
improved through the enjoyment of power? Haller writes: "You will
always find powerful people more noble, generous, and productive."[9]
"What ennobles the spirit more than the feeling of one's own superiority, the absence of fear, and the freedom from want?"[10]

We can readily understand how, with such a view of the justification and good effects of power, he saw the state and all of life resolved into an infinitely graduated scheme of power and dominance.
The levels begin with the beggar who rules his dog, and they go on up
to the prince who "enjoys the precious, edifying pleasure" of being
completely independent and who thus represents the peak of this
entire pyramid. But, Haller claims, this power can and should only
be one's own proper power, not delegated power. The power that a
prince has in his own right, Haller tells us, will be limited by the
sense of ethics and duty that is inherent in the heart of every man
and that should be especially evident in the powerful. The power
that a prince or a government exercises on behalf of a state or a nation, however, is not delegated power but is also in fact individual
power. But through the fiction and illusion of the delegation of power,
it leads to a horrible despotism and to the destruction of the entire
distribution of power that has been legally established.

We cannot deny that a sound, realistic understanding of the actual disposition of power is at work here. Haller asks, with good
reason, when the general will of the nation has ever ruled, even in

---

II, 550.—On Hegel's criticism of Haller, see Rosenzweig, *Hegel und der Staat*,
II, 190f. See also Schmitt-Dorotič, *Politische Romantik*, p. 16; Metzger, *Gesellschaft, Recht und Staat*, pp. 272f.; and Kluckhohn, *Persönlichkeit und Gemeinschaft*, p. 100.

[8] Cf. Oechsli, *Geschichte der Schweiz im 19. Jahrhundert*, I, 51ff.

[9] *Restauration*, I (2nd edn.), 382.   [10] *Ibid.*, I, 386.

revolutionary France. There the case was rather that all the factions gained their power by fighting for it boldly, and they retained that power even against the will of the people. The French soldiers who fought a war against so-called privilege were in the front ranks of the privileged in all the countries they entered. Haller cries triumphantly: "O indestructible nature!"[11] But his keen understanding of individual power developed into mere obstinacy which refused to recognize that every manifestation of actual political power is rooted in an intellectual context that becomes the broader and more imposing the more extensively power itself emerges from the narrow sphere of feudal and patrician existence and the more the autonomous power of the medieval dynasties becomes state power in the modern sense. But Haller remained caught in that narrow sphere because his entire understanding of life derived from it, and he consequently denied and opposed everything that lay beyond it. But it is interesting in this connection that he had to take grudging cognizance of forces in his glorified patrimonial state that modified it in the direction of the modern national state. The late medieval practices of indivisibility and primogeniture arose, as we know, from purely dynastic interests, but once in effect they undermined the dynastic concept of royal domination, prepared the way for the idea that the state is a closed unit that follows higher laws than the arbitrary will of the dynasties, and generally created a firm basis for larger political groups. Haller was not unaware of these consequences, and he therefore deplored their cause. If indivisibility and primogeniture had not been gradually introduced everywhere, he thought, then there would be no form of government anywhere other than the simple and natural relationship of an independent landlord to his dependents; and these false systems, those worthless concepts of a governmental power that extended over everything, could never have developed. With sound instinctive grasp, he saw indivisibility and primogeniture as a πρῶτον ψεῦδος in the modern development of the state. Yet he had to admit, on the other hand, that a patrimonial prince of the sort he approved could do nothing more reasonable than use indivisibility and primogeniture to safeguard what he had. Thus his whole system suffered from the inner contradiction that the natural greed of the powerful on which the system was based also produced the elements that destroyed it.[12]

[11] Ibid., I, 260, 265.
[12] Ibid., II, 534ff. We need not go any further into his attempt to hide this contradiction, of which he was probably aware himself.

The desire and urge for power and dominance should be stopped precisely at that point, he thought, where they threatened to overwhelm the patrimonial way of life. He was consequently an opponent of any and all large states. The scholarly mind boggles before extensive monarchies, he thought. "What good are such terrifying, closely unified masses that only frighten the rest of the world?"[13] "Smaller states are the true, simple order of nature, and one way or another she will always return to them eventually."[14] The more states that exist, the more beauty and variety we have and the more men there are who can enjoy the spiritually elevating privilege of independence. How magnificent Asia Minor was after the division of the Macedonian monarchy, and how magnificent Italy when many principalities and republics arose in it from the twelfth century on. This reminds us somewhat of Jakob Burkhardt's secret sympathy for those strong figures who emerged between the Middle Ages and the Renaissance and who made the state into a means of providing pleasure for powerful individuals.[15] But in so doing they also helped create the modern state, a fact that Haller was not willing to admit. They did this by cultivating cool, rational *Realpolitik* and the precisely calculated use of power. This was the spirit characteristic of the age of absolutism, an age which Haller and the Romantics abhorred, and it was this spirit that had not only enlarged these states externally but had also consolidated them internally and given them unity, personality, and autonomy. We saw how Adam Müller was able to appreciate to a certain extent this great development of European state personalities. Haller was not able to appreciate it at all. "What use can a doctrine have," he asked,[16] "that is as unnatural as it is unchristian, a doctrine of the absolute unity, the absolute isolation and insulation of every single state? It can have no use except to bring all states face to face with each other in enmity." He was also unable to develop any enthusiasm for an internal political structure that in the interest of the state's own power would develop the state progressively into a real community, a collective for the satisfaction of great intellectual and material needs. The idea that there was a *societas civilis* was unsympathetic to him. He spoke of "so-called state

---

[13] *Ibid.*, III, 179.   [14] *Ibid.*, II, 535.

[15] Italy's many small wars in the fourteenth and fifteenth centuries, Haller says at another point (*ibid.*, II, 103), "developed capabilities and strengthened self-confidence, that source of all great accomplishments."

[16] *Restauration*, III, 179.

goals" with scorn, and he hated the word "general" in any shape or form.[17]

If he denied the intellectual unity of the state, how could he recognize the intellectual unity of the people or nation? He does not speak of a prince's people but of "the individual human beings whose aggregate is called the people."[18] He only sees them collect and disperse, sees them draw together where they find a better living; and this living, he thinks, depends in turn directly or indirectly on the existence and wealth of the prince. "A prince's people are a scattered swarm of men, an aggregate of dependent or voluntarily subservient people with infinitely varied obligations; they have nothing in common except their common master, and among themselves they do not constitute a whole, a community."[19] He cannot, of course, completely do away with the concept of a people or nation, however objectionable he finds it. The beginnings of the national idea were already faintly evident in old feudalistic attitudes that considered the representation of the rights of the estates in dealings with the prince as a representation of the community's rights and that identified the leading classes of the nation with the nation itself.[20] Influenced by such attitudes, Haller at one point designates as "national debts" those debts that "are voluntarily taken over by the nation, i.e., by the leading and high-ranking members of the nation."[21] His loose concept of the nation will not allow him to accept the idea that there can be "national wars."[22] But the natural love a child feels for its father and a servant for his master can still cause subjects to rush to the aid of their prince, even if they are not legally obliged to do so, and to form with him "a unit, one heart and

---

[17] He makes only an ostensible exception for republics, which he discusses in the sixth volume of his work and which he treats as "communities" whose community spirit he sometimes mentions. But he conceived of them only as civil law corporations and communities, and although he was born a republican himself, he drew a balance between monarchy and republic that favored the former. See *Restauration*, VI, 546: "But how ponderous, clumsy, and awkward such a collective body is in comparison with the individual body of a single man etc." He thought the principalities were the natural states and the republics artificial institutions (VI, 10).

[18] *Ibid.*, I, xviii.

[19] *Ibid.*, II, 74f. and 119; cf. II, 366. In matters concerning an institution for the good of the people, he thought such an institution could "be created in the best and most disinterested way by the people themselves, i.e., by private persons or private organizations." His enmity toward the state brings him into a certain affinity, although not a very deep one, with Wilhelm von Humboldt and, as Metzger, *op.cit.*, pp. 273f., shows, with the early Fichte.

[20] See pp. 26f., above.   [21] *Restauration*, II, xi.   [22] *Ibid.*, II, vii.

one soul." "Indeed, in emergencies we have often seen entire nations rush to battle without being forced to do so and then fight
with honor and enthusiasm and often with a persistence that sur-
passes that of the prince and his more delicate adherents."[23] There
is in Haller's headstrong, egoistical doctrine, then, an occasional
trace of that old-style national spirit that had taken concrete form in
the battles of the Vendéeans, Tiroleans, and Spaniards and that was
alive in his own Swiss people.[24] His thinking consequently reflects in
a naïve way an older stage of national life that lay before the rise of
absolute monarchy and that had still survived under it in remote
regions where political units were small and clearly separated and
where the ideas that joined them together into a larger whole were
of a patriarchical and familial nature. These unifying ideas were
seldom the object of conscious thought, but they were capable of
bursting forth violently into palpable form. But just as these ideas
lie dormant in quiet times, they also lie dormant in the world of Haller's thought and only flare up occasionally there.

Haller is much more oriented toward the past than the Romantics
were and much less affected by the modern national trend. Neither
the idea of the cultural nation nor that of the political nation plays
a noteworthy role in his system, and we could hardly expect to find
a cosmopolitan or universalistic tendency in a man who hated the
word "general" and clung so persistently to the soil of the small feudal
state. But surprisingly enough we do find this tendency in him,
and it takes a form already familiar to us in the Romantics, namely,
the idealization of the Catholic hierarchy. He was not converted
to Catholicism until 1820; but, as he says himself, he was committed
to it emotionally from 1808 on, and his entire system was therefore
conceived under the influence of Catholic thought. His Catholicism
could not be as warm and direct as his enthusiasm for the simple life
of the patrimonial state. He was attracted to Catholicism, and, as
we know from his own statements, he needed it as a substructure
for his political system. It was the Roman church's opposition to revolutionary ideas that first won his sympathy. But he soon realized
that this ally possessed stronger weapons than he himself did. He

[23] *Ibid.*, II, vii and 81.
[24] It is interesting to see how the most heterogeneous minds came together as
late as 1814 in the common feeling of release from the threat of foreign rule.
This is evident in the fact that Rotteck's *Teutsche Blätter* reprinted Haller's article
"Was ist die alte Ordnung?" on January 22, 1814 as a "contribution completely
in harmony with the views of the German patriot as well as of the sincere cosmopolitan," although Haller's article deals only with Bern and Switzerland.

must have been somewhat drawn to the church by an awareness that the powers of the new era could not be controlled by the mere idea of the patrimonial state and by the glorification of a feudal idyll. Equally universal, worldwide ideas were needed to fight the intoxicating universalism of the times. "You call for a state of states," he cried, "a so-called cosmopolitan state. Who can provide that better than the Christian church?"[25] But the church offered more than a cosmopolitan antidote to the cosmopolitan poison of the principles of 1789. Its universal authority and power, extending beyond nations and states, were also an effective barrier against the most dangerous enemy of his patrimonial state, that is, against the modern state and the modern nation. His keen understanding of power and his protest against its uncontrolled development came together here once again. The patrimonial state had been destroyed by an expanding desire for power. New intellectual structures had been created that passed beyond that state and over the heads of individual rulers. First came the absolutistic power state, then the national power state, both permeated with the desire for inner coherence and clear separation from the outside world. In this way, the situation Haller complained of had arisen: "The borders of states and nations are more sharply drawn than ever. Every nation wants to be alone in the world, so to speak. Everyone is isolated, cut off, separated from everyone else."[26] But this had not been the case when the church had had more significance. "Were not the states within the church, so to speak, just as it was within them? . . . Did it not, in a spiritual sense, cause the border between states and nations to disappear?" He thought that the church itself could once again take up its previous office of settling the quarrels of the worldly potentates by its friendly and disinterested arbitration.[27] He saw the church serving as a means of calming the waves of modern state and national life.

"Has not the church alone been successful," he adds, "in combining variety in form with unity in spirit, in combining patriotism with true cosmopolitanism by preaching love of neighbor and tying the bond of brotherhood between all princes and peoples?"[28] If we look back now on all the political thinkers we have discussed so far, we see the utmost extremes of national thought and feeling represented, from Haller's elemental loyalties toward clan and liege on up to Fichte's pure spirituality. But at all levels of the scale, universalistic ideas were called upon for support. These universalistic ideas

[25] *Restauration*, IV, xvii; cf. V, 369. [26] *Ibid.*, IV, xxi.
[27] *Ibid.*, IV, xvii. [28] *Loc.cit.*; cf., too, V, xxii, 51, 96, 372.

will concern us now as we return to the North German, Protestant world and to the circle of men who tried to apply Haller's theories to Prussian problems. These men thought they had found the ideal sovereign and head of their party in the crown prince, who later became King Friedrich Wilhelm IV; and they also thought they had found an ideal political weapon in the young Bismarck. Since Bismarck's later achievement carried forward the ideas of this group but also negated them at the same time, we must first inquire into the ideas on the nation and the national state held by this circle before we move on to Bismarck's founding of the modern German national state.

IT IS INTERESTING to see how concurrences and contradictions among the ideas that concern us here were accompanied by the personal contact and separation of their advocates, by the forming and dissolving of intellectual commerce between one man and another. In the Christlich-Deutsche Tischgesellschaft founded by Achim von Arnim in January 1811, two of the thinkers we have treated, Adam Müller and Fichte, came together with young Leopold von Gerlach; and in the years after 1815, Gerlach became a leading member in another group of friends that made up the subsequently formed circle of Friedrich Wilhelm IV.[29] In the Tischgesellschaft of 1811, lively patriotic and literary ideas of various kinds had been represented, and only the core of the group favored a conservative, aristocratic opposition to the leveling reform efforts of Chancellor Hardenberg. In the group of young lawyers and officers that existed from 1816 to 1819 under the name of the Maikäferei[30] and that saw the formation of lifelong friendships, there was also a colorful and brilliant mélange of German and Christian Romanticism. But then a characteristic and irresistible urge for clarity and a sharp definition of positions arose. The floods of inner feeling were not abandoned, but definite channels were found for them. Thus, the

[29] Cf. my essay on Bismarck's entry into the Christian-Germanic circle, *Histor. Zeitschrift*, XC, 75f., and in *Preussen und Deutschland im 19. und 20. Jahrhundert*; Reinhold Steig, *Heinr. von Kleists Berliner Kämpfe* (1901); Nadler, *Die Berliner Romantik 1800 bis 1814* (1921); Jedele, *Die kirchenpolit. Anschauungen des E. L. v. Gerlach* (Tübingen dissertation, 1910), p. 5; Leonie von Keyserling, *Studien zu den Entwicklungsjahren der Brüder Gerlach* (1913).

[30] Named after the innkeeper Mai, at whose house, located on the castle grounds, the group met (see Ludw. v. Gerlach, I, 94ff.). Because of its members Leopold von Gerlach and Brentano, who had belonged to the Tischgesellschaft of 1811, the group could regard itself as a continuation of the earlier one. See Fr. Wiegand, "Der Kreis der Maikäfer in Berlin," *Deutsche Rundschau*, CLX.

most passionate ideas of Pietism, a glowing subjectivism that surrendered itself to both the pains of sin and the joys of atonement,
could be fused with a desire for rigid, objective principles. The
manner in which the members of the group cultivated these two
tendencies and became at first, through the enjoyment of the inner
fires, indifferent to dogmas, church, and worship, but then took
these up again and defended them energetically—this combination
of esoteric and exoteric ideals, of enthusiasm and self-control, filled
them with the consciousness of possessing something unusual and
magnificent and gave them resilience and vitality because of the
conflicts this combination evoked.

Such strong inner resources also strengthened their political conviction. They had brought with them from their previous lives a Romantic enthusiasm for everything German, a natural Prussian-
monarchistic patriotism, and a fundamental hatred for anything
that came from revolutionary France. They hated France not only
for being the oppressor of the Prussian monarchy but also for being
the oppressor of feudal freedoms and privileges and of patriarchical,
aristocratic forms of rule. They had a brilliant theoretician in Adam
Müller, but he was perhaps too brilliant and did not have enough positive substance to offer. But the first volumes of Haller's *Restauration*
amply filled the need for a powerful and manageable theory of feudal
monarchy, and this theory also opened the way for a religious impulse that overwhelmed everything worldly. Leopold von Gerlach
was so enthusiastic about Haller that he urged his friends to put in a
good word for him whenever they went into society.[31] His brother
Ludwig says of this early exciting period in 1817-18: "We fought with
passion and enthusiasm against Rousseau's revolutionary state that
arises from below, and we fought for the state that comes from
God." But the group immediately found two things lacking in Haller's
system. First, he did not go deeply enough into his religious principles; he let the living, personal God retreat behind the natural

[31] *Denkwürdigkeiten aus dem Leben Leop. von Gerlachs*, I, 6 [hereafter
cited simply as: Leop. v. Gerlach]; Ludw. v. Gerlach, I, 101f.; Hassel, *Radowitz*
I, 187. We have an interesting account of such an instance, and of how explosive
the differences of opinion were, in a letter from Gneisenau (who was conservative-
ly inclined then) to Clausewitz on March 29, 1818 (Pertz-Delbrück, *Gneisenau*,
V, 300): "It is considered idiocy here to have any praise for Haller's *Restauration
der Staatswissenschaften*, a work that contains much worthwhile material. I
recently saw the tyrant lapse into a foaming rage and some frightful bellowing in
the company of ladies when his little brother-in-law undertook the defense of this
book." The "tyrant" is Grolman, who was the brother-in-law of the Gerlach
brothers. The "little brother-in-law" is probably Leopold himself.

world that God had created. Second—and this point is of particular
interest to us—he did not develop the concept of the nation, that
beautiful blossom of the eternal kingdom of God and of man. We
have already seen how Haller's fourth volume, which dealt with the
church and theocracies, tried to fill this first gap.[32] He felt neither
inclination nor need to fill the second one. We shall come back to
this point later. In short, from the very beginning there was a tendency in this group of Prussian political Romantics to refine Haller's system and to inject into it the political and religious experience
of their own lives.

We have only insufficient information about the further development of their views during the 1820's.[33] But for the 1830's we have
a rich source in the *Berliner Politische Wochenblatt*, which appeared
from the fall of 1831 until the end of 1841 and represents a kind of
encyclopedia of politics in the form of a weekly paper.[34] As a direct result of the July Revolution, plans for a militant conservative
paper had been made in the circles of the crown prince's court. Radowitz probably gave the organ its actual form and arranged the appointment of his intellectual ally, the convert Jarcke, as the first editor. Jarcke held the post until November 1832. Major Schulz became
his successor for all practical purposes, although there were nominal
editors as well, first Major Streit (ret.), and from 1839 on, Hofrat

---

[32] He clearly did not satisfy the wishes of his Prussian friends with this any
more than he did those of Adam Müller. See Ludw. v. Gerlach, I, 127; also von
Below, *Der deutsche Staat des Mittelalters*, I, 12n.

[33] Except on the views of Joseph von Radowitz, who, as a Catholic and non-
Prussian, represented a special position from the very outset. I have discussed his
case in my book *Radowitz und die deutsche Revolution* (1913).

[34] Cf. Varrentrapp, "Rankes *Historisch-polit. Zeitschrift* und das *Berliner Polit.
Wochenblatt*," *Histor. Zeitschrift*, IC, 35ff.; Hassel, *Radowitz*, I, 43, 60, 212f.,
248; Salomon, *Gesch. des deutschen Zeitungswesens*, III, 475ff.; Kaufmann, *Polit.
Gesch. Deutschlands im 19. Jahrh.*, pp. 239ff.; Arnold, "Aufzeichnungen des
Grafen Carl v. Voss-Buch über das *Berliner Polit. Wochenblatt*," *Histor. Zeit-
schrift*, CVI, 325ff.; and the note on p. 227 of the first edition of this book.—
As a supplement to the information given there, I add from the files of the
Berliner Geh.-Staatsarchiv that after the death in 1839 of Jarcke's successor in the
editorship, Major Streit (ret.), Major Schulz took over the post. It was pointed
out by the Ministry of the Interior (cf. Varrentrapp, p. 109) that the paper
should be maintained because of its friendly position to the government on the
Cologne question, a position that had alienated South German circles. A cabinet
order of October 30, 1839 approved the appointment of Hofrat Stein as editor.
He was apparently just the nominal editor, while Major Schulz was the actual
editor. The government supported it in its last years (until 1841) by a subscrip-
tion of ten copies (which were sent to the larger provincial papers) and by small
gratuities to the editor, Stein. It ceased publication at the end of 1841 because of
a lack of circulation.

Stein. The Gerlach brothers, Leo, Haxthausen, Phillips, and sometimes even the honored master himself, Haller, were contributors
to the paper. The genesis and composition of the group indicate that
it would try to draw the Catholic and Protestant branches of political
Romanticism closely together. It also kept in touch with sympathetic
minds in France, but it still preserved its own independent position.[35] We shall soon see that divergent opinions were voiced within
the group itself and that staunch followers of Haller did not make
up its entire membership.[36] We can seldom identify the authors of
the essays with certainty, but we do not require this identification
for our purposes of determining the basic position of the group
and of characterizing the individual divergences within it. Again,
we shall select only the material that is relevant to the question of
the nation and the national state.

The naturalistic idea of power, which played a considerable but
inconsistent role in Haller's thinking, gave way to the idea of law.
Haller had said that the prince rules because of his naturally
greater power. But since God creates and rules everything, this power
should be regarded and respected as power willed by God. However, Haller is not willing to say categorically that might makes right,
and he goes on to say that the prince's power does not become legal
through prescription alone but also through the particular agreements
that he makes, formally or informally, with those who are weaker
than he and who entrust themselves to his protection. The group
realized how tenuous this bond between power and law was and
how meager these transcendent, religious justifications of power and
law were. More solid foundations were needed to support the
powers the group wanted to support; and the actual word of God as
revealed in Holy Scripture, not Haller's general theism, provided
these foundations. Wilhelm von Gerlach elucidated this position
in his articles entitled "Was ist Recht?" in the *Wochenblatt* of 1833.[37]

---

[35] It seems to me that Kaufmann, *Histor. Zeitschrift*, LXXXVIII, 437, somewhat
overestimates the influence of de Maistre, Lamennais, etc. on the German politicians of the Restoration. However, the entire problem of the interaction between
French and German political Romanticism is in need of a thorough study.

[36] As Treitschke thought, *Deutsche Geschichte*, IV, 203.

[37] Pp. 49ff. His authorship can be inferred from the reports of his brother:
Ludw. v. Gerlach, I, 208.—Somewhat later, in his *Lehrbuch der Universal-
geschichte* (1844), VI, 764f., another member of the *Wochenblatt* group, Heinrich
Leo, criticized Haller's naturalistic power theory more from a Burkean position
and saw it as a "caricature, as a transformation of Burke's ingenious doctrine into
something obvious, wooden, and therefore untrue"; see, too, von Below, *op.cit.*,
I, 14ff.

According to these articles, the privilege of authority is based on a special divine dispensation. Authority was created to combat original sin. It is a means of correction for the fallen world, "put on earth by God Himself for the control of injustice,"[38] and it is only secondarily based on the "existing and evolving constitutions and treaties" between the ruling and the ruled, agreements "that should never run counter to the fundamental principle." In this way the privilege of authority seemed to be made secure from the vicissitudes of historical development, and this was a security that Haller had not been able to offer. But the Gerlachs' attempt to remove privilege, particularly the privilege of existing authority, from the stream of history and to protect it from upheaval and revision was no more successful than Haller's attempt to make the existing disposition of power permanent and to stem the flow of natural forces. Even Wilhelm von Gerlach had to admit that injustice could evolve into justice through prescription and gradual purification: "Justice grows out of injustice as a flower grows out of the dungheap." Thus, there were invisible seeds of justice present in injustice, seeds that would attain life and maturity at their allotted time.[39] But this was not too far removed from what the Gerlachs would themselves have condemned as pantheism, the recognition of a natural evolutionary process; in the course of the following decades, whenever political authorities and the disposition of power were reorganized, their party had to face the embarrassing question of whether the revisions were to be condemned as unjust or whether they were to be recognized as a new law arising from an unjust law in accordance with God's decree.[40]

They considered everything pantheistic that sought support in worldly motives, goals, and necessities rather than in other-worldly ones. They considered historicism pantheistic because it attempted to

---

[38] *Berliner Politisches Wochenblatt* (1833), p. 60. [Hereafter cited as *BPW.*]

[39] *Ibid.*, p. 49. In Leopold von Gerlach's memoirs (I, 119), there is a similar passage that Gerlach wants attributed to a speech the king gave in 1847: "For the divine order here on earth is such that justice will arise even from injustice. To disregard this fact would be to commit new injustice."

[40] Let me cite one suggestive example of this which occurs in connection with the promulgation of the Prussian constitution on December 5, 1848, a subject that will be treated in the second part of this study. Leopold von Gerlach had opposed the measure at first, but he found afterwards "that the good Lord chose the right course with this constitutional document." Ludwig von Gerlach was unhappy about these "historico-objective pantheistic reflections" of his brother's. "The conservatives indulged in this kind of pantheism in 1866, too, and they became completely powerless because of it" (Ludw. v. Gerlach, II, 34).

understand and acknowledge the integrity of the entire course of history.[41] The glorification of the state and of absolute political goals fell under the same censure. Here they were motivated, of course, by feudal-aristocratic interests, interests that saw a dangerous enemy of feudal privilege in the absolutism of the state and even in the idea of an all-inclusive state personality. On the basis of these same interests, they regarded revolutionary power and the national state as the heir and successor of the absolutistic power state. Haller held the same view; and seen historically, his view was correct.[42] But did this justify dissolving the state completely into a collection of private shares in power and privilege as Haller had done? Friedrich Julius Stahl, who was active in the 1830's in Würzburg and Erlangen as a teacher of constitutional law and as an advocate of a conservative historical concept of the state, boldly attempted to demonstrate the state's origins in what was truly public law, to conceive of it as a community, and to place the idea of the state above the sphere of the prince's legal privileges. But for these very reasons the zealots of the *Wochenblatt* considered him a renegade and a kind of wolf in sheep's clothing.[43] He is simply reviving Hobbes's Leviathan, they said, but this time with somewhat better manners and in fashionable dress.[44] But even they could not entirely ignore the momentous lessons of history and the spirit of the state in which they themselves lived. "The modern state," they had to admit, "is a fact of world history. We are forced to recognize it, for it would be impossible to build our present national life on any principles that would run counter to it."[45]

[41] Ludw. v. Gerlach, I, 102: This merely historical theory of the state and of law (that of Savigny and his consorts) "that builds up its system . . . in a pantheistic manner and, for the most part, just on the basis of the individuality and history of nations."

[42] Cf., for example, Jarcke's articles on "Revolution und Absolutismus" in the *BPW* (1833), pp. 39ff. (*Verm. Schriften*, I, 166ff.).

[43] According to the *BPW* (1837), p. 177, Stahl's theory of the state, which spoke of the state's comprehensive tasks and of a concept of the state that took precedence over the princes, "amounted to a pantheistic deification of the state." Further polemic (Jarcke's) against Stahl and the historical school of jurisprudence appears in the *BPW* (1834), p. 259 (*Verm. Schriften*, III, 10).

[44] *BPW* (1837), p. 181.

[45] *BPW* (1833), p. 160; *ibid.*, p. 150, reads: "Haller lived in a republic where a sovereign corporation in the form of a multitude of civil law paragraphs governed simple subjects, where, that is to say, the *more intense interaction* was lacking that automatically occurs in monarchies because of an independent ruler's relationship to organically organized estates. Because of this relationship, other and deeper ties develop which make the monarchy the most perfect form of community which human beings can devise." In the question of levying taxes, Jarcke

They struggled to develop a basis for their feudal state that would still their religious and political conscience, satisfy their aristocratic claims to rule, and unite eternal revelation, historical necessity, and strong feudal interests. The solution they found could do all this only by leaving some poorly disguised loopholes between the rigid principles of the whole structure.

In a similar fashion, they tried to reconcile themselves to the idea of the nation and its significance for political life. With every concession they made, they had to exercise great caution to avoid making a slip and falling victim to the hated principle of national sovereignty. Jarcke[46] ascertained to his dismay that the *Gazette de France*, a French legitimist publication that he had much admired, was playing a dangerous game with the concept of the nation. The paper had transformed this concept into a moral entity and attributed functions to it in which revolutionary delusions repeatedly figured. He was willing to admit that the people were a unit in a certain sense because they shared a common residence, a common dynasty, a common legal system, language, and tradition, and a common experience of past centuries spent in both joy and suffering. In short, he was willing to admit "that a common national character develops and that *nationality*, a unity that makes a people into a nation, develops from that character." But none of these factors makes the nation a legal entity that has a will of its own in any legal sense, like a corporation or other business firm.

Another contributor tried the expedient of distinguishing sharply between the concepts of the people and the nation. A people, he explains, is the mass of inhabitants of a state, and as such it is not a unit, much less a legal entity. It consists only of a great number of individual legal entities that are not capable of unifying themselves into a living, individual being of a higher order. But nations are formed by a common language and ancestry, and the concept nation has even less to do with the state than the concept of the

---

advocated a position in the *BPW* (1833), p. 78 (*Verm. Schriften*, I, 192) and *BPW* (1837), p. 129 (*Verm. Schriften*, III, 371) that went beyond Haller's rigid feudal principle and represented an approach to the modern idea of the state and to the recognition of general state requirements. The *BPW* (1840), pp. 127ff., goes still further in this respect; here, among other things, the following completely un-Hallerian sentence occurs: "Princely property as such must remain dedicated to the common good." The last years of the *BPW*, influenced by the Cologne Church controversy, are, of course, generally more in line with government policy than its earlier years.

[46] *BPW* (1832), p. 246 (*Verm. Schriften*, I, 20ff.); see also *BPW* (1832), p. 3.

people. Indeed, it has nothing at all to do with it. Nationality is "a factor that is completely alien to the state and that is just as independent of the state as the state is of it."[47] "There are no national states."[48] Thus, what we have called the political nation was deprived of all active personal character and robbed of any possibility of becoming a political factor, and what we have called the cultural nation was banned from political life altogether. In this way, these dangerous concepts were deprived of their sting.

But still another view was expressed in the columns of the *Wochenblatt*. In this view, the word nation had a warmer and richer tone, and this approach did not want to separate state and nation so completely. Whoever had lived through the year 1813 with an open mind and heart would have been untrue to himself if he had forgotten what the idea of the nation—the Prussian political nation no less than the German cultural nation—had done for the state at that time. "The enthusiasm of that period," one passage reads,[49] "was not felt for the theories of the Enlightenment thinkers but for the old true freedom of our ancestors and for the independence of nations represented by their hereditary rulers." A Russian diplomat, writing in the *Wochenblatt*, launched a direct attack on Haller and reproached him with being deaf to the concept of the nation.[50] "Herr von Haller's state is only an aggregate of expressed and implied agreements. . . . How has it escaped the great man that a nation is not an accidental union of individual human beings who could just as well enter into an alliance with any other people but that it is an organic being endowed with an animating principle (i.e. nationality) and that its various contracts are only the body or form of the government?" Nationality is the spiritual bond that holds the state together. Everything that is expressed in positive law is "nothing but the matter to which the creative spirit of nationality gives varied forms, and these forms taken as a whole make up the constitution of a state." "Nationality is the source of life in every people, and anything that permits this spring to dry up condemns itself to death."

These ideas, obviously drawn from Savigny's theory, made no impression on Haller at all. He considered it superfluous in a discussion restricted purely to constitutional theory to press on to such subtleties

[47] *BPW* (1838), p. 65; similarly, *ibid.*, p. 261, and *ibid.* (1840), pp. 131 and 163.
[48] *Ibid.*, p. 200.　　　　　　　　　[49] *BPW* (1836), p. 57.
[50] *BPW* (1834), pp. 46ff.

as the obscure spiritual tendency toward unification operative in the
society of any state, and he would have nothing to do with the
idea of the nation as an organic being.[51] But the discussion was not
settled with that, and unsatisfied souls came forward again and
again who wanted more of the nation, more of this spiritual spring-
water for the state, than Haller gave them. Highly relevant political
considerations spoke for them and against Haller. The small, archaic
nations of Europe offered an example of the way in which pronounced national character created immunity against the liberal
and revolutionary spirit of the times, and it was these same nations
that clung to their old church with determination and a refreshing
strength of faith. The unity of nationality and religion that is particularly intense and persistent in the older stages of national life was
obvious in these nations. In considering the Basques, who had won
the attention of the Prussian Hallerians by their gallant fight for
the legitimate prince Don Carlos, the group noted with pleasure that
although only catechisms and prayer books were printed in the
Basque language, the entire people had a fresh view of life and a
sense of poetry that should put the civilized rabble of Paris and
London to shame.[52] Similar observations were made about the
Slavic nations. One passage in the *Wochenblatt*[53] calls attention to
the fact that the destruction of national and religious feeling would
be the surest way to drive what was left of Poland completely into
the abyss of the demonic revolution. This gives us a glimpse of the
views that stood behind Friedrich Wilhelm IV's cordial policy toward
Poland in the early years of his government.[54]

But then another line of thought appears once again, a line of

[51] He cited Adelung's meager definition by which a nation was understood to
be "the native-born inhabitants of a country to the extent that they have a common origin. They can comprise a single state or be divided into several states"
(*ibid.*, p. 234). The fifth volume of his work appeared in 1834, and Chap. 92 in
this volume sought to offer further replies to these objections. He answered the
question of the invisible spiritual basis of human society in a rather rationalistic
way here by saying that "the uniformity of belief in certain truths and certain
duties" provides "the basic bond between human beings" (V, 325).

[52] *BPW* (1834), p. 86.   [53] *BPW* (1837), p. 300.

[54] The *BPW* of 1841, pp. 221ff., objects to the political aspirations of the Poles
in Posen, but it still wants their nationality completely uninfringed upon.—On the
friendly attitude of the crown prince Friedrich Wilhelm toward Poland, see
Leop. v. Gerlach, I, 59, 73. On the Gerlachs' similar attitude in 1841, see Ludw. v.
Gerlach, I, 286; and in 1846, Leop. v. Gerlach, I, 112.—It was completely consistent with this attitude that the *BPW* also complained of the Russianizing of the
German Baltic provinces. It is significant, however, that the *BPW* did not consider the Russian national party the enemy of German nationality in these provinces, but rather the allegedly liberal Russian civil service (1841, p. 155).

thought that appealed to Radowitz in particular and eventually led him out of the party's camp. Was not the national idea also a source of strength for liberalism that liberalism alone should not be allowed to have? Liberalism, the *Wochenblatt* said once,[55] to the extent that it is founded on materialistic views, is moving toward its ruin. But the nobler souls in the liberal movement are aware of this emptiness, yearn for a positive source of life, and want to hold fast to the national element. Nothing would destroy the false and abstract conceptions of liberalism more surely than an awareness of, and an interest in, the history of the fatherland and an understanding of its old, native legal system. Thus, the point made here in the *Wochenblatt* led back to the principle that nationality, properly understood, was an excellent means of conserving the old epoch and of immunizing against the new.

Such was the conclusion that an apparently large number of the *Wochenblatt* contributors arrived at on the basis of their own experience, their emotional needs, and their political calculations. Also, it was not difficult for them to incorporate this conclusion into their other doctrines on state, church, and God, on the worldly and the eternal. They consequently achieved a broader range of ideas than Haller's simple system offered. The revelation of God, which was more positively and richly conceived of than in Haller, naturally continued to be the highest authority. The law, the law of God, that is, was still considered to be the source both of nationality and of positive contracts; but now, seen as a "moral bond that is older than all positive contracts and that is, so to speak, the mother of them,"[56] nationality was given the function of mediating between the law of God and the positive contracts, i.e., the patrimonial state. Accordingly, the law first existed as an "ethereal inspiration" before it took on concrete form in the contracts. Thus surrounded by universal, transcendent ideas on the one hand and by specific ones on the other, i.e., in a somewhat medieval context and with somewhat medieval overtones, the idea of the nation was incorporated into the political system of the group to which the future ruler of the Prussian state belonged.

But did this national idea the group was to acknowledge arise from the soil of the political nation or from that of the cultural one? The group did not consider this question with any methodological precision, and the answers to it that we have in the *Wochenblatt*

[55] *BPW* (1833), p. 244.   [56] *BPW* (1837), p. 299.

all tend to merge together. The main thing for these essentially feudal and aristocratic politicians was to acknowledge the national principle only in the most harmless form possible and to avoid every concession to the liberal national idea that would lead down the path to popular sovereignty and democracy. The stricter members of the group could not rid themselves of a certain mistrust of this dangerous contraband they had picked up. This becomes evident in the ideas on nationality that Ludwig von Gerlach wrote down in 1844 on a trip from Dublin to Liverpool, with the impressions of the Irish repeal movement still fresh in his mind.[57] He considered this movement, like the Polish one, one of those national movements that had gained the sympathy of the group because of its religious character but that had also evoked the group's concern because this religious element was in danger of disappearing. Ludwig von Gerlach is probably on the right path historically in tracing the glorification of nationalities back to Christianity or, more exactly, to the Reformation;[58] for prior to that they had been absorbed in the earlier world empires. "Developed as they are now through their languages and literatures, nationalities have assumed an important position. They compete with the universal church of God in its sublime office of being both spirit and state. Therefore, a fact of particular significance and practical value at this point is that the state is prior and superior to the nation that evolves from it. Like everything deriving from nature worship, the concept of the nation has something cloudy and murky about it; and that very cloudiness makes it sympathetic to the current pantheistic spirit."[59] He too found the characteristics of the cultural nation and the political nation not clearly separable; but despite this, he finally concluded that the nation was a product of the state. This expedient of quell-

[57] Ludw. v. Gerlach, I, 397. Concerning him, see Wildgrube, *Die polit. Theorien Ludwig von Gerlachs*, pp. 66f.

[58] A similar line of thought occurs in Heinrich Leo, who, in a memorial for Friedrich Wilhelm IV in the fall of 1848, traces the emergence of the German nation back to Boniface and the work of the church. The Reformation completed the forming of the nation, he goes on, but it also introduced a fatal disease into the roots of German unity itself. Varrentrapp, *Histor. Zeitschrift*, IC, 112f.

[59] A later comment (April 1867; II, 297) of Ludwig von Gerlach's on the concepts of state, nation, king, and nationality is also of interest here. "Before one's very eyes, these uncomprehended words transform themselves into natural substances or idols to which neither divine nor human law is applicable and which must be judged as monsters or leviathans in accordance with their own strange qualities. The 'vice of patriotism,' as my brother Leopold calls it, emerges in this way, hatched out by pantheism. I owe Haller a great debt of gratitude from 1817 on."

ing and limiting the nation was a welcome one to a legalistic and normative mind, but it stood in direct contradiction to the view of Gerlach's associates. According to this view, which we have already outlined and which derived from Savigny and the Romantics, nationality was the source of positive law and of the state. This view enjoyed the greater favor among Gerlach's friends, and it had a stronger influence on their political thinking. It was certainly "cloudy," and for that reason it seemed suspect to some. But for that same reason it seemed unobjectionable to others, for this very vagueness could help them restrict the national idea to the sphere of the intangible and purely intellectual and hinder its impulse toward political realization in modern forms. At the same time, they could also derive from it and justify by it all the older political institutions and forms that they wanted to defend. But let us refrain from excessive speculation here, and let us not forget that the national idea in this form could cross the threshold of consciousness and be accepted only because it was already intellectually available and because it had emerged forcefully from the events of the times and from the intellectual and political experiences of youth during the Romantic period and the Wars of Liberation.

Thus there arose what I should like to call the conservative idea of the national state. This idea stands in contrast to the liberal one, which drew its main strength from the ideas of 1789. Before we examine and define the conservative idea more closely, we should note a highly significant statement from the columns of the *Wochenblatt* that contains, along with the characteristics of this idea of the national state that are already known to us, other characteristics that remain for us to clarify. The passage occurs in a review of Friedrich Ludwig Jahn's *Merke zum deutschen Volkstum*, which was published in 1833.[60] The rugged gymnastics instructor, who reprimanded the Francophile liberals of the day in this book, was not unsympathetic to the politicians of the *Wochenblatt*. Some of them had even joined him on the gymnastics field of the Hasenheide twenty years earlier.[61] But they still had some reservations about his book: "We too are Germans and we too, like every right-thinking man, are full of love for the fatherland in which God has placed us. We are devoted to all the glories of German life, art, and history, and we are eager to waken as much interest in them as possible. But we think that a mere *external* unity of Germany would

[60] *BPW* (1833), p. 214.   [61] See my life of Boyen, II, 407.

destroy this genuine patriotic feeling rather than foster it. The attempt to make a so-called *grande nation* in this way would result in the most disgraceful disaster for the nobler aspects of our nationality. Indeed, we think that the German fatherland has its proper vital principle in the legally established plurality which is now to be sacrificed to the illusion of a false patriotism. We must point out to the author of the *Merke* and to all who share his glowing love for Germany and his unlimited hatred for France that national feelings, though not reprehensible in themselves, are not the highest goal. If they alone are emphasized, they will bring us to the point that the French have unfortunately reached. This state of affairs is the foulest blemish on modern France; for all agree—royalists, Philippists, and republicans—that the French are the leading nation of the world and that the left bank of the Rhine legally belongs to them . . . but there clearly must be some higher authority than national feelings, which remain heathen as long as they remain isolated. This higher authority is the recognition of a divine world order which is based on *law* and which purifies and sanctifies national feelings. This principle makes it clear to us that an injustice always remains an injustice, and no pretext, sophistry, or alleged inspiration can excuse it. . . . It also makes it clear to us that it is not permissible, under the pretext that German soil should not bear a foreign yoke, to annex German provinces that have belonged by treaty to non-German princes for a long time. Even if it was a misfortune for Germany that Alsace became French, it is better that we accept this rather than introduce without cause a new system of plundering that would be ten times worse than Louis XIV's infamous Chambers of Reunion. . . . Let us not pursue any illusions, then, and let us grant the French their monotonous unity, their departments, their centralization, and their vanity. Let us content ourselves with the superior knowledge that Germany's unity, in contrast, consists in the fact that even in the smallest parts of the German fatherland individual pulses beat, bringing nourishment to the heart."

It is characteristic of this conservative idea of the national state that it rejects the consolidation of the cultural nation on principle but that it regards the cultural nation as the fertile native soil in which varied political structures grow, both large and small but all showing genuine traces of the German spirit. We can take cognizance of the cultural nation only by the blossoms it bears in colorful profusion. The cultural nation itself, vitally productive, remains hidden in dark and impenetrable depths. This vivid conception reaches back beyond Savigny and finds its origins in the first ideals of early Romanticism. The world, we learned then, is an abyss of individuality, a plethora of unique individual life that remains coherent, united by a spiritual bond. No direct path leads, of course, from this view to the one we have before us now. But this idea had been the means of finding spiritual unity and inner coherence in the individually manifold and externally divided phenomena of life and history.

The conservative idea of the national state did not define the national state as a centralized national state but as an individual state in the form of an offshoot from the nation. Early Romanticism had not emphasized the spiritual connection between the German cultural nation and the German individual state this strongly. Like Fichte and the advocates of the *Humanitätsideal*, early Romanticism had conceived of the German nation too much as a nation representative of all humanity and not enough as a historically determined nation. But it had been interested in the individual state; it had wanted to nationalize this state in a political sense, inform it with a vital sense of community, and so raise it to a great self-activating personality. This idea, too, one that Haller's theory had threatened to bury completely, reappeared again in the group associated with the *Wochenblatt*. An essay of 1838[62] with the unequivocal title of "Notwendige Ergänzung der Staatswissenschaft" argued that along with Haller, Adam Müller must also be heard if the higher spiritual idea in the phenomenon of the state was to be understood. The essay goes on to say that the state's vital unity cannot be comprehended in words; "it can only be contemplated in its richness." The state is a "universal human life that has developed organically from one root and with its own particular tendency in time and space under divine direction and order," and it will not do, the writer claims, to understand these things only in terms of dominance, subservience, and isolated economic and legal interests. Such factors alone cannot help us understand these massive structures that history has created through the sublime spiritual fusion of princes and peoples and that determine the fate and culture of the world by means of this mysterious bond.

Romanticism brought these ideas into circulation, and political interests and experience developed them further. As we observe them running parallel to and intermingling with each other, we can understand, as we have already noted above, why no effort was made

[62] Pp. 2ff.

to distinguish clearly between a nationality that was present in the soil of the greater cultural nation and a nationality that formed the unifying force in the individual state. From a scholarly point of view, this was a failing; but from a practical one, this failing helped encourage nationalization of the state throughout the greater nation and in the individual state itself. The German individual state could thus be conceived of and felt as a genuine creation of the German spirit —valuable and unique for that very reason, like everything else that had arisen from this spirit—and also as a vital independent unit in itself. Not until this point had a concept of the state been available that could oppose the ideals of the liberal and democratic national state with meaningful national values. Political Romanticism could now play off the idea of the national spirit against that of popular sovereignty.[63] Against the defined, autonomous personality of the nation it could set the imaginative concept of a total German nationality, which remained undefined and impersonal but which was still richly and mysteriously productive. Further, it could draw on the vivid reality of the individual state personalities of Germany, every one of which had arisen through the secular cooperation of the ruling and the ruled. The spirit of old Germany and old Prussia stood up here against the new Germany that radicalism wanted to create. The liberal idea of the national state based its claim on the due rights and the will of a living nation; the conservative national idea based its claim on the national life of the past. Both ideas drew part of their strength from the great individualistic tendencies of the times, but the difference between them was that the one form of individualism was democratic and rationalistic, the other aristocratic and historicizing. The one valued the individual as the basic unit in society, state, and nation. The other valued the quality of individuality itself in the multitudinous forms of social, political, and national life. The one demanded equal rights for all in state and national life. The other assigned individuals particular functions within the state and nation according to the sphere of life in which they found themselves. The one saw the individual limited by the national will, which he in turn helped to form. The other saw the limits set by what the nation's previous generations had created. The one appealed to the consciously sovereign and controlling reason of the individual and of

---

[63] "The spirit of the nation in its mysterious depth and multifariousness," as Jarcke put it. *BPW* (November 26, 1831), p. 31 (*Verm. Schriften*, I, 36). On the term and theory of the national spirit, see pp. 158f., above, and pp. 198f., below. Jarcke is probably influenced by Puchta, *Das Gewohnheitsrecht*, I (1828).

the whole society. The other traced the unconsciously functioning
rationality of history back to the sovereign control of God. Both represented the vital interests of particular social classes; but both tried
to elevate these interests to the level of a universal ideal. The religious
universalism of political Romanticism took its stand against the rationalistic universalism of the liberal concept of the state.

We must make the political consequences of this religious universalism somewhat clearer here, for we are about to deal with the
government that tried to put the ideas of political Romanticism into
effect. We saw how political Romanticism placed the idea of the
nation between the revealed law of God on the one hand and the
feudal monarchy on the other and how it tried to control the la-
bile element inherent in this idea by the stable environment in
which it was placed. We also saw in the review of Jahn's book how
great the concern was to discourage the idea of national power
and greatness and how a war to win back territory taken from Germany could be considered unpermissible and harmful. The argument
here was that it was better to recognize a neighboring nation's claims
to the Alsace, established by prescription and agreements, even if
these claims were originally founded on a past injustice, than
to perpetrate a new injustice.[64] The vital interests, the desire for
power, and the autonomy of the nation as a whole and of the individual state as well are limited here and forever bound to higher legal
norms. It is the old denial, or at least the weakening, of the state's
right to autonomous power politics that we see recurring continually
in new forms. Political dreams of a universal political alliance between
the individual states and theoretical steps toward it lost their immediate appeal. Instead, the consciences of statesmen were now incul-
cated with the primacy of law over power and the primacy of a
universal international order over the interests of individual states.
The legal relationships between sovereigns, Wilhelm von Gerlach
says,[65] are similar to the legal relationships between sovereigns and
their subjects, for there can be no legal norms for sovereigns themselves "that do not coincide with morality and Christianity or, indeed, that are not identical with moral and Christian norms. All legal

---

[64] The author of the essay "Natürliche Grenzen," *BPW* (1838), pp. 65f., who
had called nationality in general an element alien to the state (see pp. 175f., above),
could thus declare all the more emphatically that "German nationality, high as
we may value it, cannot impose a *moral* obligation on the French people to recognize the sacredness of the German border. Only the territorial rights of the German
princes provide it with this sacredness."

[65] *BPW* (1833), p. 60.

norms, even the most specialized ones, must be derived from such legal obligations, and they must be capable of being traced back to such obligations. These legal relationships are nothing other than moral and Christian obligations that should be regulated just as all other arrangements between men should be regulated, namely, in accordance with God's will."

The "heathen" national pride of the French was not subject to such limitations. The circle of the *Wochenblatt* considered it monstrous and sinful that all the parties in France, the legitimists no less than the radical advocates of popular sovereignty, considered it France's good and self-evident right to increase her power and to openly promote her actual or assumed practical interests. Where international politics were concerned, the French parties unanimously advocated the autonomy of the state personality and bore witness by their unanimity to the inner continuity between the autonomous power state of the *ancien régime* and the autonomous national state of the Revolution. In this respect France had a considerable political advantage over Germany, where the links between the state and the nation were so much more difficult to find and where the autonomy of both the state and the nation was being checked and inhibited. Thus, according to the *Wochenblatt*, Germany and the German princes were not supposed to use certain weapons that their neighbors used without scruple in the power struggle among states. They were supposed to refrain from using them so that the integrity of the patrimonial state would be preserved.

THESE ARE THE IDEAS on the state and nation and on the principles of their behavior that the circle of Friedrich Wilhelm IV developed in the 1830's. We must be aware of them in order to understand his government, which was to have such profound effects on the destiny of Germany; for, taken as a whole, they formed a ballast of thought that burdened and encumbered his policies from beginning to end. This does not mean, however, that he accepted them completely and let his actions be determined by them. As we have just seen in the problems we have discussed so far, Christian-Germanic political theory was by no means the rigid unit it seemed to be to its opponents. It was rich in variations and nuances for the simple reason that its advocates were brilliant and perceptive people who enjoyed their paradoxes. Within their own group they used these paradoxes as a counterbalance to the dogmatic rigidity they felt obliged to employ against the unrestrained subjectivism of the period. This indulgence in the most varied notions and demands took its toll, however, when it was necessary to act in a prodigiously tumultuous world. It became evident to the group that they had lost the capacity for coherent action and that there was a confusing multitude of ways to convert their theory into practice. Leopold von Gerlach often questioned his brother Ludwig's judgment, Ludwig questioned his, and both of them questioned the king's, who doubtless questioned theirs. Each of them often reproached himself after the fact for having acted incorrectly, that is, for having applied his theory incorrectly. But the main reason for inconsistency lay in the theory itself. As we saw, it contained the seeds of a political quietism and relativism that could lame the head and hand for battle or action. They shrank back in horror and made the sign of the cross whenever their opponents committed a new injustice; then, afterwards, they could always puzzle over the question of whether and to what extent it was God's will that a new justice arise from the new injustice.[66]

Abhorrence for opposing doctrines and deeds held this relativism in check. But the inner contradictions of the system still could not be overcome. The fact that this system had been developed beyond Haller's version was both its strength and its weakness. What it gained in brilliance and ideas it lost in compactness and sharpness and in the defensive strength it needed to oppose the spirit of the times. It became too historical for a dogmatic system, and it remained too dogmatic for a historical concept of the state. Haller probably knew very well what he was doing when he kept the ideas of the state personality and the nation out of his system. If they were allowed any entry at all, however slight, the strongest forces of modern change rushed in with them, change that went beyond the patrimonial and feudal state. These thinkers wanted to create a patrimonial state while also realizing the ideas of the Prussian state personality and of the German nation, ideas that they could not neglect. But beyond that, in order to unite the entire system and to sanctify it, they wanted to raise the banner of a supreme religious ethical idea, both universal and transcendent, which was to guide not only the life of the individual but also the life of the state. There was simply too much here that could not be united,

---

[66] See p. 173, above. I have elsewhere emphasized the quietistic feature of this theory that proved crippling to action ("Die Tagebücher des Generals von Gerlach," *Histor. Zeitschrift*, LXX [1892], reprinted now in *Preussen und Deutschland im 19. und 20. Jahrhundert*), but I treated the subject too much in isolation then.

and as a result, the period dominated by Friedrich Wilhelm IV and his circle is one of a massive disintegration that begins in the 1830's, reaches its nadir in the years of the Revolution, but still continues, after staving off the Revolution, until the age of Bismarck could completely halt and redirect this basic tendency.

Our observations here have been meant to serve as an introduction to the times of Friedrich Wilhelm IV and of Bismarck. We are not far from the completion of that task. It will suffice now to characterize briefly the process of disintegration in the 1840's and then to show how the idea of the modern national state finally emerged victoriously from the mists of the universalistic and nonpolitical thinking that had previously enveloped it.

As an example of the inner dissolution of the Christian-Germanic state ideal through the absorption of elements from the idea of the national state, let us first look at the ideas that Friedrich Julius Stahl developed on the relationship of state and nation while he was teaching in Prussia in the 1840's. We have already noted that the extreme adherents of Haller considered Stahl something of a renegade in the 1830's. But these differences of opinion underwent a change while Stahl was teaching in the Berlin of Friedrich Wilhelm IV. Disagreement on Haller had put him at odds with the Gerlachs when he came to Berlin at the end of 1840, but this controversy faded. The opponents on both sides became aware of their basic agreement on a deeper level. With his essay of 1845 on the monarchical principle, Stahl was able to convince even Ludwig von Gerlach that Haller's position was a limited one;[67] and from this point on, Stahl could be accepted as an ally and as a bold advocate of the Christian state against liberalism and revolution. However, he did not renounce the eclectic and receptive tendency he had had from the beginning. On the one hand, he clung fast to the idea of a transcendent, religious basis for state life and to the justification of the feudal monarchy on that basis. As a result he thought the "historical order" was also the "divine-human order," and he found the "supra-human ordinance" that should serve as the model for all the works of men evident in historically established law and in legitimate authority. In his view, liberalism was synonymous with religious aberration, a falling away from the principles of the Reformation that preached suprahuman ordinance as the primary and incontrovertible element, not just in the narrow sphere of religion but in all things, and that saw

[67] Stahl to Rotenhan, December 5, 1849, see *Histor. Vierteljahrsschrift*, XIV, 546; see Masur, "Aus Briefen J. G. Stahls," *Archiv f. Politik u. Gesch.* (1927), 295.

in human action only the secondary element, a vital appropriation, but not individual creation.[68] But since he was more gifted in the assimilation than in the creation of ideas himself, he wanted to learn from liberalism, too. He explicitly acknowledged as positive values the following liberal principles: "The rights of man, the independence of the nation, constitutional order, the spiritual power derived from a public recognition of the value of life."[69] He explicitly and sharply rejected Haller's doctrine that made the power of the state the private property of the prince and that dissolved the state into an aggregate of its hierarchically arranged governmental relationships. He proclaimed that the state was a higher ethical order, a primal totality that contained its own laws within itself. The state is "the nation formed into a personality."[70] To the extent that Stahl wanted to see the state upheld by the feelings of the people and to the extent that he gave the state itself the role of an agency devoted to the sustaining, ordering, and promoting of the social life of the nation, he undoubtedly had the image of a genuine national state in mind. It was, of course, a conservative national state, whose subjects developed into a political nation from mere subjection and whose government was based on legitimate historical foundations. But he was not unreceptive to the more modern idea that the nation in a broader sense—the cultural nation based on the unity of national consciousness, custom, and language—was not unimportant for forming states and defining their borders. "The nation in this sense," he says explicitly, "is the natural basis of the state." He consequently demands that the natural or historical nation be the main factor considered in making new divisions of countries as long as already existing legal claims do not prevent such division. Also, if a nation like the German nation is divided into regional states based on tribal groupings, it should "strive in turn toward a more inclusive unity of these states—the stronger the better—in which the common national consciousness finds expression and security." Here he makes a distinction between what is "natural" and what is "legal." The rights of a state are completely independent of the national composition of its subjects,[71] and the "ethos" of the state, that is, the legitimate government and the historically established constitution, also takes precedence over the nation, and the nation must obey it.[72]

---

[68] Stahl, *Philosophie des Rechtes*, II (2nd edn., 1846), pp. xvff. I have treated the quietistic consequences of these ideas in my essay mentioned on p. 186n., above.

[69] *Philosophie des Rechtes*, p. xiv.   [70] *Ibid.*, p. 109.

[71] *Ibid.*, p. 134.   [72] *Ibid.*, p. xvif.

Once again the glorified autonomy of the nation was driven back behind the barriers of traditional legitimate rights; and the desire for a more effective political unity for the German nation, a desire that threatens legitimate rights, was reduced to the level of a pious wish. But it was always expressed and acknowledged nonetheless, and thus formed an alien element in the conservative legalistic and authoritarian state.

New and prophetic ideas often appear as alien elements in the midst of old and traditional ones, and the crucial point then is to what extent these new ideas are able to assert and realize themselves among the old. Such a struggle took place in Stahl's political thinking when the events of 1848 put his ideas to a test. It became clear at that time that Stahl's thinking and actions were completely imbued with the idea of an internal nationalization of the historically developed individual state, and this was an idea peculiar to the conservative concept of the national state. To a great extent this idea was able to take the place of an attachment to the Prussian soil, an attachment that was lacking in Stahl; and, as we shall see in the second part of this study, he later defended the Prussian state personality against the waves of the German national movement that swept in on it as both a friendly and a hostile element. He was also prepared to effect a constitutional reform of the Prussian state itself. This reform would have rejected pure parliamentary government, the rule of the parliamentary majority; but it would have recognized a limitation of the monarchy by representatives of the people. As a result, an independent monarchy and the will of the people would have been jointly responsible for government. Thus, despite the fact that he wanted the conservative element of the population strongly represented in the two chambers that would in turn represent the will of the nation, Stahl's constitutional program as a whole was still an important step forward toward modern constitutionalism.[73]

Characteristic elements of the conservative idea of the national state are also evident in his position on German nationality. We are not ill-disposed toward the German cause, he declared,[74] but only

---

[73] *Die Revolution und die konstitutionelle Monarchie* (1848). Salzer, "Stahl und Rotenhan," *Histor. Vierteljahrsschrift*, XIV, 214, thinks that Stahl advocated this idea on principle even before the Revolution of 1848, in his 1845 essay on the monarchical principle. Stahl does align himself in this essay with the "newer feudal and therefore constitutional system," but, as Michniewicz, *Stahl und Bismarck* (1913), pp. 36ff. and 97, shows, he still has not come as far as the concessions of 1848 in essential points.

[74] *Die deutsche Reichsverfassung* (2nd edn., 1849), p. 49. Herbert Schmidt,

toward the revolutionary one. He thought the only proper unification of Germany would be one that retained the following genuine and glorious characteristics of the German nation: the observance of established legal claims, a thoroughly articulated social order divided into classes, the independence of small regional governments rather than false centralization, the bonds of personal loyalty between princes and their peoples, the preservation of the Christian faith as the core of public life. We should note here how the historical and Romantic idea of the national spirit is once again set up in opposition to the idea of popular sovereignty. Stahl was doing more than applying a clever strategy when he raised the question of whether the constitutional draft of the Frankfurt assembly had not denied the most profound elements of German nationality in favor of cosmopolitan ideals, for his question was also a statement that contained its share of the truth. In both camps, the conservative as well as the liberal, the national idea was enveloped by universalistic ideas. On the one side these ideas were of a religious and transcendent nature, on the other, of a rational and worldly one.

This universalistic impulse was not strong in Stahl's idea of the nation, but it was not altogether absent either. The assertion of religious principles in political life helped him, just as it had the politicians of the Berlin *Wochenblatt*, to keep the German national principle under control and to protect the historical rights of the existing individual states from its consequences. Another thing we have often observed before was also evident in Stahl: The introduction of nonpolitical ideas into politics dulled the clarity of political thinking in general and weakened the understanding of what was politically possible and viable. It particularly weakened political understanding in matters that required a fresh approach. Stahl acted with sovereign political tact on the familiar ground of the Prussian individual state, and he made good use of this tact in upholding individual state interests against the unitarian tendencies of the Frankfurt constitution. But he was stronger in his criticism than he was in suggesting other alternatives. The two major questions were the relationship of Prussia to Germany and the joint relationship of Prussia and Germany to Austria. He responded to these two questions with surprising uncertainty and with completely vacillating and untenable suggestions. Should Prussia be the leading power of Germany or

---

F. J. *Stahl und die deutsche Nationalstaatsidee* (1914), has in the meantime treated these questions in more detail than is possible here.

not? His answer was yes and no. His Prussian soul said yes; his non-political and German soul said no. He said of German leadership for Prussia as it was formulated in the Dreikönigsverfassung of May 26, 1849: "Such a leading position for one state is not really desirable as an ideal or as a sound arrangement for the entire German nation."[75] But, he added, it was inevitable. In this fashion he said yes and no to the exclusion of Austria from a closely unified German federal state. Such an exclusion would not be unfortunate, he thought, if a broad confederative relationship continued to be maintained between Germany and Austria as the Frankfurt parliament suggested. But, he added, if Austria declared herself willing to fulfill all the obligations of the new federal state, she could not be denied entrance to it; then, however, the other German princes would be in a position to insist on leadership for Prussia, and Austria could not legally object to this. We hardly need to point out in what an impossible and doctrinaire fashion questions of law and power were jumbled together here. Even more naïve still was Stahl's suggestion that if Austria were willing to enter the German federal state and recognize Prussian leadership, she could be allowed a certain influence in Germany and be granted, along with other rights, the right to share in manning the South German fortifications.[76] The source of political error lay here, as it did earlier with Stein and Humboldt, in the belief that the political unity of the German nation could be created without giving the nation the firm contours of an autonomous state personality. We see here once more the important practical consequences of the fact that the German nation first felt and created her unity primarily as a spiritual unity, and we must also note again that it was a unity shaped by universalistic ideas and that recourse to such ideas diminished awareness of the realities of power.

This fact also proved fatal to the German policies of Friedrich Wilhelm IV. This is not the place to investigate all the reasons we can find for the failure of his policies and to demonstrate the weaknesses of his character, the contradictions in his intentions, the difficulties of the Prusso-German problem, and the obstacles inherent in Prussia's relationship to Germany and Europe. We want to show here only the intellectual background from which his national ideal derived. This ideal clearly bears the stamp of his own mind in the way it fuses

[75] *Die deutsche Reichsverfassung*, p. 49. Salzer, *op.cit.*, has not refuted my view. See, too, Michniewicz, *op.cit.*, p. 141; and W. Oppermann, "Stahl," *Arch. f. öffentl. Recht*, XXXIV, 92.

[76] *Die deutsche Reichsverfassung*, pp. 86ff., 91.

different ingredients and permeates everything ideal and political with a rich, decorative fantasy. But nearly all those ingredients themselves can be traced back to the ideas and concepts that we have encountered from early Romanticism on. At the head of the list is the desire to renew the Holy Roman Empire of the German Nation in both its universal and national aspects. His often-expressed idea that Austria should restore and wear the crown of Charlemagne was much more than an attempt to appease Prussia's rival with the tokens of power and to secure the reality of power for Prussia herself. It would have been an idle notion to think that such a division of the appearance and reality of power could solve the German question. But Friedrich Wilhelm IV regarded the Holy Roman Empire as more than a mere mirage. He called it a "cloud structure," but he still considered it a "great reality."[77] Describing the first year of this government, Radowitz says that the king would have made any sacrifice to restore the Empire. He even considered the possibility that a great and victorious war could prepare the way for it. "His goal at this point was voluntary submission to the imperial crown of Austria, in which he would lead the way, and the creation of an imperial alliance with the concurrence of the Pope." To this he added "the idea of a great alliance of all the European states with the clear prearranged purpose of turning its collective strength against every unjust claim and every breach of the peace."[78] We remember that similar ideas could be found in Novalis, Friedrich Schlegel, and Adam Müller; and we can easily see that Friedrich Wilhelm IV's ideas on this were more dependent on the poets and writers of the beginning of the century than on the more practical and shrewder politicians of the *Wochenblatt* and of the Gerlach circle. It is highly possible, as Simson has suggested,[79] that his idea of giving the king of Prussia the highest position after that of the kaiser and of making him the "supreme field marshal" of Germany goes back to a notion that Görres once expressed in the *Rheinische Merkur*.[80]

[77] Leop. v. Gerlach, I, 272 (January 1849).
[78] From Radowitz' notes between September 1840 and September 1841. Hassel, *Radowitz*, I, 76.
[79] Simson, *Ed. v. Simson*, p. 172.
[80] Reprinted in Görres, *Polit. Schriften*, II, 146: "Austria is deserving of the imperial crown because of her power and her former achievements. . . . The entire German nation unanimously promises the second place after Austria to Prussia; and because that royal house has devoted itself to war from the beginning and takes pleasure in war, its king will be chosen as the German field marshal." Achim von Arnim, in the *Rheinische Merkur* of February 21, 1815, also wanted to

But it is not necessary to seize on individual borrowings and influences here because the whole aura of his ideas on Germany is reminiscent of that profoundly unsettled period of national disaster and national resistance, and because he himself more than amply testifies that this period ignited the flame of German sentiment in him. He is seldom so human and, even in his excess, seldom more genuine than when he tells how his own suffering mother had instilled in him the love of Germany, how the same love that bound him to the name of this incomparable woman also bound him to Germany, and how during the past fifty years the word Germany had always filled him with waves of inspiration.[81] As far as his German ideals were concerned, he remained throughout his life the same adolescent he had been when he first seized on these ideals. He was an eternal adolescent in a good, as well as in the most unfortunate, sense, and he always lived in a mood between dream and wakefulness and in the sweet illusions of his youth. Since older and more mature men than he had succumbed to similar illusions in that past era of teeming intellectual impulses with its excess of nonpolitical political ideals, it is not surprising that the Freiherr vom Stein as well as Novalis, Friedrich Schlegel, and Görres came to life again in the German policy of Friedrich Wilhelm IV. The fact that two such fundamentally different men as Stein and Friedrich Wilhelm IV could share the same momentous errors testifies to the power of the common intellectual atmosphere that surrounded them. Let us examine these errors once again by studying their influence on these two eminent figures, one of whom fell victim to these errors at the beginning of their history, the other at the end.

The king and Freiherr vom Stein before him both shared the universalistic and idealistic view that the European states should and could form a firm community to oppose any powers that endangered peace and law. The basis of this idea was a deep mistrust of France that derived in Stein from both national and antirevolutionary feelings. The two men also shared, above all, the idea of renewing the old Empire; and even though this idea took an ethical form for one and a poetic form for the other, the fundamental historical view involved is still common to both. They were both imbued with the idea of the thousand-year continuity of German national life; they were

make the king of Prussia the imperial field marshal. Herma Becker, *A. von Arnim in den wissenschaftl. und polit. Strömungen seiner Zeit*, p. 80.

[81] To Bunsen, April 7, 1849, in Ranke, *Aus dem Briefwechsel Friedrich Wilhelms IV. mit Bunsen*, p. 217 (*Sämtl. Werke*, XLIX-L, 519). To Dahlmann, May 15, 1848, in Springer, *Dahlmann*, II, 247.

also convinced that it was essential to restore this damaged continuity and, as far as possible, to renew ties with the greatest period of Germany's past, or at least with what they considered to be its greatest period—the era of medieval imperial glory. They both invoked this period at moments that stimulated their German sentiments to the full: Stein in his memorial of September 18, 1812 and Friedrich Wilhelm IV when he prepared his reply to the Frankfurt deputation that had offered him the German crown. The king referred explicitly to the "thousand years of sanctified tradition and law" that provided the only valid basis for the election of a kaiser. "The expression 'a thousand years' is too apocalyptic for you," he said to his more prosaically inclined listeners, "but it is literally true."[82]

Still another idea shared by the two men was that historical law should be invoked to decide which of the two major German powers was entitled to the imperial crown. They both chose Austria, although they both should have chosen Prussia according to their inner commitment. This is easier to understand in the case of Stein, who had owed allegiance only to the Empire, than it is in the case of a Hohenzollern prince. But this stifling of Prussian ambition is perhaps comprehensible if we remember that Stein did not consider the Roman imperial crown that was to be restored an exclusively national crown. Instead, he saw it as a universal one that he, if no one else, conceived of as the nucleus of his envisioned European alliance of states. We will recall that Stein also had still another reason besides a historic-Romantic one for entrusting the imperial crown to Austria, and that was the need to bind Austria firmly to Germany because her interests were tending to lead her away from Germany. We find exactly the same line of thought in Friedrich Wilhelm IV. At the beginning of his reign he told his confidant, Josef von Radowitz,[83] when he revealed his imperial dreams to him: "We must force Austria to be German." Thus, he disregarded the reality of Austria's un-German policy in the belief that the egoistical interests of the individual state could be overcome by great ideas that could bind states together —ideas, in this case, that had both national and universalistic aspects. With this in mind, we can understand the remarkable contradictions in the reform program for the Confederation that Radowitz, following these same principles, put forward on November 20, 1847. On the one hand, Radowitz took cognizance of the unhappy fact

[82] Leop. v. Gerlach, I, 309; Poschinger, *Unter Friedrich Wilhelm IV.*, I, 89.
[83] Hassel, *op.cit.*, I, 76 and 311; see, too, my book *Radowitz und die deutsche Revolution*, pp. 53, 87.

that Austria was not deeply involved enough in specifically German problems, successes, and failures to commit herself completely to the German cause. Yet the author and, more important, the commissioner of the reform program did not give up the illusion that Austria, Prussia, and Germany could and must form a vital, national totality.[84] We know from Stein's case that this illusion arose not only from intellectual sources but also from realistic ones in his political experiences during the struggle for liberation in 1813. We can say in general, then, that Friedrich Wilhelm IV's German policy of reform for the Confederation, to the extent that it originated in his own thinking, was a late postlude to Stein's national policy and to the national policy of the era of the Wars of Liberation as a whole, a policy that had been magnanimous but that had sought to attain the impossible. This policy was also a prelude to the era of Bismarck in that it already contained the seeds of a hegemonic Prusso-German ambition, but these beginnings were overshadowed and quashed by a religious ethos in the concept of the state, an ethos that was binding for the king and his Christian-Germanic circle even in matters of practical politics. Prussian ambition and German national desires had to give way to the universal idea of Christian sovereignty. In his *Neue Gespräche*, the epilogue to the events of 1848-50, Radowitz has the king say: "I regard the task of creating a true community as a just desire of the nation and as a true mission for Prussia. But higher than this task, higher than everything for me, is the divine commandment that I shall not desire what does not belong to me. . . . The unification of the nation means more to me than I can say. It has been one of my fondest hopes ever since I could think and feel, but my obligations as a Christian king mean even more to me. These two things lie as far apart as heaven and earth. They are not mere maxims but commandments. Here I stand. I cannot do otherwise."[85]

An example of the practical results of the king's German policy in the months preceding the disaster of Olmütz will show once again what false directions political thinking could take if it had destroyed a sense of state and national autonomy in order to promote ideas of a universal, ethico-political community of states. In the spring of 1850 it was evident in Berlin that there was a serious possibility of armed conflict with Austria, which had just unilaterally reconvened the Bundestag. Radowitz pointed this out in the cabinet meeting of April 21, 1850. He demanded that Prussia enter a protest against Austria's

---

[84] Radowitz, *Deutschland und Friedrich Wilhelm IV.*, pp. 44, 50, 56.
[85] I, 206 (1851).

action, but he immediately added: "A congress of the participants and guarantors of the Treaty of Vienna, consulting with the German governments, can, however, obviate the danger of a breach by force of arms. Prussia could, without damage to her honor, comply more readily with the demands of such a congress than with the dictatorial demands of Austria or with the decisions of a Bundestag whose majority is dependent on Austria." In the cabinet meeting of May 7 the king agreed with this view. If Prussia follows this course of action, he said, and calls on the major European powers as arbitrators, she will "have given unequivocal proof that she will not shrink from any sacrifice to preserve the peace. She will stand as the messenger of peace in the face of Austria's militant threats."[86]

Thus, the expedient of allowing foreign powers to deliberate and decide the fate of Prussia and Germany was considered compatible with honor.

Our task here is not to censure but to understand. If we remember that even the proud Stein did not consider it reprehensible to submit the national constitution of Germany to the guarantee of foreign powers, if we call to mind once again the entire context in which these ideas emerged, if, in short, we do what we must do as observers and form our judgments on a general historical basis and not on a national one, then we see at work here a tragic fate whose causes are obscure and complex. But finally the time came for the captive limbs of the state and the nation to be freed from their shackles. We shall now examine the intellectual currents that prepared the way for this liberation.

[86] Protocols of the cabinet meetings in the Kgl. Hausarchiv. Radowitz alludes to this in his *Schriften*, II, 249f.; see my book *Radowitz und die deutsche Revolution*, pp. 342f., 417f., 429ff., 461. The king did, however, want to set certain limits to the European guarantee of the Confederation as far as the foreign powers were concerned. This is evident in his attitude toward the end of 1850, when England was on the verge of protesting against the entry of Austria and Prussia into the Confederation with all their territories. Poschinger, *Preussens auswärtige Politik 1850-58*, I, 47; Leop. v. Gerlach, I, 572.

11

HEGEL

The liberation of political thinking from nonpolitical, universalistic ideas was no more the work of individuals than its preceding subjection to these ideas had been. In both cases there were general transformations of thought and feeling in Germany, transformations so varied that the most extensive historical account cannot exhaust their richness and substance. The problem we are dealing with is only one part of the general and infinitely complex problem of the development of the modern mind and particularly of the transition from conjectural to empirical thinking, from ideal and speculative to realistic thinking. The reasons for these transformations derive from innumerable sources, but these tendencies received their strongest expression only when great personalities drew them together and made them their own. From this point of view, Hegel, Ranke, and Bismarck are the three great liberators of the state.

It may seem farfetched to name Hegel, the imposing thinker who systematized and perfected the idealistic and speculative movement, in the same breath with two great empiricists. But it was Hegel's accomplishment to unify opposing elements, to put forward a synthesis of all the ideas that affected his time, a synthesis that lasted as a unified structure as long as it was in his powerful grip but that fell apart again immediately after him. But the fact that the most varied elements were brought together under one roof in his thinking and that they were obliged to get along with each other there had, we might say, important pedagogical consequences for the future. Conservatives, liberals, and radicals, historical and doctrinaire thinkers, national and cosmopolitan thinkers could all learn from his system, exploit it for their own special purposes, and yet still retain tenuous links with those elements of it that they had rejected in this process. Then, at a later time, these links could help them find their way back to those same elements they had originally put aside or perhaps even opposed. Hegel's ideas continued to bear fruit no matter what soil they fell on. His theory of the state in particular was able to reach

197

out in the most contradictory directions and distribute everywhere some of the permanently valid truths that it contained. He stands in the foremost ranks of the great thinkers of the nineteenth century who promulgated a favorable attitude toward the state and a conviction of its necessity, greatness, and ethical dignity.

We shall focus our attention here only on those features of his political theory that are relevant to our particular problem. We feel immediately caught up again in the familiar atmosphere of Romanticism when we hear that the state is individuality, an individual totality.[1] No aspect of it can be singled out and considered in isolation. The constitution of a nation is closely bound up with its religion, art, and philosophy. These things and all the external factors such as climate, neighbors, position in the world, and so forth combine to make one substance of it, one spirit. This spiritual substance is essentially the national spirit. Here Hegel is in agreement with the historical school of jurisprudence: everything in the state arises from this national spirit.[2] But Hegel's version of the national spirit is not identical with that of Savigny or of the Romantics; it is only related to it. Hegel draws the national spirit out of the mysterious darkness of the unconscious into the bright light of his panlogism. It is not regarded as the mother of life, who is to be loved with respect, but as a wife who is expected to bear heirs to the king. The national spirit is thus rationalized inasmuch as it is seen merely as a means to an end, "a transitional stage on the way toward the state."[3] He considers state and nation so closely related to each other that the essential purpose in the existence of a nation is to be a state, and a nation that has not achieved the form of a state has no

[1] On Hegel's relationship to Romanticism, see Brie's essay, cited above in Chap. 9, note 26. See, too, Landsberg's treatment, *Gesch. der deutschen Rechtswissenschaft*, Abt. 3, 2. Halbband, pp. 347f., which correctly brings out the factors that separate Hegel from Romanticism.

[2] *Philosophie der Geschichte*, in *Werke*, IX, 44 and 50; *Enzyklopädie der philosophischen Wissenschaften*, § 540 (3rd edn.), p. 535.

[3] This is Landsberg's view, *op.cit.* Loening's view, *Internat. Wochenschr.* (1910), p. 84, that Hegel's national spirit as such is the state goes somewhat too far and puts a one-sided emphasis on one particular statement of Hegel's. On the finer ramifications of the Hegelian concept of the national spirit, see Kantorowicz, *Histor. Zeitschrift*, CVIII, 316ff. On its development, see primarily Rosenzweig, *Hegel und der Staat*, I, 21ff., 166f., and 223ff.; II, 180ff. Both Rosenzweig and Heller, *Hegel und der nationale Machtstaatsgedanke*, have closely examined the genesis and development of the Hegelian idea of the power state, a study that was not possible within the framework of my book. However, I cannot agree with Heller in all his views.

real history.[4] He certainly does not mean by this that every nation
must create a centralized national state if it is to have a history.
He means rather, in adherence to what we have called the conservative idea of the national state, that state life should emerge from the
national spirit and should be in conformance with it. But in his view
of the state—and here we are following only the historical aspect
of his thought—he puts aside all the schematizing and manipulating of the Enlightenment and all its desire for improvement by artificial means, and he emphatically asserts the singularity and uniqueness of every political system. "The state is not a work of art. It exists
in the world and therefore in the sphere of arbitrary power, of
chance, and of error. Evil behavior can disfigure it in many ways.
But the ugliest of men, the criminal, the ill, the crippled, are all still
living men. The affirmative factor, life, endures despite the failings,
and this affirmative factor is our concern here."[5] It is the national
principle, we may conclude, that gives the state this individual, pul-
sating life, whether that life be good or bad. This is not the national
principle as the French Revolution understood it. In Hegel's view, the
nation of the democratic ideal is only an aggregate of private individuals, only a *vulgus*, not a *populus*, and as a *vulgus* it is only a
crude, blind force.[6] Hegel understands the national principle historically in that the intellectual legacy of the entire past of a nation
constitutes a living force together with the nation's present and future
demands. Hegel thus concedes to the state the right of absolute autonomy and the right to assert its interests internationally so that it
can claim its position in the world. "As a single individual it opposes other individuals of the same type."[7] There is no praetor who
arbitrates and decides what is right in the affairs of states. There are
only independent powers that oppose other independent powers.
Thus, a major representative of German philosophy finally gave war
an unqualified and definitive sanction, and war received its place in
a world view that, more than any other before it, sought to grasp
the rational order of the world. Kant's idea of an eternal peace created by a confederation of states that would settle every dispute
struck Hegel as nothing more than a dream, for how could a permanent harmony of states be possible when a particular sovereign will

---

[4] *Enzyklopädie*, § 549; *Philosophie des Rechts*, §§ 349-352, in *Werke*, VIII,
434f.

[5] *Philosophie des Rechts*, § 258, in *Werke*, VIII, 320.

[6] *Enzyklopädie*, § 544.

[7] *Ibid.*, § 545; *Philosophie des Rechts*, § 330, in *Werke*, VIII, 424.

was present in every state?[8] His judgment on unions of states like the Holy Alliance was as follows: "They are always by nature relative and limited, just like any eternal peace."[9] He realized and also emphasized that there was a sense of familial community among nations, particularly in Europe, that had influenced their relationships with each other and lessened the animosity in their conflicts of interests. But we must also realize that in Hegel's view this mitigation of power struggles does not represent a restriction of autonomous power politics for the individual state personalities. It is instead a natural outgrowth of the European cultural community, of "its legislative principles, its customs, and its culture."[10] This mitigation is not forced on the states from outside and by an authority that stands above them. It grows instead from their own inner life and from their natural intellectual and ethical kinship. It too, then, is essentially autonomous in origin, not heteronomous.

Thus, a genuine empirical mind and keen historico-political insight are evident in Hegel's ideas on the relationship of states to one another. Perhaps one of the most important features of his philosophy is that, despite its basically rationalistic and speculative character, it is still so tolerant and aware of empirical forces that are by no means always rational. "The particular characters of states make themselves felt in their relationships to each other, and in these relationships the highly varied play of characteristic passions, interests, goals, talents, virtues, violence, injustice, and vices as well as external coincidence assumes its greatest dimensions."[11] This did not shake his belief that all things must ultimately serve the realization of a rational order. In accordance with rigorous principles, his philosophy of history tries to demonstrate in world history itself the stages in the development of the world spirit, to transform all of reality into spirit, and to transform the course of reality into the movement of thought itself. He built a massive structure of thought arching above the historical world, and the question immediately arises of whether he did not do history a disservice by this, whether he did not in the end violate the unique character of historical life that he seemed to have acknowledged so clearly. This raises for us the question of whether the old universalistic tendency did not appear in his view of the nation and state also, and once again obscure pure empirical insights. The answer is, of course, that this is precisely what happened.

[8] *Philosophie des Rechts*, § 333, in *Werke*, VIII, 427.
[9] *Ibid.*, § 259, in *Werke*, VIII, 321.   [10] *Ibid.*, § 339, in *Werke*, VIII, 430.
[11] *Ibid.*, § 340, in *Werke*, VIII, 430.

A major idea from the period when both cosmopolitan and national ideas came together is still alive in Hegel and takes on a new and unusual form in his philosophy of history. This is the idea of the representative nation of humanity. He did not think, as Fichte, Schiller, and, to a certain extent, Humboldt and the early Romantics had, that the German nation as such was the representative and universal nation of all mankind. His view was that there is in every epoch of world history a "nation of world historical consequence" that acts as the bearer of the universal spirit in its current stage of development. This nation, he thought, should therefore receive absolute privileges, against which the spirits of other nations had no claim. The nation of world historical consequence would also be the dominant nation of the world.[12] He was not thinking here of the actual rights of nations or of the practical matter of ruling the world. He saw the different nations gathered before the forum of the absolute world spirit; and, from this point of view, he distributed grants of ideal rights and dominance. But to the historical sensibility, such a classification and evaluation of nations will seem rigid and unacceptable. For even though all nations are not of equal value in the eyes of the historian, he still recognizes in every highly developed nation something of unique and irreplaceable historical value, because every substantial historical individuality is irreplaceable. Hegel's view led inevitably to depriving all historical individualities of their proper rights and making them mere unconscious instruments and functionaries of the world spirit.

It was this aspect of Hegel that repelled Ranke. According to this view, Ranke once said, all men were mere shadows or phantoms imbued with idea; and the successive epochs and generations of mankind were mediatized by this, as it were, and had no meaning in themselves. "But I claim that every epoch is in direct contact with God, and its value is not based on what emerges from it but is found in its own existence, in its own being."[13]

This applied to the "being" of the state and of the nation, too. Hegel, with the remarkable duplicity that permeates his entire philosophy, had both recognized and denied this being, giving it all possible freedom in the sphere of conscious reality only to limit it again in the

---

[12] *Ibid.*, § 347, in *Werke*, VIII, 433; *Enzyklopädie*, § 550; *Vernunft in der Geschichte*, p. 47. Heller, *Hegel und der nationale Machtstaatsgedanke*, p. 130, incorrectly denies the universalistic feature in this theory and says with oversimplification that "the world spirit in Hegel is nothing but a term for the ethical justification of nationalistic world power." The only point that I can grant him is that Hegel's universalism does not "further international friendship."

[13] *Über die Epochen der neueren Geschichte*, pp. 5 and 7.

most rigorous way in the higher sphere of the absolute. The state and the historical world as a whole led a double existence of apparent freedom in the realm of reality and of actual servitude in the realm of the spirit. It was a great advance over Fichte that Hegel did not tear the historical world in two as Fichte had done, and that he removed existence in the rational order to the transcendent sphere rather than wanting, as Fichte had, to realize it on earth. This relieved some of the pressure that reality had had to bear from ideas; and because of this, reality could enjoy greater freedom. But this freedom was a precarious affair in Hegel, only a concession that the philosopher condescendingly made to the world of experience. He much preferred to linger in the world of the transcendent, and he tried to force his contemporaries to judge actual historical life from this point of view, to see it with his eyes. We feel a cutting irony when he describes how states, nations, and individuals live aimlessly, deeply absorbed by their interests, but are in reality only instruments of that "inmost activity in which these figures pass away but in which spirit as such prepares and achieves the transition to its next higher level."[14] Whoever surrendered completely to the spirit of Hegel's theory always stood in danger of transforming actual life in this world into a phantasmagoria—stood in danger, too, in terms of our basic theme here, of forcefully and prematurely imposing the universal element onto the life of the state and nation. For it was universalism in its most extreme form that motivated Hegel and let the world spirit advance by means of its unconsciously functioning instruments. Thus, this aspect of his theory is still closely connected with the tendencies we have been tracing.

It was not necessary to completely dispense with the universalistic principles that had previously limited historical life in order to reestablish its full autonomy. All that was needed was to draw new and more accurate borders between the two spheres and to span the curve of universal ideas high and wide enough so that history could lead its full and undisturbed life beneath them. Hegel's attempt to do this was imposing and profound, but it was still not completely successful. As the example of Ranke will show, it was possible to go still further in recognizing the proper claims of historical individualities; it was possible to embrace them more warmly, yet at the same time to direct the spiritual vision upwards to the eternal constellations.

[14] *Philosophie des Rechts*, § 344, in *Werke*, VIII, 432.

12

RANKE AND BISMARCK

THE "NATION" BELONGS to the basic concepts that Ranke's overall view of history employs, concepts that are so remarkably fruitful because he never demands too much of them, never misuses them for an overly simple classification of historical material, and because he knows that they have no absolutely clear limits of application. When he uses them, he always hints at their origins, which keep blending continually into the infinite. Only a talent as unusual as his, only a mode of thinking simultaneously empirical, philosophical, and artistic could dispense with sharp, clear limits and firm categories without becoming blurred and unclear. A study undertaken with ordinary scholarly means cannot do without them and must make use of such concepts as "cultural nation," "political nation," "liberal idea of the national state," "conservative idea of the national state," and so forth—concepts that Ranke would probably never have used, although his historical writings lead to them often enough and are rich in observations that can easily be fitted into such categories.

It would be to go beyond the scope of this study to examine the national idea in his entire historical work. We shall instead single out one phase in his development when, as a historian and political thinker, he influenced the evolution of the idea of the nation and of the national state in Germany in a significant and, I believe, an epoch-making way. He accomplished this with his essays in the *Historisch-politische Zeitschrift*. The most important of these essays are "Frankreich und Deutschland" (1832), "Über die Trennung und die Einheit von Deutschland" (1832), "Die Grossen Mächte" (1833), and "Politisches Gespräch" (1836).[1]

[1] With the exception of "Die Grossen Mächte," which appears in Vol. XXIV of Ranke's *Sämtliche Werke* (and also now, with my introduction, in the *Inselbücherei*), these essays are all reprinted in Vols. XLIX-L of the *Werke*. Since the appearance of the first edition of my book, they have been examined from a different point of view in Otto Diether's perceptive book, *Leop. v. Ranke als Politiker* (1911). Where I deal with a problem in the history of ideas, he makes a psychological inquiry into the "relationship of the pure historian to practical politics"

What he says here about the relationship of nationality to the state and about his own inner relationship to these two forces radiates a genuine originality and a profound sensibility; and even if we were to discount these qualities, his use of language alone would still create an inimitable aura. Yet if we listen carefully, we hear echoes of almost all the voices we have heard earlier. Sometimes we think we hear Humboldt speaking, sometimes Fichte[2] or even Schiller, sometimes the Romantics, from Novalis to Adam Müller and Savigny; and there is even some affinity with the ideas of the *Berliner Politische Wochenblatt*, the extreme feudal counterweight to the historico-political disinterestedness of Ranke's magazine.[3] These influences cannot be traced by the usual literary means and by comparison with sources; and even if they are so traced, the results are still problematic. Passages in Ranke that are reminiscent of his predecessors are not necessarily drawn directly from them. They represent only the finest quintessence of the entire development of thought over the previous four decades transformed into a highly personal view. These intellectual developments were more important for Ranke than the great national experiences in the period of the Wars of Liberation, for these events did not affect his thinking in a direct and powerful way. But filtered through the medium of contemplation, they too could communicate their inner meaning to him.[4]

The earliest elements of his own national sensibility do not stem

---

and also arrives in this way at results in the area of the history of ideas. According to his views, Ranke, as an autonomous, disinterested, and fundamentally non-political (!) thinker, belongs more to the world of the eighteenth century than to the nineteenth. I have dealt with this view, which has a core of truth to it but is greatly exaggerated, in the *Histor. Zeitschrift*, CXI, 582ff. (reprinted in *Preussen und Deutschland im 19. und 20. Jahrhundert*), and I am using essentially the same text of my first edition here again because it takes into account those facts in my study on which Diether bases his argument.—Gasparian, *Der Begriff der Nation in der deutschen Geschichtschreibung des 19. Jahrhunderts* (1917), has recently treated Ranke's conception of the nation well but without any original points of view.

[2] We know that Ranke later remarked on the strong impression that Fichte's popular writings made on him in his youth. *Sämtl. Werke*, LIII-LIV, 59. There is literature on Fichte's influence on Ranke in Varrentrapp, *Christl. Welt* (1905), No. 23, and in *Histor. Zeitschrift*, IC, 50n. Also, cf. Fröhlich, *Fichtes Reden an die deutsche Nation*, p. 78, note 1.

[3] It is not at all unlikely that the members of the *Wochenblatt* party who were well disposed toward the idea of nationality (see pp. 176ff., above) learned in turn from Ranke's essays.

[4] "His intellectual destiny brought before him the greatest experience imaginable —and we are tempted to say it did so intentionally—so that he could regard it with the greatest objectivity possible." Dove, *Ausgewählte Schriftchen*, p. 153.

from these events but from the period preceding them, when the German nation suddenly felt itself to be a great cultural nation once more because of its new literature. German literature, Ranke says[5] with the authority of personal experience, "became one of the most important factors of our unity. Through it we first became aware of this unity again. German literature forms the atmosphere in which our childhood arises, our youth draws breath. It animates all the veins of our existence with a characteristic breath of life. Not one German, we must admit, would be what he is without it." Ranke's German national feeling was first and foremost of an intellectual, not political, nature. It was a feeling of inspiration, a feeling of being totally permeated and carried along, a feeling—as Ludwig von Gerlach would have skeptically called it—of a pantheistic relationship between his spirit and the spirit of the nation. "Our fatherland is with us, in us," his "Politisches Gespräch" claims. "Germany lives in us. We enact it, whether we choose to do so or not, in every country we enter, in every zone. We stand upon it from the very beginning and cannot escape it. This mysterious something that informs the lowest among us as well as the highest—this spiritual air that we breathe—precedes any form of government and animates and permeates all its forms." The subjective element seems to be completely extinguished here, the element of the conscious will that usually has an important role elsewhere in the rise of modern national consciousness. The principle is not: Whoever wants to be a nation is a nation. It is just the opposite: A nation simply *is*, whether the individuals of which it is composed want to belong to that nation or not. A nation is not based on self-determination but on predetermination.

Here we see mirrored once again in a brilliant mind that earlier stage in the development of a nation when unconscious, instinctive, rationally inexplicable processes dominate it, creating and maintaining its unity and character. If we take away the refinements that Ranke's language and thought added to this conception, we have the same view of the character of nationality as that which formed the basis of the conservative idea of the national state for some members of the *Wochenblatt* group. Nationality is a dark, impenetrable womb, a mysterious something, a force arising from hidden sources that is incorporeal itself but that creates and permeates the corporeal. The richness of personal and individual being arises from it; but, for our eyes at

[5] "Trennung und Einheit," p. 160.

least, it remains in the sphere of the impersonal. Ranke thought that
every attempt to define the limits of nationality was a restriction and
trivialization of the infinite. "Who can name it and who can profess
it?" he said, almost in those words, to whoever tried "to raise the
flag of an intellectually conceived Germanness." "Who would ever
want to capture in concepts or words what 'German' means? Who
would want to call it by name—that genius of our past and future
epochs? Such a name could only be another phantom that would lead
us in false directions."[6] One who rejected such trivial worship of the
Germanic in this way would also have to reject the attempt of the
Wochenblatt politicians to present the feudal-patrimonial state as the
flowering of the German spirit and as the Christian-Germanic state as
such. The entire tendency of his journal was against these men.[7] Unlike them, he had not conceived of the nation in a purely intellectual
and bodiless form for purposes of idealizing the crude material existence of agrarian-feudal institutions. He had not ascribed such an infinite—we might even say such a universal—character to the spirit of
the nation only to draw such a narrow conclusion. A slight but clear
trace of the spiritual universalism that filled Humboldt, Fichte,
Schiller, and the early Romantics still hovers over Ranke's concept
of the nation. What else is the nation here but a modification of human
existence as such, conceived of as both hidden and revealed? "In the
different nations, God gave expression to the idea of human nature."[8] Does Ranke not intentionally define the essence of the nation with words that could also be applied to God in the form of the
world spirit? But the name here is not the important thing. For a
man imbued with this idea of nationality, nationality was not a burden that confined him to the soil of a limited national existence.
It was a pinion that bore him to heights from which he could look
down upon his own national soil with grateful affection yet also look
up with awe at the incomprehensible, infinite forces of the universe.
There is a special evocative quality in this concept of the nation. As
we noted before, not only the epoch of the early vegetative development of nations is echoed here, but, as we have just seen, the universalistic epoch of the German national idea is also present. Thus,
Ranke himself showed an unusual instinctive awareness of historical
developments by responding to his times as he did; for, as we remarked earlier,[9] the rise of this very universalistic epoch and its

---

[6] *Ibid.*, p. 172.   [7] Cf. Varrentrapp, *op.cit.*, pp. 35ff.
[8] "Frankreich und Deutschland," p. 72.
[9] See pp. 27f., above.

national literary movement showed again the role of the unconscious, vegetative element in the development of nations. Ranke was also keenly aware of how different national development in Germany was from that in France where conscious will and rational intention dominated. Our countries, he says, are fundamentally different. They have completely different needs and represent completely different points of view. "The complete reorientation of property and law, the creation of a new nation and a new existence, the total renunciation of the past—all these things that have taken place in France have not taken place with us."[10] The contrast between German and French national development is drawn too sharply here, because the "new nation" of the French after 1789 was much more closely attached to the old nation of the *ancien régime* than these words give us to believe. This kind of judgment is rare in Ranke's historical thinking; in this instance he let his German feelings carry him too far. But his German feelings here were also personal feelings. The way in which the German spirit had developed was extremely sympathetic and congenial to him. It had grown from quiet social and political circumstances; rising simultaneously to a state of national consciousness and to the heights of human ideals.

We know how close Ranke's ties with Germany's literary epoch of Classicism and Romanticism were, and we know that the great universalistic aspect of his historical writing derived from it. We often hear the quite correct assertion that he united an awareness of the national element in history with the universalistic historical legacy of the eighteenth century; but if we remember that this awareness of the national had already come alive in the universalistic epoch itself with Herder, Humboldt, and the early Romantics, and that a clear separation of the two tendencies was impossible, then we shall be able to say of Ranke in similar fashion that his own German national feelings and his awareness of the universal existed side by side. But unlike Humboldt, Fichte, Schiller, and Novalis, he did not elevate the German nation as such to a universal, spiritual nation representative of all mankind. His consciousness and the consciousness of his time were too realistic and concrete for that. Too much had happened to shatter faith in this idealistic—but, in the long run, too ethereal—mission for the German nation. Novalis' definition of the German character as cosmopolitanism mixed with the strongest individualism could not have satisfied Ranke; but both in

[10] "Frankreich und Deutschland," pp. 62f.

his scholarly considerations and in expressing his own national sensibility, Ranke used Novalis' other statement that everything national, local, and individual could be universalized and that the common must be given a higher meaning, the known the dignity of the unknown, and the finite the appearance of the infinite. Novalis called this procedure "romanticizing" and, in the course of applying it, allowed the infinite and the universal to eclipse and obscure the finite and the national. It is characteristic of the great change in the intellectual climate that Ranke did not "romanticize" but gave reality its due. He did justice, however, not only to the reality that served particular political interests, as the *Wochenblatt* group had done, but to everything that was animated by the breath of German nationality. Pantheistic as his view of the German national spirit may seem, his pantheism is by no means mystic and purely emotional but is instead a realistic, worldly pantheism that moves directly from the realm of feeling to that of facts. Speaking of the German genius, he wrote very accurately that "we can easily see that the emotions alone accomplish nothing. As with other fermenting agents, they are there to spiritualize matter, to act on its ingredients and bring them to life. If the emotions are isolated and left to themselves they have no value, and are more a deadening and harmful influence than a vitalizing one."[11]

Because he always saw the actual and the spiritual as united and never as separated from each other, he was able to define both the relationship between nationality and state and what we have called the conservative idea of the national state more clearly and profoundly than the biased politicians of the *Wochenblatt* could. We shall turn now to his justification and glorification of the German individual state.

Like the politicians of the *Wochenblatt*, he renounced the idea of a strict political unity for Germany. In this we see the persistent strength of earlier views that did not find any value in political unity for the German nation because, emerging during the decay of the old Empire, they had never known such a value. "Fortunately, the Empire was not the nation," Ranke says of this period;[12] and his remark reminds us of Schiller's comment: "The German Empire and the German nation are two different things." But these two thinkers, separated by a generation, differ in a remarkable and instructive way in the consequences they draw from this idea. Schiller goes on to say: "The majesty of the German never rested on the

[11] "Trennung und Einheit," pp. 134f.
[12] "Frankreich und Deutschland," p. 65.

head of his prince. The German has founded his own value apart
from politics." But Ranke continues: "The vital forces of the nation had long since withdrawn from the Empire. They consolidated
themselves in the new principalities." Schiller consoled himself
with what he thought to be the indestructible ideal of the representative nation of all mankind. Ranke found comfort in the contemplation
of what he saw as the indestructible political energy of the nation
that, after the collapse of a tottering, unviable unity, seized on the
German individual state, regenerated it, and nationalized it. "What
would have become of our states if they had not drawn new life
from the national principle on which they were founded?"[13] The significance of nationality for the state was finally made clear to the general consciousness once again.

But is this nationality that is supposedly so indispensable for the
state simply the nationality common to all Germans? Is it capable of
permeating the individual state only to the extent that it permeated
Goethe's *Faust* or the Kantian philosophy? In short, is Ranke merely
applying the doctrine of the national spirit that the historical school
of jurisprudence had developed, a doctrine by which the national
spirit, invisible and uncompromising, reveals itself in many visible
individual forms, intellectual as well as political and social? Without a doubt, this is sometimes Ranke's view, and in it we clearly see
the influence of pantheism at work. Just as the nation is for him
a manifestation of human existence, so the state, he says explicitly,
is also a manifestation not only of human existence but especially
of national existence, for the state is by nature much more closely
unified than the nation.[14] He does not deny that nations tend to form
centralized national states—and this view demonstrates once again
his broader historical insight compared with the *Wochenblatt* group
—but he did not find this tendency fully realized anywhere, not even
in France and England; and he did not see it as a very strong or
promising tendency, particularly in the German nation. In his opinion, the great political task of the German nation was rather to
develop the German individual state further in as fundamentally
German a fashion—and with as little influence from foreign patterns
and theories—as possible. "We have our own great German task to
accomplish: We must develop the genuinely German state in accordance with the genius of the nation."[15] The foreign patterns to be
avoided were parliamentary government and the doctrine of popular

[13] "Die Grossen Mächte," p. 39.   [14] "Polit. Gespräch," p. 326.
[15] "Frankreich und Deutschland," p. 71.

sovereignty. He objected to the liberal idea of the national state
to the extent that this idea sought its authority in a doctrine of supposedly general validity. But unlike the politicians of the *Wochenblatt*, he did not have on hand another universal constitutional doctrine that found absolute, generally applicable values in the feudal
system. His view was that even the genuine German state could
assume a multitude of forms. He thought that the German states, like
the children of one mother, would be similar in many respects quite
of their own accord, but that it was impossible to give all German
states the same constitution.[16] In each of them, a particular principle
is at work that seeks out its own particular form.

But at this point the originally unified nationality from which these
states emerge becomes manifold. The national basis on which Ranke
wants to build the German individual state is not just the German
national spirit as such. For him, the entire German cultural nation
divides itself, in an almost imperceptible way, into as many political
nations as there are vital and independent individual states. There
are statements of his in which he must have had the cultural nation as much in mind as the political. We find, for example: "We can
only meet the threat of dominance from another nation by developing our own nationality. I do not mean an imaginary, chimerical one
but the actual, extant nationality that finds expression in the state."[17]
At another point, referring to Prussian reform legislation, he has only
the political nation in mind: "This legislation was based on the legal
will of the prince who was solely concerned with the interests of the
whole and of the nation."[18] Ranke's essay entitled "Politisches Gespräch" probably offers more of both theory and personal views than
any other of his works. Here for the first time and with startling
lucidity occurs the image of the cultural nation, that "mysterious
power" that precedes every constitution and permeates all its forms.
The state emanates out of these obscure depths. But the emanation
of the state is a different thing from the emanation of individuals
from the heart of nationality. In the latter case, as we saw, desire
or lack of desire was of no consequence. Predetermination, not self-
determination, held sway here. But in the genesis of the state, both
are involved from the very beginning: "Circumstances and opportunity, genius and good luck all work together"; and "moral energy,"
a rich and meaningful concept in Ranke, stands high among the

---

[16] "Trennung und Einheit," p. 156.
[17] At the end of "Frankreich und Deutschland," in *Sämtl. Werke*, XLIX-L, 75.
[18] "Frankreich und Deutschland," p. 65.

forces that elevate the state to universal significance. From this point on, the reader breathes only the atmosphere of the state and of the particular spirit that is alive in it. We no longer feel the strength of the nation forming the state but rather the strength of the state forming the nation, the "moral energy" at work in the state and emanating from it. The "particular state" becomes the "spiritual fatherland" of the individual;[19] and the "spirit of communal life" that accompanies us to the end of this discussion is a political national spirit, more limited but also clearer, better defined, and more personal in character than that "mysterious power" that we left behind in the profound depths. For the state, to be imbued with nationality is to be imbued with moral strength.[20]

In this way, the course of development that leads from the impersonal to personality and from predetermination to inner self-determination is completed. Ranke conceived of this inner self-determination of the nationalized state in a much broader fashion than the advocates of the doctrines of 1789 had. His concept of the national state is so elastic that it can take in the national state of the older as well as that of the modern stamp. The important thing for Ranke is not whether the political nation participates in the government in a representative and deliberative way. The essential point is its spiritual and moral role in the state in general. He does not regard pure power states, states dependent on soldiers and money, as national states at all, and he questions their capacity to survive.[21]

Everything is drawn together, then, in the idea of the individuality of the great states, an individuality that emanates from their own unique and spontaneous life. We see how different this is from the ideal of progress that Humboldt had put forward in his early work of 1792. "The human race," he wrote then, "is at a level of culture now from which it can only advance through the education of individuals. Consequently, all measures that hinder this education and that press men together into masses are more harmful than before." At first glance, Ranke and Humboldt seem to be going completely separate ways. Of culture as the central task to be achieved in world history, Ranke said: "The sole essential meaning of history is not found in the often very doubtful advance of culture."[22] And nothing pressed men together into masses more than the great power

---

[19] "Polit. Gespräch," p. 333. The word "nation" used twice more on pages 335 and 336 undoubtedly means "political nation" here.
[20] "Die Grossen Mächte," p. 39.   [21] *Loc.cit.*
[22] *Loc.cit.*

state and national state that Ranke favored. However, we cannot simplify this contrast so crassly. Ranke is not interested in the formation of great masses as such but in the spiritual personality that emerges from this formation. Individuality is the key word for both Humboldt and Ranke, but in Ranke the concept of personality includes the great collective personalities as well. We have seen the role Humboldt himself played in the explorations of the realm of individuality that the German spirit had eagerly undertaken, and in the course of time these explorations had also begun to reveal the individuality of everything that joined individuals together into masses. When Ranke says of states and nations, "True harmony will come from separation and individual development,"[23] the basic tendency of Humboldt and classical individualism is still audible in the remark; and we should not see a complete denial of the classical *Humanitätsideal* in Ranke's skeptical comment on "culture," either, particularly since the term itself is so equivocal. If we understand the concept of "culture" in an intellectual sense, then Ranke's national power state represents a genuine and noble culture. Its power and its claim to personality are not granted to it to be used arbitrarily or merely for the purpose of artificially extending its life. "The justification of its existence is that it give a new mode of expression to the human spirit, proclaim it in new appropriate forms, and reveal it anew. That is its mandate from God."[24]

We see here again a universal commandment poised over the life of great state personalities, but the epoch-making advance in Ranke's concept of the national state is that this commandment applies to the individual development of state personalities but in no way limits or weakens it. Just as Ranke did not drive the metaphysical element out of history altogether but placed it where it belonged, namely, on the vague periphery of experience, so also he did not reject the universal element in the life of the great states but located it where it no longer inhibited their free movement. Their origin in the profound depths of nationality and their telos blend into the universal, but their life itself is simply the realization of their own being. Historical research, which observes and describes their life, is necessarily universal in that nothing human can be alien to it; but it can only understand the object of its study, the individual states, if it grants them the unlimited right to act in accordance with their own

[23] End of "Frankreich und Deutschland," in *Sämtl. Werke*, XLIX-L, p. 76.
[24] "Frankreich und Deutschland," p. 73.

nature and needs.[25] A remarkable antithesis results from this. The actions of states themselves do not derive from universal motives, but from egoistical ones. However, their meaning is universal, and the mirror that reflects them must be universal, too.

As we saw, Hegel put forward this antithesis, but he had exaggerated the universal study and evaluation of history so much that empirical history became a phantasmagoria. Ranke gave back to history the blood that had been drawn from it and treated it generally with more care and respect. He was content to contemplate and intuit the universal meaning that Hegel proposed to grasp. A proper definition of limits was finally achieved here; and because of this, the ideal and the concrete, the observed object and the observing subject, were separated in such a way that justice was done to them both. We could almost call it a definition of limits in a Kantian sense, although the limits were defined only in a fluid and blurred fashion. But this flowing of the particular into the universal, of experience into speculation, was founded in the very nature of the matter itself. The important thing on which all else depended was that the realm of experience was liberated and the realm of universal and speculative attempts at interpretation was relocated further away from the center of interest.

Let us turn again to Ranke's consideration of "Die Grossen Mächte." Who is not familiar with these massive forms as Ranke sketches them for us, rapidly, but in such a way that they are indelibly impressed on us as they gather strength in themselves, clash together tempestuously, and grow in stature through battle itself? Novalis and especially Adam Müller had had an inkling of this spectacle, but it was more a vision than a clear image because their subjectivity still injected too many universalistic tendencies into it. Here we encounter the true, unobscured image of the life of these powers. Lenz has rendered the basic idea of this sketch very well:[26] "Each of these powers wants to assert its own character, the principle that informs its every organ and manifestation of life, wants to develop all its powers and strengths, both internally and in relation to the outside world. Similarities between the powers, no matter how closely they may bind states to each other, must give way to this

---

[25] "Über die Verwandtschaft und den Unterschied der Historie und der Politik," in *Sämtl. Werke,* XXIV, 291.

[26] Lenz, *Die Grossen Mächte: Ein Rückblick auf unser Jahrhundert* (1900), p. 9.

deepest of instincts. It even forms the basis for the alliances that the powers form among themselves, and it defines the limits for every friendship." The individuality and autonomy of a state are the same thing; and in Ranke's thought, this identity of individuality and autonomy is reflected in the idea that the state must be based on "special principles of existence," on nationality, on moral strength, in order to be able to assert itself and its nature. As Ranke shows, the great powers of the West had gained this nationality, individuality, and autonomy almost as a matter of course, and in what we might call a naïve fashion, as early as the *ancien régime*. But at the time of the Revolution, they were threatened by an enemy both within and without. The external enemy was the conquering French national state, which, nourished on universal, cosmopolitan ideas, tried to bring states and nations under its universal domination. The internal enemy was those universal ideas themselves which urged uniform political institutions on all nations and ingratiated themselves with these nations by an appeal to the individual's desire for equality and freedom. States threatened in their autonomy rose against such cosmopolitan oppression and leveling. They took stock of their own profound national roots, those of the political nation no less than those of the cultural nation, and called on them for aid. But the intellectual forces that Germany in particular infused into her threatened states were, as we have repeatedly seen, themselves permeated with universal ideas; and because of this the internal ally of the state was also the internal enemy of its unlimited autonomy. We saw in the cases of Stein, Gneisenau, and Humboldt how this plethora of directly or indirectly universal ideas and presuppositions invaded the sphere of practical politics. We saw how the political situation that brought the different states and nations together called the universal idea to life, and how the idea of a European community and the idea of state and national self-determination mutually supported each other and were partially congruent, but only partially, so that here again an ally could become an enemy and an act of good will an annoyance. The special political and social interests of the Restoration governments subsequently appeared as a third factor in addition to the intellectual legacy of universalistic views on the one hand and of the experience of the Wars of Liberation on the other. The adherents of the patrimonial state, as they themselves said, fought against absolutism in any form, the monarchistic absolutism of the past and the democratic absolutism of the present. As we would say, they fought against the autonomous state

personality in any form, the national state of an earlier as well
as of a modern type. They could not and did not want to draw back
from the national movement entirely, and they tried to render it
harmless by developing a conservative idea of the national state that
glorified the feudal state as the genuine product of the spirit of the
nation and of the cultural nation. It is completely understandable that
they also held to universalistic ideas of a European community of legitimate Christian powers, although these ideas were already diluted
to a certain extent. In both states and nations, this concept of community checked the desire for power that was dangerous for the
fixed forms of the old feudal life, and it also limited the autonomy
of the state personality. The concept of community gained a positive
character through the establishing of supreme legal and moral commandments that had precedence over all the egoistical power interests of states and nations, and these commandments in turn gained
a religious consecration because they were honored as the law and
revelation of God.

The historical significance and the greatness of Ranke's conception
become clear to us only when his conception is compared with this
system based on both interests and ideals. Ranke's conception retained what was fruitful in this system. It also retained—not from
this system but from the Classic and Romantic movement before it—
the idea of the cultural nation, of the national spirit, of a unique spiritual nationality that in turn created new spiritual individualities.
However, the conservative idea of the national state that he derived
from this did not lead him to a limitation of autonomy in the national state but to a justification and reinforcement of it. His national state steps into the world confidently and follows only the
voice of its inner genius in all things. The ultimate origins and goals
of its personality doubtless reach into depths and heights where
universal forces are at work, but in the bright light of its daily life
Ranke's national state pursues universal ideas only to the extent that
they correspond to its own needs. Ranke knew very well, as did
Hegel, that there was a "European community" in the life of states
among themselves, but this community was the natural result of fundamental kinship and of a common life together. It is interesting
that he found the idea of a European community alive again in the
period of the revolutionary wars. But in contrast to those who
wanted to make a permanent universal principle of this idea, he immediately limited his view of it by emphasizing how difficult its development had been and how "the states had come together only

when threatened by virtual destruction." His main statement on this reads: "Every state was, however, in the midst of its own particular development; and every single one will, I have no doubt, return to this development as soon as the aftereffects of the revolutionary wars abate."[27] Ranke has illuminated the heart of the matter with sure and brilliant insight. The era of the revolutionary wars appears here as a kind of intermezzo of universalistic politics in Europe by which the normal development of state life, which is based on the autonomy of individual state personalities, is temporarily diverted. But he predicts with complete confidence that this development will return again to its original course. His theory rejected the universalism of both the liberal and the legitimistic doctrine. He was not at all willing to concede that Europe might fall permanently into two camps of good and bad principles, for he knew that the same era that had evoked this dualistic view had also infused the great powers and state personalities of the *ancien régime* with new life. The future belonged to the autonomy of the regenerated national state, not to the universalistic principle. Thus, all the mists of universalistic ideas in which his generation had grown up dispersed here before his eyes, and the historian became a prophet who saw far into the future.

To see what lay ahead required more genius than to propose ideals of unification for Germany. Anyone who proposed such ideals, who demanded a national state for the entire German nation, had to be animated by a political passion that was not natural to the contemplative historian. For this reason, Ranke looked much further ahead into the life of the national state in general than did his limited contemporaries; but he greatly underestimated the forces in Germany that were pressing toward a closer unification of the cultural nation into a national state. We know today that the foundations of the cultural nation were capable of carrying more than the German individual states and more than the loose federal union that even Ranke had advocated. We can also easily see that this entire conservative idea of the national state, which was satisfied with the individual state nourished by the German spirit, was a reflection of the actual division of Germany and an attempt to justify this division intellectually before the forum of German national consciousness that was now irrevocably present. But all such ideas are derived from some kind of reality. They must be so derived; they must have as

[27] "Polit. Gespräch," p. 329.

much lifeblood in them as possible if they, as an intellectual force, are to affect reality again in turn. The most palpable fact in the development of German national consciousness was simply that, in the process of passing from an awareness of spiritual unity to the desire for political expression of German nationality, this national consciousness first called a halt at the limits of the individual state; and in the course of centuries, this state had created its own particular political nationality as a territorial state. Deeply rooted sentiments would have been denied if the nationality of the individual state had not been put into the scales along with all other national values. This fact does not require proof, but it gains a more profound meaning if we recall here that both Humboldt and Bismarck pointed it out[28]—Humboldt, the statesman who was most influenced by ideas, and Bismarck, the statesman most influenced by facts.

Ranke stands between them both in time and in his views. He, more than any other, performed the task of uniting ideas and facts. This connection between the three men, a connection we might call symphonic, shows that truly idealistic and truly realistic thinking are always bound to come together again. This is also the ultimate reason why Schiller's representative nation of all mankind could create Bismarck's national state. We shall consider that state now in our concluding remarks.

THE STRIKING SIMILARITY between the political program that Ranke developed in the thirties and Bismarck's mode of political thinking has already been elucidated by Max Lenz,[29] an important scholar who has done much work in both fields. He writes of the influence of these two men on the political thinking of the nation: "For us Germans, it was they who first completely overcame natural law and Romanticism in history and politics." Lenz himself would want us to take this judgment *cum grano salis*, for where have intellectual impulses of such strength and fruitfulness ever been completely overcome? They live on in what supplants them. Ranke, Bismarck, the new Germany, and we, too, have all taken our intellectual life from them. The idealistically true and the realistically vital elements they contain remain preserved for us even if we turn away from what is now only the empty shell of their former life. Ranke and Bismarck's achievement was to dispense with such empty shells and to overcome paralyzing dogmas and ideals. But in emphasiz-

[28] See pp. 143f., above.
[29] Lenz, "Bismarck und Ranke," *Kleine histor. Schriften*, pp. 383ff.

ing their achievement, we must also note the continuity between the new ideas for which they cleared the way and the old ideas whose withered branches they pushed aside.

The bridge that leads from Romanticism to both Ranke and Bismarck is primarily the conservative idea of the national state. This relationship is perfectly clear in Ranke, but I expect that it will not seem so obvious in Bismarck's case. We could cite his later ideas, where he finds the specific character of German national consciousness functioning effectively only through the medium of the "particular nationalities that have developed among us on the basis of dynastic family possession."[30] But this still does not exactly constitute what we have called the conservative idea of the national state. It is closely related to it but not identical with it. This thesis, like the conservative national idea, unites the nationality of the individual state with an overall German national consciousness; but it serves only to point out the result of national development as Bismarck saw it toward the end of his life and to impress on the coming generation what a peculiar dualism of national motives underlay the new German Reich. In the years before the March Revolution, however, the conservative idea of the national state did not recognize and did not demand a German Reich. It demanded at most, like Ranke, Radowitz, and Friedrich Wilhelm IV, a consolidation of the federal constitution; and in all other respects, it was content with the German individual state. It recognized, however, that remarkably dualistic national impulses were at work in the individual state—the particular political nationality of the individual state and the spiritual nationality of the German people. We see, then, that the forces taken into account are identical with each other or at least resemble one another but that the point of view and the interests involved are different. Bismarck made the political nation of the new Reich conscious of the forces of the individual political nationalities at work within it. In this way, the conservative national idea confronted the advocates of a German political nation with the idea of the German cultural nation and of the individual political nationalities as well.

The more general historical connection between the two points of view is immediately obvious. First, the forces of the German cultural nation and of the individual state had just created the new German political nation. Second, the conservative national idea was itself one of the spiritual means for preparing the German individ-

[30] *Gedanken und Erinnerungen*, I, 293.

ual state for assimilation into the future German national state. This idea had justified the existence of the German individual state but with reasons that pointed toward a still higher level of unification than the individual state itself. In this way, it had helped to keep alive the idea of an inner national community even in circles that had no confidence in the external political unity of the nation. This kind of justification of particularism resulted in the overcoming of particularism within the nation to the extent necessary for the creation of a larger German national state.

The conservative national idea, of course, not only prepared the way for the German national state but also retarded its progress. It retarded this progress intentionally, but unintentionally prepared the way. This double effect becomes obvious in the movement of 1848, in which the inhibiting impulse is more evident than the assisting one. The opponents of the Frankfurt constitution, both the advocates of particularism and those of a Greater Germany, presented arguments clearly derived from the conservative idea of the national state, and we have already seen in the case of Stahl how the Prussian conservative opponents in particular raised this idea as a banner and used it to appease their German consciences over the fact that they were leading a struggle against German unity.

But we can ask with some doubt whether Bismarck even had a German conscience at that time. Did he not carry on his battle purely as a Prussian particularist? His biographer Lenz says, "Everything that lay outside the black and white border posts was foreign soil for him."[31] When a Prussian peer once countered Bismarck's passionate reactionary effusions by saying there was a truth in the "national idea" that should be recognized, Bismarck answered scornfully, "Then you too have been bitten by the German dog?"[32] In the second part of this study, we shall show what dangers the German movement of the time represented for the Prussian state and for the maintenance of its particular personality and nationality. That was reason enough for a man like Bismarck, in whom the Prussian nationality and—to use his own words—its most outstanding characteristic, the warlike element, were personified, to strike out at the "German dog" and deny recognition to the German idea that endangered his native state. However, the conservative idea of the national state lay on his side of the abyss that separated him from the Frankfurt

[31] *Geschichte Bismarcks* (3rd edn.), p. 39.
[32] Ludw. v. Gerlach, II, 324.

delegates, and the acknowledgment of German nationality that this idea contained was so harmless that even a dyed-in-the-wool Prussian like Bismarck could advocate its tenets without scruples of conscience. There are, in fact, many statements of Bismarck's from these years that reflect a certain German sentiment along with the emphatically Prussian one. They have never been completely disregarded, and they have usually been interpreted as reminiscences of his youthful athletic and Burschenschaft days.[33] The persistence of such impulses cannot be denied, but all these statements can be easily placed within the framework of the conservative idea of the national state, too. This immediately raises the question of whether these statements, to the extent that they express this idea, were a genuine reflection of his true feelings or a superficial, adopted opinion, perhaps only a tactical utilization of ideas that his party had formed without him and before him.

This question is also raised by the nature of the position Bismarck held in the Christian-Germanic circle, which was also the inner circle of the Prussian conservatives. He was never completely absorbed into it. He accepted the religious and political system offered to him here only insofar as it concurred with his own personal experience.[34] He probably never spoke the language of his new friends in a purer form than in his speech on the Jewish question delivered in the United Diet on June 15, 1847. In that speech, he candidly designated the realization of the Christian doctrine as the purpose of the state. But his ideas on the possibility of achieving this are sober and practical.[35] He betrays a mode of thinking both personal and typical of the Brandenburg nobility when he speaks of the prejudice he had possessed from the cradle and when he declares that his feelings of joy and honor would leave him if he were required to obey a Jewish official. We can thus see how every element of the Christian-Germanic doctrine that he takes up is transformed in his mouth and

---

[33] See, for example, Lenz, *Die Grossen Mächte*, p. 43, on the speech of April 2, 1848: "That was the idea of his youth. He had not forgotten it even in the Revolution. But he saw the unity of Germany only in the unity of its princes."

[34] Cf. my essay on Gerlach and Bismarck, *Histor. Zeitschrift*, LXXII (1893), reprinted in *Preussen und Deutschland im 19. und 20. Jahrhundert.* Later Bismarck scholarship has been in essential agreement with this view. Even the latest thorough study, Günther Franz, *Bismarcks Nationalgefühl* (1926), uses it as a point of departure. He also agrees, in basic points at least, with my analysis that follows here. However, he gives Bismarck's view of the state a somewhat too rigid character.

[35] He emphasizes not less than three times in a row that this goal is not always achieved.

loses, entirely or almost entirely, its theoretical or doctrinaire tone. We are therefore justified in doubting from the outset that his statements tinged with German feelings really derive from his friends' theory on the relationship of Prussian and German nationality. As we saw earlier, this theory was developed from the Romantic conception of a creative national spirit that gave rise to the personal but never developed into a visible personality itself. This conception in turn was derived in part from the pantheism and panindividualism of early Romanticism and in part, too, perhaps, from the ideas of a cultural and universal nation of the spirit that Fichte, the early Romantics, and the Classical Idealists had held. We need only mention this lineage of the conservative national idea to see that it was meaningless for Bismarck. All these delicate and profound ideas could become vivid experiences for a mind inclined to contemplation but not for one, like Bismarck's, inclined to action. But were not these ideas themselves always derived from the experience of the nation, and was not the concept of a German national spirit in particular the reflection of a forceful reality? This concept was itself only reflection and speculation, but behind it lay the long, spontaneous, and natural growth of the nation. During this growth, the nation created a great deal unconsciously and only became conscious of itself when its pride, its capacity to hate, or its will was stimulated. Bismarck's account of his impressions during a trip in southwestern Germany in his youth is particularly interesting here.[36] The account was written much later, but it contains the kind of memories that are not easily affected by later events. "In looking at the map, I was annoyed by the French occupation of Strasbourg; and a visit to Heidelberg, Speyer, and the Palatinate put me in a vengeful and bellicose mood." Such basic feelings have nothing to do with that "phase of theoretical consideration" in which, according to Bismarck's own report, he experienced his first youthful awareness of German nationality. They are even more fundamental than the "Prussian officer's outlook during the Wars of Liberation," an outlook which, again according to Bismarck's own report, he also held at that time. This account of his immediately reminds us of the first speech he gave in the United Diet in 1847, in which he refused to believe that any motives other than the basic human feelings of "shame at having foreigners command in our country," of "humiliation," and of "hatred toward the foreigners" had a part in the national rebellion

[36] *Gedanken und Erinnerungen*, I, 2.

of 1813. But there can be no doubt that we have here a sample of the basic ore of national sentiment that lies still deeper than a specifically Prussian or German nationality. This is the spiritual world of the folk epic, of the heroes of *Gudrun* and the *Iliad* who cannot endure the rule of foreigners. This is a need not just for national or political autonomy but, in the last analysis, for heroic autonomy. This impulse was alive at the heart of Bismarck's plans during his entire life. It gave all his political goals their particular character and was an important contributing factor in his greatness.

It was an important factor, but not the only one. He felt along with this impulse a natural, powerful attraction to the great, historically developed spheres of influence in which he grew up, an urge to assume a position in them, to make their life his, to fuse his autonomy with theirs, to rule as a great man and to serve greatness. Growing to manhood, he found three major spheres of influence open to him: the social milieu of the Prussian nobility, the monarchical Prussian state, and the German nation. He never renounced the first, but it was deeply united with the second, which surrounded him and appealed to him most forcefully. Obliged to make a choice between the second and third, between Prussia and the German nation, he chose Prussia with all the energy and passion of his character. But the German nation was not necessarily identical with the Frankfurt assembly's national-political ideal, which was based on the liberal-democratic idea of nationality. There was, however, another concept of the German nation that he was able to accept. The idea of a German cultural nation was, as we have seen, out of the question for him. As a nobleman and Prussian, he would have nothing to do with German popular sovereignty, nor was he interested in the German national spirit of his Romantic friends. But behind popular sovereignty and national spirit lay, as historical ore, the power of the German nation, and it was to this power that he turned.

"I would have found it understandable," he wrote on April 20, 1848 to the editors of the *Magdeburger Zeitung*, "if the first expression of German strength and unity had taken the form of demanding Alsace from France and planting the German flag on the cathedral of Strasbourg." No knowledgeable person will interpret this remark to mean that he wanted to incite a national war of conquest against France. But it is not just another bold statement either. It indicated the kind of strength that was latent in him and the kind that he admired. This is still no thunderstorm, but, like similar remarks that we have already examined before, it is a distant flash of lightning. This is still not German sentiment of a political nature or even of an intellectual or ethical nature, but rather of a clearly voluntaristic nature. If we read between the lines, we find Bismarck saying: If you must have your German zeal, if you are not satisfied with the sense of well-being that your state can offer you, then I will show you what German character is when it has some force behind it. I can only be convinced by that kind of German character.

The immediate purpose of the letter to the *Magdeburger Zeitung* was to make it clear to his German and Prussian compatriots that they were suicidally foolish in granting Polish demands in Posen. We could perhaps object that he wanted to promote Prussian interests by an appeal to German feelings that he did not necessarily share himself. But we would be deaf to the natural voice of emotion if we did not recognize it even in the calculated form in which it finds expression here. He favored a purposeful, not a blind, development of German national strength, and at that point he could only find hopes of such development in the power and greatness of his own Prussia.[37] Thus he considered German nationality a great potential force, but it had reality for him only in the power politics of his own native state, not in a centralized state that had not even been created yet.

Did he have similar feelings about the other major German states? In the same letter and in his speech of December 3, 1850 on the Treaty of Olmütz, he expressed the satisfaction he felt about all the conquests by German arms in the course of the centuries and therefore about the rule of Austria in Slavic and Italian territories. We may well doubt the genuineness of his satisfaction here, but we must also admit that it was characteristic of his thinking to grant Austria's claim to the title of a German power because of her extension of German dominance and her military strength.

We must also note, finally, that his concept of the German nation at the time had some points of contact with that of his political associates Leopold and Ludwig von Gerlach. Leopold wrote in his journal on April 24, 1848, perhaps under the influence of Bismarck, with whose ideas of this same period he might have become familiar: "How hypocritical this Germanomania is and what grave wounds it has already inflicted on Germany. Prussia had spread German cus-

---

[37] It is thus understandable, too, that in the circumstances that prevailed at the time he could still not be won over to the idea of a war against Denmark that offered no advantage for Prussia.

toms and German law to the Niemen, the Netze, and the Prosna. The
Revolution is making the greatest possible effort to drive the Germans
out of all these conquered territories."[38] The situation was similar in
Bohemia, Tyrol, and Austro-Italy. "There is no mention whatever in
all this of reuniting Alsace, Lorraine, the German provinces of the
Netherlands, and the genuine German portion of Switzerland with
Germany or of protecting German nationality in Transylvania."
But in the following year, Ludwig von Gerlach agreed with Wolf-
gang Menzel's view that the only possible German national policy
would have been to declare Austria's struggles in Hungary and Italy
a German affair, to send German troops there, and to prevent altogether the armed intervention of the Russians.[39] We see immediately
how the same ideas that have a national heroic aspect to them in
Bismarck threaten to wither into a somewhat extravagant doctrine
in the Gerlachs. In the case of the Gerlachs it is difficult, indeed impossible, to separate doctrine and sentiment. In Bismarck it is
equally difficult to separate interest and sentiment. If the historian
wants to find the middle way between excessive criticism and naïveté,
he can do nothing but follow his instinct for what is alive and take
cognizance in both cases of the two tendencies that coexist side by side.

Our assumption is confirmed. Bismarck accepted the conservative
idea of the national state to the extent that his nature and his role
as an autochthon allowed and to the extent that the potential of the
German nation and the interests of the Prussian state coincided.
When he went beyond this and concurred with the national theory
of his friends, he did so primarily for immediate tactical reasons but
also because of a component of heroic sentiment that rose up in
him. But it would never have occurred to him to convert the pleasure he took in Austria's military actions in eastern Europe into actions of his own and thereby pursue a German national policy in
Gerlach's terms. Let every German state clear a path for itself with
its own sword: Austria against its Slovaks and Magyars; Prussia—
this idea came to him in these years too[40]—by telling the Germans
what their constitution should be. A few days before the Olmütz
speech, he said openly in an intimate circle of his political friends

---

[38] Leop. v. Gerlach, I, 155. Gerlach contradicts himself here, and such contradiction is characteristic of the uncertainty of his national principle. See p. 177,
note 54, above. Further material on the national concept of the Gerlachs has been
gathered in Lüttke, *Die polit. Anschauungen des Generals und des Präsidenten v.
Gerlach* (Leipzig dissertation, 1907), and in Augst, *Bismarck u. Leopold v. Gerlach* (1913).

[39] II, 47.   [40] Speech on September 6, 1849.

that Friedrich II of 1740 was a model for emulation;[41] and in the Olmütz speech itself, similar desires can be inferred.[42] He held them under firm control because he saw too many dangers threatening his state on all sides at the time. With Bismarck we are always aware of sentiments that hark back to the soldier-king and that delight in boldness, but we are also aware of a modern, practical realism that utilizes circumstances to achieve a goal and that practices self-control in order to achieve self-determination.

In this same Olmütz address he spoke that great and simple truth that swept away all the mists of political Romanticism: "The only sound foundation for a major state—and in this it is fundamentally different from a minor state—is political egoism and not Romanticism. It is not worthy of a great state to fight for a cause that does not touch on its own interests."

At another point during these same years, Bismarck also called such an autonomous policy a "Prussian national policy."[43] We would have to call this autonomous major state that he has in mind a genuine national state in the political sense even if he had not done so himself, letting all the emotional values of a "specific Prussianness" shine vividly through, for this state derives its principles of action from the internal and external needs of a politically united national community. The Prussia that Friedrich Wilhelm IV and his Romantic friends had in mind was not a national state in this sense because they did not, like Bismarck, consider the state's political egoism the only sound foundation for its policies. They subjected it to the highest ethical commandments, even in its foreign policy, and thereby limited the objectives of its power as well as its freedom of movement and even its possibilities of alliance.[44] With the nonpolitical goals that they set for the state, they transformed the means with which the state was to work; and they also transformed political thought completely, transformed ideas of what was politically

[41] Ludw. v. Gerlach, II, 116.

[42] Fester recognized this in *Histor. Zeitschrift*, LXXXV, 49f. See p. 134, note 38, above.

[43] Speech on September 6, 1849.

[44] We should note from this same period a comment of Ranke's which he made in describing the ties of Franz I to the Ottomans: "A freer management of foreign affairs, based on the needs of one's own situation, was impossible as long as policy was determined by considerations of a larger system of nations and states to which one belonged." *Französische Geschichte*, I, 117. The beginning of the third chapter of *Französische Geschichte*, with its distinction between monarchs of universalistic and ethical leanings and those of national and egoistical ones, is also a clear allusion to Friedrich Wilhelm IV.

possible and feasible and thus created a source of political errors, mistakes, failures, and humiliations.

We are near the end of our discussion. Before we make our final observations, let us consider once again the two views that struggled with each other at the threshold of our era. Every student of Bismarck is familiar with the letters he exchanged with Leopold von Gerlach in May 1857 and with the memorials he submitted to his government in May and June 1857. With these documents, we feel we are in a cool dawn, and we see the moon fading.

In Gerlach's letter of May 6, 1857[45] the universalism of Romanticism, of the Wars of Liberation, and of the Restoration emerges again, claiming to offer a valid operating principle for European politics and to prove the validity of this principle by historical example. Charlemagne's principle was, Gerlach begins, the expansion of the Christian church. He held to this principle in his wars against the Saxons, Saracens, and others, and he was rewarded for it. But his successors fought among themselves in an unprincipled manner. The great princes of the Middle Ages, however, adhered to this old principle once again; and the founding of Brandenburg-Prussian power rests on this principle, on the wars fought against nations that would not submit to the emperor, the vicar of the church. In the later period of the decay of church and Empire, only the old principle had repeatedly brought the states success, as the case of Austria and Russia in their battle against the Turks shows. The wars of the Great Elector and the first three wars of Frederick the Great also maintained the old principle, despite interests in territory and the balance of power, because they had a Protestant character; and the wars against Louis XIV were really wars against the Revolution. The worst period of Prussian politics was from 1778 until the French Revolution. That was a time dominated by the "politics of interests, of so-called patriotism." Because of the Revolution, the states were obliged to learn the old principle again, a principle that necessarily does battle with, or at least stands in direct opposition to, the Revolution in all its forms, right down to the France of Napoleon III. Prussia and Germany fared well as long as this principle was in effect. No foreign power had interfered in German affairs from 1815 to 1840.

Gerlach thought that he too was practicing *Realpolitik*, because his ideal politics allegedly always found their actual reward on

[45] *Bismarckjahrbuch*, VI, 83ff.; Kohl, *Briefe Gerlachs an Bismarck*, pp. 208ff.

earth, a point he could not prove, of course, without the most violent
distortions and oversights. He also seems to advocate the autonomy
of the nation, but this is not a genuine autonomy because it is conceived of only as the result of incorporation into the Holy Alliance,
that is, as a reward for renunciation of the true autonomy of
power. Gerlach's principle of political action led to a certain unity
and firmness that lent the appearance of integrity and that also lent
the state some credibility in times of peace. "It cannot be overlooked,"
Gerlach claimed, "that only he is reliable who acts according to definite principles and not according to shifting concepts of interests etc."
But like all heteronomous principles for action, this brought with it
monotony, rigidity, incapacity to adapt to changes of circumstances,
suppression of natural life forces and of historical development. He
looks for laws of motion not in the forces that are actually in motion
themselves but in a universal, absolute, transcendent context in
which his faith sees them.

Bismarck is just the opposite in all respects. His politics begin at the
center of the active forces themselves. Their essence is individuality,
development, and worldliness. Seen from one aspect, his policies os-
cillate from moment to moment because they are determined by "all
the nuances of possibility, probability, or intention, so that he could
remain free to form this or that alliance in the event of war, to belong to this or that group."[46] But this kind of determinism belongs
to true inner autonomy just as the external world belongs to the internal world. The one can grow and develop and assert itself only in
battle with and in opposition to the other. Thus, Bismarck's view
of the interaction between states is by no means lacking in constant
and persistent forces. These forces are the "native and natural interests" of individual states. They are not as vacillating as Gerlach claims
but are in fact much stronger than the principles that Gerlach regarded as firm and immovable. They continue to break through
all changes of governmental form and make themselves felt whether
the state is committed to revolutionary or antirevolutionary principles. Bismarck went into no greater detail than necessary with
his friend in justifying his policy of autonomy that sought "to open
every door, to keep every option unrestricted." He did not concern
himself much with the question of whether the opposition of revolutionary and antirevolutionary, of good and evil principles that Gerlach
had submitted was correct or not, and he did not feel any need to

[46] May 2, 1857, Kohl, *Bismarcks Briefe an Leopold v. Gerlach*, p. 316.

revise his own inner position on liberalism and revolution. He behaved in this controversy the way the state as a whole must behave if it obeys its own nature. He cleared the way for the most pressing and vital needs, for the greatest and most important expressions of life in states; and all the rest he left to the course of development.

He fought his friend's errors primarily by demonstrating their historical limitations. Like Ranke, he saw the era of the Revolution and Restoration as a kind of intermezzo in the life of states and in the principles of their leading statesmen. If there were a principle that formed the foundation of all politics, he thought,[47] how could it have evaded the Christian and conservative politicians before 1789? "I do not see that any politician, even the most Christian and conscientious one, would ever have hit upon the idea, before the French Revolution, of subordinating his entire political activity and his attitude toward domestic and foreign politics to the principle of opposing the Revolution, nor would he ever have examined the relationship of his country to other states purely on the basis of this touchstone."[48] He also tried to explain his older friend's error in psychological terms. "It seems to me," he said to him on May 2, 1860,[49] "that the impressions of our youth never leave us. Overwhelming hatred of Bonaparte was a major element of your youthful experience. You call him 'revolution incarnate,' and if you knew a viler term, you would christen him with that."

He thus sought out the most concrete and most vividly felt reasons behind this error. We should never forget these reasons, but our task here should be to show the wider intellectual context of this error. In our study of Stein and Gneisenau we tried to reconstruct the profound experiences of the Wars of Liberation that split the European constellation of states into two camps, but we saw how these experiences came up against certain categories of thought and feeling, particularly against the still operative eighteenth-century spirit, which had also tried to apply its universal principles to political life. The autonomous state had to fight the same battle with these heteronomous principles that the ethical autonomy of the individual had to fight with all heteronomous moral systems. The rigid power state of the eighteenth century opposed them by its very na-

---

[47] May 30, 1857, Kohl, *op.cit.*, p. 328.
[48] Cf. Sorel, *L'Europe et la révolution française*, I, 71. "Une Sainte Alliance avant 1789 est un véritable paradoxe historique. L'ancienne Europe en était incapable, et il fallut la Révolution française pour lui en donner la notion."
[49] Kohl, *op.cit.*, p. 347.

ture, and even the enlightened rulers of the eighteenth century were careful not to let themselves be overwhelmed by these principles, particularly in their foreign policy. The Revolution and the Wars of Liberation first opened gates in the life of the state through which a strong wave of universal and nonpolitical ideals rushed into politics. These ideals found particularly fertile ground in Germany because intellectual training there was especially nonpolitical and had developed the universalistic element to a particularly high degree. Romanticism summoned up the spirits of the past against the despised rational and cosmopolitan spirit of the eighteenth century, but because Romanticism itself was still rooted in that spirit, it retrieved something related to it from the past. Thus the ancient idea of a universal community of Christian states was revived,[50] and the political aspect of Romanticism became cosmopolitanism with a religious-ethical character. In the ideas of the Revolution and in the ideas of the Holy Alliance, we said, two universalisms clashed. The robust nature of the state doubtless struggled against this alien element that imposed itself on the state and that tried to bind its limbs. As a result, universalism was not wholly victorious anywhere, but it swayed the minds of leading personalities in the period of Friedrich Wilhelm IV so strongly that it had fateful effects on practical politics and on the power of the state. In the last analysis, it was a poison that the body had to cast off if the body was to function naturally again. Bismarck was the doctor who drew off this poison.

Originally, however, it had been not only a poison but also a medicine.

Let us look back again at national resistance against Napoleon. Here the nations appear in their manifold types and phases of development. Some of them, like the Spaniards, Tyroleans, and Russians, were based on an ancient nativistic foundation. They did not need any particular stimulus to erupt in enmity and hatred against the Napoleonic world empire. There was still something of the fanaticism of half-civilized nations in them, a fanaticism that rejected the modern cultural elements of this world empire. Ranke made the profound observation that Napoleon's dominance could spread more easily "where the mind was prepared for it," where the social ideas that had emerged in the Revolution and that Napoleon himself had ad-

---

[50] Enlightenment historical study had characteristically regarded the medieval idea of a "Christian republic" as the only usable idea of the Middle Ages. Cf. Samuel, *Die poetische Staats- und Geschichtsauffassung F. v. Hardenbergs* (*Novalis*), p. 257.

vocated were known. We might add that not only the social but also
the cosmopolitan aspect of the ideas of the Enlightenment had prepared the way for him. These ideas first weakened the national resistance of Germany in particular, but they then helped develop and encourage it. We are speaking here only of the higher, leading classes
of the nation, because the national feelings of the Brandenburg or
Pomeranian peasant with his militiaman's rifle were not much different from those of the Tyrolian or Spanish citizen-soldier. But in
the intellectual leaders of the nation, the national impulse had come
awake in a much more complicated way. We saw how it was permeated and entangled with universal ideals from the outset. The
higher levels of German culture at first found it impossible and insuf-
ferable to acknowledge the blatant egoism of nations. The national
emotions of this culture crept upward on the traditional cosmopolitan
trellis. Universal and spiritualized national ideas invaded the state
simultaneously and in the closest contact with each other. The national ideas gave the universal ones strength and warmth and helped
them to enter the state. Later, the universal ideas had to be put
aside to permit the Prussian national state to develop into the German national state. But they had not been superfluous. Nothing is
superfluous that carries intellectual continuity forward between two
great epochs. Nothing is superfluous, either, that can animate historical action in crucial moments. Could Stein, at the end of 1812,
have persuaded the czar to carry the war beyond Russia's borders if
he, as the European statesman that he was at the time, had been
able to appeal only to national and state interests and not to universal
ideas that went beyond such limited concerns? The cause of the nation was also the cause of European man at that time. Thus the
idea of the Holy Alliance performed its greatest concrete service when
the Alliance was still unwritten. For the universal idea in the life of
states belongs to the spiritual elements that can only become a blessing if they remain intangible breaths of life.

Book II

*The Prussian National State and
the German National State*

1

....

BEGINNINGS OF THE PRUSSO-GERMAN PROBLEM: FROM MOSER TO FRIEDRICH VON GAGERN

THE QUESTION DEALT with in Book I leads directly to a second major problem in the genetic history of the German national state, one that we have touched on before but that we must now treat in more detail.

The first part of our study showed how the idea of autonomous state personalities made itself felt in Germany in the flood of new ideas and demands that rose up from the depths of national life after the end of the eighteenth century and that sought admittance into the state, particularly into the Prussian state. The Prussian state could not wholly grant or refuse admission to these ideas. It needed them to regenerate itself and to develop new intellectual energy. Then, too, the inroads made by these ideas during the Prussian resistance were accompanied by the inroads of strong individuals into the state. In this period of crisis the Prussian state was able to use the universal as well as the national elements of these ideas, but it also had to be prepared to dispense with these universal elements again at the proper time, because they weakened its autonomy. As we suggested, though, it could well afford to retain and cultivate the national elements. With their help, it could raise itself to the position of an autonomous German national state. Now we must define this view more closely, examine national ideas in terms of their usefulness for the Prussian state, and ask whether they were compatible with its autonomy and personality. The answer to this question will be both yes and no. The course of history supports the affirmative answer. A detailed study is necessary to justify the negative one.

The idea of the nation and of the national state in Germany was anything but unequivocal, even if isolated from the universalistic ideas that came along with it. An important point we must empha-

size again is that this national idea was able to grow in the soil of
the German individual state as well as in the soil of the German cultural nation, which was trying to regain its former political unity and
confirm it properly now for the first time. This in itself could lead to
disagreement and opposition between the Prussian political nation
and a German cultural nation intent on becoming the German political nation. This opposition appears as early as Friedrich Karl von
Moser's *Vom deutschen Nationalgeist*, which we cited at the beginning of Book I. As we saw there, he found his idea of the German
national spirit seriously threatened by the "monstrosity of a militaristic-patriotic government," by the "new militaristic state law," which
—to use his terminology—had arisen in the upper and lower Saxon
territories.[1] He complained about the Brandenburg noblemen who
took a narrow point of view and wanted nothing to do with a German
fatherland. From the standpoint of the entire German nation, the
Prussian state could not appear to be a genuine national state at all,
as we can clearly see in Moser's views here; or, to put it in a paradoxical form, the more national and unified the Prussian state actually
was in itself, the less national it seemed to the rest of the Germans
and the more heartfelt their desire to be rid of it. Fichte asked in
the spring of 1813[2] how a nation as he defined it could ever be
achieved. Greece, he thought, had not achieved nationhood any more
than Germany. What prevented Greece from achieving it? "Answer:
the individual state that was already too firmly established." At another point in his consideration of this problem,[3] he suggested that if
Austria or Prussia conquered Germany there would still be no Germany but only more Austrians or Prussians. We will recall that he
considered the nationality of the German individual state a lower and
more sensuous form of nationality and that he wanted to grant it
only secondary importance, or even wanted to do away with it entirely so that only German national character would remain.[4] But
at the same time he could find no despot to enforce education in the
elements of the German character except the ruler of the Prussian
individual state. His provisional remarks thus contain all the factors
of a plan for solving the dilemma presented both by the "individual
state that was already too firmly established" and by the demand of the
German nation for unity: the ruler of the Prussian individual state himself becomes a means of achieving a new German character, and he
permits his old state and its specific nationality to be absorbed into

[1] See pp. 31f., above.   [2] *Sämtl. Werke*, VII, 549.
[3] *Ibid.*, VII, 570.   [4] See pp. 75f. and 90f., above.

this new German character. These are the consequences that necessarily follow from Fichte's premises. The history of this idea will show us that we are dealing with a central problem in the German unification movement here, and we have to admire the profound vision of a great philosopher who was, by his own principles, a thinker both nonpolitical and beyond politics but who still had hidden within him the makings of a first-rate political thinker.

This Fichtean idea was very much like Fichte the man because it was based on nonpolitical premises yet contained hidden within it a highly relevant political seed that would gradually develop. A particularly nonpolitical premise was the assumption that the most powerful and best-established German individual state could readily give up its nationality and personality for the sake of Germany. In Book I we saw how the autonomous state personality could be subjected to universal commandments and ideals. Here we see how it was possible to conceive the idea that this personality should disappear entirely and be absorbed into something greater, which it was to create, and that it should sacrifice itself to the idea of the nation—to the very same idea that, in another form, seized the Prussian state in particular and strengthened it at that time. This is an amazing entanglement of related tendencies. But Fichte's thinking was still realistic and politically sound in wanting to establish German character and German unity through the power of the most firmly established German individual state—through this state but not for it and, in the last analysis, actually against it. But this highly nonpolitical demand that Prussia surrender itself and its nationality and merge with Germany still had a sound political core to it, for how could two distinctive political nationalities exist beside and within each other without mutually endangering one another? We begin to sense here what obstacles of a political and nonpolitical nature blocked the way for even the most natural path to German unity: unification through Prussia. Prussia was both the means of and the hindrance to converting the nonpolitical German cultural nation into a German political nation.

For many who desired German unity, Prussia was only an obstacle that had to be cleared out of the way and nothing more. There is a consistent development of thought on this question similar to the one that our earlier investigation[5] showed leading from Friedrich Karl von Moser to Freiherr vom Stein. On December 1, 1812, when a new era for Germany seemed to be dawning, Stein wrote to Graf

[5] See pp. 26f., above.

Münster: "I have only one fatherland, and that is Germany. . . . In this time of great change, the dynasties are of no interest to me. They are merely means to an end. My wish is that Germany become great and strong so that it can regain its autonomy, independence, and nationhood. . . . My credo . . . is unity. . . . Put what you will in Prussia's place; dissolve it; strengthen Austria with Silesia, the Kurmark, and Northern Germany, excluding the refugees. . . . Make Austria the master of Germany. That is what I want. It is good if it is practicable." Stein wrote this impulsively and in annoyance that others expected to find only a Prussian in him. He resorted to hyperbole to defend himself against this suspicion,[6] but there is more than hyperbole in his words. Lehmann's biography has reminded us that Stein, even though a Prussian statesman, was never a whole-hearted advocate of the specifically Prussian idea of the state. If he served Prussia, it was to serve Germany; and he also demanded of Prussia that it serve Germany, too. But if Prussia proved untrue to this mission as he saw it, then Prussia's existence meant nothing to him. May it then "perish, unmourned and without lasting glory," he wrote in 1809.[7] For this reason he did not shrink, in principle anyhow, from the idea of buying Germany's unity with Prussia's dissolution.

Besides these two views of the problem, the one germinating in Fichte, the other breaking forth with momentary anger in Stein, there is still a third that, again only in its incipient phases, appears in Niebuhr's pamphlet of 1814 on the Saxon question, with which we have dealt earlier.[8] This view did not take full account of the inner self-contradictions and tensions of the problem but dreamed instead of harmonizing opposing forces. The two poles were Prussian nationality and German nationality. Niebuhr loved the one as much as the other, but only because the first was a stepping-stone to the second; and as we pointed out in Book I, he loved Prussia not because it was a united, autonomous national state, but because it was "the common fatherland of every single German," the quintessence of the German nation.[9]

[6] Cf. Lehmann, *Stein*, III, 197n.   [7] *Ibid.*, III, 29.

[8] See pp. 153ff., above.

[9] A not uninteresting variation of this is Hendrik Steffens' national-political plan of about 1815-17. Cf. Tschirsch, "H. Steffens' polit. Entwicklungsgang," *Beiträge zur brand. u. preuss. Geschichte*, Schmollerfestschrift, p. 267. He demands a loosening of the Prussian state in favor of provincial independence. He does not want this, however, in order to make a tighter political unity in Germany possible, but precisely to prevent it. He seeks to preserve the variety and uniqueness of the small states and thereby to achieve the higher, invisible spiritual unity of Germany, and it is with this unity, accompanied by all the universalistic ideas already familiar

Stein and Fichte see Prussia in the framework of their German interests. Niebuhr, too, sees it from a more German than Prussian point of view, even though Germany and Prussia were identical in his eyes. But it was also possible to believe in a German mission for Prussia from a purely Prussian point of view. This was only possible in the sense of an actual Prussian hegemony over the rest of Germany or of a hegemony exercised by a Greater Prussia enlarged with other German territories. In either case, though, the Prussian state personality would be retained. This policy, too, if it did not want to use the sword of conquest—and Prussia in her weakened condition could not dream of that—had to adopt means and to place demands on Prussia's internal life similar to those called for by policies that defined Prussia's German mission from a predominantly or totally German point of view. The way to achieve this was to increase Prussia's power by nationalization, the creation of a Prussian political nation in as strong and vital a form as possible. As the case of Adam Müller has already shown, it was possible to pursue this kind of Prussian nationality in a conservative way by cultivating the old aristocratic and agrarian structure of the society; and there was at this time no lack of men like Marwitz in the ranks of the Brandenburg nobility who would have been able to unite a conservative domestic regime with ambitious Prussian power politics in Germany and even with large concessions to the German national idea.[10] But for the most part the ideals and interests of the Prussian nobility of this period were not directed toward an expansion of Prussia in Germany or toward the formation of a unified Prussian political nation but toward the cultivation of a special provincial status. This promised them better protection for aristocratic standing and tradition than did a unified political life in Prussia with its centralizing and leveling antifeudal effects. A Prussian political nation of greater strength, one that would find the support of all classes and of both the old and new provinces, could probably not be created without greater concessions to the middle classes and the peasants and without development of the

---

to us, that he feels himself informed. Here, then, the demand for the weakening of Prussia is made on the basis of a national ideal that is completely nonpolitical and resounds with universalistic and cultural overtones. We might also recall here that even Herder, in the years when his ideas on national culture began to take shape, had ventured this statement: "The states under the king of Prussia will not be content until they are divided in brotherhood." *Reisejournal von 1769*, in *Werke*, ed. Düntzer, XXIV, 425; see also p. 490.

[10] See my life of Boyen, II, 312, and *Histor. Zeitschrift*, LXXXII, 100; Meusel, *F. A. L. v. d. Marwitz*, I, xli.

great reforms initiated during the period of the Wars of Liberation.
That was the motivating idea of the defense minister, Boyen. Few
men have sought as energetically as he to realize the essence of
nationality in political life, i.e., in the "harmony of the people with
their government"; and if he was working toward a Prussian hegemony
in northern Germany, his reasons for doing so were essentially of a
Prussian nationalistic order. For him, Prussian power politics and a
domestic liberal reform policy were only different aspects of one and
the same idea of the Prussian state and its national personality.

Thus, the paths of a purely German, a German-Prussian, and a
purely Prussian national policy came together in the larger demand
that Prussia be ruled liberally. Everyone was obliged to be in favor of
this whether he hoped to get something from Prussia for Germany
or something from Germany for Prussia, whether he wanted to be rid
of Prussian separatism in the future or wanted to see it maintained.
The future question of what shape Prussia's relationship to Germany
should take gave way again completely to this immediate question.
For example, when Gneisenau made the noble and ambitious statement in 1814 that in view of her triple leadership in war, in law and
government, and in the cultivation of the arts and sciences, Prussia
should awaken the desire in other states to be united with her, he
was probably not certain himself whether that should be accomplished
through Prussia's absorption of the other states or through a close
federal union. But the idea that Prussia must first govern herself
liberally in order to govern in Germany is an important principle of
the Prusso-German movement within and beyond Prussia from this
point on.[11] Prussia's friends as well as her enemies realized that there
was a connection between the liberal and the national-hegemonic
tendencies in Prussia. Metternich was intent on turning Prussia away
from a liberal course and simultaneously suppressing latent German
aspirations in Prussia. Pfizer's view in 1831[12] was just the opposite.
He thought the restrictions placed on public life in Prussia provided
"the major objection that the rest of Germany can reasonably make to
Prussian hegemony."

One of the greatest merits of his lucid and perceptive *Briefwechsel
zweier Deutschen* is that he uncovers a problem and defines a dilemma
of the German-Prussian idea of unity that was deeply hidden and

---

[11] See also my remarks on Gruner's plans and Hardenberg's attitude toward
them: "Zur Geschichte des Hoffmannschen Bundes," *Quellen und Darstellungen
zur Gesch. d. Burschenschaft etc.*, I, 8ff.

[12] *Briefwechsel zweier Deutschen* (1st edn.), p. 202; reprint by Küntzel, p. 175.

that could only be seen when the first great obstacle to German-Prussian unification, the coexistence of two major powers in the German Confederation, had been eliminated and when it was possible to imagine Germany without Austria and to consider how Prussia and Germany should arrange their affairs between themselves. It was clear, as Pfizer proceeds to demonstrate, that a federal state with two major powers in the federation was impossible. But beyond that, the question arose of whether a federal state with only *one* major power in the federation was possible and, if so, how. The answer appeared to be that it was possible if Prussia decided to become liberal. But this answer brought the new dilemma with it. Prussia had to become liberal to win Germany and keep it, but she could not become completely liberal if she wanted to avoid creating still other problems, and she would indeed have created these problems by accepting the consequences of liberalism and adopting a constitutional form of government. The process of forming a Prussian state would have been carried to extremes here. Prussian existence would have been even more unified than Stein and Fichte had felt it to be. The mainstays of this state would not have been simply the dynasty, the army, and the bureaucracy, but also a central parliament and a public political life of a specifically Prussian order. The Prussian people would no longer have been just a highly serviceable substratum upon which the state leaders could base their power politics. The people would not just fight the battles of their kings, but through these new political channels they could also introduce their own ideas and goals into the policies of the state. The rest of Germany would then have to reckon with more than the political will of the Prussian nation. This would inevitably make the national union of Prussia with the rest of Germany more difficult. This kind of Prussia as the leading power of Germany would be a completely different matter from a state whose central, unifying point lay in an absolute dynasty. Such a dynasty, governing both Prussia and Germany together, could be expected to subordinate the lesser interests of Prussia to the greater interests of Germany. But if it were obliged to consider the will of Prussian popular representatives in its native state, then the regulating of Prussian and German interests would be much more difficult; and dangerous conflicts between the wills of the Prussian and German peoples could be expected. Prussia without popular representation was a young tree that could still have been easily planted in all-German soil, but Prussia with popular representation had roots too strong for that.

It is interesting to watch how the line of thought that we have just reviewed in our own words developed gradually in Pfizer's mind, how it was already a latent presence in the first edition of his book in 1831, and how it took clear form in the second edition in 1832. Because he was as much a philosopher as a politician, a thinker standing on the borderline between two epochs, we can understand why he presented his ideas in the form of a historico-philosophical construction. The seventeenth letter of his book begins by saying that the Germans should certainly continue to represent the spiritual principle in world history; but to be able to do this and to gain the previously lacking foundations for their spiritual efforts they must attach themselves to the nation in an actual and vital way. He then makes the following profound and stimulating remark: "But I also think Germany has not been divided and splintered for so long in vain, and I find it remarkable in this respect that the Prussian state, formed from a number of tribes, still does not have general popular representation but only provincial diets." He goes far afield to support this claim. He first relegates all attempts to restore the Holy Roman Empire of the German Nation to the realm of Romantic dreams, shows the differences that have arisen between Austria and Germany to be insurmountable, and then focuses his attention on Prussia, which has become more closely bound to Germany by means of the same events that made Austria's separation from Germany final. It is the Prussia of the era of reform and of the Wars of Liberation that attracts him. He felt that Prussia had won a completely valid legal claim to hegemony because of what it had accomplished in this period. It was still a youthfully vital state, blooming with health and energy; but it still had, up to this point, more energy than "beauty and form of soul." It had an outer political life but no inner one. But this had to be the case. Prussia had to turn its entire political strength outward, all the energies of the state together, in order to assert itself among the world powers. "For this reason Prussia . . . still has no general popular representation." He defended the contemporary absolutistic and apparently illiberal Prussia and its "militaristic but benevolent dictatorship." But, he said, things could not continue much longer in this fashion. Prussia's power would either have to increase or exhaust itself in excessive effort, and since the awakened self-confidence of the Prussian people was not likely to let the latter possibility occur, the only alternative was growth. But if Prussia's plans were to be fully realized, this could not be growth toward selfish ends but only toward truly national ones. By means of a protectorate over Germany, gained through such growth, Prussia would establish its political existence in

Europe on an indestructible basis; and, also, it would no longer stand in opposition to the rest of Germany. A path would be opened within the country for the development of public life and for interaction and struggle between different forces. The major objection the rest of Germany had to a Prussian hegemony would thus be eliminated.

This line of thought was fruitful enough to be pursued further. The demand that Prussia grow only in a truly national way and not in a selfish one required a more profound justification. Pfizer provided this justification in the second edition of his book, which he prepared at the end of 1831. There he found still another answer to his question of why Germany's long disunity had not been "in vain" and why it was remarkable that Prussia still had no central parliament. "The main thing," he inserts here,[13] "is to give Germany, not the Prussian state, more unity," and it is of utmost importance that the Prussian state "receive no undue and harmful predominance and that the federative, republican elements of Germany thereby be preserved and maintained. Precisely because I consider a strong federal constitution the ideal governmental form that we, with our multiple nature, should strive to attain, I would almost wish for the good of Germany that the Prussian monarchy not introduce *general* popular representation but rather that it introduce freedom of the press and provincial diets that would be more than mere mirages. If the Prussian monarchy were to be completely centralized at this moment by the introduction of a Prussian central diet, then Germany might well find itself dominated not by a *dynasty* that would guarantee its unity in diversity but by the Prussian people. May God in His mercy spare us that. A ruling family can be an object of love and respect for a ruled people, but a ruling people will sooner or later be hated by the ruled. However, if the Prussian state remains divided in separate provinces, the other German states will still be able to provide the counterweight necessary for the maintenance of their freedom."[14]

Shortly before this, he interpolated an idea that is also of interest to us here: "Much as I favor liberal institutions and constitutional life, I would rather have the most violent of despots as the ruler of Germany than have the most appropriate and perfect constitutions without a national coherence of the small individual states." Pfizer will

[13] P. 214; reprint, p. 164.
[14] When Pfizer prophesies in a later passage of the second edition (in Letter 21, p. 324; reprint, p. 253) that Prussia will certainly be a constitutional state in twenty years, he certainly does not mean to modify his earlier view but only seeks to answer the objection that Prussian recognition of constitutionalism cannot be expected.

accept an absolutistic ruler, then, if that ruler is truly German; but he will not accept the rule of a state and people that constitutionally isolate themselves. That is the most important aspect of this sentence, not, as it may seem, the primacy of unity over freedom. Unity and freedom were of equal concern to him, for he adds here: "No power in the world is any longer capable of halting the progressive dissemination of liberal ideas and institutions," but the establishment of national unity can be delayed. We can conclude that he was convinced that the Hohenzollerns, who would unify Germany as absolutistic rulers, could begin like Machiavelli's *Principe* but would finally have to become modern liberal monarchs to further the true interests of their new state.[15] The despot that Fichte considered necessary to enforce education in the elements of the German character, a despot that unifies Germany with the force of Prussian power and then finally sacrifices both despotism and the Prussian character to Germany, emerges here again in a more modern and realistic form.

Pfizer belongs to those thinkers who exhaust themselves in one great effort. His later writings on the German question, despite much that is good, offer for the most part only a variation of his rich and brilliant initial work. We can imagine how difficult it was for him in the midst of his South German friends and compatriots to hold to the fine line he had drawn between thought and emotion. He felt actual pangs of conscience when he was invited in the spring of 1832 to become a contributor to Ranke's *Historisch-politische Zeitschrift*. How could he possibly remain true to the cause of freedom for the people, which drew him away from Prussia, and to the cause of the nation, which drew him to Prussia? He declined the invitation because the time had not yet come when a South German could join Prussia with honor and without betraying his own people, and he wrote at the same time of the "essentially un-German Prussian character."[16] He continued to consider the problem of how Prussia's power could be won for Germany and how the liberal desires of the Prussian people could also be satisfied without subjecting Germany to the protectorate of an excessively powerful member of the federa-

[15] See also the arguments of the second edition, p. 268 (reprint, p. 212), and those in the essay "Ziel und Aufgaben des deutschen Liberalismus" (1832), which appears as an appendix to Küntzel's reprint, p. 337.

[16] To Perthes, March 24, 1832. Parts of this letter first appeared, with some alterations in the text, in Perthes, *Friedrich Perthes' Leben* (6th edn.), III, 367. Varrentrapp later printed an accurate version of the last page, the only extant part of the original, in "Rankes *Historisch-polit. Zeitschrift* etc.," *Histor. Zeitschrift*, IC, 70.

tion. He was soon no longer satisfied with his first attempt at a solution, namely, to satisfy those desires on a German basis and not on a Prussian one alone; for he realized that a state like Prussia would not let itself be easily dissolved. In his essay "Ziel und Aufgaben des deutschen Liberalismus," which appeared in the summer of 1832, he wrote: "The reconstruction of Germany on the basis of complete legal equality seems to require nothing less than a total revision of territorial borders and of the division of states in Germany. The Prussian monarchy would have to be . . . dissolved into a few states the size of Bavaria or Saxony." Since that was out of the question, he tried to achieve the same thing with a kind of balance-of-power form of government with Prussia on one side and all the rest of constitutional Germany on the other. Prussia would then only need to expand its provincial diets into the promised Prussian central assembly, while the German territorial assemblies could join together in a general assembly representing constitutional Germany. Then "two nearly equal and similar powers would stand face to face: the advantage the one has in strength through compact unity, the other can balance with intellectual energy. Power and law would then have finally achieved equilibrium, and the fusion of the German nation as well as the recasting of the German League of Princes into a federal state would begin." Under careful scrutiny, this attempt at a solution will be seen only to postpone the actual difficulties and to make a goal of what was really only an intermediate step. It was doubtless politically wise not to demand too much at once and to leave something to the natural course of events; but to an eye not clearly focused on its objectives, the clear lines of federal unification could become blurred again, and the demand for freedom could again take precedence over the demand for unity. Then came the Confederation's reactionary resolutions of 1832 and 1834, which darkened Pfizer's hopes for Prussia all the more. The liberal in him rose up again, stronger yet, and he demanded in 1835 that Prussia, to create the foundation for its future hegemony, should first grant solid guarantees of a liberal governmental system not only by freeing the press but also by introducing a central diet.[17] Had he put aside his initial fear of a constitutional Prussia completely? We cannot say with certainty because he also clearly stated again[18] the Germans' fears of subjection to a principal ruling nation. Several years later, though, when he published his

---

[17] *Über die Entwicklung des öffentlichen Rechts in Deutschland durch die Verfassung des Bundes*, p. 372.

[18] *Ibid.*, p. 375.

Gedanken über Recht, Staat und Kirche (1842), he seemed to have actually done so. He not only repeated his demand that Prussia provide free political institutions and let them develop in its own territory as preparation for its future dominant position in the federation,[19] but he also argued against the fear of Prussian predominance in a future German national assembly as a fear originating in weakness; and, he went on, "If federal leadership is given to that German prince who alone has the power to use it effectively, then only blind envy can regard this as subjugation to the people of that prince. The rest of the Germans would become no more subordinate to the Prussian people through this than they were to the Austrians in the Empire."[20] He added to these remarks in 1845[21] that it lay "in the natural course of development that a German national assembly be preceded by the achievement of the principle of popular representation in the individual states." But he explained further, in an essay of 1846,[22] that the Prussian character, which the rest of Germany feared and which stood in the background like a threatening and debilitating specter, was alive only in Old Prussia, which was far behind the rest of Germany in population and territory. He hoped, then, that the Rhenish and liberal New Prussia, which was beginning to show its strength at the time, would keep the Old Prussian character under control and thus minimize the danger of a constitutionally unified and centralized Prussian state dominating Germany. In this way, he tried to allay the fears that he felt and that he had awakened in his compatriots. But he had still another and deeper motive. His greatness was that he did not let his extremely lively constitutional convictions and ideals dim his awareness of the vital problem of the nation as a whole; and beyond that, he also practiced the art of calculating the fate of his ideals in the thick of European reality. As a warning to himself, to his compatriots, and especially to the men governing in Prussia itself, he said that if Prussia failed to recognize its duty in Germany and remained a reactionary ally and servant of Austria and Russia, the remaining constitutional states of Germany could and would have to join together and the upshot

[19] II, 339ff.   [20] II, 346f.

[21] *Das Vaterland. Aus der Schrift: Gedanken über Recht, Staat und Kirche besonders abgedruckt und mit Zusätzen und Anmerkungen begleitet* (1845), p. 304. In his review of the second edition of my book in the *Deutsche Literaturzeitung* (1913), No. 31, Küntzel was kind enough to call my attention to this supplementary material.

[22] "Eine Stimme über deutsche Politik," in Weil, *Konstitutionelle Jahrbücher* (1846), I, 78ff.

would be a constitutional Germany dependent on France. But that would be, he said, "beginning a new national life with an attempt at national suicide."[23] In order to avoid this terrible fate he decided, I think, to risk the lesser danger that Prussia represented for the rest of Germany. We see here again how the national autonomy of Germany as a whole and the maintenance of the Prussian state personality could be mutually dependent on each other and how the one could be accepted in order to save the other. When he took up the banner of his old ideals once again in 1848,[24] ideals that now seemed near realization, he demanded certain considerable sacrifices from Prussia as the price for its future federal leadership,[25] but he did not demand the sacrifice of its internal constitutional unity. If he had been a rigorous systematician who had had to calculate the balance of powers in a constitutional federal state, he probably would have carried the ideas he had outlined in 1831 further. However, he was not a systematician but a man with a strong instinct for vital problems, a man who could maintain his own firm basic position but who could also make compromises for the sake of a higher goal.

Friedrich von Gagern, who, along with Pfizer and Welcker, is usually counted among the initiators of the idea of the federal state in Germany, developed his thoughts with greater consistency. One of the founders of the Heidelberg Teutonia of 1815, Gagern, during his time in the Burschenschaft and together with his brother Heinrich, had already had contact with a group that expected the unification of Germany from a liberal Prussia.[26] Still thinking in the

[23] *Ibid.*, I, 126.

[24] "Beiträge zur Feststellung der deutschen Reichsgewalt" (1848). This item comprises an essay already drafted before the end of June 1848 and a draft of a federal constitution which contains a remarkable attempt to bring the more closely unified federal state under Prussia into a closer constitutional relationship with Austria. Reprinted by Küntzel, *Polit. Aufsätze u. Briefe von P. A. Pfizer* (1924).

[25] Renunciation of the right to declare war and make peace; renunciation of the right to maintain an army and fleet; renunciation of the right, in effect up to this point, to form alliances and maintain embassies; renunciation of fundamental legislative functions (p. 9).

[26] Wentzcke, "Zur Geschichte H. v. Gagerns," *Quellen u. Darstellungen zur Gesch. der Burschenschaft u. der deutschen Einheitsbewegung*, I, 163ff. Wentzcke's study and Hans Fränkel's work on "Polit. Gedanken und Strömungen von 1821-24" in Volume 3 of the same journal raise the question, which still cannot be answered with any thoroughness today, of the relationship of German patriotic and Prussian hegemonical ideas of 1814-15 to the early Burschenschaft period and the post-1848 programs of politicians with Burschenschaft backgrounds. Wentzcke shows, on p. 175, for example, that Paul Pfizer, even as a member of the Tübingen Burschenschaft in 1823, had advocated the necessity of Prussian leadership in Germany. See also Fränkel, *op.cit.*, III, 314ff.

precipitous manner of youth as late as 1823,[27] he believed that all
that was needed to unify Germany was a bold and intelligent Prussian
policy. He also believed, of course, that Prussia must then let her
name disappear in that of Germany. But he did not pursue the political consequences of this idea any further at the time. A decade
later,[28] however, he offered a plan for a federal state that demands
our attention. Despite the abstract perspective he adopts in treating
his subject, there is no doubt[29] that he is thinking of Germany here,
because his discussion focuses on a federal state derived from several
monarchies. He requires this state to meet three conditions that are
of interest to us here. First, it is "desirable, if not always essential,"
that the states that submit to the joint power of a more inclusive state
not differ too much in size or power among themselves because—
and this is Gagern's main reason—"the most powerful one or ones
can easily gain so great an influence and predominance that the
other members feel oppressed or think their interests take second
place to those of the larger powers."[30] Second, it is also desirable
that the hereditary monarch who is to control the power of the higher
state not be the ruler of a particular territory, "for he should not be
allowed any local favoritism, and he should not resemble the territorial rulers in any respect." Third, it is of highest importance in a
federal state to see that no antagonism arises between the central
and territorial diets, "for this would make government much more
difficult and endanger harmony."

We can immediately see the relationship to Pfizer's thinking of
1831 and 1832 here, and this relationship may be a matter of direct
influence. Both men were seriously concerned about the dominance
of the most powerful state within the federation, and both demanded
of the ruler of the federation that his interests be identical with the

[27] Heinrich v. Gagern, *Leben Friedrich v. Gagerns*, I, 315, gives this as the date
of Friedrich's memorial "Von der Notwendigkeit und den Mitteln, die politische
Einheit herzustellen." The entire memorial is reprinted in this volume, pp. 278ff.,
and Heinrich von Gagern apparently used the chronological indications on p. 284
in establishing this date for the document.

[28] On this date for his memorial "Vom Bundesstaat" (H. v. Gagern, *op.cit.*, I,
372ff.), cf. Brie, *Der Bundesstaat*, I, 54, note 14, and Treitschke, *Deutsche
Geschichte*, IV, 260.

[29] Brie, *op.cit.*, p. 57, shares this judgment. See, too, Jastrow, *Geschichte des
deutschen Einheitstraumes* (3rd edn.), p. 138.

[30] Pfizer, too (*Briefwechsel* [2nd edn.], Küntzel's reprint, p. 209), declared
"equality of power" as one of the premises for a genuine federative constitution,
but he abandoned it as a possibility for Germany because in this case there was
no other choice "but subordination to a superior power with as many precautions
as possible against the misuse of its power."

interests of the whole. Gagern generalizes Pfizer's fear of interference from the Prussian central diet in German affairs into a warning against the interference of any territorial diets at all. What Pfizer directly and instinctively understood, Gagern converted into the formulas and paragraphs of a system. We find in him the beginnings of a federal state theory that Waitz developed further. According to this theory, the central power and the power of individual states were to be sharply separated so that each one could exist undisturbed in its own particular sphere.

Gagern also formulated his principles so sharply because his ideal of the state had a clearer unitarian aspect to it than Pfizer's. Pfizer desired unity and diversity, strength in the whole yet at the same time freedom of movement for the individual members, so that "the life fluids of the nation can flow evenly through all the veins and arteries of the federal state's great body." He considered the despotism of a single ruler over the whole only a necessary transitional phase. Gagern, on the other hand, was basically a unitarian of a naïve Burschenschaft stamp. The experience of his more mature years made a federalist of him, but he never completely renounced his original position.[31] He was clearly much more interested in the requirements of power for the federal state than he was in those for the individual states. But who, in his opinion, was to assume this power in Germany? Brie says: "We cannot assume that he ever abandoned his conviction, expressed as early as 1823, that it was Prussia's calling to unify Germany."[32] I too consider this highly unlikely. But on the other hand, "it seems," to use Brie's words again, "that he doubted whether such a large individual state could be integrated into a genuine federal state at all." For how can we conceive of a powerful king of Prussia along with a kaiser who, according to Gagern's demand, should not be the ruler of an individual state? Brie was not able to illuminate these unclear points. But they become immediately clear if we assume that Friedrich von Gagern wanted to make the king of Prussia the kaiser of the federal state but also wanted to loosen his direct ties to Prussia and dissolve Prussia into a number of territories of approximately the same size, so that, to use his words, "every territory itself could form an administrative district that would

[31] Cf. Brie, *op.cit.*, pp. 54ff.
[32] F. v. Gagern's statement on this "from a later period," which Brie cites according to Gagern, I, 316, does not originate, as H. v. Gagern himself claims here, in the period shortly before 1848 but comes instead from F. v. Gagern's memorial of 1823. See H. v. Gagern's *Leben Friedrich v. Gagerns*, I, 285, for the original passage from the memorial.

be compatible with the sound administrative organization of the entire federal state." If such steps were not taken, the government of the federal state would be an empty abstraction, and it would stand far behind the individual territorial monarchies in the "prestige and stability" Gagern rightly required for it. If we do not assume that such steps were part of his plan here, then his memorial remains pure speculation without any practical goal. We shall soon see how this idea, which we could arrive at only by an assumption, found unequivocal expression in the programs of like-minded politicians.

While Pfizer's works were read a great deal in Germany before the March Revolution, Friedrich von Gagern's ideas remained unknown. But despite the fact that he did not have any extensive influence on the public, Gagern exercised a very strong one on his brothers, Heinrich and Max. Heinrich, who later wrote Friedrich's biography, testified that the similarities in their political thinking and philosophy amounted to total agreement. "I recognized, honored, and loved in him—my leader and example!"[33] Under Friedrich's influence, Max von Gagern became convinced that historical development had raised the Prussians to the position of the leading people of Germany; and he professed this idea in his inaugural lecture as a privatdozent in history at Bonn in 1837.[34] But he was subject to still other influences in Bonn. Here he saw an alien Prussian Protestant group of administrators and scholars holding sway over a native Catholic society that included nobility, clergy, and middle class. His basic sympathies drew him to this society, and the ecclesiastical struggle in Cologne only strengthened those sympathies. He did not become a complete enemy of Prussia, but he rebelled strongly against the bureaucratic, centralizing system of the Prussian state, and as early as 1837 he felt that salvation lay in a return to what he thought to be Stein's ideal of an "independent administrative system in every province."[35] Still more influential for him than Stein's ideals, however, were the ideals of the conservative Catholic Rhinelanders who defended their provincial character and religious interests against the burdensome centralized state of Prussia and therefore denied Prussia the character and rights of a centralized state.[36] After exchanging

[33] Op.cit., I, ix; cf. also Hiemenz, "H. v. Gagern," Zeitschr. f. d. ges. Staatswissenschaften, LV, 532.

[34] Pastor, Max v. Gagern, pp. 70 and 78f.

[35] Ibid., p. 86.

[36] There is more detailed information on this position of the Rhenish "Independents" in J. Hansen, Die Rheinlande und die preussische Politik 1815-1915, in Die Rheinprovinz 1815-1915, I, 689ff. See also Chap. 4, below.

his academic position in Bonn for civil service in Nassau in 1840, Max von Gagern was converted to Catholicism in 1843. His mild and gentle idealism was able to entertain the national ideals of his brothers, Friedrich and Heinrich, along with his newly won Catholic convictions. Of greatest interest for us, however, is the fact that the idea of a loosening and decentralization of the Prussian state could be based on other interests than unitarian ones alone. Thus, while Friedrich von Gagern had purely unitarian motives for developing this idea, his brother Max had provincialistic and Catholic ones as well; and Max was soon to present his plan at a crucial moment.

2

....

THE PRUSSO-GERMAN PROBLEM FROM MARCH TO SEPTEMBER 1848

THE GERMAN REVOLUTION of 1848 is, as we know, a complex of different and differently constituted revolutions that partly achieved their goals but also left behind problems that have remained unsolved to this day. We shall concern ourselves here with the one problem that has indeed been solved, or at least seems to have been: the problem of Prussia's position in a national federal state under Prussian and Hohenzollern leadership.

One of the most important and fruitful effects of the March Revolution was that the barrier that had previously existed between the Prussian state and the rest of Germany was lowered a good deal and that a purely Prussian isolationism became impossible. But problems arose now that could not be solved by the magic formula of Prussia's leadership in Germany. Indeed, Prussian leadership created these problems; and even if one major obstacle to the national unification of Prussia with Germany—Prussia's absolutistic system of government—had been removed by the change to constitutionalism, that fact gave rise, as we have seen, to a new, still more complicated obstacle. Prussia was to become and had to become constitutional in order to adjust her internal structure to conform with the rest of Germany and to be able to lead it, but then, through her own form of constitutional life, she raised new barriers against the rest of Germany.

The members of the South German national movement were fully aware of this difficulty during the first attempt to solve the Prusso-German problem in those critical March days when Prussia considered and carried out her change to constitutionalism. Everyone looked to Prussia then with that remarkable mixture of needs, hopes, and demands that seems possible only in revolutionary times. Everyone needed Prussia as the strongest protecting power of the monarchy and of bourgeois society in the midst of the revolutionary flood. Everyone hoped to exploit this flood to wrest the founding of a Ger-

250

man federal state and a national parliament from the dynasties. Everyone hoped to win Prussia for this cause by making her the leading power of the federal state. But to insure the individual governments and the nation against a misuse of Prussian leadership and dominance, demands were made of Prussia, not only that she become liberal herself and conform to the constitutional models of southern Germany, but also that she decentralize. These ideas emerged in the negotiations toward a reform of the federal constitution which were conducted from May 7 on. A circulating legation carried out these negotiations between the South German governments at first, then between them and the Prussian government. The major participants in these negotiations were Friedrich von Gagern's brothers: Heinrich, who was appointed the leading minister of Hessen-Darmstadt on May 6, and Max, the statesman and confidant of the Duke of Nassau. Until now we have seen Max only as an advocate of decentralization at that particular time, but his brother Heinrich said later that the idea for these negotiations had originated with Max.[1]

In his first contact with the Prussian government, a letter sent to Minister von Canitz on March 9, Max von Gagern mentioned the idea of decentralization.[2] Then, on March 15 in Munich, he spoke out quite clearly against the Bavarian government: "If Prussia accepts these conditions—equal rights and freedoms for her eight provinces and a strong German parliament—then the joint power and leadership are rightfully hers and, depending on circumstances, the kaiser's crown as well." According to his plan, the king of Prussia was to be the agency of executive power in the federal state and not really a monarch. Everyone wanted to find guarantees against a "despotic dominance of the executive." "Prussia is to be held in check."[3] However, since the Bavarian government still avoided taking a stand on the matter of Prussian leadership, it also had no reason to offer an opinion about Prussian decentralization.[4] But we can certainly assume that Max von Gagern advocated Prussian decentralization in his dealings with other governments of less importance, and we can

---

[1] Speech of March 20, 1849, *Stenogr. Bericht über die Frankfurter Nationalversammlung*, ed. Wigard, p. 5883.

[2] Pastor, *Max v. Gagern*, p. 203: "Make it clear to the king that we believe he can save us if he would give to our neighbors, the Rhine province and Westphalia, and to all the provinces the same German weapons, both the iron and the intellectual ones, that we have taken up."

[3] Pastor, *Max v. Gagern*, p. 467.

[4] The only reference we find to this question is an allusion to it, and a vague allusion at that, in the agreement of March 17 in *ibid.*, p. 472, paragraph 3.

also imagine that his brother Heinrich von Gagern did not disapprove
of this. The March events in Berlin created an entirely new situation
for the Gagern brothers' program. The Prussian crown, which had
been humiliated on March 19, clung to the German idea now to
recover prestige and power. Acting on the suggestions of the new
foreign minister, Heinrich von Arnim, the king announced in the proclamation of March 21 that he would assume the leadership of Germany
during this period of danger, and he also made the significant statement that from now on Prussia would merge with Germany. Max
von Gagern could thus regard his crop as ready for harvest when he
arrived in Berlin on the afternoon of March 21. After his first conference with Heinrich von Arnim, he was able to notify his brother
during the night of March 21: "Everyone is agreeable to anything
here, and our job is easier than if the military had won. Because of
Prussia's voluntary dissolution, the eight provinces become the
equivalent of our states, the provincial diets, the equivalent of our
parliaments. The Prussians will gladly grant all rights and freedoms
to their eight provinces now." In a second conference with Arnim on
the morning of March 22, Max von Gagern tried to impress on him
even more strongly that it was essential to make the different parts of
Germany still more equal to each other and that the two major states
of Germany, if they were further consolidated by the creation of their
own constitutions and central parliaments, would lay the greatest difficulties in the path of a future German constitution. I cannot imagine,
he said in effect, how a Landtag of four hundred Prussians and a
Reichstag of four hundred Austrians, who are not even all German
Austrians, can exist alongside our future German Reichstag of six hundred Germans. The use of such faulty arrangements would be like
putting an iron gear in a golden clock.[5]

Heinrich von Arnim was able to agree so quickly to Max von
Gagern's conditions because Gagern's ideas and actions met his own
halfway. He was ambitious but without any firm position of his own,
hence easily swayed by the winds of the times. He had lost all faith
in and all respect for the old order and the powers that maintained it.
"Political affairs," he wrote characteristically on March 17, "have no
other value than the one public opinion gives them."[6] He supported

[5] *Ibid.*, pp. 191f., 226ff.
[6] *Die polit. Denkschrift v. 17. März 1848 über die franzöz. Februarrevolution
und ihre Folgen für Deutschland* (printed as a manuscript), March 20, 1848, p.
15. The summary of Arnim's ideas following this quotation is also based on this
same memorial.

the liberal principle of nationality in its most doctrinaire form. The desire and will of the people were to determine state boundaries purely on the basis of language and history. Thus, once again in agreement with Max von Gagern, Arnim considered it a Prussian obligation to help the Poles restore their national state. A statesman who had seen the firm outlines and traditions of his own state evaporate before him was bound to be receptive to Max von Gagern's thinking. Influenced by the success of the South German circulating legation, he had doubtless begun working on his own boldly ambitious national policy designed to extricate the king from the dismal circumstances of March 19;[7] and it seems very likely that his statement of March 21 that resounded throughout Germany—"Prussia will merge with Germany"—was itself only an echo of South German desires. He said later, giving a highly instructive example of the influence of philosophy on the political thinking of the time, that he had had a Hegelian idea in mind here, namely, that one thing must be done away with if it is to live on as the nucleus of a new and greater thing.[8]

[7] The legation had even influenced the policy of his cautious predecessor, Canitz. Pastor, *op.cit.*, p. 207, has also established from Max von Gagern's correspondence files the fact that on March 11 Max von Gagern sent a report to Heinrich von Arnim from Stuttgart about the king of Württemberg's favorable statement. On p. 229, Pastor also passes on a statement of Max von Gagern's from the year 1886, according to which Arnim confided to him on March 22 that he had urged King Friedrich Wilhelm IV to make his ride through Berlin on March 21 on the basis of Max von Gagern's report from Stuttgart. This statement, however, is not an entirely accurate rendering of the situation. General von Wussow and not Heinrich von Arnim first suggested the idea of a ride through Berlin. I have found Wussow's later account of this (see Bergsträsser, "Aufzeichnungen Alexanders v. d. Goltz," *Histor. Vierteljahrsschrift* [1914], p. 71) confirmed by Major August v. d. Goltz's journals of this period: "Monday, the 20th. . . . At dinner in the king's hall, I sat with General Wussow, Below, Neumann, Radziwill, and a few others at the same table, and Wussow suggested that the king take up the German colors and ride immediately with them through the streets of Berlin and among the people. The idea was to take the initiative and bring the revolution to a halt, win public favor, and call attention to the entire German fatherland and the urgent need for unity. . . . Wussow was enthusiastic about his idea. . . . Wussow spoke with Minister Arnim (Graf Arnim or Heinrich von Arnim?), who was not averse to the suggestion but did not want to bother the king with it at table" etc.

[8] Perthes, "Beitr. z. Geschichte der Märztage 1848," *Preuss. Jahrbücher*, LXIII, 541. Graf Arnim-Boitzenburg supposedly coined the formulation "Prussia will merge with Germany," but in fact he did not. As we shall soon see below, it occurs in Droysen in 1845, then in 1847 in Hoefken, "Fragen der nationalen Fortbildung des Zollvereins," *Deutsche Vierteljahrsschrift* (1847), I, 141: "But if ideas of a political hegemony are alive in Prussia, they could only be realized with the sympathy and support of the German people, that is, by means of a German policy. Then, however, Germany would not merge with Prussia, but Prussia with Germany." Ranke reports, *Sämtl. Werke*, XLIX-L, 472, that Bunsen used the expression also on March 19, 1848: Prusia would have to merge with a liberated

These overtones are clear in his demand of March 17: "If Prussia is
to develop into Germany, its Landtag must assume and fulfill its role
as a German parliament." The deputations of the German diets were
to come to Berlin with sufficient powers of negotiation, and they were
to meet and vote *in pleno* with the United Diet. This was not meant to
suggest unequivocally that a special Prussian parliament would
become unnecessary in the future, but Arnim may well have held
this view from the outset,[9] because a little later he complied readily
with Max von Gagern's requests for Prussian decentralization. The
king's proclamation of March 21 limited itself to proposing that only
"organs" of the Prussian United Diet and not the entire United Diet
meet with the princes and diets from the rest of Germany to form a
temporary German assembly of diets. This would probably have
resulted in the creation of a provisory federal parliament composed of
delegations from the individual diets. The South German governments, too, had previously envisioned the formation of a German
lower house in this way.[10] Their delegates could not very well object
to it now, but Arnim's idea of forming the German national parliament on the basis of the United Diet doubtless annoyed them a great
deal.[11] There seems to be a difference in means here but a basic similarity in the ends to be attained. Heinrich von Arnim and the South
Germans both wanted Prussia to merge with Germany, but the major

---

Germany or it would die. Around this same time, Bunsen referred explicitly to
Pfizer's idea that the German state that was to assume federal leadership would
have to renounce every policy of its own that was not a federal policy (March 21,
Nippold, *Bunsen*, II, 505; Ulbricht, *Bunsen u. d. deutsche Einheitsbewegung*, p.
48).—We even find the following prophetic statement in Karoline v. Humboldt on
February 18, 1815: "If God grants us a pure will, well-being, and His blessing,
then a time will come, I hope, when the name of Prussia will merge with that of
Germany." *Wilh. u. Karol. v. Humboldt in ihren Briefen*, IV, 474.

[9] His further statements of March 17 do not contradict this view. The king and
the diet of Prussia, he wrote on p. 17, will not fail to see their calling of worldwide importance in and for Germany. They will not accept the idea that they
"have to follow the course taken by other German diets, a course adapted to other
circumstances (!). They will not dream of tying the hands of a government in
which they are to lead Germany at the very moment when free and forceful action
is required." On p. 19, he wrote that after order had been reestablished, the plans
for a German parliament in Frankfurt am Main or in any other acceptable place
should be taken up again according to the decision of the princes and diets convened in Berlin.

[10] Draft of plans for this house in Gagern, *Friedrich v. Gagern*, II, 647. See,
too, the March 16 memorial of the South German delegates in Pastor, *op.cit.*, p.
469, and the Prussian circular of March 25 in Roth and Merck, *Quellensammlung
zum deutschen öffentl. Recht seit 1848*, I, 172.

[11] H. v. Gagern, *op.cit.*, II, 712-14; Pastor, *op.cit.*, p. 233.

problem was then whether this amalgamation should rest on a Prussian or German basis. This was the crucial point for the arrangement of the power structure within the future federal state. However revolutionary Heinrich von Arnim may have been in manipulating the traditions of Prussian politics, he still wanted to attempt unification on a Prussian basis at first.[12]

After the low point of the March Revolution and the great loss of Prussian prestige in Germany, it was inconceivable that the rest of Germany would follow the Prussian course that Arnim had pointed out. The king abandoned this course immediately when the delegates of the South German governments expressed their strong reservations about it on March 23, but what he said to them on the same occasion showed how he really felt about the matter: "The colors black, red, and gold shall not supplant my cockade, the honored colors of black and white." He declared further that a golden crown would never adorn his brow and that he would gladly hold the silver bowl for the ruler of Austria at his coronation as German kaiser. If the king did not want to be the sovereign of Germany, as Max von Gagern immediately realized, a decentralization of Prussia was no longer conceivable.[13] All Gagern's hopes were dashed, and after a few days the negotiations of the South German governments with Prussia petered out. At this point, the governments, uncertain and divided within and among themselves, let the popular movement gain the upper hand for the time being. We must try to pick up the threads of our problem again among the leaders and thinkers of this movement, and not in government circles. We pass now from the still somewhat hazy plans of the South German politicians and of Heinrich von Arnim into the bright light of clear, well-conceived programs. If we were only able to guess at a similarity of goals and a difference in means before, we shall now have the interesting prospect of seeing a single man grasp the entire problem and think it through, in terms both of goals and of the multiplicity of means.

Johann Gustav Droysen was the son of a Pomeranian army chaplain. As a professor at Kiel, he had defended the rights of the German duchies against Denmark from 1840 on, and he had been deeply

---

[12] Other political circles also objected to the idea of uniting the German constituent national assembly with the Prussian diet. As Hassel, *Radowitz*, I, 524, reports, King Friedrich August of Saxony, in his letter of March 24 to Friedrich Wilhelm IV, made "no secret of the fact that the expression 'Prussia will merge with Germany' had been understood by the princes to mean the German individual states should merge with Prussia."

[13] Pastor, *op.cit.*, pp. 232-35.

concerned about the fate of his native Prussian state and of the greater
German nation for years. In his own passionate and highly individual
way, he furthered the ethos of the Prussian reform period and the
idea of a state based on moral autonomy and on the participation of
the citizens in the state. The Prussian monarchy, he explained in 1845,[14]
has two sides to it. It is undecided whether it wants to be a "state" or
a "power," German or European, ruled by the citizens or by a dynasty.
Prussia assumed the role of a major European power at the Congress of
Vienna and thus made a pentarchical oligarchy possible in Europe for
the first time. But it also limited its own development as a German
state while still remaining unable to assert itself as a major European
power. When Droysen separated the terms state and power from each
other, "not without some sophistry," as he himself admitted, he separated things that are inseparable and made it clear that even his own
ideal of the state had a fundamental aspect that went beyond the
state itself. But he also showed his understanding of how Prussian
state individuality had been dominated by the European and universal interests of the Restoration period that we presented in the first
part of our study. In his thinking, just as in Fichte's, we can see the
close relationship of our two problems quite clearly. He rejected
European and universalistic restrictions on Prussia, but he wanted to
impose German national restrictions on it. He demanded these restrictions, thinking they were no restrictions at all but grew instead
from the inner autonomy of the Prussian state personality. If Prussia
wanted to become a state, wanted to develop a vital sense of state
consciousness, he thought, it would have to identify itself completely
with Germany and "merge with Germany." Also, the "exclusive Prussian character," he said in his lectures of 1842-43, would have "to be
absorbed into Germany."[15] In Droysen's view, the task of becoming
a state was the same thing for Prussia as the task of becoming German. But to become completely German, he thought, Prussia should
not become a state completely. When the United Diet of Friedrich
Wilhelm IV aroused opposition among liberal thinkers in Germany in
1847, Droysen considered himself to be the only commentator who
asked what the effects on Germany's national unity would have been
if Prussia had fulfilled the hopes of liberalism rather than those of
the United Diet and had formed, with a full third of the German

[14] (Hallische) *Allg. Literaturzeitung* (1845), pp. 1ff.; cf. G. Droysen, *J. G. Droysen*, I, 274ff.

[15] II, 679; cf. G. Droysen, I, 348; J. G. Droysen toned this passage down in his typical fashion in the second edition (1886), II, 482.

population, a constitutional state with all the consequences of such a system.[16] He was pleased that Friedrich Wilhelm IV had not done that. Prussia, and Germany along with Prussia, he rejoiced, is on the right path.

Then the spring of 1848 came and prompted the development of latent ideas that he had derived from Pfizer.

His *Beiträge zur neuesten deutschen Geschichte* (1849) begins with a letter of April 6, 1848 on the political situation of Germany, and he treats the problem here with typical circumspection.[17]

It was, he said, the most dismal sign of the nation's demoralization and political immaturity that it completely misunderstood the events in Prussia from 1848 on. Displeasure had been expressed because the patent of February 3, 1847 had not brought about a clearly defined constitutional system. "I still believe now, as I did then, that such a system would have made a national unification of Germany impossible from the outset. The formulations of February 3, however, by no means precluded a close union of Prussia with the rest of Germany." Clearer still are the concluding remarks in his memorial of April 29, 1848, which is included in the same pamphlet (pages 55f.): "Prussia will 'merge' with Germany; that is, instead of constitutionally isolating herself as a political individuality, she will make her unification with Germany and the unification of the other German states among themselves possible by developing a constitution based on provincial diets. In this way, her solid and extensive power organization—primarily her military and financial institutions—will provide a framework for the whole."[18]

---

[16] (Hallische) *Allg. Literaturzeitung* (1847), II, 230f.; cf. G. Droysen, *op.cit.*, I, 345.

[17] I assume that this letter was addressed to Heinrich von Arnim. Droysen himself says in his preface of October 9, 1849: "It is not of any importance for the reader to know for whom the letter that begins this book and the memorial that ends it were originally intended." A copy of the memorial that ends the book, that of April 29, 1848, is located in Heinrich von Arnim's private files (Geh. Staatsarchiv). This copy is in Droysen's hand and displays numerous variants from the printed version, which was apparently taken from the original draft. This is doubtless the same memorial that Droysen read to Arnim and Usedom on May 5. Hübner, *Aktenstücke und Aufzeichnungen z. Gesch. d. Frankfurter Nationalversamml. aus d. Nachlass von J. G. Droysen* (1924), p. 804. Arnim also communicated the contents of the document to Camphausen on May 6.

[18] This idea appears in a shorter version in the copy for Heinrich von Arnim: "By means of the development of a constitution based on provincial diets, Prussia will be able to merge with Germany." In his preface to the printed version, Droysen writes: "The conclusion of the memorial remained uncompleted after three different drafts of it had been attempted." We see from this remark how concerned he was about the formulation of this idea.

In his letter of April 6, he also considered the possibility that the present transformation of Germany might fail. "Then, of course," he said, "Prussia must be constitutionally consolidated in the clearest terms. She must form the nucleus, the primary territory of Germany, as it were, to which all who want to be German may then gradually attach themselves."

The style of Droysen's historical constructions is familiar to us. His brilliant dialectic, influenced by Hegel, likes to balance its subject on a critical point and then calculate with great precision the possible developments, whichever way circumstances turn. But it is emotion and passion that motivate this dialectic and that pursue the course of developments with breathless excitement. For him, the merging of Prussia with Germany is, we might say, a novel of the soul that progresses like a logical construction.[19] Prussia should not have a constitution. She should have only provincial diets, or at the most a United Diet, if she is to be on good enough terms with Germany to be able to enter and blend into its constitution as one soul blends into another. But if this proves to be impossible, the roles would be exchanged. Not Prussia but the rest of Germany would have to make the sacrifice, and a Prussian constitution would have to form the basis for the German one. Here, as with almost all the programs we have discussed before, we can see that the thinker's point of view goes beyond an exclusively Prussian one. There is no question about his warm Prussian patriotism,[20] nor are the existence and power of the Prussian state felt to be mere means to an end, much less obstacles to that end. A sound development for Germany and a sound one for Prussia simply represent one and the same goal for him. But the realizing of this goal still leads, by either path he considers possible, to a transformation of the original individuality of the Prussian state; and even by the second, more Prussian path, which he really considers to be an emergency solution only, Prussia does not remain the old Prussia but becomes "the primary territory of Germany, as it were."

Droysen also put forward his ideas in the Frankfurt Committee of Seventeen, which the Bundestag had commissioned to draft a constitution. He expressed his satisfaction there that Prussia had still not

[19] Diether's stimulating essay, "Ranke und Droysen," *Preuss. Jahrbücher* (October 1910), p. 19, led me to make this slight change from the wording of the first edition.

[20] G. Droysen, *op.cit.*, I, iv, misunderstood me completely in claiming that I failed to take note of this point. O. Hintze, in the *Forschungen zur brand. u. preuss. Gesch.*, XXIII, 303, makes a relevant contribution on this matter.

been organized in any central way by a constitution, for such a unified Prussia would make Germany an impossibility.[21] More precise discussion of this question of such great consequence for the future could only be opened again when the way to Prussian hegemony was free of all external impediments. The constitutional draft of the seventeen committeemen seems to disregard and even to exclude this question when it counts among the basic rights of the German people that *every* individual state shall have a representative assembly with constitutional rights. However, this does not exclude the possibility that the author of this draft, Dahlmann, whom we shall meet again later as an advocate of our idea, may not have already considered our idea at this point, too. If this was the case—and we can only guess at that, not prove it—then he probably regarded it as a *cura posterior* for which the time had not yet come. Surely the demand, in his draft, that the future kaiser reside at Frankfurt am Main had its origins in the same spirit as our idea. They were related to each other, like a mild and a strong medicine for the same illness. Pfizer himself had recommended the milder one in the spring of 1848.[22] It is also certain that critical judges saw Prussian state unity endangered in the draft of the seventeen committeemen. Professor Braniss of Breslau commented[23] that the seventeen men probably had in the back of their minds the idea that the king of Prussia would be chosen as the German sovereign and that consequently the continuance of Prussian state unity would be insured. "But we deny this. If our monarch should assume the German throne, Prussian state sovereignty would spread to the entire state. The dissolution of the inner union of our eight provinces would not be any the less complete because each of these provinces had the honor of belonging to the kaiser's dynastic holdings. On the contrary, they would have no further significant ties to each other at all, but only a more decisive one to Germany." What he anticipated as a natural consequence, others demanded now in concrete form. On May 13, the Marburg privatdozent Alexander Heinrich Fick requested as a supplement to the draft of the seventeen committeemen that the hereditary kaisership be attached to the

---

[21] R. Hübner, *Aktenstücke und Aufzeichnungen*, p. 63; see also R. Hübner, *Der Verfassungsentwurf der 17 Vertrauensmänner* (1923), p. 21.

[22] See p. 245, above, and Haufe, *Der deutsche Nationalstaat in den Flugschriften von 1848-49*, p. 169, note 2, and pp. 184ff., where journalistic opinions on the location of the German capital have been collected.

[23] *Die deutsche Nationalverfassung und die preussische Konstitution* (Breslau, 1848), pp. 16f. Cf. Wentzcke, *Kritische Bibliographie der Flugschriften zur deutschen Verfassungsfrage 1848-51*, p. 58.

Prussian throne and that the name of Prussia merge with that of Germany. Prussia was to lose her separate ministries and her separate representative assembly. Her individual provinces were to be reorganized as new states of the most independent and republican type possible.[24] Still more important was the statement of the *Deutsche Zeitung*, the leading organ of the South German national politicians. It said on May 2 that it had received frequent oral and written communications demanding that Prussia surrender her United Diet and that her eight provinces become more a part of the other small states of Germany so that Prussia's unity would not encroach on German unity. The paper called this demand an innocent expression of the particularistic spirit but speculated on May 6 that Prussia would willingly grant the demand to initiate an amalgamation of Prussian and German nationality. It did not consider the fulfillment of this demand as absolutely necessary yet and thought that the removal of the kaiser's residence to Frankfurt would suffice to prevent Prussia from absorbing Germany.

On May 27, the *Deutsche Zeitung* printed a treatment of this idea which the paper later (on June 3) called the "boldest of all plans offered so far." The author of the article was Freiherr von Stockmar, the Coburg delegate to the Bundestag, who had written this memorial as early as April 1848.[25] If Droysen's thinking made use of both a German and a Prussian point of view at once, Stockmar's point of view was purely non-Prussian and almost non-German. Having grown up under the influence of Thüringian particularism, Stockmar was certainly an ardent German patriot, but he was also a Coburg statesman, that is, a politician who saw the political life of modern Europe as a malleable object that could be shaped by political intelligence and enlightened liberalism. He served the monarchy, but it was a monarchy of a Coburg stamp—less an old, historically rooted monarchy than a modern, skillfully established one that could be brought into advantageous balance with other modern political forces. Prince Albert thought a similar balance could be found for Germany by making the kaiser's throne elective. Only this could remove the fear the other rulers of Germany had of being oppressed and destroyed.[26]

---

[24] Memorial for the German constituent national assembly. Haufe, *Der deutsche Nationalstaat in den Flugschriften von 1848-49*, p. 166, and Wentzcke, *op.cit.*, p. 85. See Haufe, p. 168, and Wentzcke, pp. 57 and 181f., on the related ideas of the Berlin philosopher Michelet in May 1848 and May 1849.

[25] *Denkwürdigkeiten Stockmars*, pp. 489ff.

[26] Springer, *Dahlmann*, II, 231.

Stockmar was not particularly interested in maintaining the sovereignty of the princes in Germany. He quite correctly wanted a strong monarchical central government for Germany, neither a rotating government nor a kaiser without dynastic holdings; but he admitted that a kaiser with considerable dynastic holdings could prove dangerous for the constitution. Consequently, his suggestion was to make a prince with large dynastic holdings the kaiser but to force him to give up his *dynastic* holdings and convert them into *state* holdings. Thus, from a different, more doctrinaire point of departure, he arrived at a solution like Droysen's: Germany should be divided into territories directly and indirectly subordinate to the kaiser. The territory directly under the kaiser would be his former dynastic holdings. The kaiser, along with the German ministry and the German parliament, would exercise throughout Germany those powers that the constitutional draft of the seventeen committeemen had assigned to the central government of the federation. The remaining governmental powers in the territory directly under the kaiser would also be exercised through the German ministry and parliament; but in the territories not directly under him, they would be given over to the individual states. Since Prussia, because of her population, location, and historical past, seemed to Stockmar best suited to serve as the desired nucleus of Germany, the former Prussian territories that would make up the territory directly under the future kaiser would consequently fall under the German ministry and parliament from now on and not under the Prussian central government. Also, Frankfurt was to be the governmental seat and not Berlin. In this way, he thought, "the Prussian character would disappear within a short time, and a purely German attitude would emerge everywhere."

Of all the plans we have discussed so far, this one of Stockmar's is the most closely related intellectually to Friedrich von Gagern's. Both men are essentially unitarians, and they regard a federal state only as a concession. The courses of their lives had caused them both to lose contact with their native roots somewhat. They both looked at Germany as Germans, of course, but still at a remove. We can understand how they desired unity and power for Germany in its moment of misery, and we can just as easily understand how they chose the wrong means of accomplishing this. Friedrich von Gagern's vague idea of a hereditary kaisership is brought down to earth in Stockmar's plan so that it can be settled on Prussia, but Stockmar's plan also crushes Prussia in doing this. Prussia is simply a means to an end. Her territory and people are needed, but the particular spirit that held them together up to this point is not needed and should be dispensed with.

It was not Stockmar's way to work for his plan in a purely journalistic manner. Through his contacts in the cabinets and among statesmen, he was able to confer directly with men in government. In May 1848 he communicated his ideas to Bunsen, Heinrich von Arnim, and King Friedrich Wilhelm IV.[27] Heinrich von Arnim, understandably enough, responded most readily to them. Bunsen had already accepted Pfizer's ideas as a basis and had spoken on March 19 of the merging of Prussia with Germany,[28] but the unitarian consequences disturbed him now. "I think," he answered his friend Stockmar on May 17, "the achievement of this goal would represent a step backwards. The federal state is above the centralized state." But the plan still made a deep impression on him, and when he met Stockmar in Cologne in the middle of August, he—who a short time before had inveighed against the drastic measures of the Frankfurt national assembly—let himself be temporarily won and agreed upon a joint plan with Stockmar which was presented to the king and which included the idea of territories directly and indirectly subordinate to the central government. Perhaps it even occurred to Bunsen himself that this might be the easiest way for the king to extricate himself from the unpleasant situation the ineffective Berlin national assembly had created for him, and it might also have occurred to Bunsen that "the constitution of Prussia, as the territory directly subject to the kaiser, and the constitution of the central government could provide the king with the upper house he desired."[29] The king could hardly have been approached from a more vulnerable flank. To form an upper house from the brilliant, old Empire aristocracy, which had owed allegiance only to the emperor, and at the same time to be rid of his difficulties with the troublesome democratic popular representatives in Berlin— those were prospects that could tempt him. On June 17 he had

[27] *Denkwürdigkeiten*, pp. 498ff. *Bunsens Leben*, II, 446.

[28] See p. 253, note 8, above.

[29] *Bunsens Leben*, II, 467. Bunsen continued to waver in his position. For a few weeks he held to the idea of letting Germany rule Prussia (cf. Ulbricht, *op.cit.*, pp. 64 and 66; Bunsen's published "Zweites Sendschreiben" of September 5 and his letter to Camphausen on September 22, Nippold, *op.cit.*, II, 479), but then he again demanded an independent Prussian ministry and a Prussian parliament that would, however, consist of the Prussian members of the German parliament (Ulbricht, pp. 64 and 80). I do not interpret the statement of August 17, which Ulbricht (p. 64) uses to support his argument, as a criticism of Stockmar's plan but as a criticism of the lack of consideration shown toward Prussia at the time by Frankfurt. On his suggestions of January 1849, see Chap. 4, below.

rejected Stockmar's plan in a friendly but decisive way;[30] but now, in August, when Bunsen presented the joint plan to him, he no longer seems to have considered it so completely objectionable. "That is a dangerous lure," he thought, "and it is important to keep a clear head and hold one's ground."[31] But we must look into the matter further before we can discuss the king's position here in more detail.

OUR STUDY WILL ATTEMPT to illuminate here those efforts undertaken to make Prussia the leading power of Germany in exchange for the sacrifice of her state personality, efforts that would not only take something from the Hohenzollerns and the Prussian people but would also give them something in return. But to understand the basis on which these tendencies could develop, we must also examine those efforts which only made demands of Prussia, without wanting, at first anyhow, to give her anything at all. The focal point here was the major struggle between Frankfurt and Berlin that began in the spring of 1848 and continued through the summer and fall. It dealt with the question of whether the Prussian state was obliged now, before the question of leadership was settled, to submit to the authority of the Frankfurt national assembly and the provisional central government that it had created. Our subject in this study is essentially a matter of negotiation, the conditions for a process of fusion between the Prussian state and the rest of Germany; but in this struggle, the opposition between national sovereignty and individual state monarchy is the central point. However, two different causes motivated this battle against the monarchy. The Leftist parties of the Frankfurt national assembly fought it primarily for democratic principles. They hoped to use the omnipotence of the Frankfurt assembly to eliminate monarchistic prerogatives both in the central government and in the individual states of Germany. But in the Center, from which the Erbkaiserpartei developed, the battle against the strongest German particularistic state was fought for the sake of future unity. Even many participants who believed or hoped that Prussia would carry forward the idea of German unity in the future felt obliged as a matter of principle to demand certain rather considerable sacrifices of her state independence during the provisional phase.

The first of these sacrifices, one that the Left demanded in Frankfurt but that the Center parties mitigated considerably, is of particular

---

[30] Stockmar, pp. 506f.

[31] From remarks written in the king's own hand in the margins of Bunsen's plan, August 1848. Hausarchiv.

interest to us here, for it has to do with the crucial problem of whether two constituent parliaments in Frankfurt and Berlin could meet at the same time and whether a Prussian constitution could be framed before the completion of the constitution for all of Germany. The advocates of democratic freedom as well as the advocates of closer unity were afraid that arrangements made in framing the Prussian constitution might interfere with their work, and this fear was shared even by Prussian patriots who wanted to raise their native country to leadership in Germany with the aid of the Frankfurt assembly.[32] The Preliminary Parliament had requested that no other constituent assemblies besides the Frankfurt one be convened. The Committee of Fifty, appointed by the Preliminary Parliament, adopted this suggestion; and at the end of April it asked the Bundestag to submit for discussion and resolution its view that constituent assemblies in the individual states should not be convened before the framing of the German constitution was completed.[33]

But this did not prevent the Prussian government from holding elections for a constituent assembly and from convening this assembly on May 2 in Berlin, an act that found no favor with Prussian democrats either. From Frankfurt, Heinrich Simon of Breslau tried in vain to dissuade Premier Camphausen from doing this.[34] Johann Jacoby asked angrily in his pamphlet *Deutschland und Preussen*, dated May 18, 1848,[35] whether the ministry wanted to make the other German states feel Prussia's predominance, now that all the other governments except Prussia had accommodated themselves? In the second meeting of the Frankfurt assembly, on May 19, Franz Raveaux from Cologne tried to avoid extremes in his approach to the subject, but on May 22 his compatriot Venedey submitted a motion that every constitution considered or ratified before completion of the Frankfurt constitution be declared null and void.[36] Robert Blum seconded this motion on May 27 with the statement: "It is highly dangerous that a constitution is being framed in Prussia, for once it is completed we are no longer free."[37] There was, then, a willingness right

[32] Hansen, *Mevissen*, II, 373f., 382.

[33] *Stenogr. Bericht über die Frankfurter Nationalversammlung*, ed. Wigard, p. 127; Roth and Merck, *Quellensammlung zum deutschen öffentl. Recht seit 1848*, I, 333; Jürgens, *Zur Geschichte des deutschen Verfassungswerkes 1848-49*, I, 66. The Bundestag's response to this was evasive.

[34] May 1, 1848; cf. Joh. Jacoby, *H. Simon*, p. 233.

[35] Joh. Jacoby, *Reden und Schriften*, II (1877), 12ff.

[36] *Stenogr. Bericht*, p. 40; see also other, less extreme amendments, *ibid.*, pp. 125ff.

[37] *Ibid.*, p. 150.

from the start to restrict the Prussian state and rob it of its right to form its own constitution. However, the more temperate majority of the assembly was satisfied with Werner's motion, which was finally passed almost unanimously on May 27. This resolution stated that the general constitution to be framed by the Frankfurt assembly would provide the standards for declaring valid or invalid any articles of the individual constitutions which did not correspond directly to those of the general constitution.[38] The majority was able to accept this resolution all the more easily because Camphausen's constitutional draft for Prussia, which was published on May 20, provided that the adjustment of any conflicts between the future German constitution and the Prussian one would be made by altering the Prussian constitution.

The idea that Prussia should have no constitution or central parliament at all was never expressed in these negotiations, but it was an assumption that played a role in them. It also played a crucial role when a provisional central government was formed in June 1848 without consulting Prussia. Usedom, Prussia's representative in Frankfurt, reported to his government on June 4 that Gagern regarded Prussia only as material for Germany, not as an independent organism. When the prestige of the Prussian government sank still lower because of the storming of the Berlin armory on June 15, Usedom was obliged to report on June 24: "Everyone in Frankfurt is asking whether it is possible to depend on Berlin and whether it might not be better to make the central government in Frankfurt as strong and unified as possible without regard for Prussia. Only in this way do people here think there is any hope of countering the growing anarchy in Germany. The Left comes to the same conclusions by a different route, since the weakening and elimination of the Prussian monarchy is the most desirable thing imaginable for them."

In wanting to postpone the framing of a Prussian constitution, the Frankfurt democrats hoped, as we saw, to subject it to the expected democratic constitution of Germany. In his attack against the Prussian ministry, Johann Jacoby played the part of advocate for the unitarian national idea.[39] Although the necessity for complete political unity has been recognized nearly everywhere in Germany, he said, an unfortunate separatistic spirit is stirring again in many Prussians, a narrow, limited provincial pride, an obstinate, petty,

---

[38] *Ibid.*, p. 155; cf. Mollat, *Reden und Redner des ersten deutschen Parlaments,* pp. 6ff.

[39] P. 15 in the pamphlet cited above.

and vain insistence on one's own sovereignty. But this kind of unitarian thinking did not go very deep. Nothing reveals more about the actual character of Prussian democracy at that time, about the primacy of its democratic ideal as opposed to the national ideal, than the change of direction it took in the course of the summer and fall of 1848. The turning point is obvious enough. It is the motion that Johann Jacoby made in the Prussian national assembly on July 7. He and his associates had been pleased that the Frankfurt assembly had chosen a German regent without consulting the princes, but had been annoyed that the assembly had bestowed the monarchical attribute of unaccountability on him. Moreover, they were thoroughly disgruntled when the Prussian government[40] afterwards recognized the Frankfurt appointment as valid but then refused to accept any further consequences of this unilateral election. All these different feelings found expression in Jacoby's motion. Had the motion been passed, the Prussian national assembly would have had to both praise and censure the German national assembly. This would have offered a classic example of the complicated entanglements that could arise if two strong parliaments engaged in high-level politics in Germany at the same time. But these difficulties did not disturb the Berlin democrats. They were perfectly willing to exert pressure in Frankfurt one day and in Berlin the next as long as they could gain as much democracy as possible by these tactics. They did not succeed in Berlin, and Jacoby's motion was defeated on July 12 by a large majority. But this majority had no firm foundations under it, and from August 1848 on the inexperienced Berlin assembly came under the influence of the originally small number of Leftists in it. When the Berlin democrats discovered that the Berlin national assembly was more useful to them than the Frankfurt one, they rediscovered their Prussian hearts. At the end of July, Gustav Rümelin heard in Frankfurt[41] that the Berlin radicals were looking toward an alliance with Prussia and were urging Prussian soldiers to deny allegiance to the German regent. The feeling among the democrats in Berlin in August 1848 was that they could do without Frankfurt. They could then frame a perfectly suitable democratic constitution for Prussia and would no longer need a German parliament to guarantee their freedom.[42] As Frankfurt had been in

[40] Statement of Premier von Auerswald in the July 4 meeting of the Berlin assembly.

[41] *Aus der Paulskirche*, p. 58.

[42] Reported by Sybel in the Hessian diet, January 1849, and cited by Varrentrapp, "Meinungen in Kurhessen über d. deutsche Kaisertum 1848-49," *Histor. Zeitschrift*, XCIV, 95.

the spring, so was Berlin now the hope and the battlefield of the democrats, especially after they had been roundly defeated on September
18 after repeated attempts to gain the upper hand in Frankfurt. "The
extreme Left," a Berlin correspondent of the *Deutsche Zeitung* reported on October 12,[43] "is agitating everywhere against the central
government and the national assembly. They do not scorn an alliance
now with the very separatistic tendencies they opposed so bitterly
before." On October 23 the Prussian national assembly adopted a resolution on the rights of the Poles in Posen. This resolution was to be
included in the constitution; it stood in direct contradiction to the
resolutions adopted in Frankfurt; and it therefore represented a crass
violation of the principle laid down in Frankfurt on May 27. On
October 24, Waldeck and d'Ester made a motion in the Berlin assembly providing that decrees of the Frankfurt central government
or constituent assembly affecting the internal affairs of the individual
territories could gain legal validity in Prussia only if they were approved by representatives of the Prussian people.

In the ranks of these democrats who had suddenly become so
friendly toward Prussia there were certainly some who honestly and
energetically held both Prussian and democratic convictions and
who could therefore protest violently against the idea of dividing
their fatherland and dissolving it province by province into Germany.[44]
But it was monarchistic and conservative Prussia that resisted such
division, and any ideas related to it, more strongly than democratic
Prussia. A remarkable state of affairs held sway, then, in the summer
and fall of 1848, when the older, more fundamental Prussia, that
is, monarchistic, conservative Prussia, rose up along with democratic
Prussia and rebelled against the authority of Frankfurt.[45] This move-

---

[43] *Deutsche Zeitung*, October 14. W. Schrader observes neatly about this situation in his *Erfahrungen und Bekenntnissen* (1904), p. 104: "The irony of history
helped bring about a peculiar reversal. The same radical representatives who, in
the spring, had most recklessly advocated total authority for the German government would, in the fall, have gladly gone back to the diets of the individual states
as a means of resisting a German constitution that did not suit them."

[44] One of these was Karl Gutzkow, who wrote in his book *Deutschland am
Vorabend seines Falles oder seiner Grösse*, begun before the September insurrec-
tion in Frankfurt and published after it: "Would to God the rest of Germany had
as many points of unity and strength as Prussia. Only the idea of Old Prussia
should be destroyed and dispersed" (p. 198).

[45] On the occasion of Waldeck's motion of October 24, an article in the conservative *Volksblatt für Stadt und Land* said on October 28: "Les extrêmes se touchent."
The extreme Right and the extreme Left, the paper said, were now in agreement
on the *form* of the Prussian relationship to the central government. "We are conservative separatists. The Leftists are revolutionary separatists."

ment began after the election of the Archduke as the German regent, and it gained momentum on July 16 when the German minister of defense ordered all German troops to participate in a symbolic parade of homage to the regent. A still greater impetus developed in July, when the part of the constitutional draft composed by Dahlmann, Beseler, and Mittermaier appeared. This draft required the individual governments to give up their right to maintain diplomatic relations and also required them to put all Germany's armed forces under the command of the central government. The Prussian General von Griesheim objected that this would destroy the Prussian army as such. His pamphlet *Die deutsche Zentralgewalt und die preussische Armee*, dated July 23, 1848,[46] voiced the protest of that Prussian military element which resisted any unitarian threats to Prussian character by an appeal to the traditions of Frederick the Great and of the Wars of Liberation. This sensational work was misrepresented when it was called merely reactionary Prussian in character. Griesheim made it clear that he would accept German unity if Prussia were in a position of leadership, but "even within a German unity, Prussia wants to remain Prussia." Thus his protest touched on those far-ranging ideas that are the subject of our study, and it concurred with a second manifesto of monarchistic Prussia, Graf Arnim-Boitzenburg's booklet *Die deutsche Zentralgewalt und Preussen* (August 1848). The statesman of March 19 wrote less colorfully and clearly than the angry soldier, but he left no doubt that Prussia would refuse to dissolve herself "into one or several German provinces." More significant still was the fact that the heir to the Prussian crown also grasped both the promising and threatening aspects of the situation for Prussia. It must have been during these weeks that he said to Ernst von Saucken in Babelsberg,[47] "Prussia must come to leadership in Germany as Prussia and not be received into it as a province, not merge with it."

Outside the circle of these high-ranking representatives of the idea of the Prussian state, there was also considerable activity among the people. On July 14, a Berlin correspondent sent the *Deutsche*

---

[46] On his authorship, see Wentzcke's study in the *Histor. Zeitschrift*, CVI, 340ff.

[47] The prince of Prussia said to E. v. Saucken in Babelsberg on November 18, 1850: "What I said to you in the summer of 1848 on this very spot is and remains my motto: 'Prussia must etc.'" G. v. Below, "Aus der Zeit Friedrich Wilhelms IV.," *Deutsche Rundschau* (December 1901), p. 389. See also the memorial of Princess Augusta from October 1848 in Bailleu and Schuster, *Aus dem literar. Nachlass der Kaiserin Augusta*, I, 119f.

Zeitung[48] a drastic account of Prussian pride that felt threatened and that asked, with gnashing of teeth, if Prussia was to expire. The *Deutsche Zeitung* itself had to admit on July 23 that the idea of destroying Prussia by incorporating her as a subject into Germany had electrified the masses; and on August 2, the paper said of this movement: "The agitation in Prussia has acquired such strength that our friends and observers there believe it is more powerful than the government itself."[49] It was in this situation that Max von Gagern appeared again in Berlin on August 12 to exert his influence, as the plenipotentiary of the German ministry, on the peace negotiations of the Prussian government with Denmark. He noted the rise of the Prussian separatist spirit with dismay, and it prompted him to recall again the idea he had expressed in March. He gave emphatic warning of the difficulties that the drafting of the German constitution would encounter if Prussia became still further centralized through a constitution and parliament. It was essential, he thought, to make the different parts of Germany increasingly similar.[50] The Prussian government did not take his advice on this point or on the Danish question either. Prussia demonstrated her independence of the Frankfurt government by ending the war with Denmark unilaterally with the Truce of Malmö, and in doing so she had the support of the population behind her. Both the state and the people of Prussia expressed their desire to remain Prussian.

In the last analysis, it was precisely this rise of Prussian self-confidence that cleared the political air again, focused the thinking of those in favor of a hereditary German throne, and set the framing of the Frankfurt constitution in motion. The national assembly in Frankfurt could not carry its unitarian policy against Prussia too far without becoming involved in the turmoil of the democratic revolution. It went further than political prudence allowed when it rejected the Truce of Malmö on September 5, but it still managed to break with the Left in time; and on September 16 it nullified its first resolution against Prussia in the matter of the truce. Then the republicans in Frankfurt rebelled and were put down. If the majority parties in Frankfurt wanted to prevent utter failure now, they could do nothing

[48] P. 1587.

[49] Cf., too, Rümelin, July 19 and 29, *op.cit.*, pp. 37 and 49ff.; Hansen, *Mevissen*, I, 568ff.; and the sources cited by Jastrow, *op.cit.*, pp. 285ff.

[50] M. v. Gagern's speech of September 16, *Stenogr. Bericht*, p. 2129; Pastor, *op.cit.*, pp. 192 and 271ff.

but ask for the help of the power they had wanted to subject to unitarian bondage only a short time before. Camphausen, Prussia's deputy to the central government, was able to report to his government with satisfaction on October 3 that the battle over the truce had unexpectedly revived the feeling that it was impossible to found a unified Germany without allowing the strongest member of the federation a position commensurate with its strength.[51] It had simply proved impossible during the period of the provisional government to impose the rigorous demands of the federal state on Prussia without giving her something in exchange. As a result, the ideas of the spring revived, and those who favored the Prussian hegemony saw their decimated ranks filling again. But there was no desire to capitulate to Prussia unconditionally either. General opinion still held that the Prussian hegemony should not and would not make Germany Prussian,[52] and the Frankfurt assembly felt strong and influential enough to demand concessions of a Prussian crown that was to become the German crown. At this point the ideas that Stockmar and Max von Gagern had advocated assumed new life, not just as interesting theses, however, but as integral parts of a party program.[53]

[51] *Geh. Staatsarchiv* (hereafter referred to as G.St.A.).

[52] Cf. *Deutsche Zeitung*, September 2.

[53] These ideas were only touched on in the deliberations of the constitutional committee of the Frankfurt national assembly in the summer and fall of 1848 (Part I, ed. Droysen, 1849) because there was still uncertainty about who would control the future central government. See, for example, Soiron's statement of August 9 (p. 167): "As long as we can find no means of destroying the large states and mediatizing the small ones, we shall still have the problem of forming a federal state out of states that are too large for a federal state and states that are too small" etc. Droysen himself reserved opinion and only suggested that the final word on the form the union of Germany and Prussia should take could not yet be spoken (p. 67).—From the journalistic side, the pamphlet *Eine preussisch-deutsche Fantasie* (Hamburg) still advocated in August 1848 that Prussia be dissolved into her provinces. Perhaps, the pamphlet said, the king of Prussia could then be elected German kaiser, not with a hereditary crown, however, but with a republican organization for Germany! (P. Wentzcke, *Kritische Bibliographie*, p. 113.)

3

•••

HEINRICH VON GAGERN'S ATTEMPT
TO WIN PRUSSIA

RÜMELIN, THE WÜRTTEMBERG DELEGATE in Frankfurt, wrote to the *Schwäbische Merkur* on October 1:[1] "The rapid and definitive establishment of a German constitution and administration is the only way to rescue Germany from the anarchy and confusion of her present condition. Of the many different plans and schemes to accomplish this, there is one that has only been discussed in private circles up till now but that may have some future. It is the old principle that Prussia should merge with Germany in a new or at least more definite and concrete form. Its basic features are as follows: All the German states excluding Austria will make up Germany proper (with thirty-three million people). The king of Prussia will be king of Germany and reside in Frankfurt. All of Prussia will be a territory directly under the king of Germany and will stand directly under the central German ministry and administration for legislative and executive purposes. The Berlin diet and the Prussian ministry will be discontinued, and only provincial diets will remain." Gustav Rümelin, a man in his early thirties at the time, was one of Paul Pfizer's close friends.[2] He was as vitally interested in both philosophy and politics as Pfizer was; but, as the younger of the two, he had a more modern outlook. Thus, it seems more than likely that Pfizer's thinking gave him his point of departure for the ideas developed above, but it is equally likely that he had been influenced by Max von Gagern, who had touched on his own ideas while speaking in parliament shortly before, on September 16. In any case, Rümelin, like Pfizer and Max von Gagern, had his roots in the soil of Southwest German political and national feeling, and it was from this feeling that the Erbkaiserpartei drew its major backing.

His other demands, among them a plan for a broader union between

[1] *Aus der Paulskirche*, p. 102.
[2] Laube, *Das erste deutsche Parlament*, III, 29.

271

Germany and Austria, need not concern us here. But it is characteristic of him that he mentions Austria's objections to this solution to the German question as an obstacle that the plan would have to overcome, but he does not foresee any objection at all from Prussia. In the narrow circles in which this plan was seriously considered, everyone was probably so convinced of the great advantages Frankfurt had to offer the Prussian royal house that there was no doubt of its willingness to pay the price for them; for it was a difficult task indeed to win the Frankfurt assembly over to the idea of a Hohenzollern hereditary monarchy for all of Germany. In case this could not be accomplished and the central government took the form of a tripartite or rotating leadership, there would be no further thought of founding a territory directly subject to the central government. This "important and fruitful idea," as Rümelin called it, of transforming Prussia into a territory directly subject to the central government was accordingly treated in October as a strategic plan for the future. It would only be presented if the central government were granted to Prussia, and it would only be useful under those circumstances.[3]

Even the advocates of a Prussian central government could only be won to this plan gradually; and, as we shall see, not all of them could be won at the same time, for the plan frightened all those who had accepted the idea of a federal state in the hope that it would develop into a centralized state. This became evident in the constitutional committee on October 13 when Briegleb, who belonged to the Coburg circle and considered himself a student of Stockmar's, presented the plan for territories directly and indirectly subject to the central government.[4] "With this concept," he remarked, "we would achieve great unity and at the same time a rapid consolidation of the small German states that would like to merge with Germany." The idea of the federal state, he went on to say, is not so generally accepted as we believed, and it does "not represent a desire but only an expedient." Waitz, who had studied the nature of the federal state in a particularly penetrating and knowledgeable way and who considered a Prussian hereditary kaisership incompatible with it, was completely against Briegleb's suggestion. Dahlmann, the leading member of the constitutional committee, did not fundamentally reject it

[3] Rümelin, October 29, *op.cit.*, p. 116.

[4] Hübner, *Aktenstücke*, p. 141, and *Die Mediatisierungsfrage in der Frankfurter Nationalversammlung* (1923), p. 31; Briegleb's advocacy of Stockmar's plan, December 13, *Aktenstücke*, p. 291. On Briegleb, see the memoirs of Herzog Ernst, *passim.*

but thought it unsuitable for the problem that had to be solved at the moment. He would not have been unhappy if everyone had come together in one state, but this lay beyond the present task. Riesser said, too, that what Briegleb wanted was precisely the opposite of a federal state. Briegleb defended himself by saying that all the individual states would by no means disappear. The ones that were capable of life would maintain themselves, and whether the academy had a name for the resulting governmental form or not was of no importance. But he was still only able to interest his listeners, not convince them.

Events had to exert their influence to clarify thinking about the relationship of a leading Prussian state to the rest of Germany. This relationship entered a new phase because of the conflict between the Prussian crown and the Berlin national assembly. As we saw earlier, Berlin was now the battlefield of democracy. The Berlin parliament held a plenary meeting beginning on October 12 to discuss the Prussian constitution, and in this meeting the democrats gained one victory after another. They held a congress of German democrats in Berlin on October 26, and their violent evening demonstrations on October 31 in front of the theater building where the parliament was in session forced the representatives inside to resolve that the Prussian government urge the central government to protect the threatened freedom of the Austrian population. But an opposing current was also in motion to drive back the Berlin assembly's desire for domination and to strengthen the power of the crown again within the monarchy. Pfuel's weak ministry resigned, and on November 2 the Berlin assembly learned that Graf Brandenburg would form the new ministry, a ministry to be chosen completely in accordance with the wishes of the king.

Up to this point, the majority parties in Frankfurt had not taken much notice of these events in Berlin.[5] The Prussian parliament was considered inferior, and its constitution, the *Deutsche Zeitung* said on October 12, was only a temporary one that would be confirmed or changed by the decisions reached in Frankfurt. The Berlin parliament attracted attention again only when it dared to defy the authority of the Frankfurt parliament on October 23.[6] The terroristic activities of the Berlin sidewalk demagogues at the end of October outraged everyone in Frankfurt.[7] In this matter Frankfurt and Potsdam were

---

[5] Haym, *Die deutsche Nationalversammlung von den Septemberereignissen bis zur Kaiserwahl*, p. 17.

[6] See p. 267, above.

[7] Camphausen's report of October 30, G.St.A.

natural allies, but because the Prussian government had shown so little strength in dealing with the Berlin parliament so far, the Frankfurt assembly, which had made use of Prussian military aid only a few weeks before in the September crisis, now thought it could look down with pity on the Prussian throne. It felt itself to be in a safe port and watched the Prussian ship of state being tossed about in the storm outside. On November 3, Camphausen sent his grave letter of warning to the ministers in Berlin:[8] "In the last two weeks, our prestige in Frankfurt has suffered proportionately as events in Berlin have indicated weakness in the government. . . . Do not blame me if I cannot at present create and maintain the regard that is due the Prussian government. The best intentions and the greatest capabilities cannot achieve that if one does not represent a power in whose power people believe. The extent of my influence in Frankfurt will depend on the course of events in Berlin."

The more serious politicians in Frankfurt were not able to enjoy having the upper hand for long. The beginning of November brought news of the defeat of the revolution in Vienna. Austria, then, was pulling herself together energetically, while the first step toward greater strength that the Prussian crown had made, the appointment of Graf Brandenburg, evoked new and unpredictable complications in Prussia. Attacks and counterattacks followed one after another now. On November 2 the Berlin assembly protested the appointment of a ministry that had not been approved by the parliament. The king's message of November 3 rejected the protest. On November 9 the assembly learned the names of the other new ministers, who were to some extent even less desirable than Graf Brandenburg, and learned, further, that its session would be adjourned and removed to the city of Brandenburg. The assembly protested all these measures and continued to convene illegally. It seemed that Prussia was in the first stages of a new revolution that might lead to a *convention nationale* of the Berlin national assembly. That would have been a triumph for the Leftists in Frankfurt, who were more interested in freedom than unity; but the framing of a constitution for Germany, the task that occupied the Center parties, would have been set back immeasurably. The Frankfurt assembly would have had a powerful and victorious rival in Berlin, and all fears of a harmful antagonism between the Prussian and German parliaments would have been proved justified. As a result, the idea whose history we are studying

[8] Private letter to Bonin, Graf Dönhoff, and Eichmann, copy in G.St.A.

here suddenly became acutely important. It also became a motivating force behind the decisions reached in Frankfurt. Recalling Rümelin's earlier statement, we can assume that the views he presented on November 18 had been a part of his thinking a week before.[9] "A complete victory for the Berlin assembly," he said, "would be disastrous for the work of this assembly. It would produce a ruinous schism in Germany and bring to temporary power a party that has no future there. In its relationship to the crown, the Berlin assembly does not clearly and unquestionably have the law on its side, nor does it lie in the interests of our assembly to unilaterally favor a dangerous rival that by rights should never have convened and that will not exist at all in the future if we manage to create a reasonable constitution for Germany. The best solution would be for Prussia to have no general constitution of her own but only provincial diets and for the Prussian central assembly to merge with the German parliament. As long as these two powerful legislative bodies exist side by side in Germany, envy and division will be inevitable. *Politics require us to consider this aspect of the situation.*"

Rümelin was somewhat too reckless in calling public attention to another aspect of the situation that he and his party associates had considered. This aspect was an awareness of their own political weakness, the realization that the omnipotence of the Frankfurt assembly was a dream, that they could exert only a moral influence, and that they consequently had to exert this influence as cautiously and temperately as possible to avoid disappointment and humiliation. But on the other hand they could not exert it too timidly. They could not merely remain inactive and watch, for the future of Germany was dependent on the future of Prussia. The pressure of events verified more and more the conviction that everything depended on Prussia and that nothing could be done without her. "If the Prussian crown falls now, most members of the Center said, you will have lost more than you have won for the German cause."[10] The *Deutsche Zeitung* wrote on November 13 that it was imperative to risk everything for Prussia, but not for Austria, "because Prussia must and will be ours at any price." Prussia cannot be allowed to fall into reaction or anarchy, the paper said. A decisive general victory of the crown in Prussia, then, could have been just as dangerous for the plans of the Frankfurt assembly as a victory of the Berlin constituent assembly.

It was a highly delicate situation, in which inaction could be just

[9] *Op.cit.*, pp. 124ff.   [10] Laube, *op.cit.*, III, 142.

as dangerous as action. Balance had to be artfully maintained, but the best minds of the assembly hoped to achieve great things with their skill at balancing. This is one of the most interesting moments in the history of the assembly. Rudolf Haym's account gives us the most information about it. It was our goal, he writes,[11] to prevent the Prussian crown from being victorious alone and without the help of the Frankfurt assembly: "A victory without us would create the impression of a victory of bayonets"; it could lead to extreme reaction. But, he continues, if we supported the Prussian crown decisively now we would do her a considerable moral service because we would remove the odium of reaction from her measures; and, in turn, our help would put the crown in debt to us. We would then gain a greater influence on her, and that would be beneficial to the cause of unity as well as to that of freedom. If the crown were victorious without us, "Prussia would feel more Prussian than ever in her regained strength. She would then create well-nigh insurmountable obstacles to unification. But if she had to admit that we were to a great extent responsible for her salvation, then she would once again be led in the direction in which we all think she can find her strength and renewed life in the future. A new, unbreakable bond would then be formed between Germany and Prussia that could be called a bond of gratitude in human terms and a bond of necessity in political terms."

We can now bring together Rümelin's ideas of November 18, presented earlier in this chapter, with these views of Haym's, which Haym describes in the party report written in the summer of 1849 as the motivating ideas of the Kasinopartei in November 1848. Even if Haym does not mention here the demand that Prussia have no parliament, he alludes to it approvingly in a later passage of his book (pages 227ff.). His ideas and Rümelin's coincide in all essential points. The goal of this clever and delicate policy was to join Frankfurt's intangibles with the tangible power of the Prussian crown, to win a strong ally for the emotions and the intellect. This policy would have offered the Prussian state a helping hand at the very moment when it was not only very willing to be helped[12] but also most free and least troubled by the burdens that, according to Pfizer, Droysen, Max von Gagern, and Rümelin, were preventing its merger with Germany. The Prussian government, in trying to rout its obstinate parliament, was moving in the very direction these men wanted it to take.

[11] *Op.cit.*, pp. 34ff.
[12] Cf. Brandenburg, *Untersuchungen u. Aktenstücke z. Gesch. d. Reichsgründung*, p. 132.

As we have seen, Bunsen had already tried to convince the king once before that he could get rid of his intractable democratic parliament most easily by following Stockmar's plan. The critical moment for this had come. Sanssouci and Frankfurt could have joined hands against Berlin: the Hohenzollern dynasty and the German national assembly against the Prussian national assembly. This was a remarkable historical moment, laden with imponderables. We see the ships, as it were, turning rapidly and the compass needles oscillating. Here, of course, the objection can be made that the compass of the Prussian state would soon show the old direction quite of its own accord. But that still does not negate the interest of this situation, and that interest lies primarily in the fact that the proud old crown of the Prussian kings could have found an ally in a movement no less popular than the popular movement she was opposing. Against a movement that wanted only freedom, she could have utilized a movement that wanted both freedom and power. She could have found common ground with the liberalism that Frankfurt offered her and that had been recast and forced in her direction by the struggle against the common democratic opponent. The monarchy could have reconciled itself to the spirit of the times; but, as we know, it would have had to take up an entirely new and purely German position, not a Prussian one.

This is, then, the essence of the policy of balance that we find in Rümelin's and Haym's statements. We do not know in detail how or by whom this policy was advocated in Frankfurt. We can only verify that it was considered at the time. Rümelin could not have been the only one with the idea of seizing the opportunity to strike a blow against the rival parliament, and we are probably not mistaken if we see a similar mood in an interesting passage from a letter that the Rhenish delegate Mevissen wrote from Frankfurt on November 17: "The mood of the assembly here favors the king and opposes the Berlin assembly, *not for legal reasons, however, but for reasons of unity.*"[13]

The idea gained support. This is evident in the less dramatic work of the constitutional committee. On November 20 the composition of

---

[13] Hansen, *Mevissen*, II, 443. Prompted by Küntzel's remarks in the *Deutsche Literaturzeitung* (1908), p. 460, I have formulated this interpretation in a more hypothetical fashion than I did in the first edition. However, I still consider it less farfetched than Küntzel's. According to Droysen's journals (Hübner, *Aktenstücke*, p. 831), "the future of Prussia, her dissolution for the sake of the German crown," was also discussed in a meeting of the leaders of the Erbkaiserpartei at Beseler's on the evening of November 15. This, too, cannot be understood in any other way than as a debate on the ideas we have been treating.

the Staatenhaus was discussed. Half of this house was to be made up of members appointed by the governments, and the other half, of members appointed by the representative assemblies of the individual states. Beseler submitted that the small states should be united with or attached to the larger ones for purposes of these elections. Then he brought up another question in connection with this. It would probably be a mistake, he said, if the major states were directly represented through their central diets. A division of these states into provinces and representation in the Staatenhaus by these provinces would perhaps be preferable. Dahlmann had suggested, he went on, that in Prussia, Austria, and Bavaria the members of the Staatenhaus be apportioned by districts (provinces) and that half of them be appointed by the governments, half by the diets of the districts. "In this way," he concluded, "we would begin to draw the small states together and to disperse the large ones; this could be the beginning of an important development."

Animated plenary meetings on the Prussian question took place in the Frankfurt assembly from November 13 to 20, but no one, of course, openly advocated Rümelin's ideas. The moment was not appropriate for revealing his plan. The fear of imminent reaction in Prussia was still too real and the ultimate goal of a hereditary Hohenzollern crown for Germany too uncertain. Under these circumstances, no one dared demand of the Prussian people that they give up their own constitutional desires. Thus, it seems possible, although we cannot prove it, that the attacks against the Berlin national assembly by Bassermann on November 18 and by Wilhelm Jordan on November 20 were directed at the very existence of the assembly as well as at its most recent sins. But perhaps this deep design we are assuming here was too subtle for the Frankfurt assembly, which counted among its failings a lack of statesmen as party leaders. We were, Haym complained,[14] "neophytes in the art of bringing our own and others' interests adroitly together and of winning the support of power for freedom." The motion that Haym and the members of his party made on November 13, in an effort to win the majority of the assembly, was harsher toward the Prussian crown than it could afford to be if the crown was to be won and put in debt to the assembly.[15]

[14] *Nationalversammlung*, p. 38.

[15] Waitz's motion, *Stenogr. Bericht*, p. 3254. He demanded primarily "that the Prussian crown select a ministry that enjoyed the trust of the country." He thus expressed a lack of confidence in the Brandenburg ministry here at the outset. Cf. Haym, *Nationalversammlung*, p. 22.

From the narrow path that could perhaps have led it to greater power, the assembly fell back, as it had so often before, into the realm of mere desires for freedom. The influence of the Augsburger Hof, the party that stood farthest to the left among the Center parties and that had Biedermann and the emotional Riesser as members, seems to have steered the Frankfurt assembly to the left both times when the Prussian question came to a vote.[16] Thus, on November 14, influenced also by news of the shooting of Robert Blum, the assembly resolved to urge the Prussian government, first, to revoke the removal of the Prussian parliament to Brandenburg as soon as the freedom of its proceedings could be guaranteed in Berlin, and second, to appoint a ministry that enjoyed the trust of the country. Then, on November 20, after the Berlin parliament adjourned on November 15 with the resolution to suspend taxation, the Frankfurt assembly declared this resolution, "which endangered the state," null and void, but still repeated its desire for the appointment of a more popular ministry in Prussia and assumed the role of protector for all the rights and freedoms that had been promised to the Prussian people. This was an implicit guarantee of the right of the Prussian people to their own constitution and representation. "A certain aspect of popular opinion," Haym writes, "drew our assembly away from the path of greatest prudence." Haym is referring here to the demand for a change in the ministry. This demand weakened the government that the assembly wanted to strengthen,[17] but Haym's statement also applies to the surrender of our idea. The fulfillment of liberal demands placed on Prussia made the fulfillment of political demands impossible, and at this point, when the Prussian parliament hung on the body of the Prussian state like a partially severed limb, the chance to realize these political demands could not have been better.

The results of this political campaign, then, were of little consequence. The votes cast in the Frankfurt assembly were, as Haym said, strong enough to wound the Prussian government but too weak to influence its next moves. The help that was granted was "not given willingly enough to enforce gratitude from those who were helped." The poor impression was made still worse by the regent's proclama-

---

[16] *Ibid.*, pp. 24 and 37. See also Pastor, *A. Reichensperger*, I, 276, and Saucken's letter of November 28, published by G. v. Below, *Deutsche Rundschau* (July 1905), p. 101.

[17] It is worth noting here that Haym, a member of the committee that made this motion, explicitly refused to have any part in it and had originally planned another motion that did not ask for a change in the ministry. *Stenogr. Bericht*, pp. 3438f.

tion of November 21, which elaborated the contents of the resolution of November 20 unnecessarily and in a condescending and demanding fashion.[18] The Prussian government was justifiably annoyed that the German ministry sent this proclamation directly to the Prussian provincial governors and thereby actually treated the Prussian state like an aggregate of German provinces. As we noted, the Prussian government would gladly have received assistance from Frankfurt. But as Graf Bülow, then chief of foreign affairs, wrote to Camphausen on November 26:[19] Since the national assembly and the central government have taken a position half on the side of the Prussian government and half on the side of the opposing party, it has become impossible for the Prussian government to dispose of this affair in concurrence with Frankfurt. *We must take care of it independently now, as a purely internal affair.*

The advocates of an alliance between Frankfurt and Prussia still had hopes that personal negotiations between the delegates who had just been appointed in Frankfurt and Berlin could repair the breach. It was only in the course of these negotiations, however, that the full consequences of Bülow's statement became clear.

On three separate occasions, representatives of the Frankfurt government came to Berlin. The first arrival was Undersecretary Bassermann, who stayed for a few days beginning on November 9.[20] Simson and Hergenhahn arrived on November 20, and then, on the evening of November 25, Heinrich von Gagern, the president of the assembly, whom Simson had summoned from Frankfurt.[21] Bassermann, Simson, and Hergenhahn came as official German delegates on behalf of the regent. Gagern came with the approval of the German ministry[22] but apparently not in any official capacity.[23] Bassermann, Simson, and Hergenhahn negotiated with limited authority. Their task was simply to carry out the instructions of the German ministry headed by Schmerling. They were not to pursue any policies that went beyond repairing relations between the provisional central government and the Prussian government and settling the conflict

[18] "Prussians: The Frankfurt assembly represents the entire German nation. Its word is the supreme law for all!" etc. Cf. *Stenogr. Bericht,* p. 3510.

[19] G.St. A.

[20] *Stenogr. Bericht,* pp. 3252 and 2366. Cf. Brandenburg, *Untersuchungen,* pp. 133f., and A. v. Harnack, *Bassermann und die deutsche Revolution,* pp. 76ff.

[21] B. v. Simson, *Ed. v. Simson,* pp. 133f.; Brandenburg, *op.cit.,* p. 141. Droysen's journals, November 24, in Hübner, *Aktenstücke,* p. 832.

[22] Simson, *op.cit.,* p. 134.

[23] His request for leave, submitted to the Frankfurt assembly on November 24, suggests this (*Stenogr. Bericht,* p. 3537).

between the Prussian government and the Berlin assembly.[24] Accordingly, in the conference held with the Prussian ministry on November 21, Simson and Hergenhahn explained that the purpose of their mission was, first, to urge that the Prussian assembly be reopened in Berlin rather than in Brandenburg on November 27, since order had been restored in Berlin, and second, to urge that the crown appoint as soon as possible a ministry that would enjoy the confidence of the country to a higher degree. It is understandable that these amiable overtures from the Frankfurt delegates were not well received by the Prussian ministers. But on this same occasion the Frankfurt delegates saw an entirely new and unexpected perspective open on the solution of the Prussian constitutional question and on the future relationship of Prussia to Germany. Graf Brandenburg said that the Prussian government might possibly promulgate a liberal constitution for the Prussian state—we are following the report on this conference that Camphausen received from his government[25]—if everyone in the government believed that no positive results could possibly be achieved with the Prussian assembly before the completion of the Frankfurt constitution. Graf Brandenburg emphasized that this was merely a possibility that should be kept in mind. As we shall see later, it was indeed only a possibility even then. But the Prussian ministers had revealed a weapon here that frightened the Frankfurt delegates. Because of it, Simson returned to Frankfurt the next morning to urge as rapid a completion of the constitution as possible[26] and also to bring Gagern back to Berlin to exert his influence on the Prussian government.

What was it that had troubled Simson? His son relates[27] that Simson thought the promulgation, if it took place, would also be regarded by the people as a victory for the ministry. This can hardly be what worried Simson so much that he brought Gagern to Berlin. If the ministry really gained the trust of the Prussian people, then the desires of the Frankfurt assembly, expressed on November 14 and 20, would have been satisfied and the stumbling block removed that the German

[24] We cannot establish with any certainty whether Simson and Hergenhahn's associates had given them additional secret instructions to find out what Prussia's attitude was on the question of a hereditary German crown for Prussia. Arneth, *Schmerling*, p. 251, claims this was the case, but the Prussian records contain nothing concerning this matter.

[25] Bülow's instructions to Camphausen, November 22. G.St.A. Cf. Simson, *op.cit.*, p. 134.

[26] Bülow refers to confidential communications he had received to support this.

[27] *Op.cit.*, p. 134.

delegates had been sent to remove. It is more likely that the act of promulgation itself was objectionable to them. Promulgation was an evil word in the ears of every good liberal. "A promulgated constitution is no constitution at all," Welcker wrote in his *Staatslexicon*.[28] The excellence of what was promulgated could not make up for its arbitrary and despotic origin, and it lacked guarantees for the future.[29] We can easily understand, then, why Hergenhahn made a renewed effort to negotiate a Prussian constitution and why, on November 23, the German minister Schmerling, acting on Simson's reports, instructed Hergenhahn "to oppose decisively any ideas of promulgation."[30] The Austrian Schmerling, who did not want Prussian leadership for Germany, cannot be suspected of opposing the promulgation for any reasons other than constitutional ones. The members of the Kasino-partei, however, are not free of this suspicion. It is very likely that the objections to a special Prussian constitution which Rümelin had expressed on November 18 and which Beseler, following Dahlmann's line of thinking, had raised on November 20 in the constituent committee, sprang up again now. On November 23 Dahlmann withdrew the motion he had made three days before on the formation of the Staatenhaus—the motion proposing the dissolution of Prussia into provinces—because he thought the moment unpropitious for it. Dahlmann clearly did not want to offend Prussia at this particular point, because in the last analysis Germany could not do without her. He added, however, that he still thought his motion contained an essential and important point;[31] and on the next day, November 24, shortly after Gagern and Simson's departure for Berlin, Rümelin wrote: "We must be prepared for the eventuality of a promulgation, although it would be a disaster." There is no doubt that the disaster he saw lay primarily in the constitutional isolation of Prussia. Up to

[28] X, 100 (1848).
[29] On November 21, Radowitz, following the general opinion in the Frankfurt Center, also pointed this out to the king: The entire legal basis for Your Royal Highness is "the principle of mutual agreement both in the relationship of Prussia to the new German government and in the relationship of the crown to its own people. Nothing in the world could compensate for the damage that would be done if this legal basis were destroyed. No matter how good the actual substance of the promulgated constitution might be, such a constitution will always be regarded as a breach of all legal principles and promises. It will set the crown completely adrift and perpetuate the revolution forever. Men here like Vincke, Schwerin, Dahlmann, and Gagern, who differ greatly in their political positions but who are irreproachable in their intentions, share this opinion with me" (Hausarchiv). Cf. my book *Radowitz und die deutsche Revolution*, pp. 180f.
[30] Simson, *op.cit.*, pp. 135 and 141n.
[31] Hübner, *Aktenstücke*, p. 248.

this point, completion of the Prussian constitution had not lain in the foreseeable future. It was hoped that the German constitution could be completed before the Prussian one. Rümelin and his adherents were therefore able to back the Frankfurt resolutions of November 20 without reservation and in the hope that the Prussian promises of freedom would be realized by a German constitution, not a Prussian one. Now the separate Prussian constitution had become an immediate threat. Only a few hours after Simson's departure from Berlin, however, Hergenhahn was able to send reassuring news to the ministry in Frankfurt. He reported that the idea of a promulgation, if it had ever existed, had been given up, and that he had been reassured on this point by completely reliable sources.[32] The Prussian ministers were clearly disturbed when they saw the explosive effect their innuendo had produced, and they denied what they had suggested twenty-four hours before. This did not mean, of course, that they had actually given up their idea just to please the Frankfurt delegates. That would have been highly improbable in itself, and the instructions sent to Camphausen on November 22 show that it was not the case. Their purpose was to calm unsettled nerves and to mitigate fears of an imminent promulgation. However, the intention of promulgating a constitution was by no means expressly denied; promulgation was mentioned as a "possibility to be kept in mind and discussed." But had the political situation out of which the idea of promulgation had grown suddenly changed in the twenty-four hours that had elapsed between November 21 and 22? Had prospects for a peaceful agreement with the obstinate Berlin assembly improved? Not in the least. What Simson told his party associates on November 23 or 24 about the situation in Berlin, then, was completely correct, and what Rümelin consequently wrote on November 24 was equally correct: "Both parties still stand in sharp opposition. The ministry will not give in, and the national assembly will give in even less." But despite this hopeless situation, Rümelin added that the promulgation "can probably still be prevented."[33] What was the basis for this hope? It was certainly not Hergenhahn's unequivocal report of November 22 that the idea of a promulgation had been completely abandoned, a report that we know proved false. If Rümelin had already received this report, he would have had not merely a hope to offer but a fact. He therefore must have had his own special reasons for this hope.

Perhaps we can get to the bottom of the matter if we assume that

[32] Simson, *op.cit.*, p. 140, note 2.   [33] *Aus der Paulskirche*, p. 125.

Simson and Gagern already shared Rümelin's opinion on the harmful-
ness of a Prussian parliament. We cannot prove this assumption in the
case of Simson, but in Gagern's case, which is more important, we
can. As early as October 26, he made a statement in the Frankfurt
parliament that could well have come from his brothers, Friedrich
and Max: "In my opinion, we need impartial, comprehensive leadership at the head of our federal state. This automatically excludes the
idea of a Prussian hegemony."[34] On November 20, Camphausen wrote
from Frankfurt to the Prussian undersecretary of state and chief of the
foreign office, Graf Bülow:[35] "Heinrich von Gagern is recommending
Max von Gagern's old plan now too, namely, Prussia alone as leader
but with provincial diets instead of a general diet in Prussia." This
report is highly significant. Does it not also cast light on Gagern's
trip to Berlin? As we remember, Simson made his hurried trip to
Frankfurt to bring Gagern to Berlin and to urge the most rapid possible completion of the Frankfurt constitution. This suggests on the
one hand that the hereditary German crown for Prussia was to be
settled upon as soon as possible, and it suggests on the other hand—
to reconstruct the situation as I think it existed—that Gagern was
to use the hereditary crown as bait to dissuade the Prussian government from promulgating a constitution for Prussia. This would account, then, for Rümelin's optimism. I do not share the opinion generally held up to now that Gagern was obliged to oppose and wanted
to oppose just the illiberal idea of promulgation. I think instead that
he meant to oppose a separate Prussian constitution altogether. Only
from this perspective does his mission become completely understandable and gain a coherence and deeper motivation. The previous
view held that Gagern's trip to Berlin was primarily motivated by
Simson's report of intentions to promulgate a constitution and that
Gagern also took this opportunity to use his personal influence to
urge the king to accept the Frankfurt crown. According to our view,
though, the Prussian and the German aspects of his mission to Berlin
stand in the closest causal relationship. His struggle against promulgation was a struggle against obstacles that threatened to rise suddenly in the path of Prussia's merger with Germany. This must have
seemed to him a momentous occasion indeed when he could per-

[34] *Stenogr. Bericht*, p. 2900. A few years later, when he found this remark mentioned in Eigenbrodt's *Aufzeichnungen*, he commented: "I was thinking of a
gradual merger of the territories as provinces under one ruler who would be
capable of fulfilling the same obligations for all the provinces. That is the opposite
of a hegemony." Bergsträsser, *R. C. Th. Eigenbrodt*, p. 233.

[35] Brandenburg, *Untersuchungen*, p. 281, and Caspary, *Camphausen*, p. 264.

sonally guide the king up the mountain from whose heights the glory of the new German empire could be seen.

In the early morning of the day when the king spoke with Gagern, he found in the Herrnhuters' scriptural readings for that day the words: "And the tempter came to him."[36] We know how urgently this tempter tried to persuade the king in frequent discussions to accept the German crown, how he cried out to him: "Cursed above all be patience!"[37]—how the king embraced him but then afterwards looked back on him with mixed feelings of "admiration and revulsion." Gagern was not just the leader of the Erbkaiserpartei who was trying to win the monarch his party needed for its plans. He also represented a Germany that was trying to persuade the Prussian state to sacrifice itself and its personality. The blood of this state personality was needed to nourish Germany; and it was thought that if this state did not sacrifice itself, it would take away the breath of life from the rest of Germany. The Prussian state was to be the *ver sacrum* of Germany.

But now we must provide some concrete facts and not just metaphors. As we have already shown, Gagern's opinion at this time was that Prussia should not have a central parliament, and in view of this fact we can be sure that he must have been a convinced opponent of Prussian plans for promulgating a constitution, whatever their form or content. We can further assume with reasonable certainty that Gagern, who was prompted to go to Berlin by news of these plans, departed with the intention of opposing them and of advocating his own plan of "Prussian leadership but without a general diet." But we must then ask whether and in what way he advocated this plan in Berlin and whether he really made the granting of the hereditary German crown to Prussia completely dependent on the fulfillment of these conditions.

The opinions of Gagern's associates offer our first area of inquiry. We must first call attention to the fact that when the Frankfurt correspondent of the *Allgemeine Zeitung* reported Gagern's trip to Berlin on November 24, he saw it as a direct attack against the existence of the Prussian national assembly:[38] "On the basis of this situation (in the Frankfurt constitutional discussions), Gagern can offer new suggestions to the king of Prussia concerning the constituent German (he writes 'German' but means Prussian) assembly. Who can deny that these constituent assemblies in the individual states are the greatest obstacle to the creation of order and of a constitution for all of

---

[36] Ludw. v. Gerlach, II, 32. [37] Simson, *op.cit.*, p. 136.
[38] Supplement to No. 333, November 28.

Germany?" The question arises of whether this report is really based on information from Gagern's circle or merely on hypothesis. Also, is it directed against a permanent constitutional isolation of Prussia or only against the current Berlin national assembly? A literal reading of the text speaks for the latter interpretation, but on the basis of what we know of Rümelin and Gagern's views, we cannot completely reject the other interpretation either.

We find another source that demands our attention in the *Politische Briefe und Charakteristiken aus der deutschen Gegenwart*, which appeared in 1849 and was written, as we know, by Gustav von Usedom. Usedom, a later rival of Bismarck's, was the Prussian representative to the Bundestag at the time of the regent's election and was *persona grata* with Friedrich Wilhelm IV. He wrote at the end of his book, in the concluding letter dated Christmas 1848:[39] "Frankfurt has made several offers of the German crown to Berlin on the condition that Berlin agree to divide the Prussian state into three, five, or eight parts and to replace the Prussian parliament with the Frankfurt one." Since Gagern's offer was the most important and urgent of the offers of the German crown that Frankfurt made to Berlin in 1848, it is likely that Usedom is referring to Gagern's offer as well as to other such offers. However, we cannot prove this unequivocally. More significant here are the suggestions that General von Willisen, who went to Frankfurt on a military matter, sent to the king from Frankfurt on November 30.[40] The advice he gave him was essentially based on ideas from Gagern's circle. He recommended letting the assembly in Brandenburg adjourn of its own volition until the constitution was completed in Frankfurt. "If we consider, Your Majesty, that we shall be the leaders of Germany when the constitution is completed, then it seems not only unnecessary but even harmful if an almost equally large national assembly exists in Prussia along with the main German parliament. The two would be in constant conflict." We shall come back to his other suggestions later, but for the present we must note that at the same time Gagern was negotiating in Berlin, the demand for Prussia to forgo its own parliament became louder in Frankfurt. The *Deutsche Zeitung* during early December even gives an impression of planned, coherent propaganda. On December 2 the

---

[39] P. 283.

[40] Hausarchiv. The close contact that Willisen had with Gagern's circle in Frankfurt is evident in his concluding words: God has mercifully ordained that the king at least parted ways with Gagern and Vincke in peace.

paper published an article of November 30[41] that read at one point: "To keep pace with the course of events, the (Prussian) crown should dissolve its own assembly. It should disavow the rumored intentions of promulgating a constitution. It should state that it will not recognize or convene any constituent assembly for Prussia before the constitution is completed in Frankfurt." The editorials of December 5 and 6 are even clearer. The editorial of December 5 recommended that Prussia both renounce its own parliament and settle for provincial diets in its federal territories in exchange for federal leadership. If Prussia adopted this policy the present conflict could be avoided, and the inner strengthening of Prussia would prove advantageous for German unity rather than detrimental to it. On the next day, in an obviously more nervous tone, the paper wrote to the following effect: Let's put our cards on the table. A Prussian hegemony over Germany is just as impossible as a Prussian merger with Germany as long as Prussia continues to be a separate state in itself and as long as Prussia as a major power maintains a general parliament to rival the German national parliament.

But we still have no evidence that Gagern himself took this position in Berlin.[42] We recall, however, that the Prussian ministers thought it prudent to conceal their ideas of promulgation from the Frankfurt representative on November 22. They probably did so with Gagern in any case so that he could be allowed to think he had temporarily won his objective of blocking a Prussian constitution without a battle. An account that the Coburg diplomat Meyern sent to Herzog Ernst

[41] "Frankfurt, Kremsier und Brandenburg II," column "From the Neckar," perhaps by Gervinus. Cf. Mathy's literary remains, pp. 451f.

[42] The earlier major source for Gagern's negotiations in Berlin was his own oral account as presented by Jürgens, *Zur Geschichte des deutschen Verfassungswerkes,* I, 216ff. The new publications (Edwin v. Manteuffel to Ranke, 1873, in Dove, *Ausgewählte Schriftchen,* p. 256; Leop. v. Gerlach, I, 253-56; Ludw. v. Gerlach, II, 32f.; Simson, *op.cit.,* pp. 134ff.; Bergsträsser, *Eigenbrodt,* p. 240; Pastor, *Max v. Gagern,* pp. 480f.) have supplied us with some interesting items that will not all stand up to critical scrutiny. A noteworthy example of this kind is Leopold von Gerlach's claim (taken up after him by his brother Ludwig) that Gagern had the intention of becoming the premier of a Prusso-German ministry. This idea was indeed expressed, and this fact has been confirmed by Gagern's letter to his wife on November 28; see Pastor, *loc.cit.:* "Even Vincke wanted to become my subordinate!" But this letter also confirms the report of the *Deutsche Zeitung* (supplement of November 29 and regular edition of November 30) that Gagern had refused to form a Prussian cabinet. Vincke and his friends probably initiated the idea, and Leopold von Gerlach interpolated the rest afterwards. An entry in Droysen's journal on December 4 (Hübner, *Aktenstücke,* p. 835) and a letter from P. Pfizer to Gagern on December 11 (Küntzel, *Polit. Aufsätze u. Briefe von P. A. Pfizer,* p. 57) still refer to the plan.

in the middle of December supports this view: "Gagern is supposed to have returned from Berlin expecting that the Prussian constitution would be delayed until the proclamation of the Frankfurt one so that the king could accept the German constitution for Prussia at the same time that he accepted the German crown."[43] Gagern's letter from Frankfurt, dated December 14 and written after the promulgation had actually taken place on December 5, 1848, completes the chain of evidence. He wrote to the German delegates, Hergenhahn and Simson, who had remained in Berlin:[44] "The promulgated constitution is not viable in itself; and seen in terms of the entire fatherland, it is impossible."

Thus, as we have just heard from his own lips, Gagern condemned not only the act of promulgation in itself but also the contents of the document promulgated, condemned it, indeed, from a German point of view. He could not condemn the document for being reactionary in character, because it had turned out to be surprisingly liberal. Gagern himself admits in his letter that the king had apparently won public favor with it at the moment. What he found unacceptable about it for all of Germany, then, was not a lack of liberalism but the constitutional isolation of Prussia.[45]

We can therefore feel sure that the main purpose of his trip to Berlin was to prevent this. He probably did not have an opportunity to win his point, because his opponent avoided the confrontation. As a result, the combination of imposition and supplication that was directed at Prussia and that we have deduced both from the context of the affair and from the sources has not taken on a very concrete form. I believe, however, that we have properly grasped the intellectual forces at work behind this situation.

[43] Ernst II, *Aus meinem Leben*, I, 323.

[44] Simson, *op.cit.*, p. 146. Brandenburg's general considerations (*Untersuchungen*, p. 142, note 1) do not detract from the validity of the different sources I have drawn upon to establish Gagern's position.

[45] Droysen's ambivalent reaction, on December 7, to the publication of the promulgated constitution was typical: "My feelings are mixed. I reject the thing, and yet it seems very liberal. It's a good example of cutting a Gordian knot" (Hübner, *Aktenstücke*, p. 835).

4

....

THE PROMULGATION OF THE PRUSSIAN CONSTITUTION OF DECEMBER 5, 1848

THE CAMPAIGN of the Frankfurt delegates in Berlin had failed. On December 5, Prussia received its constitutional government and its separate parliament. There is no doubt that this drove a wedge between Berlin and Frankfurt, between Prussia and Germany. The Prussian government had done just the opposite of what Droysen, Stockmar, Rümelin, and Max and Heinrich von Gagern had thought necessary to incorporate Prussia into the German federal state. This casts an entirely new light on the act of December 5. The significance of this act for the German problem is much greater than we have previously thought it to be. By announcing its decision to remain an independent state personality under any circumstances, no matter what course Germany took in the future, Prussia struck a serious if not fatal blow against the Frankfurt constitution; for, as we shall see in more detail later, the Frankfurt delegates' demand that Prussia give up its political independence was closely connected with the basic ideas of that constitution. But first we shall have to inquire into the genesis of the events of December 5, into the men and motives behind them, and into the relationship between these motives and the German question.

The publication of papers from the estates of the Gerlachs, Otto von Manteuffel, and Camphausen has provided important information about the events that led up to the promulgation, and I have made an effort to gather all the material available in the archives at the present time. But despite this, we are still unable to give a satisfactory account of these events.[1] We have only a partial knowledge

---

[1] The following study had already been written in the version of the first edition when Goldschmidt's work, "Die oktroyierte preussische Verfassung," *Preussische Jahrbücher*, CXXV, 197ff., appeared. Goldschmidt's study and mine have certain points in common; however, his is based only on printed sources. He was also able to make use of my lecture "Preussen und Deutschland im 19. Jahrhundert," which had already appeared in the *Histor. Zeitschrift*, XCVII, and which presented the

of the political deliberations carried on about the promulgation at the highest levels of the Brandenburg ministry. Leopold von Gerlach's account shows that the initiative for the proclamation originated in the ministry alone. The idea of promulgating a provisional constitution of a liberal nature came up in the ministry's deliberations on November 12. The reason this idea was suggested was that the Berlin national assembly had not wanted to comply with the adjournment and relocation in Brandenburg ordered on November 8 but was still meeting in Berlin on its own authority. The ministers found themselves immediately confronted with the question of whether it was possible to frame a constitution with such an assembly at all and whether dissolving the assembly and holding new elections might not just make the situation worse. In any case, a decision for promulgation had still not been reached.[2] The inclination toward it was stronger on November 16.[3] The ministers wanted to dissolve the Berlin assembly, which had passed its resolution against the ministry's right to levy taxes the day before, and ask the king to promulgate a constitution.[4] They worked out a draft for it in great haste, but the king opposed their plan from the very beginning. Because of this and because of other considerations we shall hear more of later, they were in tempo-

---

major conclusions of my research here. Goldschmidt and, after him, more thoroughly still, Seitz, *Entstehung und Entwicklung der preussischen Verfassungsurkunde i. J. 1848* (1909), have treated the contents of the promulgated constitution itself, and I refer the reader to their work on this subject.

[2] Graf Bülow to Camphausen, November 12, in Brandenburg, *Untersuchungen*, p. 275. As early as November 13, Varnhagen (*Tagebücher*, p. 285) records the rumor that the king intended "to proclaim a constitution that was supposed to satisfy everyone with its high degree of liberality."

[3] Leop. v. Gerlach, I, 242.

[4] If these steps were indeed taken, the ministers intended to let the retention of their posts depend on a vote of confidence from the newly formed parliament. In the cabinet files of the G.St.A. there is a draft, dated in November, for a public statement of the ministry which was probably written in the days after November 16. This draft justifies the previous steps taken by the ministry; admits that the dissolution of the assembly and the publication of a constitutional document, for both of which the ministry assumed responsibility, would be exposed to varying judgments and many attacks; hopes, however, for a favorable reaction from the people, etc. "The undersigned ministers will meanwhile submit to the convened parliament, prior to all other deliberations, the question of whether they enjoy the trust of the parliament. If this question should be answered negatively, the ministers will immediately submit their resignations to His Majesty." In any case, this document is identical with the "ministerial decree" that Leopold von Gerlach saw on the evening of November 20 and that "ends with an expression of the ministers' willingness to submit to the majority in the parliament" (I, 246f.).

rary confusion on November 18 about what course to follow next.[5] However, on what must have been November 20, they went ahead and presented the completed constitutional draft to the king. This time his opposition to it bordered on violence.

On November 23 he declared: "I find it bad, impractical, and highly dangerous."[6] He found it incompatible with his responsibility before God to sign and swear to such a thing.[7] We can understand his indignation because the basic materials of the ministerial draft were taken from the preliminary drafts of the Berlin national assembly.[8] He also found the act of promulgation itself beneath the dignity of a king and tinged with *mauvaise foi*. He therefore directed the ministers on November 23 to make another attempt at conciliating the assembly that had been moved to Brandenburg and, above all, since the general mood of the country was improving every day, to stall for time. Then "negotiations can be undertaken with the good and the evil but in a manner worthy of a king and with full confidence of victory for all time."

Our instincts are probably not incorrect if we assume Radowitz' influence here. The king had explicitly asked for his advice on the question of promulgation,[9] and Radowitz gave it on November 21. As we know, he spoke vigorously against promulgation on the grounds that it would be regarded as illegal, and he also encouraged further negotiations with the assembly in Brandenburg. At the same time, he drew the king's attention away from the Prussian question and directed it toward the German one. He quoted Gagern, and Dahlmann's views and urged the king to accommodate the Frankfurt assembly, which now had so much moral weight on its side. In this same letter to the king, Radowitz outlined Gagern's plan of forming both a loose and a

---

[5] Leop. v. Gerlach, I, 244; Bülow to Camphausen, November 18, in Brandenburg, *Untersuchungen*, p. 280.

[6] Poschinger, *Denkwürd. O. v. Manteuffels*, I, 46. That the letter was not addressed to Manteuffel but to Graf Brandenburg becomes evident from Leop. v. Gerlach, I, 249.

[7] Leop. v. Gerlach, *loc.cit.*

[8] Seitz, *op.cit.*, shows that Waldeck himself had relatively little to do with the so-called "Waldeck charter," the constitutional committee's draft, and that Peter Reichensperger had a larger part in it. He also suggests strongly, p. 140, that the ministers used the version of the Waldeck charter that had been modified by the central committees [*Zentralabteilungen*] as a basis. They called on Professor Keller to help in working out the draft. Gerlach, I, 680, and Goldschmidt, *op.cit.*, p. 204.

[9] Boddien conveyed the request. Cf. Leop. v. Gerlach, I, 244. The opening of Radowitz' letter of November 21 (see p. 282n., above) also refers to this.

centralized federation and of placing Prussia at the head of the centralized federal state. We can well imagine that these considerations of his friend and adviser had their effect on the king. We have shown elsewhere[10] how currents and crosscurrents followed one after another in the king's German policy and how he regarded Gagern and the Frankfurt parliament with both sympathy and revulsion. If we are correct in assuming Radowitz' influence, then the strong words the king used on November 23 to condemn promulgation contain the first fruits of agitation against it in Frankfurt.

Could the king have been won over to the further implications of the ideas Gagern and his circle advocated? We have seen with what means Bunsen tried to make Stockmar's plan palatable to the king in August. "Yes, it is true," the king replied, summarizing Bunsen's argument again:[11] " 'As the ruler of Germany, the king would escape the difficulties that *his* (!!!) incompetent constituent assembly has caused him, because the German constitution would become the constitution of Prussia, which would in turn be the territory directly subject to the kaiser.' I see the point of this argument. But the king (who surveys the entire situation) is obliged to reject this lure from the West and to turn back to the East, saying: Lead us not into temptation!— The prospect of 'the noble members of the upper house' does not attract the king. His own lands provide enough such men to surpass the English upper house. But the king does not 'desire' such an upper house one bit more or less than he desires (in his own and in all the German lands) the realization of that truly extant government of a thousand years duration, which, through the might of its institutions, has made our German people, whether they were aware of it or not, the leading nation of the world on both sides of the ocean (since the decline of the Romans)."

He was interested in Stockmar and Bunsen's idea, but he was also highly distrustful of it. If this idea had been realized, it would have been incompatible with the king's own national ideal. It was based on the liberal idea of the national state, on the new, growing German national spirit that was searching for the most effective possible guarantees of national political unity. The king's national ideal, however, was derived from the Romantic and conservative idea of the national state and found high, irreplaceable values in the secular achievements of the old German national spirit, in the Holy Roman Empire of the German Nation, and in the rich variety of the German individ-

[10] In my book *Radowitz und die deutsche Revolution.*
[11] The king's marginalia to Bunsen's plan, August 1848; cf. p. 262, above.

ual states as well. As his statement shows, the king thought of these values more as cultural values, more as the rich adornments of a spiritual view of the world, than as political values or as elements of power and power relationships. He considered his own monarchy to be among the highest products of the German national spirit, and he had no intention of sacrificing it to the idea of German unity. He wrote to Camphausen on July 16, 1848,[12] "I will not make the slightest concession whatever to certain demands this neo-Teutonic creature has made for the dissolution of Prussia." He wrote to Bunsen on Easter Sunday of 1849[13] that the great majority of his Prussians were true to his colors and were willing to accept "Germany only as an acquisition but by no means as an object into which they *are to be absorbed*." He then added[14] that if he accepted the German crown, he would run the risk of "selling my honor cheaply by dissolving Prussia—*that glorious historical creation of God's*—for all time and in obedience to an *assembly* that totally disregards the highest traditional authorities of the fatherland." To understand the significance of these words correctly, we must remember that they were written at the moment when the king was breaking his connection with the Frankfurt assembly and formulating in the clearest possible terms the principles that separated him from them. In the previous year, his feelings toward the Frankfurt assembly had been remarkably different from those toward the Berlin assembly. In private conversations he had sometimes had friendly words for the Frankfurt assembly,[15] but never for the Berlin one. In the spring of 1848, he was willing to let the Frankfurt assembly constitute the lower house of the future German parliament as it saw fit.[16] That was allowing a great deal, and he would never have granted this to a Prussian popular assembly. He was, then, sometimes prepared to make greater concessions to the constitutional trends of the times for Germany than for Prussia. This is understandable. To a certain extent, Germany was for him a new political territory in which his political imagination, historically oriented as it was, could still move more freely than it could on Old

---

[12] Brandenburg, *König Friedrich Wilhelm IV. Briefwechsel mit L. Camphausen*, p. 188.

[13] Ranke, *Aus dem Briefwechsel Friedrich Wilhelms IV. mit Bunsen*, p. 273 (*Sämtl. Werke*, XLIX-L, 520).

[14] May 1, *ibid.*, p. 278 (p. 523).

[15] See, for example, Leop. v. Gerlach, I, 269, 270; Ludw. v. Gerlach, II, 32; Nippold, *Bunsen*, II, 491; Ranke, *Friedrich Wilhelm IV. und Bunsen*, p. 242.

[16] That was offered in exchange for the fact that the princes would constitute the upper house as they saw fit. He suggested this to Dahlmann on May 3, 1848. Springer, *Dahlmann*, II, 241.

Prussian soil. He also had a certain historical and Romantic respect for the German nation in its totality, but the main thing he demanded from the Prussian people was devotion to the patriarchal system.

There was perhaps a bridge that could have linked the plans of the Gagern circle, which we have already discussed, to those of the king. The Gagern plans wanted Prussia to have no constitution and to content itself with provincial diets. The prospects for making this idea palatable to the king were not hopeless. Using an approach like Bunsen's, Willisen tried to do this in his previously mentioned letter of November 30 to the king: "The German parliament can adequately provide for everything that comes under the name of freedom of the people. Such large assemblies are more a hindrance than a help to the administration. For all these reasons, it would be a good thing if we returned to provincial diets."[17] The king had considered utilizing the provincial diets for his own purposes since the beginning of the revolutionary period. When it became necessary after the March events to reestablish the authority of the crown, his friend Radowitz had suggested to him, on March 28, that a revival of individuality and autonomy in the different parts of the country would accomplish this. "This would provide," he said, "a major counterweight against the revolutionary element."[18] The king seized on the idea eagerly. On March 31[19] he wrote Minister von Auerswald that he wanted "the organization of the country to have precedence over the invention of a so-called constitution. My efforts of the last eight years to give the country and the individual provinces independence in the management of their own affairs must be realized now, and these efforts will find the understanding and approval of everyone. In short, I want self-government. Therefore, the provincial diets are not to be abolished but reformed." Now, when his ministers wanted to press a liberal constitution on him again, he found an antidote against modern constitutionalism in the idea of the provincial diets, just as he had earlier. On November 23 he wrote to his ministers[20] as he had written to Auerswald before: "The constitution will have little or no influence on the mood of the country, but the announcement of the intention to initiate self-government in the communities, districts, and provinces will have a definite influence on it." But on December 5 he explained

---

[17] He added: "This would also dispose of the jealousy of the rest of Germany toward a Prussia that seemed to be too strong. This could all be easily accomplished on the wave of enthusiasm Your Majesty's elevation to the German throne would occasion. However, these plans should not be revealed now."

[18] Hassel, *Radowitz*, I, 578.   [19] *Ibid.*, p. 579.

[20] Poschinger, *O. v. Manteuffel*, I, 47.

to Professor Walter of Bonn "how he had wanted to return to the institution of the provincial diets after the dissolving of the assembly but in such a way that a *broad* representation of clergy, educators, scholars, and even of people without suffrage would be achieved."[21]

These were favorite ideas of his that had always had a place in his thinking. Even after he was forced down the path of modern constitutionalism, he continued to look back with longing on the old Prussian provincial diets that had formed the basis of his own political life. He tried to find his way back to them and to the United Diet that had been formed from them. They were his own true children, but the constitutional government of Prussia was, and remained, a stepchild for him.[22] This aspect of the king's thinking offered the best point of contact with the plans of Droysen, Rümelin, and Gagern. Two worlds of political thought met here despite their very different origins. Both considered English self-government good and worthy of imitation, although the king was attracted to it by its aristocratic side and the liberals by its bourgeois side. The king and these Frankfurt leaders were also united in their aversion to a constitutional isolation of Prussia, but the king's Christian-Germanic state ideal was completely alien to them. Or, to put it more precisely, because they favored both modern constitutionalism and the unitarian ideal, they rejected a separate Prussian constitution which threatened to smother the German one. But had the king himself not declared after the March events that "constitutionalism will have to be accepted for Germany's sake"? The burden of this concession, which he had had to make for Prussia then, would have been lightened for him if he had been obliged to make it only for Germany now and had been able to retain his beloved provincial diets in Prussia. The Frankfurt leaders would have had to make concessions to him about the membership of these provincial diets; and to satisfy him completely, they would have had to grant him the United Diet too.[23] But Droysen's views in the spring of 1848 had already suggested that the United Diet could continue to exist for

[21] F. Walter, *Aus meinem Leben*, p. 265.

[22] Cf. his letter to Grossherzog Friedrich Franz von Mecklenburg-Schwerin on January 7, 1849 (Hirschfeld, *Friedrich Franz II.*, I, 288). He pointed out to him "how, during our difficulties with the provincial diets and the United Diet, I have carefully avoided declaring the dissolution of the old form of government under the diets. I cannot see what useful purpose that would serve. Destroying is so easy, but we often wish in vain that we could have back what has been destroyed."

[23] Some of the most active advocates of the Christian-Germanic wing wanted it back then, also. Ludw. v. Gerlach, II, 26, 28. Manteuffel mentioned later (1856), too, that in the fall of 1848 he had wanted to return to it. Leop. v. Gerlach, II, 438.

certain limited purposes; and on January 1, 1849,[24] Gervinus made a suggestion that took the king's desires into account. Gervinus suggested permitting at least a surrogate of the United Diet, like the one the king himself had tried to create in the early years of his government. To avoid the problem of having two major German assemblies, Gervinus went on to explain, Prussia could reconstruct its central diet and convene it every four years. However, general representative committees made up of one eighth of the total membership would meet every year in Berlin to act on matters of joint concern.

This compromise would have preserved the Prussian state in a loose form. Bunsen suggested a very similar compromise when he was staying in Berlin in 1849. He did not demand that the Prussian parliament disappear entirely but only that "it cease to have a significant political position as soon as the German parliament was constitutionally established as the official parliament of the federal state." If Bunsen's report is fully credible, the king was apparently more receptive then than he had been in August 1848 both to this idea and to the concomitant prospect of being rid of the constitutional machinery in Prussia itself.[25] Given his particular political and philosophical orientation, he certainly never would have agreed to anything more than this. He never would have allowed the name of Prussia, the Prussian crown, or the idea of a Prussian people to disappear completely. But we can show that the compromise just discussed here won favor with some who shared the king's position and who also had a spark of Prussian ambition in them along with strong conservative leanings. The *Kreuzzeitung* of October 26, 1848 wrote:[26] "If Prussia, under whatever name, assumes the leadership of Germany, it also assumes responsibility for representing Germany internationally in peace and war, and the link between its diplomatic and military institutions and those of Germany will automatically be established. Domestically, Prussia might have to do without a separate national assembly. But since such an assembly is more an encumbrance than an aid for Prussia under the present circumstances, this loss could be sustained *provided the Prussian provinces would be assured their*

[24] The column "From the Rhine" in the *Deutsche Zeitung* of January 4, 1849. On Gervinus' authorship of these columns, see Springer, *Dahlmann*, II, 317.

[25] Nippold, *Bunsen*, II, 492. In his journals, Bunsen appears rather uncertain and muddled about the king's attitude in August 1848 (Nippold, II, 468 and 471). Cf. pp. 262f. and 290f., above.

[26] Supplement to No. 101, "Noch einmal Berlin und Frankfurt." The article was probably not written by Stahl, who ordinarily signed his essays with an "S," and the style alone indicates that it cannot have been written by Bismarck.

desired independence by the freest possible governmental development at the local and diet level and provided the unity of the provinces as well as the perpetuity of the Prussian name would be preserved by a *forceful government* acting within the limits defined for it by German legislation."

These ideas awaken curious associations. In the years after the Wars of Liberation, when the question of the Prussian constitution was in its first great crisis, the old feudal, conservative elements of that period, too, had wanted to settle for provincial diets because a quiet, isolated provincial life benefited them more than a strongly centralized and energetic state life.[27] At that point, renunciation of a central and liberal Prussian constitution and renunciation of the development of Prussian power had gone hand in hand. This conservative position in both foreign and domestic affairs was still advocated by some of the Prussian conservatives and by the Gerlachs in particular. But we can see from this article in the *Kreuzzeitung* that still other combinations were possible. Not only could Rümelin and Gagern's plan be translated into conservative terms if the emphasis were shifted to the preservation of separatistic provincial existence, but the plan was also capable of exciting Prussian ambition. It spoke both to the great-grandchildren of the aristocracy of the territorial period and to the grandchildren of Frederick the Great's officers, and it sought to win them for a modern federal state that was both national and liberal.[28] As we have just seen, the task of uniting the dominant political motives of three centuries—the provincial spirit, the Prussian national spirit, and the German national spirit—was a task that could appeal even to a writer for the *Kreuzzeitung*. It is doubtful that he could ever have seen his goal realized at the time because the alliance of these three ideas was in danger of coming under the exclusive influence of the most recent one. But this was an experimental effort in the direction of what another contributor to the *Kreuzzeitung* achieved later, but then, of course, under Prussian leadership.

[27] Cf. my biography of Boyen, ii, 310ff. and 348, also p. 237, above.

[28] In 1844, Leopold von Gerlach (I, 100) said against the king's plans for a general diet: "Unlike France and England, Prussia is not so constituted as to be a compact monarchy. Prussia consists of fragments from the German Empire and can only become a unit in union with Germany. Thus, government by provincial diets would be natural for Prussia." We see again the idea of a government organized along provincial lines for Prussia joined to the idea of incorporating Prussia into Germany. But this is presented in a strictly and purely conservative fashion, without the additional element of a Prussian desire for power that the article in the *Kreuzzeitung* contains.

In any case, though, we can say that the demands of Rümelin and Gagern were not doomed to meet with immediate rejection by the king or by his political followers, the Prussian conservatives.

But despite this, we know how much stood in the way of an understanding between Frankfurt and the king. We only want to suggest here that Rümelin and Gagern's demands did not necessarily destroy the possibility of an understanding from the outset. But another Frankfurt demand probably did destroy it. As we recall, Frankfurt demanded, on the basis of the resolutions of November 14 and 20, that the king dismiss Brandenburg's ministry, the very ministry that had rescued him. That was an encroachment on rights of the Prussian crown, rights that had just been reinstated by the actions of these loyal men that Frankfurt wanted dismissed. It is clear how disastrous those Frankfurt resolutions were for Rümelin and Gagern's plans. The king was between Scylla and Charybdis. On the one side were the ministers with an objectionable liberal constitution for Prussia; on the other was Frankfurt with its outrageous demand that the ministers be dismissed. On November 17, Gerlach had weighed one evil against the other: "I finally came to the view that the course the ministry wanted to take was really the wrong one but still not so bad that one should part company with the ministry on that account."[29] On November 21 the king himself was still undecided about which was the greater evil. He said "he could not bring himself to carry out the complete disorganization of the country—not only carry it out but also take an oath on this rag of a constitution—nor could he relinquish the ministry."[30] The fate of the ministry remained undecided for several days. On November 25 or shortly before, Manteuffel drafted decrees that the king could use after the convention of the Brandenburg assembly to make the dismissal of Brandenburg's ministry known to the country.[31] The ministry had, in effect, put its resignation

[29] Leop. v. Gerlach, I, 243.   [30] Ibid., I, 245.

[31] Three drafts by Manteuffel for a decree to be issued after November 27 are in the G.St.A. The first and second drafts were conceived against the eventuality that the assembly convened without a quorum on November 27. The first draft provided that, in such an event, the deputies should be summoned to convene and the session postponed until December 11. The second draft adds to this the statement that the king had dismissed the ministers Graf Brandenburg, Ladenberg, Manteuffel, Strotha, and Rintelen "at their request" and provided for the formation of a new cabinet. The third draft was conceived against the eventuality that all the representatives appeared for the opening session. It, too, announced the dismissal of the ministry and the postponement of the session until December 11. The dating of these three drafts, which were apparently all written at the same

in the king's hands. But the king did not accept it, and he doubtless did not accept it because the Prussian crown's dismissal of the Brandenburg ministry at this moment would have represented a humiliating concession to the Frankfurt authorities. In Gerlach's words, it was the Frankfurt "column's attack on the flank" that gave the Brandenburg ministry respite and strengthened its position with the king again. "I see now," Gerlach noted on November 25, "that the present ministry must be retained despite its wretched constitutional project."[32] Ministry, camarilla, and king, then, drew closely together at this point. On the next day, November 26, Graf Bülow wrote to Camphausen that if the Prussian government agreed to Frankfurt's demands, it would surrender Prussia's independence to the central government and it would also sacrifice the authority of the crown within Prussia itself. The question was decided on that same day. The king, particularly offended by the proclamation of the regent,[33] wrote to him that he would retain the Brandenburg ministry.[34]

With this step, the fate of the ministry's constitutional draft was decided. Promulgation was not to take place immediately. Instead, further efforts were to be made with the assembly that was to convene again on November 27 in Brandenburg. The plan now was to present the assembly with the ministers' constitutional draft,[35] which had been repeatedly revised to suit the king's wishes.[36] But it became clear after a few days that nothing could be achieved with this assembly.[37] A quorum could only have been formed by making

---

time, is based on the notice of engrossment, dated November 25, on the first draft. —See also Oberstleutnant Fischer's report of November 26 in Caspary, *Camphausen*, p. 266.

[32] *Op.cit.*, I, 253. His brother Ludwig proved to be the poorer *Realpolitiker* of his party when he began to doubt later whether it had been correct to retain the ministry in spite of its constitutional plans. *Ibid.*, I, 259. Cf. Ludw. v. Gerlach, II, 32 and 97f.

[33] Simson, *op.cit.*, p. 138; see also the reports from Berlin in the *Deutsche Zeitung* on November 27 and December 1.

[34] Leop. v. Gerlach, I, 254.

[35] This becomes clear from a copy of the draft that was reedited later, after the draft had been presented (G.St.A.). A Berlin correspondent of the *Deutsche Zeitung* suggests on December 3 (supplement to issue of December 7) that Vincke's influence was most crucial in effecting this. A Berlin column dated December 7, which appeared in the number of December 12, offers a similar view.

[36] On these revisions, see Goldschmidt, *op.cit.*, p. 204, and Seitz, *Entstehung und Entwicklung der preussischen Verfassungsurkunde i. J. 1848*, pp. 137ff.

[37] Seitz demonstrates, *ibid.*, pp. 128f., that the minority in the right wing of this assembly advocated promulgation early in December, and he indicates that they were probably influenced to do so by the ministry.

concessions to the democratic majority. Consequently, on the evening of December 4 the ministers were able to put through the order
to dissolve the assembly, and at the same time they secured the signa-
ture of the still deeply troubled king on their constitutional draft,
which went into effect the next day as the promulgated constitution.[38]

Qui trop embrasse, mal étreint. The Frankfurt assembly had brought
about just the opposite of what they had wanted to achieve. They
had only confirmed the Brandenburg ministry instead of toppling it
and, as a result, had cleared the way for the promulgation they
abhorred. Indeed, they had actually provoked the promulgation. The
Russian envoy, Baron Meyendorff, reported from Berlin that "the
intolerable tone that the central government assumed in all its public
decrees regarding Prussia" had been one reason why the publication
of the new constitution was not delayed.[39] But all this illuminates
only one side of the events leading up to December 5. Without the
persistence of the ministers, the promulgation would never have come
about. Therefore, an inquiry into their deeper motives is of great
importance here.

We must first ask what is known about the attitudes of the individual
ministers. It is reported that Ladenberg and Rintelen worked for the
promulgation.[40] As the king himself said, he thought Rintelen was
the one who "misled" the other ministers.[41] Edwin von Manteuffel,
though, considered Ladenberg to be more the liberal element in the
ministry than Rintelen.[42] The minister of defense, Strotha, also seems
to have belonged to the liberal wing of the ministry.[43] Otto von
Manteuffel was the only one who represented the Right. He resisted
the promulgation longer than anyone, not because of any aversion to
promulgation itself but because, as he later explained, he wanted to
return to a United Diet; and this would not have been possible without the king's approval either. He thought of resigning but finally
remained and, with his typical bureaucratic detachment, participated
in the preparation of the constitutional draft to which he objected.[44]

[38] Cf. Hansemann to Camphausen, December 10, in Brandenburg, *Untersuchungen*, p. 285.
[39] *Deutsche Revue* (September 1905), p. 274.
[40] Leop. v. Gerlach, I, 245; Ludw. v. Gerlach, II, 31.
[41] Leop. v. Gerlach, I, 250.
[42] *Ibid.*, I, 260. Cf. Ludw. v. Gerlach, II, 28. Later, in 1851, Leopold von Gerlach also considered Ladenberg the motivating force behind the constitution (I,
680).
[43] According to Otto v. Manteuffel's later report, in Leop. v. Gerlach, II, 438.
[44] Leop. v. Gerlach, I, 243, 259f., 708, 827; II, 438, 733. Ludw. v. Gerlach,
II, 31. Poschinger's claim, I, 46, that Manteuffel propagandized for the promulga-

He remained, he said three years later, because Graf Brandenburg pointed out to him that the person and attitude of the ministers were more important now than any "slip of paper" like the constitution. Brandenburg may indeed have said that, and it may have had its effect. We know that Leopold von Gerlach had similar thoughts at the time and consoled himself with the prospect of eventually getting rid of this weak constitution.[45] It was probably a consideration of great importance not only for Gerlach and the king but also within the ministry itself that the collapse of the Brandenburg ministry at this point would represent a defeat of the crown in the eyes of the Frankfurt assembly and of the crown's opponents within Prussia. We can assume for the present, then, that since Ladenberg and Rintelen, supported by Strotha, wanted the constitution in such a determined way, Brandenburg had gone over to their side[46] and thereby influenced Manteuffel to stay too.

We can thus focus our attention on Ladenberg and Rintelen as the main advocates of promulgation. What do we know of their political leanings? Unfortunately, very little. Gerlach's view that they wanted to promote essentially liberal principles seems doubtful to me. As a representative in the Berlin national assembly, Rintelen had claimed the constitutional state to be the best and only possible state, but he had also repeatedly and energetically opposed radicalism.[47] His activity as minister of justice and his harsh measures against the representatives of democracy in the judiciary[48] give an impression of anything but liberal inclinations. The main idea that influenced his and Ladenberg's thinking will become clear to us later. However, the names of this minister of education and of this Catholic minister of justice awaken associations that may not be the most important ones but that are still worth consideration. Did the implications of Article 12 in the promulgated constitution have some influence on them? "The Protestant and the Roman Catholic churches," the article reads, "as well as all other religious organizations, will order and administer

---

tion of a liberal constitution thus seems to be completely unsubstantiated. On p. 56n., he absentmindedly cites the one Gerlach passage that refutes his own claim. Manteuffel's part in the draft is documented in the relevant cabinet files in the G.St.A.

[45] Op.cit., I, 249, 256.

[46] Ludw. v. Gerlach, II, 31, also saw the situation in these terms: "Brandenburg followed them passively."

[47] Cf. Seitz, op.cit., pp. 132ff.

[48] Rintelen's decree of December 8, 1848. Deutsche Zeitung, December 23, supplement.

their affairs independently and will retain the possession and use of the institutions, foundations, and funds intended to further their cultural, educational, and charitable works." This article was taken over almost to the letter from the wording the central committee of the Berlin national assembly had given to Article 19 of the so-called Waldeck charter. The article gave the church its desired religious freedom along with the degree of political independence that the church wanted.[49] This was the great gain that ultramontanism won in the Revolution of 1848. Ultramontane interests cleverly took this gift from the hands of doctrinaire liberalism, which underestimated the dangers of a Roman church freed of its bonds. Ultramontane demands had been victorious in Frankfurt, too, but not completely victorious. Article 14 of the basic rights, which was first presented on September 11, also promised that "Every religious community (church) will order and administer its affairs independently." But to the annoyance of the ultramontane faction, it added the provision that the church, "like every other organization in the state, will remain subject to the laws of the state."[50] This provision, which left the way open for new state legislation concerning the church, was absent from the Prussian constitution.[51] The constitution of December 5 thus represented another victory for the cause of clericalism. The question of *cui bono* seems to have turned up a hidden clue here. Is it possible that Catholic influence was at work in the genesis of the promulgated constitution? The provision objectionable to the Catholics was, of course, absent in the drafts of the national assembly that served as a basis for the promulgated constitution; and the Catholics, led by the indefatigable Archbishop Geissel of Cologne, had already achieved their desires in committee negotiations within the assembly. But the actual realization of these desires still depended on the final seal of approval, and this became the crucial point now. The decision of the ministers to accept in the constitution the broad provisions for religious freedom that the assembly's draft contained was clearly a highly political decision whose background requires examination.[52] It is not likely

[49] Roske, *Die Entwicklung der Grundrechte des deutschen Volkes vom J. 1848 etc.* (Greifswald dissertation, 1910), pp. 103 and 127; Schnabel, *Der Zusammenschluss des polit. Katholizismus in Deutschland i. J. 1848*, p. 96.

[50] At the second reading, which took place in December 1848, the phrase "like every other organization in the state," which was particularly offensive to the Catholics, was struck. Cf. Pastor, A. *Reichensperger*, I, 260f.

[51] Article 11 was only a weak gesture in this direction: "The exercise of religious freedom will not be allowed to interfere with social and political duties."

[52] I offer this as an argument against the formalistic criticism which Roske, *op.cit.*, pp. 127f., brought against my view.

that Ladenberg, an opponent of the Pietists,[53] consciously served Catholic interests; but there is no doubt that his ministerial adviser Aulike, the chief of the Catholic division of the Ministry of Education, actively furthered them,[54] and the warm interest that the Catholic Rintelen developed in the promulgation project is not completely free of this suspicion either.[55] Immediately after the promulgation, suspicions of secret Catholic influence were aired. The Hanoverian statesman Stüve wrote on December 13:[56] "The church is now completely in favor of the new Prussian constitution. This seems to have been brought about deliberately, and all the signs suggest this is the case."

Since an assumption of this kind was made, we must determine to what extent it is supported by everything else we know about the strategy of Catholic circles in Prussia.

We must note first that there was no general agreement about this strategy. In the summer of 1848, as the Prussian ship of state seemed to be foundering before the cliffs, the Catholic *Rhein- und Moselzeitung* praised the choice of Archduke Johann as German regent and expressed the desire that he take up the central government of Germany with a strong hand. Also, since he now needed a dotation, a territory directly subject to the central government, the paper suggested the Prussian Rhine province as suitable for this.[57] The paper won the hearty approval of its readers with these suggestions, and all the hatred that the ultramontane Rhinelanders felt toward Prussia vented itself in the paper's columns. The least it demanded of a future

[53] Wippermann, *Allg. deutsche Biographie*, XVII, 501.

[54] He substantiates this himself. Cf. Schulte, *Lebenserinnerungen*, p. 63; Vigener, *Ketteler*, p. 124, and, in addition, the sources collected by H. Oncken in *Forschungen zur brand. u. preuss. Geschichte*, XXII, 314. He passes on Diepenbrock's report that the king wrote the guarantee of church property into the constitution in his own hand after the committees had already struck it in the draft. Roske shows this report to be incorrect by demonstrating conclusively that the preliminary version of the promulgated constitution, i.e., the resolutions of the central committee, already contained the passage in question here.

[55] According to Ludw. v. Gerlach, II, 27, Rintelen was supposed to have been only a "nominal Catholic." His son, Geh. Oberjustizrat Dr. Rintelen, was kind enough to comment on this for me: "That my deceased father was merely a nominal Catholic is completely incorrect. He was a true Catholic but a child of his times. Intense faith was rare then among most Catholics, especially in Berlin."

[56] Stüve and Detmold's correspondence, p. 145.

[57] July 21, 1848. The idea of the Rhineland breaking away from Prussia had been in circulation since the critical days of March. Cf. Caspary, *Camphausen*, p. 172, and *Histor. Zeitschrift*, LXXXIX, 35; Hansen, *Mevissen*, I, 524, and in the *Rheinprovinz 1815-1915*, I, 717; Stüve and Detmold's correspondence, p. 43. On the *Rhein- und Moselzeitung*, see Mönckmeier's work (1912).

Prussian constitution was that the Rhine province not be too closely
united with the other Prussian provinces, and it had hopes that a
central German monarchy would put an end to Prussian willfulness.[58]
In the turmoil of September, when there were even rumors of a military mutiny in Potsdam, the paper predicted the imminent collapse
of the Prussian state. "Prussia is rapidly hurrying toward an abyss.
No human power can save it from this fall."[59]

The Koblenz *Rhein- und Moselzeitung* was considered the organ of
the lower clergy, while the *Rheinische Volkshalle*, which appeared
in Cologne, was thought of as the organ of the higher clergy and of
the Rhineland aristocracy.[60] This paper was more subtle than the
other and knew how "to deal advantageously with the ruling powers."
But in the difficult days of November, even this paper said[61] that
the Prussian monarchy was falling into two parts that did not really
belong together, the predominantly Catholic West and the Protestant
North. "Instead of the one Berlin diet, two separate ones should convene, one for the Rhineland and Westphalia and one for the East; and
on the basis of the general constitution formulated in Frankfurt, they
should establish their own institutions. This plan would bring three
great and indisputable advantages. It is in accordance with nature;
it prevents an otherwise inevitable division between Germany and the
Prussian national assembly; and it is capable of creating a desperately
needed alternative to the terrible breach that is imminent between the
king of Prussia and his subjects. Citizens of the Rhineland and Westphalia, do what lies in your power to further this plan."

The idea of dissolving Prussia politically occurs in this camp too.
It was even partially supported with the same arguments used by
those favoring a hereditary German crown, but the assumptions and
goals were, of course, completely different. One could object here
that we have only the idle desires and fantasies of Catholic news-
paper writers before us and that we cannot believe that more serious
politicians like the Reichensperger brothers shared such ideas, even
though their connections with these two papers can be proved.[62]

[58] July 21, 22, 27, and *passim*.   [59] September 23.
[60] Its establishment was decided upon on April 11, 1848, in a meeting of the
"Borromäusverein" that was called mainly on the initiative of A. Reichensperger.
Pastor, *A. Reichensperger*, I, 231. Schnabel, *Zusammenschluss des polit. Katholizismus in Deutschland i. J. 1848*, p. 39.
[61] "Deutsche Reform," November 29 (article from Cologne, November 26). Cf.
J. Hansen, *Die Rheinlande u. die preuss. Politik 1815-1915*, in *Die Rheinprovinz
1815-1915*, I, 729.
[62] See Pastor, *op.cit.*, I, 230, and Mönckmeier, *Rhein- und Moselzeitung*, pp. 37f.

But feelings and desires that had been entertained for a long time by certain citizens of the Rhine province were expressed in these ideas. Two ways were open to the Rhinelander in dealing with the Prussian state, which he felt to be alien to him in many respects. If he were modern and liberal, he could try to import Rhenish liberalism into all Prussian political life; and, to be consistent, he would also have to fight for the centralization of Prussia as well as for its liberalization. Hansemann, Camphausen, and Mevissen, the leaders of Rhenish liberalism, did just that. However, the Rhinelander with Catholic leanings, and particularly the conservative Catholic aristocrat of the Rhine, wanted to keep the Prussian centralized state at arm's length under any conditions, whether it were bureaucratic or constitutional in form; and he therefore demanded the highest possible degree of provincial autonomy. Oddly enough, Max von Gagern's plan for de-centralizing Prussia could draw on two sources, a German unitarian one and a Rhineland Catholic one. The *Rhein- und Moselzeitung* stated in 1846 that "clear-sighted Catholics" were against a representative government for Prussia and favored provincial independence. For this reason, the United Diet of 1847 was not looked on with favor in these circles.[63] After the March Revolution, when everything was in flux, these ideas of dissolution and separation seemed to be possibilities for the future. At the end of June 1848, when Archduke Johann was elected as German regent and when Berlin seemed to be under mob rule, August Reichensperger took note of both these facts and asked: "How much longer will it be before the Rhineland declares itself subject to Germany alone?"[64] Professor Ferdinand Walter of Bonn, who shared Reichensperger's views and who was in the Berlin assembly, wrote from Berlin on June 4[65] that if a republic were really proclaimed in Prussia and gained stability, "then the delegates of the Rhineland and Westphalia will not let our beautiful provinces be dragged in the wake of the Berlin republic but will go home and frame our own constitution there—*with all due consideration for the king's rights, of course. We all agree on that point.*" This sounds

---

[63] See pp. 248f. above, and Mönckmeier, *op.cit.*, pp. 46ff. and 129ff.; Helene Nathan, *Preussens Verfass. u. Verwalt. im Lichte rheinischer Achtundvierziger*, pp. 28f.; Hemmerle, *Die Rheinländer u. d. preuss. Verfassungsfrage 1847*, pp. 31f., 156ff., 198; Treitschke, *Deutsche Geschichte*, IV, 553.

[64] To his friend Thimus on June 29, in Pastor, *op.cit.*, p. 249. See also Böhmer's letter to Hurter, Frankfurt, August 5, 1848 (Janssen, *Böhmers Leben*, II, 515): "When Brandenburg-Prussia comes into conflict with the central government here, which will happen sooner or later, the Rhine province will secede. The republic could then begin to flourish in the Southwest."

[65] *Aus meinem Leben* (1865), p. 188.

very loyal to the king. If we read between the lines, though, we may suspect that this loyalty is not undeviating; but Walter did not really think it would be put to the test he envisions here. Walter Rogge, a bold and clever journalist to whom we are indebted for many shrewd observations, claimed[66] that even at the beginning of September, Walter still had not dismissed the idea of separation for the Rhine province and of a German federal state with complete decentralization.[67] As late as November 19[68] Walter himself thought it "possible that the crown, because of its determined adherence to its measures, would lose the Rhineland." Walter did not want to see this happen, and he condemned "his countrymen's blind hatred of Prussia," but we can still see that this possibility caused him considerable thought.

There is no doubt that he and his adherents were more concerned about the church than about the Prussian state. He himself indicated[69] that he thought the most important features of the Prussian constitution were the paragraphs dealing with the church and the schools. Politically, he and his close friends leaned more toward the side of the old order, belonged to the parties of the Right in both the Berlin and Frankfurt assemblies, and watched developments from this quarter. We would do them an injustice if we imagined them guided only by tactics and calculation and if we gave no credence to the emotional foundations of their royalism. But the principle they followed and to which they all submitted in cases of doubt was free of such emotional ties and allowed the formation of alliances with the conservatives as well as the democrats. In the Rhineland, the hatred of Prussia made contact with the Left possible, and the *Rhein- und Moselzeitung* attacked the promulgated constitution of December 5 with arguments that every democrat could have subscribed to. But still another view also appeared in the paper's columns. "Of great significance for Catholics," the issue of December 10 reads, "is the fact that the clergy, as far as we have been able to hear its opinion, has been openly pleased with the promulgated constitution, particularly since this constitution proclaimed by the king grants religion its rights, whereas the Frankfurt resolutions had been highly restrictive to Catholics." Nothing could have pleased the Catholics more than receiving from the old state authority itself what they had hoped to receive from the new liberalism. Even though several of the Catholic

[66] *Parlamentar. Grössen*, I, 46ff.

[67] The fact that there is nothing about this in the passages Walter cites from his letters of this period by no means disproves it.

[68] *Aus meinem Leben*, p. 244.   [69] May 22, *ibid.*, p. 180.

politicians, for example, Peter Reichensperger, their most important representative in the Berlin assembly, did not approve of the way the promulgation was carried out,[70] Brandenburg's ministry still found ready and willing helpers in Reichensperger and his adherent Walter. It was they, the leaders of Prussian Catholicism in the Berlin parliament, who traveled to Frankfurt on an unofficial mission in November and December and sought favor there for the policy of Brandenburg's ministry.[71]

Walter Rogge says, "Even if we ignore the unproved rumors about definite agreements between the Catholic clergy and the government, the fact still remains that the same delegates who were concerned about the interests of the one true church also belonged to the extreme Right." As soon as the ultramontane elements had realized that the Prussian state was not unstable, as they had at first thought it to be, they had gained concessions, Rogge believed, by helping to subdue the hydra of democracy. Even if Rogge is correct in this, we must also add that it was not just a shrewd estimation of the power constellation that probably caused politically minded Catholics to change their course. After the experience the Catholics had had in Frankfurt with the antichurch democrats, they had good reason for not wanting them to be victorious now. Walter wrote on November 19: "If the wrong side wins in Prussia, culture, humanity, and religion will be lost in Germany for a long time to come."[72] If we put ourselves in their position, we can imagine, although we have no sources to go on, that still another consideration had occurred to them. Friedrich Wilhelm IV was the ruler whom they could use, who had already given them something, and who could give them much more. However, the majority of Catholic politicians still did not want him as the kaiser of Germany. This would have been too great a concession to the

---

[70] See his essay "Die preussische Nationalversammlung und die Verfassung vom 5. Dez." (1849), pp. 37ff. (This is also reprinted in his *Erlebnisse eines alten Parlamentariers*, pp. 239ff., a work that is rather obviously meant to recount his own and his sympathizers' services to the Prussian monarchy during the year of the Revolution.) However, his brother August wrote on December 11: "As far as one can tell, this 'bold step' (the promulgation) was really the most effective means of calming the storm." Pastor, A. *Reichensperger*, I, 279.

[71] P. Reichensperger, *Erlebnisse*, pp. 185ff.; F. Walter, *Aus meinem Leben*, p. 269.

[72] *Aus meinem Leben*, p. 244. "Where the democrats win," remarked the Rhenish Oberpräsident Eichmann, "the influence of the clergy disappears." J. Hansen, *Die Rheinlande u. die preuss. Politik 1815-1915*, in *Die Rheinprovinz 1815-1915*, I, 731.

Prussian Protestant element in Germany.[73] But to support this particular man as the king of Prussia could well appear to be in the Catholic interest. Also, if they were really aware of what was at stake in the struggle between the Prussian and German constitutions—which, of course, seems very unlikely indeed—then their support of the promulgated constitution could have helped eliminate the possibility of a hereditary German crown for the Hohenzollerns.

As early as November 18, Bishop Diepenbrock of Breslau wrote a pastoral letter to influence the Catholics of his diocese in favor of the government. But his words of January 22, 1849 show that even this benign church leader was capable of regarding the support he lent the ministry as a pact that could be both formed and dissolved: "These gentlemen should not think they can reward us for supporting them by playing cat and mouse with us now."[74] I do not mean to say that the gravitation of the Prussian Catholics to the side of the government was nothing but a contract and business arrangement. I repeat that such processes of adaptation tend to be the result not of conscious calculation alone but of a total complex of politico-social thought and feeling. I also concede readily that the consideration Brandenburg's ministry showed for Catholic interests in the promulgated constitution does not necessarily point to secret Catholic influence. The ministers could also have thought it a matter of sound political strategy at this critical moment to secure the Catholic population, particularly the undecided Rhinelanders, for the monarchy.[75]

To understand the genesis of the promulgation at all, we must be particularly careful to take both the internal and external situations into account. Was it still possible then, or possible once again, for Prussian statesmen to depart from the constitutional path that Prussia had followed since March 18? A robust personality like Bismarck might have been able to do it. At the time, he suggested buying off the entire peasantry and winning it for the government with a generous redemption and credit law; then, he claimed, the representatives would accept anything, even a constitution with four estates and a hereditary or appointed upper house.[76] The idea of bringing peasants

---

[73] It is well known how coolly the election of the kaiser in 1849 was received in the Catholic Rhineland. See also Hansen, I, 734.

[74] Reinkens, *Diepenbrock*, p. 415.

[75] H. Oncken, *op.cit.*, p. 315, makes this point well.

[76] Leop. v. Gerlach, I, 244 (November 19). Seitz's assumption, *op.cit.*, p. 136, that Bismarck approved of the promulgation of the liberal constitution at that time cannot be brought into line with this; and in any case, it cannot be proved. His view that Bismarck favored the promulgation of a liberal constitution as early as

and landowners, the entire rural population, under one roof and
playing them against the liberalism and democracy of the cities
smacks more of a modern conservative party leader than of a truly
modern conservative statesman. It is uncertain whether this would
have been Bismarck's final decision if he had been responsible for
acting on the matter. In any case, though, we must emphasize that
his party in general proved totally incapable of offering a positive,
well-thought-out alternative to oppose the ministers who were eager
to promulgate a constitution. The behavior of Bismarck's party at
the time gives the impression of helpless consternation. One man
suggested the United Diet, another something else, but they did not
come to any common plan. Ludwig von Gerlach later complained:[77]
"We were against the promulgation in principle, but perhaps we
should have had a constitution on hand that could have been promulgated *in eventum*. This would, however,"—he then adds very typi-
cally—"have brought with it the danger of a loss of character and of
being misunderstood." We have a clear view here of the political
impotence of the Christian-Germanic circle, impotence that originates
in the principles of their system. These men were better suited to
reaction than to action, and their tongues failed them at the moment
when they should have spoken. Thus, both planned tactics and inner
weakness were at work when Leopold von Gerlach decided that the
retention of Brandenburg's ministry was more important than its
paper constitution.[78]

But perhaps a feeling more Prussian than Christian-Germanic in
nature awoke even in Leopold at that point. "The king and even
Leopold," his brother reports, "hesitated to completely deny the
promises made in March."[79] This was the difficult situation in which

---

September and was perhaps even the originator of the idea also stands on shaky
ground. From Gerlach's account (I, 199-200), all we can establish is that in September, along with other possibilities, Bismarck and Gerlach also discussed that
of a liberal promulgation. The idea was obvious enough, and the important point
of discussion was not the idea itself but its implementation and the spirit of its
implementation. That the Bismarck of this period was basically indifferent to the
policy of December 5 is also the opinion of Erich Marcks, who was kind enough to
call my attention to the relevant parts of his Bismarck biography.

[77] II, 28.
[78] His quietistic remark on November 21 is typical (I, 247): "I sometimes think
it had to work out this way so that an end could finally be put to absolute constitutionalism." Even later, he thought he could justify his tactics to himself, but
as Ludwig von Gerlach asked reasonably enough from the standpoint of the party:
"Where is the statesman, the head of the party?" (Ludw. v. Gerlach, II, 98).
[79] *Ibid.*, II, 28; see also Goldschmidt, *op.cit.*, pp. 205f.

all who were responsible for Prussia's destiny at the time felt themselves to be. They could not go backwards. They had to go forward on the road they had taken in March and somehow make good the king's word. Graf Brandenburg's honest and straightforward character probably felt a particularly strong obligation here. In response to Leopold von Gerlach's warnings, he called attention to everything the king had allowed to happen from March on. His common sense told him that they were not in a position to do what was best and would simply have to do what was possible in the hope "of carrying on later from this first provisional basis with God's help, with prudence, determination, and consistency."[80] We can imagine that he and his adherents wanted to preserve the power and authority of the king as well as make good on the constitutional promises. They had good reason to despair of the Berlin assembly. Could any better results be expected if the assembly were simply dissolved and new elections held? What could be accomplished with another, equally obstinate assembly? A Berlin correspondent of the *Deutsche Zeitung* wrote on December 3[81] that a second assembly would be far more threatening in its power than the first one, which had now fallen from its position of absolute authority. The ministers may have had similar fears and may have reverted to the expedient they had discussed earlier[82] of promulgating a liberal constitution with monarchical guarantees. This may have seemed to them to be the surest and most effective means of creating an advantageous relationship between the crown and a new national assembly, of appeasing the country, of dispelling the fear of reaction, and of preventing a new revolution. They later explained their move in an unofficial circular:[83] "The important thing was to restrict absolutism both from above and below. The implementation of new elections with the purpose of arriving at a state constitution would have indefinitely prolonged the conditions that held sway since March." We must also take into account the date, November 16, on which the ministers' idea of promulgation

[80] Leop. v. Gerlach, I, 250 (November 24); see also, I, 261; Ludw. v. Gerlach, II, 29f.; see, too, Fr. Heinemann, *Die Politik des Grafen Brandenburg* (Berlin dissertation, 1909).

[81] Supplement of December 6.

[82] Suggested ca. September 1 by Edwin v. Manteuffel (Anschütz, *Verfassungsurkunde f. d. preussischen Staat* [1912], I, 47); see also Leop. v. Gerlach, I, 199 (September 16); Abgeordneter Landrat v. Moeller's letter to Mevissen, Berlin, November 11, 1848, in Hansen, *Mevissen*, II, 442.

[83] *Warum der König also handeln musste und dass er wohlgetan hat, eine Verfassung zu geben*, Berlin, December 6, 1848, publication of the Deckersche Hofbuchdruckerei, in the Ministry of the Interior's files, to which I was given access.

took firm shape. This date stood under the influence of what had happened the day before in Berlin. The ministers must have wondered then if the country would follow the call of the revolutionary assembly. Characterizing the mood of the country, a Prussian general staff officer said:[84] "Things looked bad for the king until the resolution against the ministry's right to levy taxes." The storm clouds of agitation that hung over the lower classes of the population were still so dense on November 16 that the outcome seemed questionable indeed. Thus, both prudence and loyalty may have led to the idea of meeting any new revolutionary outbursts with tangible liberal concessions instead of with a rule of the sword like the one Austria had just experienced. There was no doubt that public opinion demanded such concessions. Even Leopold von Gerlach had to admit:[85] "It is clear that public opinion is still on the side of constitutionalism." With the reliable army that was available, a military dictatorship could have assumed command, but it is to the credit of the Prussian statesmen and leaders that no one urged that course. In this connection, we should also ask which tendencies were predominant in the army. Obviously the army did not take an active part in politics itself, but it is equally obvious that it had an indirect influence on political leadership. A witness we have heard from earlier reported on October 21 that the army naturally remained loyal to the king and that a decisive majority in it favored liberalism but not radicalism.[86]

Each passing day after November 16 helped clarify the domestic political situation. The resolution against the levying of taxes had an effect just the opposite of the one intended. A wave of royalistic sympathy swept through the country. By the end of November and beginning of December, it was obvious that the revolutionary assembly had no support in the country and that new outbursts were not imminent. Promulgating a constitution was no longer tantamount to evoking the immediate danger of revolution. We would think that the ministers could have achieved their goal of pacifying the country and winning its favor now with less radical means; and because they were sure of moral victory, they actually did once more momentarily seek a means of forgoing promulgation. Graf Bülow wrote to Camphausen: "There is no reason to use a *dernier moyen* that would

---

[84] December 7, 1848, "Potsdamer u. Berliner Briefe eines preussischen Offiziers aus dem Jahre 1848," *Deutsche Rundschau*, XXVIII (1881), 264f.

[85] I, 247.

[86] *Deutsche Rundschau*, XXVIII (1881), 253.

bring great dangers with it."[87] But despite this they immediately returned to the idea of promulgation, although the original reasons for it were no longer pressing. As the idea was freed from immediate pressures, it changed in character from an expedient to a bold, but nonetheless organic and significant, measure. While the originally menacing cliffs faded away, new shores that were both threatening and attractive hove into view, and with each passing day the idea of promulgation became more interesting. It became more interesting because, along with the originally dominating but now less important domestic Prussian motives, German aspects of the situation became more prominent. They had probably never been absent. The intention of turning a quickly drafted Prussian constitution against a Frankfurt one that might contain features unacceptable to Prussia had doubtless played a role from the very beginning.[88] On November 21 the Frankfurt delegates learned of the ministers' promulgation plan, and from this date on the plan became, as we have seen, directly antagonistic to the Frankfurt constitution. Berlin, ministerial Berlin, used the idea to strike out against Frankfurt, although it also had to struggle with Potsdam at the same time. The ministers now stood embattled on two fronts that soon became three, because they were also obliged to take notice of warnings from the prince and princess of Prussia.[89] The princess, following the opinion of the heir to the throne, did not reject the promulgation out of hand, but she did call it an "extreme and dangerous step" and predicted fearful scenes of internal instability, of the collapse of the dynasty, and of civil war. It is a great political achievement that the ministers did not let themselves be swayed by all these opinions from both right and left and continued on their course. We noted above that the Frankfurt government's intolerable attempts at interference had strengthened the ministers' decision to promulgate the constitution. These efforts sought to bring Prussia under German government. Gagern and Rümelin's enticing plan had the same goal. Interference and enticement were the means used to win the upper hand over Prussia. The interference illuminates the significance of the enticement, and the enticement that of the interference. The situation looks

[87] Brandenburg, *Untersuchungen*, p. 280.

[88] Brandenburg, *Untersuchungen*, p. 138, grasped this point accurately.

[89] Princess Augusta to Manteuffel, November 24, with an enclosed memorial whose contents, as she said, the prince "had examined and approved." Poschinger, *O. v. Manteuffel*, I, 40ff.—On Hansemann's influence on the prince and princess in favor of promulgation, see his letter to Camphausen on December 10 in Brandenburg, *Untersuchungen*, p. 284.

this way in historical perspective, and the ministers probably saw it this way also. Their promulgation policy thus became a defense against the demand to absorb Prussia into Germany. One could object here that the ministers simply carried through what they had already planned before they had any idea that Gagern wanted Prussia to do without a separate constitution. This does not lessen the historical importance of their action. It is a frequent occurrence in the course of history that an act originally planned for different reasons takes on a completely new and unexpected significance and purpose because of the new circumstances that it encounters and that bring it to maturity. It then produces effects that go far beyond its original premises. This was the case here.[90] The old Prussian state concept took a strong stand against the modern national Germany and even did so with modern weapons.

But in this strangely complex struggle, it was possible for the combatant to defend himself energetically with one hand and offer the other to his opponent in friendship. At the point when Gagern was staying in Prussia and the promulgation was being prepared, Frankfurt was both friend and foe for Berlin. In recalling the events leading up to March 18, Hermann Oncken suggested years ago that the promulgated constitution had made such great concessions to liberal desires because Prussia needed her Frankfurt allies even if she did

[90] With these additional remarks, I hope to refute the criticism that G. Anschütz, *Verfassungsurkunde f. d. preussischen Staat*, I, 48ff., has brought against my view. He misunderstands me when he claims that I see the rejection of the Frankfurt offers as a major, causally determining motivation in the ministerial promulgation policy. I have always emphasized that this policy originally and primarily arose because of internal political reasons in Prussia. However, I still claim it is possible, indeed probable, that the ministers effected the promulgation policy forcefully only after they had been aggravated by the Frankfurt attempts at interference and after they had learned through Camphausen's report of November 20 about Gagern's plans for a Prusso-German constitution, plans that they rejected on principle. As I showed above, it is impossible to determine whether Gagern negotiated personally with the ministers on this question or not. In any case, though, it should be noted that when the Prussian representative in Vienna, Graf Bernstorff, spoke with Schwarzenberg about the promulgated constitution and Gagern's offers in Potsdam, he specifically emphasized "that Prussia's influence and power in Germany can only be great if Prussia is great and powerful both in itself and as an independent state" (personal report to the king, December 9, 1848, in Ringhoffer, *Im Kampf für Preussens Ehre*, p. 79)—a clear reflection of the differences that existed between Berlin and Frankfurt.—Even E. Brandenburg, who tries to tone down my view on other points, is obliged to say of this period at the end of November: "The ministry probably overcame its last reservations about the promulgation only now, when Prussia's independence seemed immediately threatened" (*Untersuchungen*, I, 143).

not particularly care for them.[91] The situation cannot be reduced to such simple terms any more, for we know that the promulgated constitution also put a decisive end to the plans of the Gagern circle. But the highly liberal contents of the constitution offered some compensation for the blow the constitutional isolation of Prussia had struck against Gagern's adherents, and the ministers probably conceived of its contents as compensation as soon as they were aware of Gagern's desires. But even before Gagern had made his effort and before the ministers knew what conditions it entailed, they must have been considering the future position of Prussia in Germany. From the beginning, they must have conceived of the future Germany as a federal state. Otherwise they would not have included in their original draft the provision from the Waldeck constitution that allowed future German federal law to limit the Prussian crown in its foreign policy and in its right to make treaties.[92] Nor would they have included the proviso that alterations of the current Prussian constitution could become necessary.[93] We should not ignore the fact that these reverences before the future German constitution were also regarded as the fulfillment of the March promises that Graf Brandenburg felt obliged to keep. Later, in justifying his German policy, he even referred to the edict of March 18, saying that it "could not be ignored."[94] Clearly, though, he did this not because of scruples alone but also because of Prussian ambition;[95] the German constitution that he and his colleagues had in mind and that they would be willing to submit to can only have been a constitution that would also take Prussian pride into account. The entire German policy of the ministry makes

[91] *Histor. Zeitschrift*, LXXXVIII (1902), 506.

[92] Poschinger, *O. v. Manteuffel*, I, 50. Draft of constitutional commission ("Waldeck charter"), Article 47. This provision was struck at the wish of the king, who found it, and with good reason, "highly questionable" at that time.

[93] Article 111; see also the state ministry's personal report to the king on December 5, 1848 (Poschinger, *op.cit.*, p. 59). It was this particular proviso that evoked Prince Schwarzenberg's strong reservations, and he remarked to Graf Bernstorff that he "could only understand such a subordination of Prussia's own political institutions to Germany as an expression of the (Prussian) government's desire and hope of seeing Prussia placed at the head of Germany." The liberal contents of the constitution as a whole were also seen from this same point of view in Vienna. Bernstorff's personal report to the king, December 9, in Ringhoffer, *op.cit.*, p. 78.

[94] Leop. v. Gerlach, I, 289 (February 9, 1849).

[95] See Bismarck's judgment on Graf Brandenburg in *Gedanken und Erinnerungen*, I, 66: "His Prussian patriotism was primarily nourished by memories of 1812 and 1813, and for that reason it was permeated with German national feelings. However, the decisive factor was his dynastic and Borussian feelings and the idea of increasing Prussia's power."

that clear. It will suffice here to examine documentation of this policy from the periods shortly before and after the promulgation.

On November 23 the king expressed annoyance that Brandenburg did not want to take any action on the German question.[96] That is to say, Brandenburg did not want to pursue Prussia's German policy in league with the German kings the way Friedrich Wilhelm wanted him to, but preferred to do so by working together with the Frankfurt parliament and by utilizing it. He agreed completely with Camphausen, who pointed out that the important thing at this stage was to strengthen the parliament, now that it no longer had the power to be dangerous, and at the same time to subdue the individual states. If this was not done, the egoism of the individual states would destroy any German constitution and unity.[97] Prussian ambition was particularly evident in the unofficial circular of December 6, 1848 that sought to justify the promulgation: "The constitution of Germany will be completed in a few weeks. When the eye of the German people then looks about to see in whose hands the highest authority should be laid, should Prussia stand there with lamed strength, vacillating between absolutism and anarchy? No, the situation of the fatherland, the situation of the world requires a *strong* and *ordered* Prussia. But only a *free* Prussia can be strong."[98] Not too long after this, probably on December 14, Graf Brandenburg said explicitly to a friend of Gagern's that he thought the simplest and best solution to the German question would be to have Prussia at the head of the German federal state with a council of the kings as support.[99] When Bunsen came to Berlin in January 1849, he found the ministers thinking along these same lines. They were highly in favor of establishing Prussia as a protective power at the head of Germany, but they were considerably put out when Bunsen expressed the view that the Prussian parliament would have to forgo a political role in the German federal state.[100]

In summary, we see that internal Prussian interests went hand in hand with German interests from the beginning, just as they did in the events leading up to the patent of March 18. The Prussian inter-

[96] Leop. v. Gerlach, I, 250.
[97] Sybel, *Begründung des Deutschen Reiches*, I, 261.
[98] *Loc.cit.* See also the article in the *Preussische Staatsanzeiger* of December 9 in Simson, *Ed. v. Simson*, pp. 143f.
[99] Simson, *op.cit.*, p. 157. The dating of this report from an unnamed politician is essentially based on the statement on p. 154: "Hergenhahn will let you know how welcome my reports . . . were for him." Hergenhahn departed from Berlin on the morning of December 14 (*Deutsche Zeitung*, supplement to No. 323. On the authorship here, see *Histor. Zeitschrift*, LXXXIX, 192).
[100] Nippold, *Bunsen*, I, 492; see pp. 00f., above.

ests were more immediate and pressing at first, but they gradually
gave way in importance to the German interests. We have good
reason to believe now, too, that the news of what was proclaimed in
Kremsier on November 27 also had its influence on the Prussian
ministers. If Austria did not want to give up its political unity but
wanted instead to confirm it even more strongly, then the founding of
a German federal state without Austria and with Prussia in a position of leadership seemed to be the solution that Austria's decision itself dictated. Graf Brandenburg actually conceded to that same
friend of Gagern's on December 14 that the unification of Germany as
a federal state should not be delayed by Austria's separate status.[101]

The events of December 5 seem highly unusual and significant
indeed now that we can survey all their implications. Prussia actually
did the same thing that Austria had done on November 27. Both the
old powers, victorious over internal revolution, consolidated their historically created unity on a new constitutional basis. In doing this,
they defied the Frankfurt constituent assembly and asserted their
state autonomy over claims of national sovereignty. But the situation was such that even the refusal they offered the Frankfurt assembly was originally meant to further the Frankfurt constitution. It
was Schwarzenberg's Kremsier plan itself that had encouraged
Gagern's party to attempt the founding of a German federal state
without Austria. But if it were to be founded without Austria, it
would have to be founded with Prussia. Prussia's declaration that it
was a centralized state and intended to remain one doubtless threatened the foundations of Gagern's plan. Gagern's party demanded
that Prussia, if it were to become the leading power of Germany, be
liberal and constitutional but not entirely and independently constitutional. The contradiction within this demand recoiled on those
who made it. They received both more and less than they had desired.
Prussia became as liberal as they could possibly have wished, even

---

[101] The news of Franz Joseph's accession to the throne came on the evening of
December 4. As Leop. v. Gerlach, I, 259, reports, the Prussian princes saw this as
an "Austrian bid for the German crown" (see also Bailleu and Schuster, Aus dem
literar. Nachlass der Kaiserin Augusta, I, 327). It is not impossible, as a Berlin
correspondent of the Deutsche Zeitung assumed on December 7 (p. 2503), that
this news had had some influence on the decision reached that evening to publish
the constitution. See, too, Walter, op.cit., pp. 265f.—Hintze's belief (Preuss. Jahrbücher, CXLIV, 392f.) that the Saxon statesman Carlowitz had worked in the
formation of the promulgation policy for a unification of Germany through the
governments finds no further substantiation than the short mention of it in Bismarck's Gedanken und Erinnerungen, I, 53; and strictly speaking, this passage
does not even specifically refer to the idea of promulgation.

though it did so in a way they were obliged to condemn. But the Frankfurt assembly could do nothing about this, and they were forced to stand by a Prussia that they needed and that had declared its willingness to help them in their work. The situation had become completely reversed. The Frankfurt assembly wanted to exploit Prussia; but now, through the act of December 5, Prussia initiated a policy that amounted to exploiting Frankfurt for Prussia's purposes. Prussia had caught in its own sails so many of the national and liberal winds that impelled Frankfurt that it finally took the lead, and at the same time the "trim Prussian frigate" still sailed ahead on that great ocean current which had carried her since the days of the Great Elector and of Frederick the Great. The Frankfurt assembly had no choice; it had to follow this same course. There is already something of Bismarck's spirit in this act of December 5. It was at once conservative and creative: conservative in decisively preserving Prussian character, creative in its utilizing of national and liberal forces. These forces were utilized but also held within limits that made them compatible with factors that had developed in the course of history and still remained alive in it.

Considered from the point of view of its contents, the promulgated constitution did not represent an ideal compromise between the old and the new. Its basic material was schematic liberalism imported from France and Belgium,[102] and the contribution made by the ministers in working out their draft was limited to incorporating into the national assembly's draft a number of important provisions for preserving royal authority.[103] If the path that Stein and Humboldt had pointed out for the framing of a Prussian constitution had been taken, then something better, more organic, and genuinely Prussian could have been created. But this development had been interrupted, and its body of ideas had sunk out of view for the men of that era and for the men who had to produce a constitution now in these troubled times. If they were going to fulfill liberal demands, they were practically obliged to accept whatever conditions the liberals imposed on them at that particular moment. Even Bismarck did not act differently when he passed universal suffrage in 1866.

---

[102] R. Smend, *Die preussische Verfassungsurkunde im Vergleich mit der belgischen* (Göttinger Preisschrift, 1904), provides an interesting comparison of the final form of the Prussian constitutional document with the Belgian one from the point of view of constitutional law.

[103] On this, see Goldschmidt, *op.cit.*, p. 204, and Seitz, *op.cit.*, pp. 137ff. On Article 108, see Hansen, *Die Rheinlande u. die preuss. Politik 1815-1915*, in *Die Rheinprovinz 1815-1915*, I, 739.

The ministers' draft was a product of haste and pressure, and it was faulty as a result. Its great value is evident only within the context of its creation and in the future course it set for Prusso-German politics. But this positive aspect of the draft is in a certain sense anonymous. We can show that the majority of the ministry consisted of men who desired an understanding with Frankfurt and the founding of a Prusso-German federal state, but we cannot say which of them was the leading and compelling figure. Graf Brandenburg's German views have emerged quite clearly for us; but if we look at his later German policy, we feel that he did not deliberately shape it but simply let it take its course. He was probably influenced by Graf Bülow, the chief of the foreign office, who pulled together with Camphausen and who won the king's displeasure in the following months because of his zealous efforts toward an understanding with Frankfurt. We also know that in the spring of 1849 Rintelen favored Frankfurt and a hereditary German dynasty,[104] and that Ladenberg later advocated Radowitz' unification policy. We know practically nothing about Strotha's views on the German question. Manteuffel, as we know, took an unwilling part in the entire promulgation policy.

But perhaps there was still another unobtrusive influence present. There is no doubt that Major von Manteuffel, the king's aide-de-camp, exerted some influence too. As early as September he had suggested the promulgation of a constitution to the king, and he supported it again now.[105] In November he drove back and forth between Berlin and Potsdam, conferring with Brandenburg and Strotha, with Adjutant-General von Rauch,[106] and sometimes with Leopold von Gerlach as well. On November 20 he urgently requested Gerlach to convince the king not to resist the constitutional plan of the ministers, and he took pride in having personally brought about the deletion of a constitutional oath for the army from the constitution.[107] He let Gerlach think that the important thing at the moment was to gain time and create order and that such a constitution would not be permanent. But more important than such *argumenta ad hominem*

---

[104] Leop. v. Gerlach, I, 304, 306; Friedjung, *Österreich von 1848 bis 1860*, I, 507.

[105] Anschütz, *Verfassungsurkunde f. d. preussischen Staat*, I, 47.

[106] Keck, *E. v. Manteuffel*, p. 94.

[107] Leop. v. Gerlach, I, 245. The first drafts of the constitution still did, in fact, contain the constitutional oath for the army (Poschinger, *op.cit.*, I, 53, and G.St.A.), and in the constitution of December 5, 1848 there was still a provision that the "promised oath of allegiance to the constitution for the army" would be effected after revision had been completed.

is Manteuffel's remark on this occasion "that he had had the advice of little Ranke." If I am not mistaken, Major von Manteuffel is referring here to views of Ranke's contained in a memorial reprinted in Volumes XLIX-L of his works (pages 592ff.).[108] The date given to the memorial there is the end of October 1848. This cannot be correct because the memorial refers to events that took place in November.[109] I believe it was written at the same time that the ministers' promulgation plan was taking shape. The "best-informed," Ranke says, "do not

[108] Ranke himself later (1885) commented on his political memorials of those years: "I was called upon indirectly sometimes at somewhat desperate moments. Manteuffel, who was an aide-de-camp at the time and later became a field marshal, functioned as the go-between. And I gather that the king took what he said into consideration and resolved himself to take a firmer stand" (*Sämtl. Werke*, LIII-LIV, 74). See also Wiedenmann, *Deutsche Revue*, XVII, 2, p. 113, and Varrentrapp, *Histor. Zeitschrift*, IC, 111.

[109] P. 595: "The most recent events are of the greatest importance here. The assembly refused to recognize the ministers the crown had appointed and demanded that they be removed from its midst." This can only refer to the resolution of the assembly on November 2 and the well-known delegation it sent to Sanssouci. It had been planned to deny the Pfuel ministry a vote of confidence, too, but this was not done. Cf. Unruh, *Skizzen aus Preussens neuester Geschichte*, pp. 73f. The memorial itself must have been written after the middle of November because it speaks of the assembly in the past tense, already refers to "the declaration of public opinion in favor of the crown," and also mentions the idea of promulgation. The fact that the most recent revolutionary act of the assembly on November 15 is not mentioned does not invalidate this dating if we consider the broad perspective from which the situation is viewed. Diether, *L. v. Ranke als Politiker*, pp. 345ff., however, thinks the date of the memorial should be fixed between November 3 and 9 or between November 3 and November 10 at the latest. I do not deny the strength of some of the reasons he cites for this, but he himself must admit that he cannot name any specific incidents from this period that contain a "declaration of public opinion in favor of the crown." Ranke, however, speaks in such strong terms (p. 596) of the "nation's" decisive and general expression of opinion in favor of the crown that we can only see this as a reference to the change of mood that began to set in from November 16 on. Wiedenmann's note, which Diether uses as the main prop for his argument, is of no chronological importance here. It says nothing against my dating at all. Furthermore, Diether's dating would make it difficult to explain Ranke's statement on p. 593: "Austria is able to do this and seems to want to do it at this point" (sc. exclude itself from Germany). As I mentioned in the first edition, p. 427, this certainly does not have to be a reference to the Kremsier plan of November 27. But I am no longer satisfied with the attempt I made then to explain it on the basis of Metternich's efforts in England, where he was at the time, to urge the separation of Austria and Germany, efforts of which Potsdam had been aware since mid-November. Ranke's statement "Austria is able to do this and seems to want to do it at this point" must refer to specific acts of the Austrian government itself that could be interpreted in this way, and the earliest and perhaps only act that could be interpreted in this way was the shooting of Robert Blum on November 9, an act that was immediately considered in Germany to constitute a breach with the Frankfurt assembly.—Thus, the memorial must have been written not long after that and shortly after November 15.

seem to consider the path of unification possible, and they prefer to grant a constitution based on the proposals and drafts already made." Ranke approved of this, provided the concept of popular sovereignty did not gain a foothold. That was an unnecessary warning because the attitudes of these particular ministers made this danger completely improbable anyhow, and the warning was probably meant to serve more as a reassurance for those who were wary of a modern constitution in any form at all. It was to those people that he primarily addressed himself: "We must look dispassionately at constitutionalism as a form of government under which modern men want to live. We must frame the constitution in such a way that we can manage with it." However, he did not find the most pressing reason for Prussian constitutional government in the demands of his contemporaries or in internal Prussian affairs, but in the relationship of Prussia to Germany. Prussia, he said, can no longer move ahead by means of its own strength as it did in Frederick's time. Part of its power and of its significance in Europe lies now in its relationship to Germany. If Prussia wanted to isolate itself at this point, it would have to abandon the Customs Union. Prussia has the choice "of exerting influence or receiving it." The only way for Prussia to exert it, he thought, was for Prussia to assume the leading position in Germany. But to be able to exert it, Prussia would have to fulfill the constitutional ideal now.

Ranke probably did not know of Rümelin and Gagern's demand that Prussia fulfill this ideal for Germany but not for herself. In any case, he did not know how serious this demand was. But he would not have recognized it anyway, for he rejects it implicitly when he says: "The German kaisership is conservative by nature, has always been so, and will always be so. If the highest authority in Germany does not want to open the way for a republican revolution, it must resolve to recognize the independence of the individual states and the concept of principality." Gagern's plan did not necessarily have to lead to a republican revolution, but a German kaisership based on the subordination of the largest individual state in it cannot really be called conservative either. The entire spirit of Ranke's assessment radiates Prussian self-confidence and state consciousness. This is Ranke's old conservative idea of the national state that we met in the first part of our study, but now on a higher level than before. This idea no longer sees invisible but politically effective ties binding the nationality of the most powerful individual state to the more inclusive German nationality.

Here we have what we have been seeking: an explanation and justification for the policy of promulgation, for the promulgation itself, and especially for what was to be promulgated. The explanation and justification are made on the basis of the broad perspectives and the keen historical and political understanding that we take for granted in Ranke's writings. But we cannot take for granted, even with this great master, his ability to sense and understand his own time so well that he could prescribe a formula for it that did justice to both the established past and the shifting present. Also, this memorial is not just a personal opinion. It served an immediate political purpose, was meant to be seen by the government, and can therefore be regarded as a Prussian state document. On the basis of the facts mentioned above, there can be no doubt that Edwin von Manteuffel, who provided the impulse for the memorial, conveyed either the document or its contents to the ministers with whom he was in touch. Ranke was in close contact with the group that wanted to promulgate a constitution. As he reported later,[110] he was even requested, in the name of the king—and, I would imagine, at Edwin von Man-teuffel's suggestion—to help draft the constitution. However, he declined to do so. At the time, he did not think that "the thing," the constitution, would survive long. This conservative skepticism prevented him from participating in a project that his political insight led him to approve. But he did prevail upon himself to draft a royal decree for the promulgation.[111]

We cannot say that Ranke's ideas in this memorial were simply taken over by the ministers, but we can say that they provide a fuller rationale for the ministers' action and confirm our view of it.

We should also point out here that this central political problem brings the strikingly contrasting points of view in nineteenth-century German historical studies into sharp relief—the opposition between Ranke and the representatives of so-called political history. Johann Gustav Droysen, Max Duncker,[112] and, as we shall soon see, Dahl-

[110] To Wiedenmann, *Deutsche Revue*, XVII, 2, p. 344. I imagine that the request was made during the days after November 26, when the king began to weaken in his resistance against promulgation. I assume further that Wiedenmann must have misunderstood or made an error when he has Ranke mention a "suggestion of Otto v. Manteuffel's." Ranke probably meant Edwin v. Manteuffel, with whom he had close contact. Wiedenmann also misinterprets Gerlach's remark (I, 245: "Ranke *a consiliis*"), cited above, as referring to Otto v. Manteuffel.

[111] *Op.cit.*, p. 598. The dating of December 5, 1848 given there is, of course, only the final date of the draft. It was doubtless written in the last days of November or the first days of December.

[112] Duncker's memorial for the Kasinopartei on the question of leadership was distributed shortly before Christmas 1848 (Haym, *Duncker*, p. 98). It is reprinted

mann all stood in the ranks of those who wanted to destroy or at least
undermine Prussia's political unity for the sake of Germany. They
wanted to unify Germany with Prussia's help but also at Prussia's
expense. Ranke wanted to unify Germany with Prussia's help, too,
but he also wanted to preserve Prussia's historically formed political
individuality. Droysen, Duncker, and Dahlmann were more deeply
rooted in their own time in taking the ideal of a modern German
national state as their basis and in respecting historical, territorial
Germany only to the extent that their concept of a constitutional federal state permitted such respect. Ranke reached deeper into German history and drew together the old conservative German empire,
the territorial epoch, and the new, developing constitutional and
national Prusso-Germany into a unified, uninterrupted evolutionary
process. In them, there is more desire and passion, traces of that same
passion that Stein wanted to use earlier to divide Prussia. In Ranke,
the composure of historical contemplation is joined with the detachment of hardheaded political calculation. He takes his position high
in the watchtower of the Prussian state, while the others try to storm
those heights from the flatlands of the German nation. One who saw
the German question from a Prussian point of view could not be as
fiery and passionate in his desires as they could, because he already
had something. They thought they had nothing, and in their hunger
for the nation they wanted more than they could have, because they
wanted everything. But without the hunger of these have-nots, the
desire of the Prussian state for total fulfillment could easily have
faded, and Prussia could easily have remained nothing more than
Prussia. Without the forces that those men helped to create, neither

---

completely in Hübner, *Aktenstücke*, pp. 727ff. Haym, *Nationalversammlung*, II,
217ff., prints excerpts from it. Duncker writes: "If we master this situation quickly
and in a statesmanlike fashion, every conflict between dynastic and state power
can be avoided in the leadership we want to provide for the federal state. The
dangerous friction between a major state assembly and the German assembly can
be avoided, and instead of the feared Prussian hegemony, the dominance of Germany over Prussia . . . can be achieved." W. Stolze, *Quellen u. Darstellungen
zur Gesch. der deutschen Burschenschaft*, VII, 132, doubts that Duncker was ever
prepared "to extinguish Prussia itself for the sake of greater unity." But Jürgens,
op.cit., I, 481, testifies clearly that in December 1848 Duncker voted for a Prussian
hereditary kaiser "only under the condition that Prussia be dissolved into provinces
and not retain a Prussian general assembly." In the course of the following year,
however, Duncker gave up this position (cf. Küntzel, *Deutsche Literaturzeitung*
[1908], p. 458, and Jürgens, *op.cit.*, I, 482f.); and later, in 1861, he spoke out
clearly against the dissolution of Prussia's political unity. Cf. Westphal, *Welt- und
Staatsanschauung des deutschen Liberalismus*, p. 210, note 4.

Ranke nor Bismarck after him would have been able to project his thinking beyond the borders of Prussia. If the others had not prepared the way, these men would not have been able to see so far and to build so well.

Still another observation should be made here. Droysen and Duncker, who both wanted to dissolve the Prussian state in 1848, afterwards became the Borussian historians κατ᾽ ἐξοχήν. This is easy to understand. As early as the spring of 1848, Droysen had given indications of what his future development would be. We saw that he had both German and Prussian leanings from the beginning and that he saw a solution to the problem only in the clear alternatives of a Germany either predominantly German or predominantly Prussian. After the first possibility had failed, it was no breach of character for him to move decisively to the Prussian side. The more dispassionate Duncker did the same thing, but probably on the basis of a realistic adjustment to the new situation. During all this, however, the old master, Ranke, in his calm preeminence, continued to spin the thread of world history.

I should like to take this digression from our subject still another step further, because this additional step immediately leads us to a new view of our subject. Might we not say that our problem, in a different form, is implied in the very way that Droysen explained and realized the new concept of history? It was characteristic of this historical view to idealize Prussia's autonomous power politics in past centuries and to imagine them to be determined by German national ideas to a greater extent than they really were. In wanting to derive Prussia's historical calling for Germany from its goals in actual politics, he failed to recognize the true nature of this state.[113] Thus, he unknowingly and unintentionally committed the same offense against the autonomy of the Prussian state personality that he had knowingly and intentionally committed when he demanded the dissolution of Prussia for the sake of German unity in 1848. He dissolved it intellectually, as it were, and satisfied his own emotional need that way. He believed that Prussia had already achieved a partial ethical merger with Germany in the past, and he tried to use historical research to prove this. We see, then, that his later historical views have a direct connection with his political actions of 1848. If closely examined, his Borussian point of view was really non-Borussian, or at least supra-Borussian; and the "political history" he advocated had an ex-

[113] The beginnings of this idealization are evident in the essays of 1845 and 1847, cited above on pp. 256f. and in the lectures on the Wars of Liberation.

tremely nonpolitical side to it; for it was un-Prussian and nonpolitical
thinking to ascribe policies to the Prussian state that did not arise
from its own true character. If we fully grasp the basic source of his
error, we can see again how powerfully the nonpolitical thinking of the
eighteenth century continued to influence the thought of this historian who wanted to be strictly political in his approach. Droysen
received the immediate impact of these intellectual currents, and we
can still clearly see their influence today in the popularized versions
of his historical view, just as we can see the traces of a massive wave
on the beach long after the wave itself has ebbed back into the sea.

....

5

THE PERIOD FROM THE
PROMULGATION OF THE CONSTITUTION TO
THE ELECTION OF THE KAISER

WE LEAVE BERLIN and Prussia now to return to Frankfurt, the focal point of the efforts that concern us in this study.

As we have often seen before, a certain ambiguity is integral to the very being of these efforts; and their advocates, after the defeat they had suffered on December 5, were in the fortunate position of being able to register a gain along with their loss. The Prussian state's every true expression of power also strengthened the Frankfurt Erbkaiserpartei. In an extensive memorial to his government on December 14,[1] Camphausen could note with satisfaction that Prussia's prestige in Frankfurt was making a strong recovery, that the number of Prussia's friends was growing, and that the measures of the present Prussian ministry had been crucial in bringing this about. On the same day, Heinrich von Gagern offered some interesting reflections on the gains and losses that resulted from the promulgation.[2] He thought the greatest disadvantage of it was that the other German states would be forced to make just as many concessions as Prussia had. He was afraid that the promulgation would disturb the basis of the voting laws, i.e., that it would no longer be possible to prevent general suffrage in Germany now that Prussia had set a democratic example. On the other hand, he too could count it a gain that the Prussian government's winning over of public opinion had had an influence on the Frankfurt opposition and had tamed it. As we already know, he condemned the promulgated constitution as unviable in itself and impossible for Germany. But for that very reason he did not consider it too serious an obstacle to his plans. In any case, he thought it rested on a poor foundation because it was simply promulgated and not properly

[1] G.St.A. (Brandenburg, *Untersuchungen*, pp. 290ff.)
[2] Simson, *Ed. v. Simson*, pp. 146f.

325

agreed upon. "I hope," he went on, "that it will never go into effect. The next great difficulty will then be to dispose of it altogether."

We can understand, accordingly, why his party did not undertake a direct battle against the Prussian constitution and why it even opposed the effort of the radicals in Frankfurt to conduct such a battle.[3] The plan was to take care of the essentials first, to secure the hereditary German crown for Prussia, and only then to begin doing away with the Prussian constitution.[4] But now it seemed advisable to those who formulated this plan to prepare public opinion in Germany and Prussia to accept these two things. They had to appeal to the Germans with the idea that the Hohenzollern hegemony was not equivalent to a hegemony of the Prussian state, and they had to prepare the Prussians for the fact that the elevation of their royal house would put them in a new relationship to it and that they would become citizens directly subject to the German crown. On December 11, the *Deutsche Zeitung* went into these matters in detail after it had cleverly pointed out the good aspects of the promulgation along with the bad two days before. This editorial is probably the most impressive formulation these ideas ever received.

The inevitable course of affairs, the paper wrote, will bring Prussia into a position of leadership in Germany sooner or later. The only question remaining is how Prussia can be organically assimilated into Germany. As the leader of the federal state, the king of Prussia will find himself doomed to eternal vacillation between two positions, two governments, two parliaments, and two residences. This cannot be

[3] This effort crystallized in Wesendonck's motion of December 7 to declare the promulgated constitution null and void. On the night of December 7, in a consultation at Beckerath's, the Gagern group decided to recognize the Prussian constitution as valid. Hansen, *Mevissen*, II, 448. In the constituent committee, the idea of dividing Prussia into provinces was, of course, discussed in the following weeks. Cf. Hübner, *Aktenstücke*, pp. 266, 284, 286, 291f., 294 (Soiron), 298f., 303 (M. v. Gagern), 305, 364; also Haym, *Nationalversammlung*, II, 233, 241; Jürgens, *op.cit.*, II, 325.

[4] Accordingly, we find reported in Haym the basic drift of Duncker's memorial from the period before Christmas 1848 (mentioned above, p. 321n.): The adjustment of the relationship between the Prussian individual state and the entire federal state could well be left to take care of itself in the future, and it had to be seen as a gradual yet at the same time an inevitable adjustment. Haym, *Nationalversammlung*, II, 228. It is true that the *Allgemeine Zeitung* of December 15 reads: "According to reports of the tenth from Berlin, serious negotiations were underway between Frankfurt and Berlin on a plan to grant the German crown to the king of Prussia provided Prussia were truly dissolved, i.e., provided Prussia renounced its state assembly and only the old provincial diets remained." However, I am unable to find any substantiation for this in Prussian files I am familiar with.

permitted. "Prussia must surrender itself to regain itself twofold." "Lose yourself and gain the world." We can have only *one* major government in Germany, only *one* parliament. Fortunately, Prussia has retained a provincial organization that has a natural and legal basis. The future hereditary kaiser should grant the eight Prussian provinces greater autonomy under governors selected from the princes of his family and from other eminent circles. He should enlarge the powers of these provinces, which are no longer Prussian provinces but German territories, to the point of almost complete internal independence. The German constitution, which remains to be revised, will continue to grant this same independence to the territories of the princes. The kaiser's foreign ministry will be the only one in Germany. His ministry of defense will be responsible for the territories both directly and indirectly subject to the central government, more so in the case of those directly subject to it, less so for those indirectly subject to it. The other ministries will function similarly. An organization into districts would also be possible. The smallest territories would be incorporated into this system with the greatest possible preservation of their separate existences. This is the picture this writer sketches of a vital, centralized state formed out of eight territories directly subject to the central government and eight indirectly subject to it, the former under hereditary rulers, the latter under appointed governors. "The heart leaps for joy at this very idea." For the time being, however, it is desirable that the unfortunate Berlin or Brandenburg parliament not come into existence again. The kaiser's residence must be Berlin in the future, but every other year the German parliament must convene in Frankfurt, and during the parliamentary session the German government must be located there too.

"Only in this way will the princes and people be fully convinced that they belong to Germany and not to Prussia."

The writer of this article is probably the young Heinrich Kruse, who edited the *Deutsche Zeitung* from December 2 on and immediately brought new life to it with his "outstanding editorials." However, no lesser a personality than Dahlmann was the major influence behind Kruse, and Kruse conducted a lively exchange of ideas with him.[5] As we remember, Dahlmann had fundamentally agreed, in the constitutional committee, to the idea of loosening Prussia's political unity, but at the time he did not think it possible in practical terms. Also, in the national assembly on December 6, he had only men-

[5] Springer, *Dahlmann*, II, 317.

tioned as a future possibility that the Prussians might have to do
without their general assembly and be satisfied with provincial assemblies.[6] Now he went a step further. At Kruse's request, he wrote
a "New Year's contribution" for the *Deutsche Zeitung* of January 1
that forcefully called the attention of Germany to the great project
that was now nearing completion in Frankfurt. "Seek protection with
the powerful! . . . At the moment, Prussia possesses the power. We
must simply recognize this as a fact of history that cannot possibly be
altered." Germany must join with Prussia; but if this is to be accomplished, he continued, the Prussian people must, by merging with
Germany, achieve once again, but to a still greater extent and more
consciously, that transformation of their character that made the creation of Prussia from Brandenburg possible before. Dahlmann not only
repeated his previous demand that the German parliament should
not convene on Prussian soil but also added: "A Prussian national
assembly will quickly prove to be impossible. To establish a legislative assembly for half of Germany here and one for all of Germany
there would only be to evoke a struggle between forces that would
mutually destroy each other."

There is no need to doubt any longer that these ideas, which the
most important contributor to the Frankfurt constitutional drafts
proclaimed in such ringing tones, had become the common property
and leading principles of a large group in the Erbkaiserpartei.[7]

Speaking somewhat obliquely but still directly enough for the
knowledgeable, Heinrich von Gagern expressed his views to the parliament on January 11, 1849. He dealt with the Austrian question and
pointed out in this connection that the very regional groups that had
an established political life and a proud history of their own would
have to make particular sacrifices for German unity. For this reason,
he continued, complete unity could not be achieved quickly through
the pronouncement of a decree. Prussia had been reproached for
desiring a hegemony, but recent events seemed to indicate that just
the opposite was true, "for everything we call specifically Prussian

---

[6] *Stenogr. Bericht,* p. 3859.

[7] It will suffice to cite the issues in which the *Deutsche Zeitung* continues to
discuss this idea in the following weeks: No. 34 of February 3 (Berlin column of
January 31); No. 49 of February 18; 2nd supplement to No. 80 of March 21. We
need not go into the polemic of other publications against this idea. Cf., for
example, the December 24, 1848 number of the *Deutsche Reform,* which had been
appearing in Berlin since October: "The new kaisership is meaningful only if
Prussia continues to exist in an unweakened condition." See, too, *Die Grenzboten*
(1848), IV, 494; and other publications.

resists absorption into Germany and would prefer to continue on its separate path. But I hold the firm conviction that the great majority of thinking Prussians realize that Prussia can only continue to exist with close ties to Germany and that Prussia must seek its future in Germany." He refused to consider the idea of a Prussian hegemony, just as he had on October 26, 1848. Hegemony, he said, is the guardianship of a large state over smaller ones. He wanted "throughout our great state a true, strong, and beneficent government that would assume responsibility for important national interests."

On January 15, 1849 the debates on the paragraph of the constitutional draft dealing with "the chief of state" began in Frankfurt. We shall not be disappointed if we expect to see our main idea discussed, advocated, defended, and attacked on the floor still more frequently now. The men who had advanced it still did not formulate it concretely and precisely, and they had good reasons not to do so. It would have made their task considerably more difficult, and it would have made the desired understanding with Prussia particularly difficult if they had made their demand now that Prussia give up its separate parliament. Because of December 5 their opportunity had been lost, and they were obliged to bide their time again. Thus, it was more the opponents than the advocates of a hereditary German crown for Prussia who were responsible for bringing up the subject, no doubt with the intention of luring the Erbkaiserpartei into an embarrassing position and exposing it. Schüler, a democrat from Jena, introduced these tactics on January 15.[8] If the Prussian dynasty were to rule over Germany, he said, it could only do so if one of two conditions were fulfilled. Either the other dynasties would have to be dissolved and all Germany become Prussian, or the Prussian state would have to dissolve itself into its individual provinces. Biedermann, who belonged to the left wing of the Erbkaiserpartei and who was not reluctant to make somewhat radical statements,[9] did not wait long with his answer. I believe, he said, that one or the other of these alternatives could be realized. Indeed, perhaps both could be realized, and I would be the last to regret that. But he also added, for safety's sake,

[8] As early as September 1848, he had proposed, in the constituent committee, a provision that would have made it possible to literally eradicate the constitution and representative assembly of every individual state by means of federal legislation. Droysen, *Verhandlungen des Verfassungsausschusses*, I, 333 and 414.

[9] "He stood firmly by the principles his theory outlined for him; and, consequently, in the matter of 'centralizing' the German state, he often stood alone in the Augsburger Hof, where there was only a desire to 'concentrate,' only a desire for a federal state in the strictest sense." Laube, *op.cit.*, III, 35.

that it was not the task of the Frankfurt parliament to destroy and reform the individual state governments. This debate continued on the next day, opened this time by the Catholic August Reichensperger from Cologne. Almost all the advocates of a hereditary German crown for Prussia agree, he said, that Prussian unity must perish if German unity is to arise from it. Prussia should be divided into its provinces and suffer the fate of the old man who let himself be hacked into pieces and thrown into a sorcerer's cauldron in order to be rejuvenated. He, Reichensperger, an inhabitant of one of the new Prussian provinces, was in agreement with many Prussians from the old provinces in rejecting this dangerous experiment. But was this "new" Prussian really speaking as a Prussian here? In this same speech, he made no secret of the fact that he, as a Catholic, had objections to a hegemony of the Protestant North. We have a glimpse here into a remarkable state of affairs. The Catholics consciously acting in the Catholic interest supported the Prussian state because this Prussia with its promulgated constitution and religious freedom promised them more than a unitarian Germany with the Protestant North as its nucleus.

Ostendorf, the Soest delegate from the Erbkaiserpartei, formulated the reply to Reichensperger. This Westphalian with his traditional Prussian way of thinking did not deny, either, that it would be historically inevitable for Prussia, placed at the head of Germany, to gradually dissolve into its parts. He agreed with Reichensperger that this "would be neither possible nor advantageous for Germany at the moment, but the inexorable development of history will gradually bring it about." Welcker, whose sympathies were for a Greater Germany at that time, had good reason in the following meeting on January 8 to note mockingly that the Erbkaiserpartei was hoping to catch a lot of mice with this bait.[10]

But it cannot be denied that there were several mice in the assembly that were attracted by this bait. Schüler's speech on January 15 shows that he could have been won to the side of the hereditary Hohenzollern crown if one of the two alternatives he presented had been realized, and two other representatives of the Left, Vogt[11] and Raveaux,[12] said unequivocally on March 18 that if the dissolution of the Prussian state into provinces were a real possibility, this would be an enticement for them too. Raveaux said to the Center, "Various advocates of our position would speak out for the hereditary German

[10] Stenogr. Bericht, p. 4770.   [11] Ibid., p. 5821.
[12] Ibid., p. 5833.

crown if what had been previously discussed were really carried out. But no one wants to do that; no one can do it."

Although the Left, as we shall see later, had good reason to be interested in the dissolution of the Prussian state, we can assume a definite mistrust of such a move on the side of the Greater German and particularistic opponents of the hereditary German crown. It had become perfectly clear that what was happening to Prussia now could also happen to the other particularistic states of Germany tomorrow or the next day. It was Edel from Würzburg, a member of the Catholic group, who clearly understood the unitarian consequences of this idea and warned against them on January 23.[13]

Then the advocates of a Greater Germany changed their tactics. Instead of opposing this idea, they snatched it up. This fighting the Erbkaiserpartei with its own weapons was one of the many strategies they used in the weeks before the election of the kaiser to confuse the Erbkaiserpartei and, ultimately, to make the German constitution unacceptable to the king of Prussia. In the constituent committee, the Austrian Sommaruga resubmitted a motion[14] that Dahlmann had made there on November 20 but had then withdrawn three days later. On February 20, Sommaruga asked for the following provision: In those states made up of several provinces, each province having a separate constitution or administration, the members of the Staatenhaus that are to be appointed by the assembly of the entire state should not be elected by the general state assembly but by the provincial diets. The Erbkaiserpartei was in an uncomfortable situation. Beseler replied that he recognized the importance of this matter and hoped that things would develop that way. But he thought it was too early to take this step yet. He tried to point out, with little success, that the present provincial organization of Prussia did not correspond to the constitutional premises contained in Sommaruga's proposal; and he also pointed out, with better success, that one would have to interfere with the general assemblies of all the individual states, and such interference would be even less welcome to the others than it was to the Prussians. The motion was finally passed, by twelve votes to eleven, after a long debate in which Welcker supported it because of South German vindictiveness toward the North. However, when this paragraph was edited two days later, the Erbkaiserpartei was able to dilute it so much that it tentatively allowed, but did not oblige, Prussia to let the provinces name the members of

13 *Ibid.*, p. 4838.   14 Hübner, *Aktenstücke*, pp. 531ff.

the Staatenhaus.[15] But when the paragraph came before the plenary session for a second reading, the opposition carried the day; and on March 26, over the votes of the Erbkaiserpartei, the motion of Pretis and Möring from Austria, Edel from Würzburg, and others was passed. It read that "in those states made up of several provinces or territories, each province or territory having a separate constitution or administration, the members that are to be appointed by the popular representatives of these states will not be appointed by the general state assemblies but by the assemblies of the individual territories or provinces (provincial diets)."[16] As Otto von Manteuffel rightly thought, this was devised as a means of destroying Prussia's unity.[17]

There were similar attempts of this sort that were not as successful. The Austrian representative Werner from St. Pölten made the motion on March 19[18] that if the hereditary German crown were offered to the king of Prussia, then an accompanying condition of this offer should be "that the Prussian state as such cease to exist immediately and be divided into four separate states belonging to Germany."[19] A similar tendency was evident in the motion the Bavarian delegate Müller from Würzburg made on March 20.[20] This motion proposed arranging and securing the necessary changes in the Prussian constitution, particularly the elimination of the Prussian parliament, by means of negotiations with the Prussian government.

After all these questions and motions, Gagern, as prime minister for Germany, was obliged to take sides. "I agree completely with that," he said in his major speech on the same day.[21] "If a Smaller Germany [*Kleindeutschland*], as it is called, is to achieve its goals for the present and the future, then its center must be in the center and not in the

---

[15] *Ibid.*, pp. 537f. See also, on pp. 660f., the suggestion of the constituent committee for the second reading: "Half the members of the Staatenhaus will be appointed by the government, and half by the representative assemblies of the states concerned or by the representative assemblies of their provinces. Whether and how such representation will be effected by the provinces will be left to the legislation of the individual states etc." Cf. Bergsträsser, *Die Verfassung des Deutschen Reiches vom Jahre 1849*, p. 50.

[16] § 88 of the final constitution. Cf. *Stenogr. Bericht*, p. 6024.

[17] To Radowitz, May 16, 1849.

[18] *Stenogr. Bericht*, pp. 5834ff. Two days before, Schüler had made a similar motion in the constituent committee, also without any success. Hübner, *Aktenstücke*, pp. 658, 660, 747.

[19] And these four would be under governors to be appointed by the king of Prussia. This motion, then, follows the suggestion of the *Deutsche Zeitung* of December 11, 1848.

[20] *Stenogr. Bericht*, p. 5868. Jürgens, *Zur Geschichte des deutschen Verfassungswerkes*, II, Part 2, p. 223, calls it "ironic and scornful."

[21] *Stenogr. Bericht*, p. 5885.

North." A cry of "Hear! Hear!" from all sides interrupted him. "I have no illusions," he immediately said in a conciliatory fashion. "I do not think that if a federal state is formed with Prussia at its head, the immediate result will be the decentralization of Prussia by means of dissolving the Prussian general assembly as it now exists. But no one who takes cognizance of the historical analogies can have any doubt that such a decentralization, such a merger with Germany, will be the gradual and inevitable result."[22]

His view was seconded on the next day[23] by Gabriel Riesser.[24] Prussia, Riesser said, is an artificial state, but Germany is a national state, a natural state; and just as nature is stronger than artifice, so the natural strength of Germany will prevail over the artificial strength of Prussia. This predominance of Germany, however, can only come about through the gradual process of a free and noble Prussian surrender to Germany; "but never again can we force conditions on Prussia that negate its existence; never again can we demand of Prussia that it negotiate its very existence with us; I tell you outright that for the sake of Germany as well as of Prussia we should not want to see Prussia's stability the least bit weakened until Germany is securely and firmly established for all eternity."

That was the last important statement made on this subject in this historic battle of words, and it also marks the temporary conclusion of the efforts we wanted to recount here. Highly political motives

[22] Jürgens, op.cit., II, Part 2, p. 175, reports from the period around March 13: "In private, Gagern admits openly now that the German question has become a Prussian one, that he fears it will not be possible, as it was planned, to dissolve Prussia by making its king the kaiser of Germany. However, he adds that for him and his associates the condition of division and plurality of states is so intolerable that they would rather become Prussian . . . than remain in their present condition." Although Jürgens is not a reliable source for the statements of his political opponents, it is at least possible that Gagern said something of this sort in a moment of passion. This does not mean, however, that he had to give up the hope he expressed in the speech cited above.

[23] After Schüler had already expressed his skepticism about Gagern's hopeful statement, Stenogr. Bericht, p. 5896.

[24] Ibid., p. 5907. Rümelin took a similar position in the Schwäb. Merkur on March 18. "The adherents of the Erbkaiserpartei want Prussia to fall apart into its provinces and cease to exist as an independent state in all essential respects. This would necessarily come about anyway, but to demand it now as a condition to be immediately fulfilled is equivalent to crushing this entire course of development before it has a chance to get underway. And perhaps that is what they desire after all." Aus der Paulskirche, p. 199. As a contrary example we might also mention that the eccentric Grävell, who had backed Prussian independence in the fall of 1848, demanded the dissolution of the Prussian state in the Prusso-German federal state in February 1849. Haufe, op.cit., pp. 170f.; Wentzcke, op.cit., pp. 216f.

forced the thwarting of an idea that the advocates of a hereditary
German crown for Prussia had set in motion and that they now saw
being used against them by their opponents. The attitude that
Schwarzenberg's Austria now assumed toward the Frankfurt constitution gave reason to expect that a hereditary German crown for Prussia would not be established without a struggle. Beseler said in the
constituent committee on March 15 that Prussia was facing a war,
just as it had been in 1756, and he thought that Prussia could and
was obliged to take this struggle on itself. Hergenhahn added on
March 17 that the consequences would be disastrous if the division
of Prussia were decreed at such a critical moment.[25]

Thus, the members of the Erbkaiserpartei gave up their hopeless
and, at that point, even dangerous effort to melt down Prussia, the
rocher de bronce. They also gave up their questionable tactics of proposing more concrete demands, which they made in the hope of per-
suading some of the Leftists and particularists to vote for Friedrich
Wilhelm IV. If they had given in more to these groups, the election
might have been won by a more impressive majority, but then probably some of the delegates more sympathetic to Prussia would have
left them. The crown that they finally offered the king was already
weighted down enough with devious concessions to the Left. It was
clear that the Left had different ideas about the dissolution of Prussia than the Erbkaiserpartei did. The Erbkaiserpartei wanted Prussia
to merge with Germany; the Left wanted Prussia to perish.[26] The
rapacious glances that the Leftists were casting about must have
been warning enough to the Erbkaiserpartei to proceed cautiously
and not to destroy the only wall that could protect them from the Left
now and in the near future.

But they were not ready to regard what they had postponed as
irretrievable. They comforted themselves with the idea that the inevitable course of history would eventually bring about what they
had been unable to demand. The constitution was created from this
point of view. It was meant to be understood that way, and that is
the way those who come after must understand it and interpret
it. I think we do indeed cast a new light on the constitution if we
always keep in mind that a great number of the men who offered

---

[25] Hübner, *Aktenstücke,* pp. 649 and 660.

[26] The republican Struve had already said in *Grundzüge der Staatswissenschaft*
(1847), I, 56: "Prussia will decline as soon as the German nation is awakened to
new life."

the Frankfurt crown to Friedrich Wilhelm IV hoped that its acceptance would eventually lead to the dissolution of Prussian state unity.[27]

But would it necessarily have had this result? Or was this possibility with which the Erbkaiserpartei finally contented themselves
nothing more than a cheap philosophical consolation? We shall try
to answer this question in the following chapters of our study. Our
main goal here will be to bring what we have already grasped of
the premises as well as of the consequences of this plan into a broader
context and to measure all this by the standards that history itself has
given us—the accomplishments of Bismarck.

[27] In an "Ansprache an seine Wähler" on June 15, 1849, Max von Gagern said
in summary: "Our party's plan that the House of Hohenzollern, in exchange for
the hereditary crown of a new German empire, give up the isolated, overly
extended Brandenburg kingdom that once destroyed our old German empire—
this plan of the majority, this plan that was victorious in the German constitution
of March 28 etc." Pastor, *Max v. Gagern*, p. 310. Even if he is generalizing too
strongly here, what Baumgarten said in 1870 about the mood that determined the
vote of March 28, 1849 can only have been true for a small portion of the
Erbkaiserpartei: "We believed in Prussia's *enduring* existence, and for that reason
we gave her the throne." *Hist. u. polit. Aufsätze*, p. 298.—Among most recent
studies, Lenz, "1848," *Preuss. Jahrbücher*, XCI, 543, and *Kleine histor. Schriften*,
p. 394, and Laband, "Das deutsche Kaisertum" (a speech, Strasbourg, 1896), pp.
23f., have shown the most agreement with my conclusions here.

6

···

FROM HEINRICH VON GAGERN
TO BISMARCK

WE POINTED OUT at the beginning of our study that the idea of "Prussia at the head of Germany but without a general diet" was both a political and a nonpolitical conception, a national and a nonnational one. It misunderstood and violated the autonomy of the state personality and the right to existence of the political national-ity that had sprung up on the soil of the individual state. In doing this it showed that the nonpolitical mind of the eighteenth century still had a profound influence on it. But it did these things for the sake of a new political and national need that had awakened in the German cultural nation. What was developing collided with what was already established. The liberal idea of the national state, which called for the sovereignty and political unity of the entire nation, collided with the conservative idea of the national state, which wanted to protect the living political structures of the past.

But this delineates only the general categories in question here. It does not show the actual life that these categories circumscribed. In Book I we tried to present the life of the conservative idea of the na-tional state. The life of its liberal counterpart is in need of more detailed description now. Doubtless, by its very nature, this idea has an antipathy to the particular and individual aspects of the German individual state and a strong affinity for the more general. This na-tional-philosophical idealism that was prepared to sacrifice the par-ticular to the general was especially evident in those advocates of our idea who were willing to see Prussia merge with Germany even though they themselves were born in Prussia and were deeply attached to it. Droysen, Duncker, and Haym belong to this group. It is worth noting that they were all basically scholars and philosophers, and it may have been the influence of Hegelianism that enabled them to make the step from a lower to a higher form of national existence. But we also have evidence[1] for the fact that practically all the influential Prussians in the assembly, even dyed-in-the-wool politicians and statesmen like Vincke, Schwerin, and Flottwell, fell victim at one time or another to the doctrine that Prussia would have to make sacrifices. But they held this doctrine only intermittently; and if this view had ever become a matter for serious consideration, it probably would have split the Prussian branch of the Erbkaiserpartei in two.[2] The fact is, our idea does not really originate in the Prussian wing of the Erbkaiserpartei at all. If we are looking for its sources, we cannot neglect the Catholic Rhineland, where Max von Gagern had once been influenced in this direction; but we must first turn to south-western Germany, where Pfizer first advocated the idea and where Heinrich von Gagern and Rümelin had their roots. Here, along with the more general intellectual basis for a liberal conception of the national state, we also find specific and concrete factors at work that

[1] Notes written by the representative Boddien on January 17, 1849 (they were intended for King Friedrich Wilhelm IV, and his remarks appear in the margins [Hausarchiv]): "If men like Vincke, Schwerin, Flottwell, etc. and almost all important Prussians declare themselves in favor of a hereditary German crown, they do so in the conviction that this crown can fall to Prussia alone. They are caught up in this idea that they have repeatedly declared: Prussia will and must give up its own general assembly, i.e., must reduce its state parliament to provincial diets. Prussia would thus make the great sacrifice of its history and of a fundamental aspect of its independence by taking up the leadership of Germany." As evidence of the circulation our ideas had in the circles of the Prussian liberals, we may cite, despite their party coloring, the words Kleist-Retzow threw out to his opponents in the great Olmütz debate in the Prussian lower house on December 3, 1850: "There is so much talk of Prussia's honor. If I look at the people who talk most about it . . . I find some among them who have demanded that Prussia be divided into its provinces, that it should, in any case, be subjugated to and merged with parliamentary majorities beyond Prussia itself." *Stenogr. Berichte*, p. 53.

[2] From the vivid sketch that Radowitz made on March 20, 1849 of the two tendencies within the Erbkaiserpartei (Jürgens, *op.cit.*, II, Part 2, p. 659), we can see in any case that the truly Prussian hegemonic or Greater Prussian tendency had certainly remained alive or had come alive again. Among its adherents, we must mention primarily the group of Rhenish-liberal leaders, Camphausen, Hansemann, and Mevissen. Recent publications, Hansen's book on Mevissen above all, provide us with considerable information on their political plans. They had fought so energetically for the merging of the Rhineland with the Prussian state and also for the permeation of this state with Rhenish-liberal ideas that the idea of the Prussian state became precious to them itself as a consequence of this. We find in them no trace of Gagern and Rümelin's idea of dissolving Prussia, and Hansemann actually spoke out against this idea (*Das preuss. u. d. deutsche Verfassungswerk* [1850], pp. 291f. and 353f.). In his discussion of the first edition of this book, H. Oncken, *Forschungen zur brand. u. preuss. Geschichte*, XXII, 313, called attention to Gustav Freytag's protest, made from a Greater Prussian point of view, against the Erbkaiserpartei's inclination to dissolve Prussia. I would object here, however, that despite this, Freytag was still prepared to make the "sacrifice" of letting the Prussian name disappear in that of Germany.

will help us understand Pfizer, Gagern, and Rümelin's mode of thought.

Contemporary observers did not fail to see how much the southwestern territories, which had formerly been called the "Empire," had contributed to the Frankfurt parliament in both leading men and ideas.[3] Here both the pleasant and unpleasant aspects of territorial division could be most deeply felt; and, oddly enough, the one accompanied the other. Here the memories of the old kaiser and Empire were still most alive; and here the mixture of particularistic and national feelings was strongest.

Here the deeds of Frederick the Great had once been able to awaken pleasure and pride in this great man and in the new sense of life he had injected into the national culture. But as Goethe described his own attitude, he was "all for Fritz, but Prussia meant nothing to me." The genius of Frederick the Great and the genius of the Prussian state could be seen separately; and, as the case of Friedrich Karl Moser in his later years shows, a man who favored kaiser and Empire could regret what Frederick the Great had done but still recognize his greatness.

The vicissitudes of the Napoleonic era had obscured this old idea of empire but had not completely destroyed it.[4] However, as it rose up again it became more modern and took on liberal and constitutional elements. These central territories of the old Empire were also the border territories that had been most subject to the influence of French ideas. These new rights, or claims, to freedom were established possessions that no one was willing to give up again. It was not necessary to be pro-French to value these French achievements. One could admire Napoleon and also abhor the thought of a return of Napoleonic domination. Here again it was thought possible to separate great historical phenomena from the political soil in which they arose. People accepted whatever seemed good without wanting to submit completely to those who had produced it. They were politically eclectic, and the old and new philosophical currents encouraged this tendency to separate ideas from their roots and to pick

---

[3] "I would ask you to keep in mind that the present awakening of the idea of German unity has its origins in the small states of the Southwest." Usedom, *Polit. Briefe u. Charakteristiken aus der deutschen Gegenwart* (1849), p. 171. See also Jastrow, *Geschichte des deutschen Einheitstraumes* (3rd edn.), pp. 277f.; Baumgarten, "Wie wir wieder ein Volk geworden sind," *Hist. u. polit. Aufsätze*, p. 244.

[4] Cf. Max von Gagern's statement of June 15, 1849, cited above on p. 335n., in which he speaks of the "isolated, overly extended Brandenburg kingdom that once destroyed our old German Empire."

fruit in every garden. They were still not aware that great historical personalities and enviable political institutions drew sustenance from their native national soil. This was not understood because political life here was anything but native in its origins. In the form they had then, all the political structures of southwestern Germany were artificial creations that could only sustain themselves by means of a calculated political eclecticism once the support of their creator had been removed. The only indigenous concept of the nation that southwestern Germany possessed consisted of old, faded memories of the Empire, which, through their very lack of clarity, excited political fantasy more than they sharpened political insight.[5]

Thus, Napoleon and the ideas of 1789 were the forces that dominated political thinking in southwestern Germany. They were the standards that were arbitrarily applied to men and affairs. Pfizer's *Briefwechsel zweier Deutschen* was one of the first reactions of the German spirit against French thought,[6] but Pfizer is still much indebted to French thought nonetheless, and we are immediately reminded of Napoleon when Pfizer says that he would be willing to accept a national tyrant during a transitional period.

Let us evaluate the attitude of the southwestern Germans toward the Prussian state on the basis of all these factors. Frederick the Great took second place behind Napoleon, whose stature had never been equalled in Prussia. Memories of the Confederation of the Rhine were more persistent for southern Germans than those of the Wars of Liberation, in which they had had little part; and as far as political institutions were concerned, they still continued to see Prussia only as an absolutistic state of soldiers and bureaucrats despite all the reforms Prussia had effected. Even if the southern Germans granted some importance to the Prussian reformers and their ideas, they still tended to see them as a temporary phenomenon that was alien to the true nature of the Prussian state. It is an old but still current belief in southern Germany that Prussia is obliged to draw many of her best minds from the non-Prussian parts of Germany.[7] Thus, in the eyes of the southern and western Germans, Prussia was and continued to be an artificial state. They were not unaware of the

[5] Cf. Baumgarten, *op.cit.*

[6] See, too, his essay of 1846, *Konstitut. Jahrbücher* (1846), p. 113: "Many still seem to believe with all honest conviction that without the French Revolution time would have stood still in Germany and we should be grateful to France for tossing us a few suggestive ideas and importing a few fermenting agents into Germany after destroying the entire independent development of German national life."

[7] Cf. *Denkwürdigkeiten des Fürsten Chlodwig Hohenlohe*, I, 114.

beam of their own artificiality, but this still did not prevent them from seeing the mote in the eye of their neighboring state. Even Pfizer, who had more praise for Prussia than most southern Germans, thought Prussia had still developed only an external life but not an inner one.[8] But who among these people had any firsthand experience of Prussia at all? When Heinrich von Gagern went to Berlin in November 1848 to offer Germany's proposal to Prussia, he did not even know the lady he was to court, because he had never been to Berlin before.[9]

Pfizer called longingly on the eagle of Frederick the Great to protect the deserted and homeless with his golden pinions. In the painful situation of being without a state himself, he did not reach out for help to the most powerful German state but to the rulers of this state. In a sense, he too was more for Fritz than for Prussia. He fought for a national monarchy of the Hohenzollerns but not for a hegemony of the Prussian state, and the leaders of the Frankfurt Erbkaiserpartei whom we have already mentioned followed him in this. They persisted in believing that they could separate what belonged together. But if we look back, what a conglomeration of historical remnants we find in their remarkable false assumption that they could win the Hohenzollerns but dissolve Prussia. Particularism and memories of the Empire, Frederick the Great, 1789, Napoleon and the Confederation of the Rhine, rationalism and eclecticism tinged with natural law —all this was fused together by the desire to emerge from this fragmented life and to achieve a full and proper political existence.

This federal state idea of 1848, then, bore an essentially Southwest German stamp. The idea did not originate in any particular state,[10] and it took no state into consideration in its goals. But concrete conditions and facts can explain this disregard of the state for us, and perhaps there are still other concrete political factors that will help explain how these ideas we have treated could also take hold of North German and even Prussian minds.

There is no doubt that the efforts we have described were essentially sound politically. The parallel existence of two major constitutions and two powerful parliaments within the same political framework would have made political life difficult under any circumstances, and two great driving forces alongside one another could not avoid coming into conflict. There is no better argument for the

[8] See p. 240, above.
[9] Cf. Kaufmann's article on Gagern in the *Allg. Deutsche Biogr.*, IL, 665.
[10] Jastrow, *op.cit.*, p. 280.

validity of Gagern's ideas than the fact that it was precisely the Prussian opponents of his plan who rejected it for the same reasons that led him and his party to propose it. Gagern's Germany said to Prussia: If you want the leadership of Germany, then you will have to give up your constitution and parliament because two major constitutions competing with each other will be impossible in the long run. Bismarck's Prussia answered: For that very reason I have no use for your German crown. Bismarck said in the Prussian diet on April 21, 1849: "I cannot imagine two constitutions existing side by side in Germany and Prussia for very long." His fellow party-member Stahl held the same view:[11] "I have always considered a German parliament a good idea, but it cannot be realized without a total change of prevailing conditions." The idea could not be achieved, he thought, because the parallel existence of the major state assemblies and the German parliament seemed impossible without rivalry and struggle and because the reduction of the assemblies to provincial diets seemed equally impossible.

If Germany had struggled to win Prussia in 1848-49, Prussia struggled to win Germany in 1866. If Prussia had previously demonstrated her strength by repulsing that attack, she now faced the task of demonstrating her strength not only by a military victory but also by solving the problem that the men of 1848 had vainly tried to solve. At the founding of the North German Confederation the old problem came up again immediately. Various speakers touched on it in the Prussian Abgeordnetenhaus on September 11 and 12, 1866, when the electoral law for the Reichstag of the North German Confederation was under discussion. Twesten, who reported on behalf of the commission, said: "It is perfectly clear that two parallel parliaments with similar and overlapping areas of jurisdiction are completely impossible and untenable in the long run." We shall have to return later to a completely new motif that arose in the debates, but the old opinions of 1848 were also brought up again at this point and continued to be discussed in the following years. Their former leading advocate, Heinrich von Gagern himself, spoke up again and made the familiar suggestion of altering the Prussian constitution in such a way "that the center of gravity be removed from the Prussian parliament and relocated in the provincial diets so that the federal parliament would be assured of the authority it could never gain in competition with

[11] *Die deutsche Reichsverfassung* (2nd edn., 1849), p. 23.

a Prussian parliament of any political significance."[12] We should note
here in passing that Heinrich von Gagern held to the basic ideas of
his earlier years more closely than it is commonly thought. However,
if this close relationship is to become clear, Gagern's earlier ideas
have to be formulated somewhat differently than they usually are.[13]
At this later date his conception must have sounded like a voice
from the grave, but some of the living held the same view, too. "How
many men of integrity," Treitschke wrote a few years later,[14] "still
hoped in the spring of 1867 . . . that the Prussian diet would be dissolved, the firm structure of the Prussian state weakened, and all her
provinces directly subordinated to the federal government just as
Weimar and Mecklenburg were." Bismarck remarked in the Reichstag
on April 16, 1869: "I remember the time not so long ago—and I
would not be surprised if there were some advocates of this plan
sitting in this room now—when the division of Prussia into small
parts was considered as a basis for a free and unified organization of
Germany." This idea was revived again for two reasons. The first was
the disproportionate advantage that Prussia had within the federal
state due to the fact that she held four fifths of the federal territory.
The second was the need of the newly annexed Prussian provinces to
assert their own existence by exercising a certain degree of autonomy.
There was consequently a return to the idea of 1848, which had
favored the coexistence of a strong central government and strong
provincial autonomy and also favored the elimination, or at least the
weakening, of excessively strong individual states. In general, these
desires were treated in a more cautious and modern fashion than
they had been in 1848, and the middle course by which the National
Liberal Party's program of June 12, 1867 drew them together was
prudently conceived. "Our goal is to invest the parliamentary functions of the state as completely as possible in the Reichstag. Even the
Prussian diet should gradually become accustomed to a role that can
in no way limit the prestige and effectiveness of the Reichstag." Thus,
a general political leitmotif emerged from an immediate constitutional

[12] From Mohl's report to Freydorf, May 4, 1868, in Lorenz, *Kaiser Wilhelm und
die Begründung des Reichs*, pp. 589ff.
[13] Wentzcke's essay cited above on p. 245n. has shown this continuity in more
detail, and it has clarified particularly, too, the relationship between the Prussian
and Austrian aspects of Gagern's national plan. I did not go into these aspects in
my study because my main purpose was to bring the problems to a focus and put
aside everything that was not essential.
[14] "Das konstitut. Königstum in Deutschland," *Hist. u. polit. Aufsätze* (5th
edn.), III, 539.

demand. It had become evident that Bismarck's Prussia was made of harder stuff than the Prussia of Friedrich Wilhelm IV. Outside Prussia, farther away from the rock that was to be split, much more was desired. We shall not consider at all here the excessive demands of the Württemberg democrats who saw in the dissolution of Prussia the essential basis for German freedom and unity, for they wanted national unity only in a loose confederate form anyhow.[15] But in the hope of realizing a firm national political unity, the Bavarian liberal Marquard Barth revived Rümelin's old demands in their most fundamental form in September 1866.[16] He thought, however, that an organizer like Stein would be needed to carry them out. With this pious wish and the naming of this particular name, he demonstrated his sound historical instinct as well as the instinct of a *Realpolitiker* full of doubts. In southern Germany, though, the question continued to be a matter of interest. At the end of 1868, Treitschke pointed out that the demand that the Prussian diet surrender its functions to the provincial diets was repeatedly voiced in the South German press.[17] It is of great interest here that even Grossherzog Friedrich of Baden took up this idea and advocated it during the war year of 1870 as part of his ideal for a future Germany. On September 12, 1870 he told the Oldenburg cabinet secretary Jansen[18] that in his view Germany was moving toward a centralized state but was not ripe for it yet. The important thing now, he explained, was to use the idea of the German crown to break down that worst of all particularisms—Prussian particularism. In the long run, though, he thought, neither a Prussian lower house nor even a Prussian upper house would be able to survive under the German crown and alongside the German

[15] Cf. Rapp, *Die Württemberger und d. nationale Frage 1863-71*, pp. 99f.

[16] H. Oncken in the *Forschungen zur brand. und preuss. Geschichte*, XXII, 315ff., and in the biography of Bennigsen, II, 107ff. In the same passage, the related demands of the Hessian Fr. Oetker can be found, and in II, 206, M. Barth's statements from December 1870. Further journalistic sources are available in Gerh. Ritter, *Die preussischen Konservativen u. Bismarcks deutsche Politik*, p. 250. In the same volume, pp. 251ff., are sources of the concurrent revival of the Old Prussian conservative interest in creating the highest possible degree of provincial independence.

[17] "Zum Jahreswechsel 1869," *Zehn Jahre deutscher Kämpfe*, p. 225 (3rd edn., I, 253).

[18] Jansen, *Grossherzog N. F. Peter von Oldenburg*, p. 161. Brandenburg, *Briefe u. Aktenstücke z. Gesch. der Gründung d. Deutschen Reiches*, I, 42f. There is brief mention of his unitarian plan in his journals from Versailles, January 28, 1871, in Oncken, *Grossh. Friedrich I. von Baden*, II, 344. The Grossherzog expressed similar ideas on the limiting of particularism, "especially in Prussia itself," on the German ministry, and on the German army to Chlodwig Hohenlohe in 1875. *Denkwürdigkeiten Hohenlohes*, II, 153.

parliament. It could only be of advantage to the federal consolidation of Germany if Prussia should find herself obliged to fall back on the system of the provincial diets.

Treitschke, who was living in southwestern Germany at the time, considered such desires the expression of a conscious or unconscious particularism. We know from 1848, and we shall come back to this point later, that they could indeed have particularistic roots. But at the same time Treitschke also considered the complaints about the inevitable friction between the two parliaments thoroughly justified. "It remains a mystery," he said immediately after the victories of 1866, "how a German and a Prussian parliament are to exist side by side for very long."[19] His doubts were reinforced when only a North German, and not a German, federal state was created. He also thought that the North German Reichstag and the Prussian diet, which were both essentially Prussian representative assemblies, should merge as completely as possible. The Prussian and North German parliaments should both be chosen through the same elections, and they should have the relationship to each other of a smaller to a larger parliament.[20]

[19] "Polit. Korrespondenz," July 10, 1866, *Zehn Jahre deutscher Kämpfe* (3rd edn.), I, 115.

[20] "Polit. Korrespondenz," September 10, 1866, *ibid.*, p. 179; see also pp. 205 and 252. As early as 1848 (see p. 262n., above), Bunsen had suggested this middle course, and so had Paul Pfizer afterwards, in 1862 (i.e., "that the same representatives should represent the Prussian people in Berlin and in the German parliament" *Zur deutschen Verfassungsfrage*, p. 137). In doing so, they called attention and gave their approval to the efforts of 1848-49 with which we are familiar. The representative Groote advocated this same idea together with Treitschke on September 11, 1869 in the Prussian Abgeordnetenhaus. The Free Conservatives and the National Liberals also took it up again at the beginning of 1869. Kardorff's motion of January 28, 1869 was: "in regard to defining the voting districts and determining the method of voting and the number of representatives, to bring the composition of the Prussian Abgeordnetenhaus into harmony with that of the Reichstag and thereby to make a closer organic relationship between the two bodies possible." Hennig's motion for national reform wanted to go further and extend the reform to the Herrenhaus as well. *Stenogr. Berichte 1868-69*, II, 1294f. Bismarck's essential argument against the motion on January 28, 1869 was that, within the Prussian constitution, a threat to the Prussian crown's right to dissolve the parliament would exist. He realized clearly, then, that the motion amounted to a fundamental change in the role of the Prussian crown. See, too, Gerh. Ritter, *Die preussischen Konservativen u. Bismarcks deutsche Politik*, pp. 259ff., on the highly unitarian attitude of the Free Conservatives in this question. During the war of 1870, the Oldenburg cabinet secretary Jansen wrote in his anonymous brochure *Die Revision der norddeutschen Bundesverfassung u. d. Oberhausfrage* (cf. Ott. Lorenz, *Kaiser Wilhelm*, p. 355), p. 20: "The political circles of Prussia are already beginning to realize that the existence of both a North German Reichstag and a Prussian diet side by side cannot be maintained indefinitely and that, if I may express myself in this way, the mediatizing of the Abgeordnetenhaus and of the Herrenhaus by means of a revision of the Prussian constitution is only

He retracted this suggestion after the events of 1870 because it would have piqued the smaller states too much, but he still thought it might be taken up again at a later time.[21]

He did not think it would be taken up again merely for reasons of political expediency[22] but for the same basic reasons that had once motivated Friedrich von Gagern and Stockmar's suggestions, namely, unitarian ideals. The great difference was, of course, that they conceived of their unitarian ideals from a non-Prussian point of view and Treitschke conceived of his from a Prussian one. "Whoever sees the centralized state and the autonomous administration of strong provinces as elements of the state in the future will have to leave Prussia's monarchical and military traditions intact."[23] In the last analysis, this is not much different from what Gagern and Rümelin had worked for and what the editorial that appeared in the *Deutsche Zeitung* of December 11, 1848 had envisioned. The same thing would have resulted, too, from the German constitution of 1849, which reduced the individual states to subjects of the central government and allowed them independence only in regulating their territorial interests. But where Gagern and Rümelin wanted to dissolve Prussia to reach that goal, Treitschke wanted to preserve Prussia carefully as a solid foundation that could support the eventual development of the other states. The difference between him and the men of St. Paul's

---

a question of time. Such a mediatization will be taken up and will have to be taken up as soon as the features of the German federal state have taken on firm contours."

[21] "Das konstitut. Königtum in Deutschland," *Hist. u. polit. Aufsätze*, III, 556f.

[22] "How they interfere with each other; how the diet, at every step, has to take into account deliberations that it knows of only by rumor; how neither of the two representative assemblies has its corresponding adequate government, its adequate budget; how the people become exhausted by the all-too-frequent elections and lose any understanding of the parliamentary deliberations that change in rapid series; how the strength of men in politics is wasted by the excessive length of the parliamentary period of office, which could easily be shortened within only one assembly; how this waste of time, which is the basic weakness of all parliamentary government, threatens to smother the political activity of the nation" etc. *Ibid.*, III, 556, partially taken from his article "Zum Jahreswechsel 1869," in *Zehn Jahre deutscher Kämpfe* (3rd edn.), I, 251f.

[23] *Hist. u. polit. Aufsätze*, III, 533. His formulation of the German goal of the future had already been anticipated in 1848. Soiron said in the constituent committee on December 13, 1848: "If a centralized state develops from this, the people will doubtless have nothing against it, for we shall then have self-government of the communities, districts, and provinces everywhere. The people will not fear or hate this centralized state, and they will see their individualism preserved in it. The individual governments under this central government will lose their importance. General interests will come under the jurisdiction of the centralized state; local ones under that of self-government." Hübner, *Aktenstücke*, p. 294.

Church in Frankfurt was not one of ends but of means. They wanted Prussia to merge with Germany. He saw Germany merging with Prussia in the future. The link between Treitschke's ideas in 1848 and in 1871 is therefore a remarkable one. He took his ultimate objectives from the ideals of the older generation that could only envision a powerful national state in the form of the most centralized state possible, but his political and historical realism taught him that the impulse for reaching these objectives would now have to come from Prussia and not from Germany.[24] This was the solution the brilliant Droysen had anticipated in 1848 when he suggested that Prussia consolidate herself rigorously if the amalgamation of Prussia and Germany proved impossible at that time.[25]

One alternative after another presented itself. The Droysen-Treitschke alternatives represented alternative means for achieving an identical end. The Gagern-Bismarck alternatives of 1849 represented alternative ends themselves. The choice was Germany or Prussia, and Bismarck chose Prussia at that time. He left the complicated problem of Germany unsolved and was content to have taken care of Prussia. Then, when he did solve the German problem in 1866 and 1871, he did not do so within the framework of the alternative that Droysen had considered the only alternative. He did it by means of a synthesis. The old period of either/or, of dialectical thinking, and of inviolable ideals was over. The period of the modern, realistic both/and begins here. Bismarck's synthesis of the Prussian and German constitutions and of federative and unitarian demands was no rigorously symmetrical work of art. It seemed formless and complex, but it was viable. Prussia and Germany received their constitutions and their own parliaments, and they managed to make allowances for each other. This was achieved by means of a few simple but

---

[24] He pointed this out as early as his essay "Bundesstaat und Einheitsstaat" (1864), *Hist. u. polit. Aufsätze* (5th edn.), II, 156.

[25] Fundamentally not far removed from these views of Treitschke's and Droysen's is the view that Konstantin Rössler developed in 1872 when he reviewed Stockmar's *Denkwürdigkeiten* in the *Zeitschr. f. preuss. Geschichte*, IX, 447. He even went so far as to approve Stockmar's "ingenious" project of 1848 (see Chap. 2, above) because he assumed it would not harm the Prussian state organism. "A territory directly subject to the German crown has already been established in Germany, and the greatest progress that German state development could make internally would be to grant the Prussian state this position officially. There is little danger for the Prussian state organism in this, because the educable of the non-Prussian members of the Reichstag, if the Reichstag functions as the Prussian parliament, will become only the more Prussian, only the more unitarian, only the more centralistic in their thinking." More unitarian, perhaps, but more Prussian, too?

highly ingenious safety measures that Bismarck introduced to ensure the integrity of Prussia and Germany.

If we look back, we see that there were two main reasons why the demand was made on Prussia to renounce her parliament and her state unity. The first was the fear that the Prussian parliament would infringe on the German one. This fear arose from the view that the parliamentary majorities, through their power to control taxes and budgeting, would actually determine government policy and the composition of the ministries. This fear arose, that is to say, from the so-called parliamentary doctrine. Two actively governing parliaments side by side, it was thought, are an impossibility. They would bring the entire machinery to a halt. This assumption that constitutionalism actually was, or had to be, the same thing as parliamentary government was held by nearly everyone who was interested in any form of modern government at all. Stahl is a classic example. He wrote in 1849:[26] "Hardly anyone would object to the statement that the political ideal of the conservatives after the March Revolution is none other than parliamentary government—the debasement of the king to the executor of the parliamentary majority's will." This was not his own position, but he considered himself an exception.

The force with which liberal demands erupted in 1848 and the appeal of the Revolution alone do not fully explain the prevalence of what I would call a prejudice against parliamentary government. The experiences that Germany had already had with parliamentary government also played a role here. The political life of the South German states, available for all to see, was far from being a model of parliamentary government; and for this very reason it had the effect of a warning example. Everyone saw how the bureaucratic ministries had their will with oppositional parliaments and how the approval of the annual budget was reduced to a "vapid farce." That was the way Fürst Solms expressed it in 1848.[27] A former Hallerian, he had acted as marshal of the Herrenkurie of the United Diet in 1847 and 1848, and he considered such a parliamentary farce beneath the dignity of

[26] *Die deutsche Reichsverfassung* (2nd edn.), p. 7. See also J. Hansen, *Die Rheinlande u. die preuss. Politik 1815-1915*, in *Die Rheinprovinz 1815-1915*, I, 723.—Heinrich von Gagern's speech on October 26, 1848 (*Stenogr. Bericht*, p. 2897), gives the basic argument for his view that constitutionalism amounts to dominance by the majority.

[27] *Geschichtliche Anmerkungen*, published in November 1848. On Solms, "who conducted himself so miserably in the second United Diet and in Erfurt," see Leop. v. Gerlach, I, 568, and G. Kaufmann, "Der Vereinigte Landtag in der Bewegung von 1848," supplement to the *Allg. Zeitung* (1906), Nos. 25 and 26.

a state like Prussia. But he also thought that if a parliament had the real power and not just the ostensible power to approve the budget, this would lead to a government whose ministries would be controlled by the parliamentary majority.

The ineffectual parliamentary constitutionalism of the South German states[28] was not a sign that the governments actually had any power. Other factors made such an unparliamentary constitutionalism possible and actually encouraged it—the reactionary Bundestag, both reactionary major powers, the Vienna resolutions of 1834, in short, all the ills of Germany before the March Revolution. These ills were associated with unparliamentary constitutionalism and made everyone despise it. But beyond that, this system of moderate constitutionalism was only able to win public favor through great positive achievements, through historical deeds; and such deeds could not be achieved in the stuffy atmosphere of the smaller states. It makes a considerable difference whether a large, energetic state or a small one puts into effect an institution like this which involves sacrifices. The military adventures of the eighteenth-century princes were ugly and ridiculous because they did only on a small scale what Friedrich Wilhelm I and Frederick the Great did in a way that earned the respect of their contemporaries and of posterity. Even the army of Friedrich Wilhelm I would not have been regarded as a truly important historical accomplishment had it not undergone its baptism of fire in the Silesian Wars, and moderate constitutionalism would have gone without historical sanction too had it not had its baptism of fire in the period of conflict between crown and parliament in 1862-66 and in the wars of 1866 and 1870. Through his accomplishments for the nation, Bismarck rescued the honor of the discredited governmental form of moderate constitutionalism and broke the prejudice against parliamentary government. It thus became possible for the Prussian and German parliaments to exist side by side in Bismarck's constitution without interfering with each other too much. If these two flywheels had been larger, they would have come into contact and inhibited each other.[29]

[28] "A still unclear mixture of old dynastic rule and of popular representation." Radowitz, 1847, *Gesammelte Schriften*, IV, 171.

[29] On the development of the idea of moderate constitutionalism since 1848, see Koser, "Zur Charakteristik des Vereinigten Landtags von 1847," in *Festschrift zu G. Schmollers 70. Geburtstage*, pp. 328ff.; Michniewicz, *Stahl und Bismarck*, pp. 95ff.; W. Schmidt, *Die Partei Bethmann-Hollweg und die Reaktion in Preussen 1850-1858*, pp. 98ff.; Jellinek, *Regierung und Parlament in Deutschland* (1909); and Hintze, *Preuss. Jahrbücher*, CXLIV, 399. On the preliminary phases in the

The second prejudice that Bismarck had to overcome in order to preserve Prussian state unity within the German federal state was what I would call the prejudice against unitarianism. This is a more complicated phenomenon, and the cure for it that Bismarck prescribed was more complicated, too.

We must return again to the ideas of Pfizer, Friedrich von Gagern, and Stockmar. They all wanted a federal state whose central government recognized no interests other than those of the federal state. They wanted to use Prussian power as the substratum for this state, but they did not want a hegemony of the Prussian state or of the Prussian king as Prussian king. Treitschke said, still completely under the influence of this doctrine: "Hegemony goes against the nature of the federal state."[30] Georg Waitz's theory of the federal state forms a connecting link between Treitschke and the other three thinkers. In this theory, the ideas of his predecessors and the efforts of the Erbkaiserpartei are gathered and purified as in a reservoir. The totality of political power, he taught, is divided between the government of the entire federal state and the governments of the member states. The central government is responsible for the political problems of the nation; the governments of the member states are responsible for the political problems of the territories. Within their own spheres, each of the two types of government is sovereign and independent; and they must consequently be sharply separated from each other. The unmistakable mark of a true federal constitution was, he said, that the head of state had no dependent relationship with the individual states.[31] Strictly speaking, Waitz would also have had to insist that the monarch of a federal state not be a monarch of an individual state, and in 1848 he actually had had reservations about a hereditary German crown for Prussia.[32] When he gave up these reservations, he

---

development of this idea, see Meisner, *Lehre vom monarch. Prinzip*, pp. 192 and 310ff.

[30] *Hist. u. polit. Aufsätze* (5th edn.), III, 536. See, too, "Bundesstaat und Einheitsstaat," *ibid.*, II, 156: "A German kaiser and king of Prussia would first of all consider the interests of his home state in exercising his monarchical veto against the German parliament." That would, however, "arouse the just indignation of the other German states." "It would be humiliating to the understandable sense of identity possessed by the non-Prussian peoples to have to put up with a protector." Drawing the consequences from this, he thought a federal state made up of monarchies contained no guarantee of permanence but would gradually evolve into a centralized state (*ibid.*, pp. 143, 146).

[31] *Allg. Monatsschrift* (1853), p. 505.

[32] Haym, *Nationalversammlung*, II, 236, and Jürgens, *op.cit.*, II, Part 1, p. 325. Waitz's speech of March 19, 1849 (*Stenogr. Bericht*, p. 5838), reads: "I used to

consoled himself with the argument that favoring a ruler in this way
was not equivalent to favoring his state as well. But he was doubtless aware that this did not solve the problem. "If we choose this
expedient," he wrote,[33] "it will bring considerable changes with it
in more than one respect. In actual life, if not in the constitution, it
will put the citizens of this state in a different position than their
partners in the federal state. We cannot predict what influence this
would have on the destiny of the nation as a whole. However, I do
not find that it is contrary to the nature of the federal state." These
were faint presentiments of possible future developments. I would
venture to guess that the loosening and weakening of the Prussian
state were among those "considerable changes" he predicted.[34] How
else could the head of the federal state be in no way dependent on
the individual states as Waitz so emphatically demanded? Would he
not also have to be free and independent of the influences of his own
individual state if he were to devote himself only to the interests of
the federal state?

Waitz's theory of the federal state, which was the dominant theory
until Bismarck, has been characterized as an "essentially doctrinaire
imitation put together from the models of others."[35] But that is not
really the case. As we can see, this theory is directly related to the
actual political efforts we have described. There are foreign prece-
dents for it, too,[36] of course, but it was developed essentially to meet
the practical problems of incorporating the Prussian state into the
German federal state without letting Prussia stifle Germany and of
creating a federal state without a hegemony of the most powerful
state. Waitz solved these problems in a unitarian fashion. The "whole
state" in the federal state is a straightforward, unified centralized state
in all the areas of its jurisdiction, and its central government has to
be unified because it has to be free in its own sphere. It is clear

---

think, gentlemen, that a rotating chief of state was suitable to the nature of a
federal state. But I have changed my mind on this point." Hübner, *Aktenstücke*,
offers considerable evidence for this change in his position.

[33] *Allg. Monatsschrift* (1853), p. 528.

[34] The limiting words "if not in the constitution" do not invalidate my point. He
is not speaking of the Prussian state as such here but of the citizens of this state,
and if the individual provinces of the Prussian state received a position like that
of the other individual states, then these citizens could appear to have the same
status "in the constitution" as their equals in the federal state did.

[35] Anschütz, *Bismarck und die Reichsverfassung* (1899), p. 13.

[36] The North American federal constitution, or the conception of it that de
Tocqueville had presented.

that Waitz's federal state is not simply identical with the Frankfurt federal state of 1849. He allows the individual states a genuine independence in their own spheres that the Frankfurt constitution did not allow them. But both Waitz and the Frankfurt constitution share the basic unitarian idea of forming a unified central government independent of the member states.

Mistrust of the largest state, Prussia, is a major source of this unitarianism; but there are also particularistic motives hidden in it, paradoxical as that may seem. Paul Pfizer provides a case in point. He was afraid that a hegemony of the Prussian people would not only interfere with the rest of Germany as a whole but would also be particularly harmful to the duly distinct ways of life of the individual states and peoples. In Pfizer's compatriot Rümelin, this Swabian fear of being ruled by Prussia is particularly evident. He once made the revealing statement that a Prussian hereditary crown was like a plunge into cold water for the southern Germans, and they would need some time to adjust to it. We know what sort of plans he had to make the cold water tolerable. Friedrich von Gagern's interest in having the member states of the federal state as much the same size as possible may well derive from the desire to accommodate the justifiable particularism of the individual states. There may have been a stronger undercurrent of particularism in some members of the Erbkaiserpartei of 1848-49 than was previously suspected. Their attestations that they wanted to preserve the inalienable life of the individual states[37] are usually not believed because their actions seem to deny this claim. They would have had to restrict the other individual states if they wanted to diminish the dangerous predominance of the largest individual state. In that case, all the individual states would have been somewhat diminished, but at least the largest state would not have been able to oppress its partners still more. Then, if the Prussian state dissolved of itself, as they hoped, the other states would have been completely freed of their troublesome, overly powerful partner.

[37] See, for example, G. Beseler's speech of February 13, 1849 (*Stenogr. Bericht*, p. 5184): "I and my friends have been repeatedly attacked for wanting only a centralized state in the federal state. That, gentlemen, is not what we want. What we do want is a strong federal state that will make the totality strong and healthy but that will also allow the parts to be healthy and strong in their own spheres." See also his statements in the constituent committee on October 14 (Hübner, *Aktenstücke*, p. 144): The federal state could indeed evolve into a firm unit in the course of a historical development that could not be prevented. But he did not think that this was imminent or even possible, and within the federal unity, particularism could still exercise a beneficial influence.

We cannot document this line of thought with statements from the members of the Erbkaiserpartei themselves, but that the idea of Prussia's dissolution could be seen from a particularistic point of view as a guarantee for the individual life of the other German states became evident in the acceptance this idea found in the clearly particularistic camp. The Württemberg minister Römer, who made no secret of his particularistic viewpoint, registered on March 21, 1849 what was almost a complaint that the Erbkaiserpartei had again given up its demand that Prussia be divided into provinces.[38]

As we saw before, it is highly doubtful whether the fulfillment of this demand would have given the particularists of the medium-sized and small states what they wanted in the end. Prussia's dissolution would have opened a breach in the system of the old territorial states that would have let the unitarian flood pour through. On January 23, 1849, Edel from Würzburg[39] very appropriately asked the assembly to consider what effects the absorption of Prussia into Germany would have. In such a case, German legislation would have to be so comprehensive that it would also become Prussian legislation. It would then follow that particularistic legislation in the other territories would come to an end, and these territories would be forced to become part of a legislative unit with Prussia.

The leaders of the Erbkaiserpartei had not wanted to encourage the completely centralized state yet; but they saw it coming, some with more certainty, some with less; and they were not afraid of it.[40] They were interested not only in freedom but also in Germany's power, her security in the midst of the European powers that encircled her. Dahlmann even said on January 22, 1849 that it was "for the most part the power Germany had lacked before" that she desired now. "Germany as Germany must finally become one of the great political powers of this continent."[41] In the Committee of Seventeen, as early as April 18, 1848, Droysen had said: "If there is no powerful

---

[38] *Stenogr. Bericht*, p. 5894: "Prussia should, moreover, remain a legislatively independent state in the future and not merge with Germany as we used to be constantly assured it would." He consequently feared Prussian particularism and the dominance of so powerful a government.—Gervinus, too, had at first (editorial in the *Deutsche Zeitung* of May 2, 1848) interpreted the demand that Prussia give up its diet as an "expression of the particularistic spirit." See Chap. 2, above.

[39] *Stenogr. Bericht*, p. 4838.

[40] See Chap. 3, above, and Hübner, *Aktenstücke*, pp. 291 (Briegleb), 294 (Soiron), 299 (Beseler). In October 1848, Waitz, who was still an opponent of the hereditary German crown at the time, argued against the possibility of a centralized state. Hübner, p. 280.

[41] *Stenogr. Bericht*, p. 4821.

kaiser, then I shall take up the cause of a republic this very day."[42] The hereditary German crown was to establish and guarantee Germany's power. But to establish and guarantee the hereditary German crown itself these men thought it necessary to provide that foothold for unitarianism with which we are already familiar: Prussia would eventually have to become directly subject to the German crown— a step that would mean the beginnings of a centralized state. Thus, the realization of the Frankfurt constitution and of the conditions and expectations bound up with it would not have been the conclusion but the beginning of a new, unpredictable development in German political life.[43] How many problems and conflicts would have required resolution in order to bring the central German government, Prussia, and the individual states into harmony. Germany's strength could have exhausted itself in these domestic problems. Motivated by the need to solve difficult problems, the concept of power that had animated the leaders of the Erbkaiserpartei might have brought about a stronger concentration of national energy and consequently an earlier solution to the problem. But it might also have had to lie dormant for a long time, until the domestic evolutions and possible revolutions had come to an end.

Such a strong impulse, perhaps too strong an impulse, was contained in the unitarian origins of our demand. But still, its basic idea of combining the unity and power of the whole with the freedom of the parts was sound and intelligent. The demand was strongly tinged with particularistic features, but these features were more than just a basic aspect of German character. This union of particularistic and unitarian interests was precisely what Germany needed and what Bismarck then gave her. He created this union by making the individual states themselves, in their totality, the pillars of the central government. The essence of his achievement was, to use Anschütz's incisive formulation of it, "to make the established, particularistic state consciousness of the German individual states available as such to the concept of Germany and to reach this goal mainly by placing the highest governmental power of Germany in the hands of the confederated German state governments." The institution of the Bundesrat was the

---

[42] On the subject of power, see Hübner, *Aktenstücke*, pp. 53 (Gervinus), 291 (Briegleb), 294 (Soiron), 299 (Beseler), 305 (Tellkampf), 506 (Beseler).

[43] The constituent committee's report on the section entitled "Die Gewähr der Verfassung," submitted by Waitz on January 30, 1849 (*Stenogr. Bericht*, p. 4956), says correctly that "the growing together of Germany and the states cannot take place without causing significant changes in their relationships, and a considerable length of time will probably pass before it is fully effected."

expedient that disposed of all the difficulties that had plagued the
Frankfurt assembly. The ruler of the most powerful individual state
could be given the executive power of Germany without the rest of
Germany and the other states having to fear that they would be
stifled by Prussia and without Prussia having to surrender her own
unity. Germany, Prussia, and the individual states were all satisfied;
everyone had received his due. The power of the new German throne
and of the Prussian state behind it was, of course, able to grow beyond the limits set for it by the constitution. There was no way to
prevent such actual changes in the distribution of power. Living political forces themselves were the decisive factor there. As a result,
the Bundesrat did not carry out the tasks it was designed to accomplish. But the individual states still had in it a dike that the unitarian flood could not at first overcome.

We should note how the institution of the Bundesrat played a role
in destroying the prejudice against parliamentary government and
how all the factors involved worked together in a coherent way to
accomplish this. The German Reichstag of Bismarck's time could not
achieve a parliamentary regime because it did not work with a responsible German ministry but with the Bundesrat and the German
chancellor. Bismarck had good reasons for opposing the demand for
German ministries. He said at one point[44] that they would "not be
possible except at the expense of all the agreed-upon rights that the
confederate governments already exercise in the Bundesrat. The most
important governmental rights of the member states would be absorbed by a German ministry which, because it would be responsible
to the Reichstag, would always be subject to the influence of the
current majority in the Reichstag." German ministries that did not
have definite roots in a single state, he explained at another time
in the Reichstag,[45] would provoke a violent reaction of particularism,
especially of Prussian particularism. "The primary and most powerful
opponent of the German minister would be the Prussian finance minister." This is the very point that troubled Rümelin and Gagern.
The creation of central German ministries would have immediately
revived the problem whose history we have already traced.

But why, we must ask, did the men of 1848 not arrive at this solution for the problem? Why did they exert themselves so persistently
on the steep, unitarian path instead of taking the convenient federal-

---

[44] Prussian declaration in the Bundesrat, April 5, 1884. Mittnacht, *Erinnerungen
an Bismarck*, New Series, p. 41.
[45] March 10, 1877.

istic path? Why were they so anxious to prevent the individual states from having any part in the central government? They give us the answer in their own words: They were afraid of creating another Bundestag. Max Duncker asked:[46] "How can such an assembly made up of representatives bound by the instructions of their governments govern any differently than the Bundestag has—that is, slowly, clumsily, wretchedly, or not at all—even if the majority is to rule in this council of princes?" The princes of the federal state, Dahlmann said, could not be allowed complete control of the upper house "if we are to prevent it from being another Bundestag that would oppose all the needs of the people with an irrevocable veto."[47] This kind of federalism, then, was seen in exactly the same light as moderate constitutionalism. They were both so discredited by the experience of recent decades that no one dared to entrust the future of the nation to them. We see, then,—and this is my point here—that the political errors of the thinkers of 1848 essentially sprang up from the unhealthy soil of the period before the March Revolution.[48] Not ideologies but actual experience gave rise to these errors. Doctrine followed quickly on the heels of experience and formulated what experience dictated or seemed to dictate. Some members of the Erb-kaiserpartei were certainly aware, as Duncker himself admitted,[49] that "the principle of the federal state demands for all the members an *equal* share in the government of the whole." But precisely because they thought, for pressing political reasons, that they had to deny the member states this share in the federal government, they were forced to accept a different concept of the federal state. If they were going to create a "federal state" at all, they were obliged to accept another concept of it, namely, the one Waitz had presented and outlined in his speech of March 19, 1849.[50] This brings us to the second political source of Waitz's theory. We can see now more clearly that what he calls a federal state was really not a federal state at all but a cen-

[46] *Zur Geschichte der deutschen Reichsversammlung in Frankfurt* (1849), p. 51.

[47] Springer, *Dahlmann*, II, 223. See, too, Binding, *Der Versuch der Reichs-gründung durch die Paulskirche* (1892), p. 46: "It cannot be denied that unhappy memories of the Bundestag, whose revival was to be avoided under all circumstances, were crucial in preventing the recognition that was properly due the states and their governments."

[48] Cf. Pfizer in the *Briefwechsel* (2nd edn., reprint, p. 211): "As long as there are princes in Germany who form a federal parliament, this parliament will continue to function within the previous framework of reaction."

[49] *Op.cit.*, p. 51.

[50] *Stenogr. Bericht*, p. 5837. Hübner's work is also useful on the development of Waitz's concept of the federal state.

tralized state that simply relinquished certain political functions to the governments of the member states, which were strictly separated from it in all other respects.[51]

Waitz's theory had hidden the federalistic concept of the federal state so thoroughly that Bismarck seemed to have brought something entirely new to life.[52] He did create something new in the sense of giving it concrete form, but the idea for it had already been present, and it will be worth our trouble to follow the course of its growth at the time of the March developments.

In the very first stages of these developments, we find that federalism still had some chance of success. In those previously mentioned negotiations that were initiated by the South German governments in the first half of March 1848 and that Max and Heinrich von Gagern had played such an active part in, the delegates from Württemberg, Hessen-Darmstadt, and Nassau presented the Bavarian court with a plan that asked for a federal parliament composed of two houses. The representatives of the German princes in the federation would make up one house; the representatives of the German people would make up the other. The first house would receive its instructions from the princes; the second would be independent. The approval of both houses would be necessary to pass a resolution.[53] In this plan, the Prussian leadership of the federation can only have been conceived of as that of an executive agency, not as that of a constitutional monarch.[54] We have here already several of the essential features of the system Bismarck created in 1866, because the kaiser of the new German state was not in fact a real monarch in a constitutional sense either.

[51] He tried to get around this problem himself by understanding federal state to mean a joint existence of the "central state" and the individual states.

[52] Anschütz, op.cit., p. 14: "It was Bismarck's accomplishment and merit . . . to have made an entirely new concept of the federal state effective in the German constitution."

[53] Memorial of March 16, 1848, in Pastor, Max v. Gagern, p. 469. This idea was also presented in the speech that Heinrich von Gagern gave in the Hessian parliament on March 24, 1848. H. v. Gagern, Ein öffentl. Charakter (1848), p. 264.

[54] This is confirmed in the agreement of March 17 between the circulating delegation and the Bavarian government (in Pastor, p. 472): "In any case, more extensive power should be granted to the head of the federal government, and the head of the federal government should be made responsible for executing the resolutions passed by the federal constitution (sic)." The Prussian government actually received another version of this plan. The hazy wording of this version makes it possible to interpret a legislative role for the leadership of the federal state into the plan. Cf. Pastor, p. 237, and the Prussian circular of March 25, 1848, in Roth and Merck, op.cit., I, 172.

That this opportune moment for a federalistic solution was missed can also probably be counted among the unfortunate effects of March 18 and 19. In the plan of the Heidelberg Committee of Seven for the Preliminary Parliament,[55] there were still plans to have a senate from the individual states above the house representing the people. But a few weeks later, the constitutional draft of the Committee of Seventeen made a major change. According to this draft, which was Dahlmann's work, the upper house was to be composed both of representatives of the individual governments who would not be bound by their governments' instructions and of representatives of the individual state parliaments. This deprived the individual state governments of their part in the legislation of the federal state, and they were reduced to mere electoral bodies for the upper house.[56]

Thus, federalistic and unitarian ideas that were originally bound together went their separate ways. Federalism became the leading principle of all those who wanted a directorial or a rotating government at the head of Germany.[57] This party was made up of the anti-Prussians and particularists from the less important states. Now, however, the unitarians could only conceive of the chief of state's hereditary office as that of a constitutional monarch; but from the federalists' point of view, such an arrangement was unacceptable. Though not of primary importance here, a theoretical preference for the form of constitutional monarchy doubtless played a role in driving the federalistic concept into the background. In addition to all this, there was also the intoxicating atmosphere in which the Frankfurt parliament lived during its first months, an atmosphere that dulled its vision and obscured the political realities of the individual states.

The development just sketched here began in southwestern Germany and came to an end in Frankfurt. There the federalistic element it had originally contained disappeared. This element, then, cannot have entered Bismarck's world of thought from the Southwest. But in these same years, and independent of this development,

---

[55] H. v. Gagern, *Fr. v. Gagern*, II, 750.

[56] Mathy stood more or less alone on June 24, 1848 when he asked for a further development of the Bundestag into a Staatenhaus (*Stenogr. Bericht*, p. 519; cf. Sybel, *op.cit.*, I, 181), and he was not even asking for a Bundesrat as Bismarck was to suggest it later, i.e., with delegates bound by their governments' instructions, but for an assembly that "could pass resolutions without any particular instructions and by a simple majority." On similar plans, see Biedermann, *Histor. Taschenbuch* (1877), p. 127, and Jürgens, *Zur Geschichte des deutschen Verfassungswerkes*, I, 134ff., 147, 153, 157ff., 171.

[57] See, for example, Rotenhan's motion of January 15, 1849, in Binding, *op.cit.*, p. 46.

a federalistic solution was under consideration in Prussia, too; and here we can find a connecting line that leads directly to Bismarck.

The earliest unequivocal proof of this is a book entitled *Über die Reorganisation des Deutschen Bundes*, written by the young Graf Robert von der Goltz, who later made a name for himself as Prussia's representative to the government of Napoleon III. Goltz claims to have written down his essential ideas before March 18,[58] and he admits that he is drawing on his experience in North America. His suggestion was to form a federal government with a king-protector (from Prussia), a house of ambassadors from the individual states, and a house of popular representatives. For the most part, the executive power would be invested in the king-protector, the legislative power in the parliament made up of both houses. The ambassadors would be bound by the instructions of their governments, and no law would be valid without adoption by both houses and approval by the king-protector, who would have only a delaying veto. As we know, this kind of federalistic structure was incompatible with pure parliamentary government, and it is to the credit of Goltz's insight that he rejects such a parliamentary system. Some of his other suggestions, however, would have considerably weakened the position of the king-protector and the natural influence of Prussia in the federation.[59] But these ideas combining hegemony and federation that this near-conservative democrat advocated are highly interesting.

But it is not Goltz that I would name as a possible source for Bismarck's ideas. Stahl is a more likely candidate. In an editorial in the *Kreuzzeitung* of August 30, 1848, Stahl argued that the upper house in Germany should only take the form of a Fürstenhaus and not be just a Staatenhaus. He said that the princes were indeed subject to the sovereign German government but that they must also have a share in this sovereign government as princes. In his book of 1849 on the German constitution, a book we have mentioned earlier, he formulates this more precisely. There it is very plainly stated:[60] Monarchical states as such can only be suitably represented if the upper house is made up of the princes themselves or of delegates bound by their instructions.[61] What he wanted was something like the plenum

[58] The preface is dated April 8, 1848.

[59] And more than any other, the impossible suggestion that all the states should have an equal vote in the house of ambassadors.

[60] *Die deutsche Reichsverfassung*, p. 28; see, too, Michniewicz, *Stahl und Bismarck*, pp. 133f.

[61] However, they should never be allowed to postpone voting because they

of the Bundestag but with a different distribution of votes, for in a federal state—and here his sound understanding of the nature of power takes him further than Goltz—the larger states had to be better represented than they had been up to then in the Bundestag. Another passage anticipates one aspect of Bismarck's later achievement:[62] The subjects of the individual princes will only develop love and sympathy for the central government if they know their princes have a share in it. That is exactly what Bismarck said later, in a somewhat cooler tone, in the chapter "Dynastien und Stämme": "As a rule, German patriotism needs the mediation of dynastic ties to become active and effective."[63]

Since May 1849, of course, Radowitz' union policy was making serious efforts to blend the requirements of both hegemony and federation and to prepare the way for a moderate constitutionalism in both Germany and Prussia. In general, his goals were excellent, and the elements to be mixed together were the right ones, but the proportions in which they were to be mixed were wrong. Stahl and Bismarck therefore had cause to complain that the union constitution, like the Frankfurt one before it, gave too little to the Prussian state and actually decreased its power to the advantage of its weaker partners in the federation.[64]

This was mainly the result of Prussia's unfavorable position in the legislative branch. An assembly of princes together with a Reichstag was to exercise the legislative power. But Prussia had only one out of six votes in the princes' assembly, or as it was finally planned, only one in five. She was bound by the majority decisions of that assembly, and only in questions of amendments to the constitution did she have a veto against objectionable decisions of the princes' assembly and of the Reichstag.[65] If Prussia wanted to assert her will against her partners in the princes' assembly, she had to seek support in the federal state parliament. But if she did that, she ran the danger of

---

lacked instructions. Bismarck furnished this same precautionary clause in Article 7 of the German constitution.

[62] P. 42.

[63] *Gedanken und Erinnerungen*, I, 290.

[64] Stahl's speech in Erfurt on April 12, 1850, *Siebzehn parlam. Reden*, p. 150.

[65] See §§ 76, 77, 82, 99, and 194 of the Dreikönigsverfassung and Radowitz' explanatory memorial of June 11, 1849 on it (contained, with other items, in Blömer, *Zur Gesch. der Bestrebungen der preuss. Regierung für eine polit. Reform Deutschlands 1849-50*, p. 40). The Erfurt parliament then improved Prussia's position by revising Articles 82 and 99 and thus unequivocally granting the veto in legislative matters to the head of state, that is, to Prussia.

succumbing to the influence of the parliament. If Prussia played the one cleverly against the other, she could perhaps assert her independence; but it would always be threatened on the one side by the federalistic elements represented in the princes' assembly and on the other by the unitarian and popular elements represented in the parliament of the planned federal state.

Then, on April 15, 1850, in the Erfurt Volkshaus, Bismarck made a remarkable motion.[66] The assembly of princes, he suggested, should be transformed into a merely advisory group, a Vereinsrat for the chief executive (i.e., for the king of Prussia); but through constant orientation in all matters it would still have a certain share, although not a very significant one, in the executive power of the federal state, and that executive power would be in Prussia's hands. The Staatenhaus of the parliament, however, which Radowitz had constructed after the model of the Frankfurt constitution and which was therefore almost completely untouched by the influence of the individual state governments, was to be replaced by a Fürstenhaus which would be made up of the princes themselves or their authorized delegates and which would have the same distribution of votes as the plenum of the old Bundestag. Accordingly, the three essential organs of the federal state would have been the king of Prussia as the head of state, with his advisory ministers; the Fürstenhaus, in which Prussia would no longer be represented; and the lower house. The remarkable feature here is that Prussia as head of the federal state would be more sharply separated from her allied principalities in the federation than she was in Radowitz' constitution or in Bismarck's later German constitution. The intention was apparently to keep the allied principalities at a distance and preserve Prussia's own freedom of movement. Each of the three organs—chief of state, Fürstenhaus, and lower house—were to have an equal share in legislation. But we can see immediately that this formal equality of the three legislative bodies was most advantageous to the one that also wielded the executive power and had the most power in general behind it. Prussia would have been in a much better position to divide and conquer, to play the princes against the lower house and vice versa, than she would have been under Radowitz' constitution.[67] Prussia's power is

---

[66] Kohl, *Polit. Reden Bismarcks*, I, 232ff. Stahl and Ludwig v. Gerlach, among others, backed him on this motion.

[67] The provision that the governing princes in the Fürstenhaus should either appear in person or be represented by a prince of their own or of a related house was ingeniously thought out to achieve this tactical advantage. Not the individual states but the individual dynasties were to supply representatives, and in this way

really greater here than in Bismarck's later German constitution, but that was justifiable because the population of the smaller states came to only five million as against Prussia's sixteen million. The whole scheme would have amounted to a *societas leonina*, the domination of the smaller states by their larger federal partner. Radowitz clearly recognized this aspect of Bismarck's motion, and he warned the Erfurt parliament that it would lead to Prussian control of the smaller states. With this type of federal constitution, Prussia would have become the territory directly subject to the central government, but she would have assumed this position as a powerful nucleus united in herself and sound in her inner structure.

"I think this suggestion," Bismarck said at the time, "removes a major part of the serious difficulties that prompt us Prussians, or at least those Prussians who think as I do, to say that we want a federal state but would rather not have it at all than have it with *this* constitution." But Bismarck would have seen only part of his wishes realized in this motion, not all of them; and we can imagine that he was not pleased about the concession he had had to make to constitutional and parliamentary concepts. But all he wanted to do was to point out a better route than the poor one the Frankfurt assembly, the Gotha group, and Radowitz had chosen; and he did it without any particular enthusiasm and in an almost annoyed and careless fashion. At the beginning of his speech supporting his motion, he said: "If it actually should happen that we dress German unity in the threadbare coat of a French constitution," then I will at least tell you, his speech implies, how it could be done if need be. He acted the part of a self-sufficient Prussian who would be content with the black and white flag of his fatherland alone, but the drift of his motion suggests that this apparently thoroughgoing Prussian nobleman nursed a desire for power that went beyond Prussia to include Germany. Thus, we can probably assume, further, that he did not think the right moment had come for utilizing the movement for German unity to the advantage of Prussian

---

they could escape the influence of their territorial parliaments as much as possible. Bismarck's draft appealed to the dynastic and antiparliamentary attitudes of the princes with this measure, but it also drove a wedge between the princes and their territorial parliaments and thus weakened the parliaments and the political significance of the Fürstenhaus. As a result, the Fürstenhaus, caught between the head of state and the lower house of the federal state, would naturally have to seek its support with the head of state in most cases.—Cf. my book *Radowitz und die deutsche Revolution*, p. 403f., on the significance of Bismarck's motion among the various attempts made in these years to provide a Greater Prussian conservative solution to the German question.

power politics, and he found this moment particularly inappropriate because he thought the unity movement still too deeply colored by liberal ideas he disliked. Its parliamentary bias made it unpalatable for him, and in order to overcome his prejudice against parliamentary government, he first had to overcome his anticonstitutional prejudice. He made a first step in this direction with his Erfurt motion. With this proposal, he fulfilled unequivocally, if unenthusiastically, the desire of his liberal contemporaries for a central federal parliament. Thus, this motion was still not the first act of his future German policy, but it was an interesting overture, and the coming theme was first sounded here. The motifs of Prussian hegemony, unitarian constitutionalism, and federalism were all drawn together in such a way that assured the dominance of the first but also allowed the other two some importance.

The federalistic motif was our point of departure for examining Bismarck's Erfurt motion. We saw that the Fürstenhaus received more the appearance of power than power itself. But it received enough power so that the dynasties of the small states on which Prussia was then still almost totally dependent could assume a secure but also a dignified and honorable role in the federal state. This was Bismarck's first attempt, then, to solve the problem he later solved through the institution of the Bundesrat. This early attempt was typical of him, too, because the gift he offered the princes combined strategy and generosity. His party friends may well have felt at the time that there was more generosity than strategy in this offer. But they also had to admit, and were completely correct in doing so, that Bismarck's motion contained a willing and ample recognition of the federalistic element and thus carried out part of their political program. Stahl took the floor after Bismarck on April 15 in Erfurt and said: "The reshaping of the federal constitution that Representative Bismarck suggests is the very one I have advocated in print from 1848 until now."[68]

[68] Michniewicz, *Stahl und Bismarck*, p. 160, correctly emphasizes here that Stahl was far from accepting the hegemonic aspect of Bismarck's motion. I should like to call attention to another excellent little study by Triest, who was a government adviser and a representative in the Prussian upper house as well as in the Erfurt Volkshaus: *Das Parlament zu Erfurt* (Berlin, 1850). According to a note in Landfermann's copy, which I used, the book must have appeared on February 1, 1850. Even at this early date, the book suggests a uniting of the assembly of princes and the Staatenhaus. "The peers of a federal state are the states themselves that are united into a federation. These states can only be properly represented if their governments alone are responsible for appointing representatives to the Staatenhaus. . . . The governments would thus have the authority in the Staatenhaus

Thus, even the Prussian conservatives of the time had a share in the political thinking that went into Bismarck's later achievements. All the vital forces of the nation contributed to it.

It was not from the division but from the preservation, not from the death but from the life of the Prussian state that the institutions of Bismarck's Germany grew, and it was these institutions that fulfilled the wish of Pfizer and his followers to foster variety within unity and to protect the unique existence of individual states. The Prussian conservatives were able to grant the dynasties and peoples beyond the black and white border markers their due because they understood from their own experience what importance dynasties and regional groups had in Germany. In this way, the robust character of the Prussians guaranteed the preservation of the character of other German regional groups.

---

to veto the legislative resolutions of the chief of state, and they would have the right to provide their authorized delegates with instructions. The voting on a resolution may not, of course, be delayed . . . by these instructions."

7

FURTHER DEVELOPMENT OF
THE PRUSSO-GERMAN PROBLEM[1]

HAVE WE COMPLETELY SOLVED the problem our study set for us? We have examined both the ideas and the presuppositions of 1848 and 1866, and the last five decades have proved the historical viability of Bismarck's solution. But without wanting to minimize the political value of that solution, we must also add that the state of affairs it created is still far from ideal. Treitschke's fear of excessive parliamentary activity has been confirmed. This is without doubt one of the reasons why the level and the prestige of parliamentary government has sunk in Germany. Is it not likely that Bismarck might have predicted that too? As we saw, certain restrictions had to be put on parliamentary government. But would Bismarck not have welcomed even further limitations of parliamentary power in Germany, limitations beyond those absolutely necessary? That Bismarck would attempt to impose such limitations was the very fear that arose in the Prussian Abgeordnetenhaus after the victories of 1866 when the basic tendencies of the new system began to emerge. Virchow said on September 11:[2] "A clever government will always be able to bring about a rivalry between institutions and a mutual weakening of the parliamentary bodies." On the next day, Twesten, who was less extreme politically, concurred in Virchow's opinion. He was afraid that the parallel existence of German and Prussian representative assemblies would result in a "Caesarism of the government's power that would be able to by-pass the conflicting resolutions and competencies of the two parliamentary assemblies with the greatest of ease."[3] This was a worry that was still remote from the situation and thinking of 1848. At that time, only the two extremes of absolutism

[1] In order not to obscure the character of this chapter, I have left it in the form I originally gave it in the period before World War I. Consideration of later developments will be found in the short supplements added to the third and sixth editions. (This note was added to the seventh edition.)

[2] *Stenogr. Bericht* (1866-67), I, 288.　　[3] *Stenogr. Bericht*, p. 322.

and parliamentary government caused concern, and it was thought desirable to prevent friction between two states with parliamentary governments. But the possibility of a modern absolutistic government in Germany did not occur to anyone, the possibility that a strong monarchy would be able to exploit even liberal and national ideas as instruments of power and gain its ends at the expense of democratic and parliamentary institutions. But in the meantime, Napoleon III had shown that this was possible, and no one thought Bismarck incapable of following the same path. These liberals of 1866 were not the first to suspect Bismarck of Bonapartism, and this suspicion was by no means unfounded. As we know, Bismarck had always shown an unusually strong interest in Napoleon III, primarily because he needed him as a piece in the chess game of his foreign policy. But his resorting to universal suffrage—a translation of *suffrage universel* into East Pomeranian, as the wits remarked—shows that Bismarck was also able to learn from him in domestic politics.[4] In the years of conflict between 1862 and 1866, he had even considered "creating" a ministerial majority in the Abgeordnetenhaus by promulgating universal suffrage in Prussia. His intention of establishing the parliament of the North German Confederation on the basis of democratic suffrage did not reduce the fears of the Prussian Abgeordnetenhaus in the fall of 1866 but rather increased them. Skeptical of what Bismarck wanted to do with the new democratically elected parliament, the Prussian Abgeordnetenhaus saw to it that the parliament of the North German Confederation had only a deliberative role in framing the constitution of the Confederation, while the Prussian Abgeordneten-

---

[4] Unruh, *Erinnerungen*, p. 273, objects to the imputation that Bismarck wanted to imitate Napoleon III's methods, and he cites as evidence for his argument a statement of Bismarck's from this period which suggested that such election tactics, although possible in France, would be impossible in Germany: "The Germans would not put up with that." Bismarck may well not only have said that but also have thought it. However, there is no doubt that the idea of establishing a direct relationship between power and the masses has a Caesaristic element to it. He was able to do without Napoleon III's election tactics because he could count on the monarchistic leanings of the masses and on the social influence of the large landowners upon the rural population (cf. Oncken, "Bismarck, Lasalle und die Oktroyierung des gleichen und direkten Wahlrechts in Preussen," *Hist.-polit. Aufsätze*, II, 167, 176, 181). At that time, he preferred democratic suffrage to three-class suffrage (*Dreiklassenwahlrecht*) for the very reason that it promised undemocratic results. See, too, the often-cited passage from his message to Bernstorff on April 19, 1866 (Sybel, *op.cit.*, IV, 318). It is of interest in this connection that as early as the end of 1861 Napoleon III recommended the introduction of *suffrage universel* to the Prussian government because "in this system the conservative rural population can vote down the liberals in the cities." Ringhoffer, *Im Kampfe für Preussens Ehre*, p. 456.

haus reserved for itself the right to approve or reject the resulting constitutional draft.[5]

But not much was gained by this, and Bismarck had his way in the end.[6] It is likely that this governing with two parliaments—this riding first on the German horse, then on the Prussian one—was a concealed *arcanum imperii* of Bismarck's.[7] Recalling the 1862-66 period of conflict between crown and parliament in Prussia, he hoped at first to sail farther with the German winds than with the Prussian ones. On March 28, 1867 he called the Prussian three-class system of suffrage the worst of all voting systems, and he was able to work successfully for a long time in the Reichstag with the representatives elected by universal suffrage. But he had no serious intention of making suffrage for both parliaments identical,[8] and if we look for the reason why

[5] Sybel, *op.cit.*, V, 438ff.

[6] Bismarck's comments to Friesen, Saxony's representative, at the deliberations on the draft of the constitution for the North German Confederation in January 1867 are highly characteristic. He threatened to ally himself with the liberal— indeed, even with the radical—parties if the governments offered him no support, but at the same time he enticed the governments by claiming that his true goal was "to destroy parliamentary government through parliamentary government" and thereby to strengthen the weakened position of the governments. Von Friesen, *Erinnerungen*, III, 10. See too, Brandenburg, *Reichsgründung*, II, 236f.

[7] It is possible that he, too, had temporarily considered a simplification of the twofold parliamentary machine. Cf. his speech of January 28, 1869: "The royal government and the authorities of the Confederation have concerned themselves from the beginning with the simplification of the machinery created in 1866, and the question of how this could be done, of how it is possible, has occupied our attention on many occasions before today." The crucial point is, though, that he did not pursue this idea any further.

[8] He did not take any action on his speech of January 28, 1869, in which he raised the possibility of reforming Prussian suffrage. However, as Oncken, *Bennigsen*, II, 112, clearly saw, Bismarck made a certain concession to the loosening and decentralizing tendencies in the Prussian state by establishing the Hanoverian provincial fund in 1868. The Prussian conservatives immediately opposed the act in typical fashion, but they probably did so more because of a general political instinct and an envy of the new province than because of opposition to provincial self-administration as such.—Brandenburg, *Reichsgründung*, II, 272, thinks there is a fundamental difference between the provincial self-administration that Bismarck initiated and that which the unitarians of 1848 had in mind. Bismarck, he thinks, allowed the provincial diets freedom only in local, nonpolitical administrative matters, while the unitarians of 1848 had wanted to transform the provincial diets into representative *political* entities, to the detriment of the Prussian central parliament. This is not quite correct. The more unitarian the unitarians of 1848 were, the less they cherished the intention of granting political privileges to the provincial diets. Max von Gagern, in whom this intention appeared very strongly, was essentially more provincialistic than unitarian (see Chap. 1, above), and that is even more true of the plan in the *Kreuzzeitung* of October 26, 1848 (see Chap. 4, above). We can say, however, that the realization of the unitarian plans of

he avoided a reform of Prussian suffrage at the time, we will see that
he feared it might also ignite a struggle for reform of the Herrenhaus.[9] He would not tolerate any interference with this house, which
had served him so well from 1862 to 1866. This Old Prussian mainstay of power had to be retained in the German federal state, too.
Thus, little as Bismarck may have cared for the three-class system of
suffrage, it at least helped him preserve this mainstay. It also became
directly useful and indispensable to him when, in changing the course
of his domestic politics, he was able to play the Prussian Abgeordnetenhaus off against the less cooperative Reichstag.[10] But enough
of these hints, which would all require a special study in their own
right.

The point is that Bismarck was able to govern with this system.
Those who came after him were able to govern with it, too, and they
did not consider closing the yawning gap between suffrage for the
Prussian Abgeordnetenhaus and suffrage for the German Reichstag
either.[11] The question arises of whether this state of affairs was as
desirable for those who were governed as it was for those who governed. This particular problem within our political system still remains
unsolved. Thanks to the ingenious safety precautions that Bismarck
took, immediate causes for friction between the Prussian and German
parliaments were satisfactorily eliminated; and now the united Prusso-
German government, as the third and strongest power, was free to
pursue its political aims over the heads of both parliaments. But, we
might say, it pursued these aims, and had to pursue them, more according to the maxims of foreign than of domestic politics. The Abgeordnetenhaus and the Reichstag became two distinct powers that went

---

1848 would have given the provincial diets political significance because of the
vacuum that the lack of a Prussian central parliament would have created.

[9] R. Augst, *Bismarcks Stellung zum preussischen Wahlrecht* (1917), p. 106.

[10] Bismarck said to Professor Thudichum on September 2, 1887: "The Prussian
Abgeordnetenhaus provides important support for the government if there should
be a majority in the Reichstag that opposes the government. This became clear
in the question of the measures against the spread of Polish influence. Furthermore, the joint existence of two different systems of suffrage provides us with a
valuable opportunity to compare their effects, and a great advantage of the Prussian system is that no Social Democrats are elected." Bismarck, *Werke*, VIII,
569.

[11] That Kaiser Friedrich's thinking as crown prince was German-unitarian is
well known and need only be mentioned here. On November 10, 1871, he asked
Chlodwig Hohenlohe "whether I thought the Reich would consolidate itself. The
kaiser's unwillingness to give up Prussian ways and his role as Prussia's king and
the efforts of the Brandenburg nobility to encourage this unwillingness made him
uncertain on this point." *Denkwürdigkeiten Hohenlohes*, II, 74.

their separate ways and developed their own wills to an ever greater extent, so that the government sometimes had to bargain with one, sometimes with the other. As in international dealings, the government could not afford to let either one be too strong or too weak if it were to be the decisive power itself. Much can be accomplished this way, but it is very difficult to achieve what should be the goal of a sound domestic policy: unity in all areas of public life. A dominating personality like Bismarck was able to harness together the federal parliament and the Prussian parliament, German desires and Prussian desires, to achieve the most important and pressing objectives of his domestic policy; but for objectives that stood at a farther remove, that were less urgent but that could be of importance in the future, even he often had to let things take their own course. Even under him, then, there was no lack of harsh disagreements in domestic politics. In the very first years of the North German Confederation, the contradiction between two irreconcilable aspects of his government had aroused criticism: the reform activities of his federal chancellorship and the reactionary spirit of his Prussian ministerial colleagues Lippe and Mühler.[12] This schizophrenia became still more pronounced after 1890 than it had been before. The contrast became strikingly clear in the period when Caprivi put through the liberal trade agreements in the Reichstag and the conservative school policy in the Abgeordnetenhaus.

There were, of course, still deeper reasons for these harsh disagreements. It was not just the tactical value of the *divide et impera* principle that spoke for governing with two different systems. To a certain extent, the inner genesis and structure of Prusso-German power dictated this solution. The strength of the Old Prussian military monarchy created the German Reich, and the monarchy clearly used the strength of the national and liberal movement but without acknowledging this movement as a decisive guiding principle. For the most part, the German Reich has been maintained up to now by the same agencies that founded it. The firm center of domestic politics, the citadel of the entire stronghold, as it were, has always been the Prussian military state and everything connected with it—its royalistic and aristocratic traditions and its support of those social classes that provide the nucleus of the officer corps. These were always the guiding principles. The political interests of the other classes were not neglected, but they have never been allowed to become dominant. A

---

[12] Oppenheim, *Waldeck*, p. 250. See, too, *Aus Ed. Laskers Nachlass*, I, 52.

full commitment to the other classes would have meant giving up a firm basis of power. The other classes could not be relied upon for unwavering dependability and performance. They could not be trusted to provide such good officers and to approve all military measures immediately. In the early years of the Reich, Bismarck could do without the political help of the Prussian conservatives temporarily because National Liberalism provided him with enough. At that time, he could still use the old slogan that "Prussia must merge with Germany,"[13] and he was even capable of inventing the new slogan that Prussia was more in need of Germanification than Germany was of Prussification.[14] More significantly still, he even tried at one point to shift the center of gravity from Prussia to the Reich. He tried, as he said, to stop being the Prussian premier because he thought himself strong enough as Reichskanzler. But he did not cling to this error long, and in 1877 he had to admit that the main influence it had been granted him to exercise he "had found up to now in the power of the Prussian crown and not in the power of the Reich."[15] After the high tide of the Reich, he saw its ebb tide coming; and the ebb tide came quickly enough with his defeat in the Kulturkampf, the failure of liberalism, the rise of Social Democracy, and the threat to agriculture, particularly to the Prussian landholders. The means of helping these landholders came from the same system that was to provide the Reich with new income and new sources for satisfying its urge for power. A wave of Prussian conservative thinking flooded the Reich again. The new German and liberal national ideas lost ground, and the Prussian Abgeordnetenhaus again became more influential than the Reichstag. Prussia's three-class suffrage, which produced liberal majorities in the sixties and seventies, has since become suffrage of the propertied class and particularly of the landholding class. Since the election of

[13] December 4, 1875, Poschinger, *Bismarck und die Parlamentarier*, I, 75.

[14] March 14, 1877, *ibid.*, I, 104; Kohl, *Bismarckregesten*, II, 140. See also his speech of April 26, 1876 ("It is my duty as Reichskanzler to oppose the development of a Greater Prussia that would be detrimental to the authority of the Reich") and, in a similar vein, that of May 18, 1876.

[15] Speech of March 10, 1877. But even in December 1877 he was still speaking to Bennigsen about the "danger of the Prussian particularistic state draining the Reich and the Bundesrat dry." Oncken, *op.cit.*, II, 327. On the effects of a possible separation of the Reichskanzler's post from that of the Prussian premier, see the Bavarian federal delegate Graf Lerchenfeld's remark to Bismarck in February 1890: "The mortar of the Reich holds so firm because there is a constant certainty that Prussia will also desire what the chancellor desires. What would happen if a representative of Prussia sat next to the chancellor in the Bundesrat and said, after the chancellor had spoken, that he was of a different opinion?" Delbrück, *Bismarcks Erbe*, p. 114.

1879[16] it has produced a reasonably stable distribution of party power in the Prussian parliament, while universal suffrage for the Reichstag, subject to the double pressures of socio-economic and religious forces, has produced a division in the rest of Germany that has led in turn to the political impotence of nearly every faction that was not predominantly Prussian-conservative or religious in character. This was all the more reason for the government to seek support among those who were organized and unified.

Thus, behind the new opposition between agrarian and industrial Germany, the old opposition between Prussia and the rest of Germany was still alive. The comments Pfizer made on this situation in 1832 are still relevant today. Events have taken a course different from the one he feared at the time. It is certainly not the Prussian people as a whole that are oppressing the rest of Germany through their control of parliament. He had shared the political categories and illusions of his time when he took the concept of "popular representation" so seriously and literally and was unable to imagine it as anything but a unified and powerful people standing behind a unified and powerful representative assembly. In the last analysis, the introduction of parliamentary institutions in Prussia has probably divided the Prussian people more than it has united them. The aspiring classes have been driven back, and the domestic situation has been controlled by the alliance of a strong monarchy with the strongest social and political elements within the monarchy's own state. Thus, the structure of Old Prussia and of a national state of older cast as such—to use the terms of our previous discussion—becomes evident in the modern forms of the present Prussian national state. It is a striking demonstration of the vitality of such a state that this vitality has persisted to the present day. But the old mainstay of this state is no longer what it used to be. We have noted the unusual double role that the monarchy has assumed since the events of 1866 and 1870. The monarchy is both Prussian and German. As we noted, it is able to shift alliances, to sail before the Prussian winds today, before the German ones tomorrow. But its most basic feature is that its double nature prevents it from achieving inner unity. It is a political power with two souls, and it provides us with the remarkable

16 After the conservative Prussian parliamentary elections of 1882, Treitschke wrote: "The well-designed system of our state cannot become effective if the two most powerful and representative bodies of the Reich are not ruled by the same spirit. The sharp conflict between the outlook of the Reichstag and the Prussian parliament will make itself felt all too soon." *Deutsche Kämpfe*, New Series, p. 210.

spectacle of a national state government with a double nationality. But for this very reason, we must ask if this state of affairs offers any prospects of enduring historical stability.

We have to keep in mind the fact that the dominance of Prussia in the Reich and of Old Prussian conservative tendencies in Prussia is not based on power alone, nor is it really the result of social and economic factors. It is based on the first and most important requirement for the government of a great European state. At this point, Friedrich Naumann's ideas become relevant to our discussion. He claimed that the moment the new German liberal and middle-class industrial substructure became strong enough to support the power politics and power requirements of the federal government, the Old Prussian substructure would become superfluous and the tension could be resolved between the modernized Old Prussian national state and the still incompleted and still just emerging German national state.

The pure historian will draw less rash conclusions than the agitator Naumann, who was inspired by the noblest of political passions, and he will not give too much credence to the signs of the times that point toward such a resolution. The astounding vitality of the Old Prussian spirit can survive the present crisis, too. But the influence of international affairs on the planning of domestic political life always has been and always will be unpredictable. Recalling once again the initial ideas in this book, we should also note that a single historical moment and a single historical personality can determine a nation's course in defiance of all formulas and laws. Naumann's intelligent prophecy, which anticipates the political victory of the new German industrial state, has only conjectural value, but it is a conjecture that deserves serious consideration. The conservative agrarian state that the government still cannot do without is threatened by the unpredictable demands of a world situation that has been changing now for years, sometimes violently, sometimes quietly; and this state will continue to be perpetually threatened by the waves of overwhelming economic transformation. At some point, driven perhaps by the storms of a world political crisis, this flood will be able to destroy the artificially constructed dikes of the present. Then the question will be whether the new world of liberal and industrial Germany will have the political and national stability to take the place of the collapsing one.

At that point, the idea whose history we have been examining will become relevant again. In a Germany that entrusts its power interests to the middle class and the industrial population, the Prussian state will play a different role than it did in the time of Bismarck and his successors. It will not need to be dissolved, and what we have called the political nationality of the individual state will by no means have to disappear. But the idea of the Reich will increasingly overshadow the idea of the individual state. The individual states will dry up, so to speak. For all practical purposes, they will be reduced to provinces of the Reich,[17] which is what they are already in the area of modern federal socio-political institutions.

One of those transformations in the constitution that do not affect the external form of the constitution could occur here.[18] Even an equalization in suffrage between the German and Prussian parliaments would not necessarily bring about the victory of the idea of the Reich over the previously dominant forces in Prussian political life. The struggle that has broken out in recent years for a Prussian suffrage reform has also become a struggle for this goal, and it may bring us nearer to it. But the historian knows that such higher goals can still be reached even if the immediate goal, in this case the external revision of suffrage, is achieved only partially or not at all. For if we judge this situation in the broadest perspectives and with all the current trends in mind, we will realize that parliamentary government in general is in a crisis now that is much more dangerous for its

[17] An adherent of Naumann's submitted the following postulate in 1905 without realizing to what historical context his idea was related (*Strassburger Zeitung*, February 6, 1905): "If Graf Posadowsky said the individual states would be reduced to provinces of the Reich if all the resolutions were carried out that the Reichstag has adopted, then we must openly admit that this will have to come about sooner or later, because the present federal constitution is unnecessarily impeding the unification of the financial and economic energies of the nation, a unification that economic development is furthering despite all obstacles, and the constitution will gradually prove to be untenable. We need only think of the federal financial reform to illustrate this. In any case, Prussia as a province of the Reich would have to be governed in a more progressive fashion than is the kingdom of Prussia now, that stronghold of reaction in contemporary Germany."— If we saw before how anti-Prussian particularism had added its voice to the unitarian demand for the dissolution of Prussia in 1848-49, we can also find a parallel situation to this in very recent times. On May 19, 1908, the cabinet counselor Schimmelpfeng stated at the convention of the Hessian Rechtspartei that his party believed "the German Reich will only become a reality through the development of an independent, self-sufficient central government. And then, too, by the dissolution of Prussian state absolutism, the possibility will be created for the German nation to achieve a true integration of her peoples, an integration in which a fitting place will be assured for Hesse and its royal house by virtue of their nature and history." *Tägl. Rundschau*, May 21, 1908.

[18] Cf. Jellinek, *Verfassungsänderung und Verfassungswandlung* (1906).

real substance than for its forms.[19] A decline of parliamentary government in general would provide a possible superficial solution to our problem by ameliorating the rivalry between the two major German parliaments.

Such a development would not represent a sharp break with the past. Bismarck's constitution is elastic and adaptable enough to prevent such a break. If his constitution made the Prussian state a firm pillar in the German federal state, it also raised the Prussian crown itself out of its purely Prussian sphere, stripped it of its purely Prussian character, and assured it the possibility of merging into the Reich.[20] The Prussian crown continues to hesitate, but it will be faced constantly and ever more urgently with this crucial question. Financial control and armed forces are the alpha and omega of a state's political autonomy. If the universal tax system already provided for in the original constitution of the Reich (Article 70) should ever become a reality along with the already existing armed forces of the Reich, and if the new German idea, the idea of a totally integrated Germany, were fully realized in both these areas,[21] then the monarchy would be able to complete its transition from a Prussian to a German basis.

The individual state, and Prussia in particular, blocks the path of such a development today with apparently irrefutable arguments.

[19] "The most overwhelming constitutional change of recent history lies hidden in a momentous and undeniable fact that the violent, forward rush of modern history has taught us. That fact is that, quite apart from the parliaments, quite apart from these artificial creations that have sprung up in recent times, the two basic, indestructible forces in the state, the government and the people, have begun to encounter each other face to face" (*ibid.*, p. 80).

[20] Cf. Jellinek, *Das Recht des modernen Staates*, I (2nd edn., 1905), 763: "Since the federal state is sovereign, there are no limits set to the expansion of its jurisdiction in regard to the member states. This expansion can go as far as the destruction of the member states' political character, and the federal state can accordingly transform itself into a centralized state. . . . Should a nation inclined to become a centralized state be legally bound to let a federalistic form shape its political affairs forever? History cannot be mastered with a kind of federalistic legitimism." —Another teacher of constitutional law, Hatschek, *Bismarcks Werk in der Reichsverfassung* (1906), p. 13, writes: "We are presently in a phase of development that is gradually leading us out of the old federalism of the constitution of the Reich and into a *unitarian* course." Besides Laband, "Gesch. der Entwicklung der Reichsverfassung," *Jahrbuch für das öffentliche Recht* (1907), Triepel, in *Unitarismus und Föderalismus im Deutschen Reiche* (1907), treats this point incisively. (See my remarks on Triepel's book in the *Histor. Zeitschrift*, C, 618ff.)

[21] O. Bielefeld's instructive study, "Das kaiserliche Heer," *Archiv f. öffentl. Recht*, XVI, 2, 280ff., shows that great incongruences between Prussian and German fundamental principles still exist in the constitutional role of the German army.

A truly universal and satisfactory tax system for the Reich, it is said, would threaten the financial basis of the individual states. But what the Reich requires, the power and existence of the nation also require; and the more pressing these necessities become, the more quickly and decisively a way will have to be found to provide sufficient means for both the Reich and the individual states, for both power politics and cultural policies. The most recent broad financial legislation for the Reich in 1913 indicates that this path will lead not in a federalistic but in a unitarian direction.

Treitschke's view that the new German Reich would develop into a centralized state was, then, by no means wide of the mark, although he made his prediction on the basis of vastly different premises than we would use today.

But we do not even make a claim to prophecy. However, the historian may put the living forces of the present into historical perspective and suggest the possibilities of their further development. Today, both the Old Prussia and the new Germany are living forces. The forms by which they influence each other and cooperate with each other may disappear, or they may remain and take on a different substance. The goal to which everything is directed is an all-inclusive community of the German national state, a community so strong that it is able to tolerate, utilize, and overcome all the separate nationalities of its individual members.

Epilogue to the Third Edition (Spring 1915)

....

EVEN IN THE FIRST edition of this book in 1908, the concluding remarks led from historical study to political interpretation. Only a few sentences have been added to the text of the first edition on the basis of the experience of recent years. I am printing the concluding pages again in the identical form they received shortly before the outbreak of the World War in order to give historical permanence to what I thought then in contrast to the views the momentous course of world events now suggests to us. However, between an old and a new epoch, new observations on the further development of the Prusso-German problem already urge themselves on us.

The possibility of a great decisive struggle for Germany's future stood before us when this book was first written. What I expressed then—hopefully, but not necessarily expecting its realization—has now become a gratifying fact. Industrial Germany, with all the masses it comprises, has demonstrated its will and strength to defend the German national state against a world of enemies. A great, new, and indispensable task has also been set for the conservative agrarian state in which the unique character of the Prussian state found its social base. We are indebted to it not only for the human resources that it has always supplied in times of military challenge but also for supplying our national provisions, for defeating English plans to starve us out. At the same time, the unfortunate tensions have been reduced that existed between the conservative powers of Prussia and the liberal demands of the rest of Germany and also between all the middle-class parties, primarily the conservatives, and the democratic-socialistic demands of the industrial masses. These conflicts have by no means disappeared; they will continue to exist as long as vital national and social forces stand behind them. They will even be able to exert a fruitful and progressive influence as long as a common ground of political necessity is recognized by all parties. And precisely because we have found this common ground again now, it is of great importance for all parties, and for the government particularly, to find a new orientation. A fresh outlook must be the motto if we are to solve all the questions that bear on these conflicts.

What form in particular will the relationship of Prussia to the German Reich now take? We saw before that the most important reason for maintaining the "Prussian" system was one of power politics. In the last analysis, the requirements of power politics will continue to determine the constitutional life of the German Reich; and Prussian militarism, by virtue of which the "Prussian" system was able to maintain itself, will necessarily continue to be our defense in the world. But without reducing its capabilities, its forms can be somewhat modified and tempered in order to provide the broadest and strongest possible foundation for the defensive forces of the nation. The liberal middle-class citizen and the Social Democratic worker will happily serve in the army in peacetime, as they do now in time of war, if confidence is placed in them and if they are granted all the rights that they can claim as defenders of the state. We shall be able to take up Scharnhorst and Boyen's ideas of a citizens' army again without sacrificing the solid kernel of the professional army that Kaiser Wilhelm I and Roon created. The problem is not easy, but it can be solved, and a modern man who is ready to give up his doctrines in the face of experience will solve it more easily than the men of the nineteenth century who were all too ready to let their experience harden into rigid doctrine.

The solution of this problem is the prerequisite for solving the further problem of bringing Prussia and Germany together in a truly organic and harmonious relationship. If our military succeeds in completely synthesizing the citizens' army and the professional army, then our state will also succeed in completely synthesizing the political systems of Prussia and of the Reich, for there will then be no more need to protect Prussian individuality anxiously under all circumstances. Mistrust of the social forces of the new Germany maintained Prussian individuality. The confidence in them that is emerging from this war will permit a tempering of Prussian individuality to the point where the entire new Germany will be able to regard Prussia with trust. This war has shown in an overwhelming way how deeply and inseparably Prussia and Germany are intertwined with each other. The exchange of their intellectual characteristics will continue to become more intense. The best feature of the Prussian character, its capacity for rigorous organization, has now become a general German characteristic. Now that the war has mixed Germans of all regional origins together more intensely than ever before, it will be easier for the freer social views of the rest of Germany to enter into the Prussian character. To avoid being dried out and petrified by the will and intellect, our intellectual culture desperately needs an influx of artistic feeling. It is also good for the state, as Pfizer put it, to have "beauty and form of the soul" as well as strength. The North German can find this aesthetic complement in the South German. The German type of the future will not lead to a featureless mixture of the territorial groups; instead, it will be able to unite the virtues of the North German and South German natures more frequently than was the case before.

But if this is to come about, some superfluous features of the Prussian system will have to be done away with. Prussia must set about the task itself, and it can be accomplished only on the basis of self-knowledge and Prussia's own will. Since the majority of the Social Democratic working class has identified itself with the German national state, the reform of Prussian suffrage has become the most pressing necessity for the state and the nation. If we do not effect this reform, or if we settle for only a nominal one, then the incipient return to health and the change of spirit in our working masses will probably come to a halt again. The only person who can desire that, however, is someone who is not concerned with the entirety of the state but only with his own accustomed social dominance in the state. The Prussian state with its rigid organization, with its monarchical and military traditions that inform all national life, still contains defenses enough against excessive radicalization. But faced with the question of whether it should look for its source of strength in external authority or in an inner confidence established between government and people, it should not hesitate for an instant. The Prussian state should not repeat the mistakes of the period of reaction after 1815. It should act in the spirit of the 1808 reform of city government, not in that of the Teplitz and Karlsbad resolutions of 1819.

The second great step in the final reconciliation of Prussia and Germany and of the previously dominant social classes in Prussia with the broad masses of the people is the energetic continuation of the program to increase the agricultural population of the East. Whoever seeks to do away completely with large landholdings in the East not only undertakes the impossible but also causes actual harm and attacks indispensable social and political sources of strength. However, it is in the interest of national independence to reduce large landholdings. The agricultural base that has made us economically independent of foreign trade now, at such a critical moment, must make itself as independent as possible from foreign labor in the future. The more we succeed in this, the freer we shall be in our future relations with Russia. Also, a more healthy mixture of small farm and large estate holdings will not put an end to differences in the social and intellectual life of the upper and lower classes, but will tend to provide more social levels between the extremes and thereby bridge the gap that now divides them.

The history of the idea we have examined here shows that the internal relationship of Prussia to Germany cannot tolerate any radical and extreme actions, but neither can it be left entirely to the play of the forces involved. As at the time of the promulgation and of Bismarck's founding of the Reich we are in need of great statesmanlike control exercised by a moderate but firm hand.

The Prusso-German Problem in 1921[1]

■■

THE PROBLEM OF PRUSSIA'S RELATIONSHIP to the Reich is incredibly complex because every attempt at a complete solution brings negative effects with it in some other sector and threatens deeply rooted interests involving power and even existence itself. This became evident in a moving way in the attempts of 1848-49. Bismarck's solution was only able to pass as a complete solution because superior insight, based on superior power, was able to put aside the momentarily less important and less urgent issues and create a certain *unitas in necessariis.* The will of the Prussian state and the will of the Reich were, at least in the most important points, so closely merged and so dependent on each other that the machinery could function and both the will of Prussia and the will of the Reich could mutually support and maintain each other. We know now that in the course of development the harmony between the needs of Prussia and those of the Reich was again disturbed and that the cumbersome and complicated constitutional system was not able to meet the demands and tests of strength the World War imposed on it. But one thing remained constant until the end, one great and incomparably valuable asset—a strong state authority exercised over the entirety of both Prussia and the Reich, an authority administered in both by one man. The government of the Reich was strong by virtue of the fact that the most powerful individual state stood behind it.

Today we complain about weakened state authority. Many of the reasons for this weakness, which is a result of defeat, of the Revolution, and of the enemies' terms, are obvious and do not require further discussion here. But one of the most important reasons is seldom understood with complete clarity. This is that the will of Prussia and the will of the Reich have again parted ways, that two major governments exist in Berlin, governing alongside each other and often against each other. It is ridiculous, for example, that the Organisation Escherich is forbidden in Prussia and permitted in the Reich. At every step, in affairs of major and minor importance, the two organisms and their representatives come into constant conflict. It is pointless to

[1] First published in the *Deutsche Nation* (March 1921).

object here that this is merely a result of the differently constituted
majorities in the Prussian parliament and in the Reichstag up to now,
and that identical suffrage in Prussia and in the Reich would produce
homogeneous governments. Even the most homogeneous governments
in Prussia and in the Reich will not be able to put up with each
other in the long run. The very arrangement itself will inevitably produce contention. There are many interests that one and the same
statesman would deal with differently depending on whether he held
a ministerial post in Prussia or in the Reich. Also, two-thirds of the
Reich's population always stand behind the desires of Prussia and
thus lend them force that the desires of Bavaria, Württemberg, or other
governments cannot have. How can a strong and unified authority be
created in the Reich on this basis? We must constantly keep in mind
that the strength of the central government under Bismarck's constitution was achieved with the support of Prussia and that a central
government will always be weak if Prussia does not support it but
persistently rivals it instead.

After the November Revolution, the answer to the problem seemed
to be the dissolution of the Prussian state. The collapse of the dynasties
seemed to have removed the largest obstacle to the establishment of
a truly German centralized state, and Treitschke's old evolutionary
goal of a "centralized state and self-administration of strong provinces"
seemed to be within grasp, even though this situation came about in
a way that would have reduced Treitschke to tears. The dissolution of
Prussia into its parts could be tolerable even for those of Prussian
allegiance, provided their German allegiance was stronger than their
Prussian one, for the new German unitarianism promised to provide
something to take over the role Prussia had formerly played.[2] But
we have seen in the meantime that this "something" has not yet been
provided; a truly strong unified central government has not yet been
created. We shall have to take this hard fact into account in the
future. The Weimar constitution may indeed look unitarian enough,
and it seems impossible to outdo our tax legislation in its unitarian
directions. Also, the Reichsrat has much narrower jurisdiction than
the old Bundesrat. But despite all this—as informed circles testify—
it has still come about that the Reichsrat is in fact stronger today
than the Bundesrat was! Alongside the written constitution an unwritten one has taken immediate shape, and it is this unwritten one that

_____

[2] Immediately after the Revolution, I treated the Prusso-German problem from
this point of view in my essay "Verfassung und Verwaltung der deutschen Repu-
blik," *Neue Rundschau* (January 1919).

represents the actual distribution of power. Thus, it has become evident that the obstacle to unitarian development was by no means exclusively or primarily located in the dynasties. We see instead that there is a massive vitality and resistance in the organisms of the individual states themselves. In the first flood of unitarian feeling and because of Germany's pressing need, they grudgingly let Erzberger's unitarian financial reform pass. But a reaction against this reform is distinctly possible, and this bulwark of unitarianism cannot yet be regarded as firmly established. Then too, as long as we live in such overwhelming debt and poverty and under the terrible oppression of the victors, the unification of finances cannot provide any unlimited source of power and authority for the central government. And what is the situation in Germany of that other source of political power, the army? The crippling of our armed forces, which has been imposed upon us, is clearly another of those factors that impede the restoration of complete political authority and, above all, of the authority of the central government. In addition, not content with everything our enemies have devised to restrict and humiliate us, we have helped them along with our own blind party hatred. Instead of joining forces with the leftist parties and building a strong new political authority by means of democracy and a republic, the only path open to us, the right wing parties have done their best to discredit the republic in the eyes of their members.

If we compare our domestic situation now with that of two years ago, at the time of the Spartacus struggles, we have reason to be grateful for what the new republican central government has accomplished. But the hope that the new unitarian spirit of the Weimar constitution would provide the central government with as strong a power base as it had in the old constitution of the Reich has not yet been completely fulfilled. The façade of the new building looks unitarian, but behind it particularistic forces are already beginning to make themselves at home again.

Under these circumstances should we not finally concentrate on destroying the strongest of all particularisms—the Prussian one? We must, of course, attempt to render it harmless, but that does not necessarily mean that the Prussian state should be destroyed. Such destruction is not as easy as it may have appeared to be in November 1918, and such an operation would be fatal for our weak and wounded state and our national organism. In the present situation, a spontaneous dissolution from within, a victory of the desire for independence in the Rhineland, Hanover, Schleswig-Holstein, and Upper Silesia, is not desirable either. The danger is too great at this point that if Prussia were to fall apart now, eight or nine new particularisms would spring up to replace one large one. What, then, is the heart of the matter in the desire of the provinces for independence? It is the old, fundamental struggle for local government that the nobility fought against the territorial rulers in the seventeenth century. The people want to govern themselves and be governed by their own local administration. They do not want to let Berlin force any imported presidents, councilors, and so forth on them. This is easy enough to understand, and in modern times it is not as harmful as it was in the limited and isolated circumstances of the earlier territorial states. We can also hope that the independent provinces of the future will see the practical value of being open-minded in the choice of their administrative staffs, just as the large cities today often find their best administrators outside their own city limits. However, we still cannot completely depend on this hope being fulfilled. This liberality in the choice of city administrators is practised today by large North German cities that live in the atmosphere of a large Prussian state. But such liberality is reputedly rather rare in South German communities. Now, even if we assume that the capability of the administration would not suffer essentially from selection on a more nativistic basis, it is still clear that that valuable group of men with interprovincial and nonparticularistic leanings—men that have previously developed among Prussian administrators and teachers—will become considerably smaller. As a refutation of my argument here, one could point to the narrow-mindedness and rigidity of officials from the region east of the Elbe, qualities that such officials do not lose in the West either, and, on the other hand, to the more pleasant and local nature of South German administrators, who are selected on a more nativistic basis. I would answer, however, that it is probably even more essential for a North German than for a South German to wander around in many different areas and smooth off his rough edges in them. But it would be useful and beneficial for both.

Even more important than interprovincial administrators, though, is the interprovincial composition and mixture of the secondary school and university faculties that are responsible for educating the leading classes of the nation. Provincial narrow-mindedness is much more harmful here than it is in administration. The intellectual level of the secondary schools and, more crucial still, that of the universities would sink if they became institutions for residents of the territories alone. We should not take this danger lightly, for the desire to provide for local residents first and foremost lies deep in every population, and it is familiar to anyone who has ever worked at the university of a small state.

I draw the following conclusions from these considerations: Since the demand for autonomy in the provinces cannot be suppressed and since it is useful to the extent that it is focused on decentralization of the administration and on reviving interest in local political activity, considerable allowance should be made for it. But measures must be taken to prevent a dangerous separatism from developing. For this reason, certain concessions will, unfortunately, have to be made to the provinces in the autonomous formation of their own bureaucracies. However, I would consider the dissolution of the Greater Prussian school and educational system catastrophic. I would add as a corollary to this point that I do not consider the dissolution of the Greater Prussian state desirable in the near future.

A remarkable antinomy arises from this. In the present situation, the existence of Greater Prussia proves to be both an obstacle to and a means toward realizing the demand for national and political unity. But this has always been so in the history of the German movement for unity. The complexity and ambiguity of the Prusso-German problem derives from Prussia's position as both the strongest particularistic state and the strongest advocate of German unity. These are the two souls of Prussia, two souls that have grown together in such a remarkable fashion. The stronger soul was doubtless the particularistic Prussian one. For Bismarck, German national policy was originally a means for furthering a clearly conceived, far-reaching Prussian egoism. The unitarian course that Bismarck's constitution followed more and more was based to a great extent, as Triepel has demonstrated so well, on Greater Prussian particularistic motives. Now, at the end of this course, could not a gradual and peaceful development loosen this tangled knot somewhat and create a tolerable state of affairs between Prussia and Germany?

This has been considered possible indeed, and this development has been conceived of in approximately the following terms: The desire of the provinces for autonomy should to a great extent be fulfilled. By developing their own local administrative machinery, they should gradually learn to stand on their own feet so that they can eventually become independent "territories" within Germany just like the other individual states. According to this scheme, the dissolution of Prussia into its parts would occur gradually, not immediately, and in the meantime a Prussian central government and representative assembly should continue to exist to handle the reduced tasks of the state as a whole. But then, of course, the intolerable state of affairs that we criticized at the beginning of this chapter would also continue to exist for a long time; that is, two major governments in Berlin would continue to govern side by side yet incohesively, and they would inevitably continue to interfere with each other. The difficulty would perhaps not be as great as it is now, because the areas of competence would be reduced. But would not the provinces that were gradually emancipating themselves then become new centers, forming their own political wills, and thereby create a highly complicated and difficult state of affairs? Having just entered into their majority, would not these provinces add new sources of friction to the ones already existing between the will of Germany and the will of the entire Prussian state as a whole? In short, the transition to complete independence for the provinces and complete centralization for the German state can be long and difficult, and it is more than likely that our grandchildren will finally have to solve the problem of subduing the will of the Prussian state. As long as a Prussian representative assembly elected in Prussia and a Prussian central government derived from this elected assembly continue to exist, inertia will continue to support them. How can they be put aside? Even empty and lifeless governments can prolong their lives unduly and block the way for innovations.

The final goal of this process, the total absorption of the Prussian state into the provinces, does not seem completely desirable to me for the reasons mentioned above. It would only be desirable if Greater Prussia, condemned to slow death, would leave a generous legacy to Germany, especially those valuable assets that the educational system and cultural institutions of a major state represent and that Prussia now enjoys. We cannot tell today whether this would in fact occur or not. The final results of this entire development remain completely indeterminate and hazy. I do not deny that this possible scheme of development has the advantages of being moderate and easily applicable and that it could perhaps lead to good results eventually. But it does not heal the critical illness of the present, the intolerable dualism of the Prussian and German will.

This illness demands a rapid cure, for the enhancement or decline of state authority and our entire internal consolidation depend on it. Precisely because there are so many undeserved and fateful realities that oppress our present central government and keep it weak, it must be raised up and strengthened in those areas where we are al-

lowed freedom of action. It can only become strong again through
the same means Bismarck used to make it strong originally, that is,
through any practicable union whatever of Prussia and Germany.
We have no other choice today, because the dissolution of Prussia
is neither attainable nor particularly desirable. This time, however,
the union of Prussia with Germany will be formed under a different
aegis than it was in Bismarck's time. Prussia was the dominating
partner in the union then; this time it will be Germany. Instead of a
Prussian hegemony in Germany, we will have a German hegemony in
Prussia. The will of the Prussian state must be subdued by letting
Germany directly influence and regulate it in such a way that the
tracks will run parallel to each other in the future and not cross each
other. There are many forms by which this can be accomplished.
However, they will have to be considered throughout in connection
with the desire for a change in the parliamentary basis of the Prussian
government, a change which will probably not take place immediately but will definitely take place sometime in the future. For as
long as a Prussian representative assembly elected within Prussia
exists, it will always want to exert its influence and will always
threaten the harmony between Prussia and Germany. We thus return
again today to the idea that Treitschke and the Free Conservatives
suggested in the period of the North German Confederation (Kardorff's motion in 1869): The Prussian parliament should consist of
the Prussian members of the Reichstag. This would not, of course,
make all friction impossible between the Prussian parliament and the
plenum of the Reichstag, but the source of most of the difficulties,
and of the most dangerous ones, would be eliminated. It could then
perhaps be further established that the German head of state would
also be eo ipso Prussian head of state. In this way, he would be able
to exert an important and harmonizing influence on the formation
of the Prussian government. But I find the brilliant suggestion made
in the January issue of the Deutsche Nation even better than this.
There it was suggested that the Prussian ministries, after their spheres
of activity are reduced by the expansion of provincial self-administration, be converted into state secretariats that would then all be responsible to one, and indeed the only, Prussian minister. This minister
would also be a member of the German state cabinet. By means of
this solution, the new relationship between Germany and Prussia
would display most elegantly its similarity to and its difference from
Bismarck's constitution. Formerly, the German Reichskanzler, in his
capacity as chief of the state secretaries of the Reich and as Prussian

premier, created a union between Prussia and Germany. Now, the Prussian chief of state would do the same thing in his capacity as chief of the Prussian state secretaries and as a member of the German cabinet. To use geological terminology, we can say that the elevation of Germany and the subsidence of Prussia would become patently clear.

The most elegant and plausible solutions, of course, are often the most difficult to put through against the resistance of the inert masses. In the *Deutsche Politik* of February 4, 1921 the former German minister Preuss approved the goals of this solution, as one might have expected, but he warned against alterations of the constitution because they could weaken the foundations of public law, which had been laid with great pains, and because they could evoke all manner of undesirable opposition. How much effort would be required, for example, to convince the newly elected Prussian popular assembly that it had no right to exist at all and would do well to disappear again quickly. If our parties and electorate were more mature, if a deeper understanding of the significance and urgency of the Prusso-German problem were not so much the esoteric privilege of small, enlightened groups, then we might be able to expect our parliaments to undertake such thoroughgoing changes in the constitution at the present time. But as things stand now, we have to make allowances for human weakness and lack of receptivity. However, it is becoming a more and more pressing duty for our party leaders to study the Prusso-German problem more energetically than they have done before and to waken the interest of their adherents in it.

Thus, we must try to be modest and reduce the demand for reform to a minimum of what is really required. We must do without a completely ideal solution and without beauty and consistency from the point of view of constitutional law. We must attempt to create, by means of the simplest and most practical steps possible, a unity between Prussia and Germany in the most essential areas, even if we are obliged to do this with uncertain and seemingly provisional measures. Here, we come to a suggestion that Preuss has publicly advocated also. The main area of conflict between Prussia and Germany is domestic administration. If the same man were to head both the German and the Prussian ministries of the interior, the conflicts themselves would not be completely eliminated, but their resolution would be made considerably easier. No articles of the Prussian or German constitutions stand in the way of an actual uniting of these two ministerial offices or of any other ministries either. All that is

required is that the majority parties of both the Reichstag and the
Prussian parliament force themselves to see the necessity of such an
emergency attempt to close the gaping chasm between Prussia and
Germany. It would be worthwhile to make the attempt. If the measure
is successful and proves to be practical, then everyone would readily
carry it over into the next formation of governments in Germany and
Prussia. A good habit could be developed out of it, a fundamental
principle of the unwritten constitution. There are examples enough
in modern constitutional history of how originally provisional measures developed through usage into basic institutions. But if the attempt is not successful and if it collapses at its first test when the Prussian and German majorities part ways, then no great damage will
have been done, and then perhaps the view will finally prevail that
we will have to dig deeper and find more permanent means of putting
an end to this problem. Most important of all, though, discussion must
be stimulated and kept alive so that those who are asleep will eventually be wakened.

Fundamental resistance due to threatened interests need be feared
from only one corner, but it is a corner that has to be taken very seriously: the governments of the smaller states. With some good reason,
they see in this possible new arrangement a mediatizing of Prussia by
Germany and a great gain in power for the German government. They
fear that this strengthened government will now turn against the
remaining individual states. The nightmare of the coming centralized
state oppresses them. What can we say to alleviate these worries?
Hardened particularists who forget Germany's needs in their concern
for their own individual state can never be convinced and won over
to our reform. It is tempting to fling some of Treitschke's fury about
the sins of the lesser states at them, but that would achieve very little.
It is not wasted effort, however, to appeal to the patriotism of the
present representatives of the smaller states, to appeal to their sense
of responsibility for all Germany. They would bring down upon themselves a harsh and intolerable judgment from the bench of Germany's
future if they allowed the highest public institutions of Germany and
Prussia to remain in a condition of weakness and division, of mis-
directed and senseless struggle alongside and against each other.
Moreover, it is completely uncertain and highly doubtful that the
mediatizing of Prussia by Germany would really represent the death
blow to the individual states that they fear it would, for we cannot
overlook the fact that the extension of all the measures now directed
toward creating a new union between Prussia and Germany will also

mean a simultaneous and extensive growth in autonomy for the Prussian provinces, and this victory of the idea of autonomy will benefit the autonomous existence of the other individual states as well. In its new position, Prussia will be a source of both unitarian and particularistic influences, just as it always has been in the past. Germany will, of course, gain greatly in strength through its union with what remains of the Prussian state, but this will be a gain in strength that will also serve the clearly defined interests of the individual states. Everyone suffers from weakened state authority, and restored state authority at the heart of Germany will animate all its member states as well. They should not try to renew the shortsighted policy of the territorial states in the old German Empire, a policy of searching for liberty at the cost of the central government. Berthold von Henneberg, elector of Mainz, warned his peers in 1500 that if they did not devote themselves more selflessly to the Empire, the iron rod of foreign domination would fall on them. Today, when we are already living under this iron rod, it would be an insult to the representatives of the non-Prussian individual states if we even questioned their willingness to make sacrifices for the sake of the nation as a whole.

A Note on Terminology

IN TRANSLATING this book I have not hesitated to break with the terminology of the original if I could achieve greater clarity by doing so. The word "Reich," for example, is used throughout the original to refer to the Holy Roman Empire, to the German Empire of 1871 to 1918, and to the empire, or unified Germany, that the Frankfurt parliament hoped to create. Rather than translate all three uses of "Reich" with "Empire," I have used "Empire" for the Holy Roman Empire, "Reich" for the second Empire, and "Germany" for the projected German state of the Frankfurt parliament.

With personal titles I have let expediency be my guide. If there were obvious English equivalents, I used them. If not, I left the titles in German. The results are "prince" and "minister" on the one hand, "Landrat" and "Oberregierungsrat" on the other.

In dealing with the various parliamentary bodies mentioned, I established the general policy of retaining the German terms for organizations formally constituted as legislative bodies and of using English terms for those that were not. Thus, I have used the Bundestag of the German Confederation, the Herrenhaus and Abgeordnetenhaus of Prussia from 1850 to 1918, the Bundesrat and Reichstag of the German Reich from 1871 to 1918, and so on. Conversely, for the Frankfurt and Prussian constituent assemblies I have used the terms "parliament" and "national assembly" interchangeably, following Meinecke's usage of "Parlament" and "Nationalversammlung."

Having established these rules, I then proceeded to violate them in a few instances where violation seemed all to the good. Reichstag and Landtag, for example, can appear as the titles of specific bodies, or they can be used as general terms meaning simply "parliament" or "diet." If they are used in this general sense, they are usually translated as "parliament" or "diet" in accordance with established policy. However, in a few passages of this kind it seemed desirable to keep the distinction between a *Reich*stag and a *Land*tag clear, and in those cases I have retained the German words. This same violation of the rules occurs in Book II, Chapter 6 in passages dealing with Frankfurt and Erfurt plans for a Staatenhaus or Fürstenhaus.

There are also violations in the opposite direction. In the same passages of Book II, Chapter 6, the formally constituted Fürstenkolleg of the Dreikönigsverfassung appears, but I have translated it into "assembly of princes" to avoid confusion with the term Fürstenhaus. Also, throughout the book, the Prussian Vereinigter Landtag appears as the "United Diet" because the term is generally known in English and the use of the German in this case would confuse more than it would clarify.

In short, the guidelines established do apply in general, but I have abandoned them in cases where circumlocution could be avoided or clarity achieved by doing so.

I hope the glossary will help illuminate any terms that still remain obscure despite, or because of, the policies just outlined here.

ABGEORDNETENHAUS Lower house of the Prussian parliament from 1850 to 1918.

ASSEMBLY OF PRINCES (FÜRSTENKOLLEG) Upper house made up of princes of the individual states under the Dreikönigsverfassung.

AUGSBURGER HOF A political party in the Frankfurt parliament named after the inn (Augsburger Hof) in which its members assembled. It was one of the parties of the center, but tended more to the left than any other of this group.

BUNDESRAT Federal council consisting of delegates appointed by the governments of the individual states of the North German Confederation and, later, of the German Reich (1871-1918).

BUNDESTAG A body composed of delegates appointed by the governments of the member states in the German Confederation (1815-1866); the Bundestag met in Frankfurt. Its possibilities for decisions were limited because a unanimous vote was required before action could be taken.

DREIKLASSENWAHLRECHT Three-class suffrage in Prussia. Elections for the Prussian Abgeordnetenhaus were held under this system, which divided the voters into three groups according to the amount of taxes they paid.

DREIKÖNIGSVERFASSUNG Constitution adopted in 1849 by Prussia, Saxony, and Hanover to bring about the formation of a smaller German union under Prussian leadership, excluding Austria—after the rejection of the German crown and the Frankfurt constitution by Friedrich Wilhelm IV. In November 1850 in a conference at Olmütz, Russia and Austria forced Prussia to abandon the plan for a smaller German union under Prussian leadership.

ERBKAISERPARTEI Political party in the Frankfurt parliament which favored giving a hereditary German crown to the king of Prussia.

ERFURT VOLKHAUS The lower house of the parliament meeting in Erfurt in 1850 in order to work out the details of the constitution for the smaller German union championed by Prussia.

FÜRSTENHAUS An upper house to be made up of princes of the individual states; no house by this name was actually constituted.

GERMAN CONFEDERATION (DEUTSCHER BUND) Confederation formed at the Congress of Vienna in 1815, dissolved 1866.

HERRENHAUS Upper house of the Prussian parliament from 1850 to 1918.

HERRENKURIE Upper house of the Prussian United Diet.

KASINOPARTEI The political group in the Frankfurt parliament which included the chief champions of German unification under Prussian
leadership.

KULTURKAMPF Bismarck's struggle with the Roman Catholic Church in the
1870's for control of educational and ecclesiastical appointments.

LANDTAG In general, the diet of a "Land" or individual state; also, in the
combination "Provinziallandtag," the diet of a province within a "Land."
Cf., too, "United Diet" (Vereinigter Landtag).

LEAGUE OF PRINCES (FÜRSTENBUND) Formed in 1785 by Frederick the
Great to maintain the composition of the Holy Roman Empire as established by the Peace of Westphalia in 1648. This term is also used
sometimes in a general sense to designate the German Confederation
established in 1815.

NATIONAL SPIRIT This term is used to translate both "Nationalgeist" and
"Volksgeist."

NORTH GERMAN CONFEDERATION (NORDDEUTSCHER BUND) Formed in 1867;
the constitution of the North German Confederation became, almost
without change, the constitution of the German Reich in 1871.

ORGANISATION ESCHERICH An organization of citizen-volunteers founded in
March 1920 by the Bavarian forester Escherich to protect law, order,
and property in case of disturbances by left-wing groups; disbanded in
June 1921 at the demand of the Entente.

REGENT (REICHSVERWESER) Archduke John of Austria was elected regent
of Germany in 1848 to serve while the Frankfurt parliament was framing the new constitution.

REICH Used in this translation to mean only the second "Deutscher Reich"
(1871-1918).

REICHSRAT In the Weimar Republic, the house representing the "Länder"
or constituent states; parallel to the Bundesrat in the Reich.

REICHSTAG In general, any legislative assembly; specifically, in the North
German Confederation, in the German Reich, and in the Weimar
Republic, the elected representatives of the people as opposed to the
representatives of the individual state governments.

SPARTACUS STRUGGLES The Spartacus League was a group on the extreme
left of the German Socialist Party. It formed the kernel of the Commu-
nist Party. The Spartacus League tried to seize power in Germany by
force in the winter of 1918/19.

STAATENHAUS Projected upper house for a united Germany, representing the
governments of the individual states; plans for such an upper house
were discussed in the Frankfurt and Erfurt parliaments, but no house
by that specific name was ever constituted.

UNITED DIET (VEREINIGTER LANDTAG) A central Prussian diet composed of
members from all the Prussian provincial diets, convoked in 1847 by
Friedrich Wilhelm IV.

TRANSLATOR'S NOTE: This index has been taken over directly from the 1962 Oldenbourg edition of *Weltbürgertum und Nationalstaat*. The index in that volume does not attempt to be exhaustive; it lists only persons and the titles of sources that Meinecke used. I have left all these titles in German in the index, assuming that anyone who cares to refer to the works cited should not have to translate back into German to do so. Since most of the titles are in German in the text and notes, conflicts of language occur only with items like "memorials" and "journals," which appear as "Denkschriften" and "Tagebücher" in the index. I should also note that several titles in the index cannot be found in the text or notes. These discrepancies usually occur where Meinecke has given volume and page numbers in collected works without citing the specific titles in question.